THE
VIRGINIA CAMPAIGN
1864 AND 1865

THE

VIRGINIA CAMPAIGN
1864 AND 1865

THE ARMY OF THE POTOMAC

AND

THE ARMY OF THE JAMES

BY

ANDREW A. HUMPHREYS,

BRIGADIER-GENERAL, CHIEF OF ENGINEERS, AND BREVET
MAJOR-GENERAL U.S.A.; CHIEF OF STAFF, ARMY OF THE
POTOMAC; COMMANDING SECOND CORPS, ETC., ETC.

WITH A NEW INTRODUCTION

BY

BROOKS D. SIMPSON

DA CAPO PRESS
NEW YORK

Library of Congress Cataloging in Publication Data

Humphreys, A. A. (Andrew Atkinson), 1810–1883.
The Virginia Campaign: 1864 and 1865: the Army of the Potomac
and the Army of the James / by Andrew A. Humphreys; with a
new introduction by Brooks D. Simpson.—1.st Da Capo Press ed.
   p.   cm.—(Campaigns of the Civil War)
Includes index.
ISBN 0-306-80625-8
   1. Virginia—History—Civil War, 1861–1865—Campaigns. 2.
United States—History—Civil War, 1861–1865—Campaigns. I. Ti-
tle. II. Series.
E476.5.H86   1995
973.7′3—dc20   94-48356
                                      CIP

First Da Capo Press edition 1995

This Da Capo Press paperback edition of *The Virginia Campaign*
is an unabridged republication of the edition originally published
in New York in 1883 as *The Virginia Campaign of '64 and '65*,
with the addition of a new introduction by Brooks D. Simpson
and two maps especially commissioned for this edition.

New introduction copyright © 1995 by Brooks D. Simpson

Published by Da Capo Press, Inc.
A Subsidiary of Plenum Publishing Corporation
233 Spring Street, New York, N.Y. 10013

All Rights Reserved

Manufactured in the United States of America

INTRODUCTION

The historian of the Second Corps of the Army of the Potomac noted that the final commander of that corps, Andrew Atkinson Humphreys, was known to all in that army. "His high military scholarship, his intimate acquaintance with all arms and departments of the service, his fiery yet disciplined courage"—these qualities served as examples to others. Assistant Secretary of War Charles A. Dana thought him "the great soldier of the Army of the Potomac" as the Wilderness campaign opened; Joshua L. Chamberlain called him "the accomplished, heroic soldier, the noble and modest man." Yet somehow Humphreys has not received the attention he merits. Aside from a biography prepared by his son, there is no extended study of his career. Although he wrote about the war, he wrote little about himself, in contrast to some of his fellow generals. Indeed, most people know Humphreys best as the author of this fine study of the campaigns that resulted in the capture of Richmond and the surrender of Robert E. Lee and his Army of Northern Virginia to the armies under the command of Ulysses S. Grant.[1]

Born in Philadelphia in 1810, Humphreys attended West Point and graduated in 1831 as a second lieutenant of engineers. In 1861 he joined the staff of George B. McClellan, serving as his chief engineer during the Peninsula campaign. At the beginning of the Antietam Campaign in September 1862 he took over a division in the Fifth Corps; he led it in action at Fredericksburg and Chancellorsville. Transferred to division command in Daniel Sickles's Third Corps, he positioned his division along the Emmitsburg Road on July 2, and gave ground grudgingly under the weight of James Longstreet's attack that afternoon. One officer said that Humphreys was "without a superior on the field of battle—full of fire, and yet in absolute equipoise"; another general appreciatively noted his "conspicuous courage and remarkable coolness."[2]

Humphreys's performance at Gettysburg confirmed the decision of George G. Meade to name him chief of staff of the Army of the Potomac. Indeed, Meade had tendered the offer to Humphreys prior to the clash, but Humphreys thought it a mistake to assign a new division commander on the eve of battle. The declination would result in much heartache for Meade, for Daniel Butterfield, who had headed the army's staff under Meade's predecessor, Joseph Hooker, would bedevil Meade after Gettysburg with charges that the army commander desired to retreat rather than battle Lee. On July 8 Humphreys, convinced that it would be some time before he would command a corps, accepted Meade's invitation.[3]

Many of those who encountered the new chief of staff found him a remarkable man. Newspaper correspondent Charles A. Page commented that Humphreys's "quiet, unassuming demeanor, smile sweet as a woman's and voice impressively low" gave listeners "the idea of tremendous power in reserve." A staff officer in the Sixth Corps recalled that Humphreys's "blue-gray dauntless eyes threw into his stern face the coldness of hammered steel"; he had "the austere charm of dignity and a well-stored mind."[4] Theodore Lyman, a volunteer aide on Meade's staff, found Humphreys knowledgeable and a gentleman, but a bit short-tempered: "When he does get wrathy, he sets his teeth and lets go a torrent of adjectives that must rather astonish those not used to little outbursts." Nevertheless, Lyman concluded that "there never was a nicer old gentleman, and so boyish and peppery that I continually want to laugh in his face."[5]

Humphreys was a model of the professional officer and an exemplar of much that was commendable about the Army of the Potomac. However, his service as McClellan's chief engineer inevitably meant that he was associated with Little Mac, an association that did not always serve him well. It was also a misleading one. Unlike McClellan, Humphreys seemed to love combat—he once called soldiering "a godlike occupation." Unfazed when under fire, he remarked, "Ah, war is a very bad thing in the sequel, but before and during a battle it is a fine thing!"[6]

Humphreys performed well as Meade's chief of staff, but his abilities as a combat commander were not forgotten. At one point Ulysses S. Grant toyed with the idea of placing him in charge of a corps of black infantrymen; eventually, however, Humphreys replaced Winfield Scott Hancock as the leader of the Second Corps in November 1864. With his elevation, engineers had taken over the entire Army of the Potomac, for Meade and his corps commanders all hailed from that branch of the service—although by war's end Gouverneur Warren would find himself displaced by the hard-bitten artilleryman Charles Griffin. Humphreys proved a most able corps commander, blocking Lee's retreating columns and helping to hem the Confederates in at Appomattox. After the war Humphreys rose to chief of engineers, a position he held until his retirement in 1879; he then turned to writing about the war. He had intended to cover the period between Gettysburg and the arrival of Grant in his volume for Scribners's *Campaigns of the Civil War* series, but space considerations forced its separate publication. He died just after the appearance of this volume in 1883.

The Virginia Campaign of '64 and '65 covers one of the most misunderstood periods of the war—the confrontation between Ulysses S. Grant and Robert E. Lee. To this day most people still treat the ensuing campaign as a relentless slugfest in which Grant, a plodding butcher, displayed less generalship than bull-headed determination in hurling column after column at Lee's entrenched veterans in mindless frontal assaults; in the end, it was his vast superiority in numbers which overwhelmed the gallant Lee and his army. Several camps contributed to this image of the 1864 campaign. Confederate chroniclers, intent on exalting Lee and in denigrating Yankee generalship, welcomed a perspective that suggested that might overcame right. They joined forces with veterans of the Army of the Potomac who still cherished the memories of the romantic war under George McClellan and shared their hero's desire for bloodless solutions (although somehow they overlooked Antietam). Postwar political opponents of Grant found common ground with some of Grant's own officers who grew disillusioned with their chief and now sought to share the true story. Decades later, in the wake of global conflict, military historians, following the lead of J. F. C. Fuller and Russell Weigley, embraced Grant's approach as the pragmatic and realistic implementation of a strategy of modern warfare. Whether guided by a desire to attack Grant or by a determination to treat him as a progenitor of twentieth-century practices, these studies failed to assess the campaign on its own merits, in context, and from Grant's perspective.

Recently, historians have examined with more care the final year of the war in Virginia. One hundred years after the appearance of Humphreys's book, Herman Hattaway and Archer Jones presented an incisive critique of the prevailing orthodoxy. Other historians have offered their own revisions, emphasizing that Grant's campaign was based upon different initial premises and changed in response to events. Their work opens the door for new understandings of this campaign. Yet it should be kept in mind that Humphreys contributed important insights into the conduct of military operations that did not always appear in later accounts of the struggle. In clear, concise prose he explains why Grant decided to advance across Lee's right instead of his left (ease of supply); that his ultimate objective was the severing of Lee's supply links to the Confederate heartland, not the grinding away of his army in a continuous battle of attrition; that a move via the James or York rivers at the outset of the campaign in the style of McClellan's 1862 offensive, even if it led to the capture of Richmond, would have left Lee's army intact and ready to inflict damage; that a crossing of the James was in Grant's mind from the opening of the campaign rather than emerging as a spur-of-the-moment improvisation; and that any campaign against Lee would result in heavy fighting and long casualty lists sooner or later. If Humphreys had a bone to pick with Grant, it was not in the latter's decisions but their implementation—which is understandable in light of Humphreys's position as Meade's chief of staff. Here and there he offers his own opinion on operations, but in most cases his criticisms are short and muted—a marked contrast to his reputation as an expert in profane expression who shared his gift with all in earshot.[7]

Humphreys also intended his work as a rebuttal to Adam Badeau's *Military History of U. S. Grant*. Badeau, who had joined Grant's staff in 1863, became his official biographer; Grant had aided his efforts by appointing him to office as well as by furnishing him information and reviewing his manuscript. The first volume of Badeau's history appeared in 1868; the second and third volumes, covering Grant's tenure as general in chief, came out in 1881. Badeau was obsessed with reversing previous estimates of the relative size of the opposing armies as well as the casualties each suffered; although in many cases these earlier estimates were offered to support the claim that Grant possessed overwhelming numbers and frittered away life on the battlefield, Badeau went to the opposite extreme. Humphreys challenged this and other aspects of Badeau's narrative, often with success, to say nothing of ill-concealed glee and disgust with Badeau. In so doing, he revealed that a sense of grievance against Grant remained among some veterans of the Army of the Potomac; he chose to omit a discussion of how that army adjusted, not without protest, to life under Grant, how Grant's unfamiliarity with the officers and men of the army shaped his decisions, or how, in the words of one veteran, Grant grappled with "the Army of the Potomac's one weakness, the lack of springy formation, and audacious, self-reliant initiative." Command relationships and the implementation of directives are essential to understanding these operations, and Humphreys was in an ideal position to comment on them.[8]

Humphreys also proved reluctant to comment upon the tensions in the Grant-Meade relationship as well as the problems each general had with various subordinates. He was quite aware that both Grant and Meade grew exacerbated with the dilatory behavior of Gouverneur Warren: during the battle of Spottsylvania* Grant had suggested that Humphreys replace Warren as head of the Fifth Corps.[9] Rather, Humphreys treated Warren sympathetically in discussing the circumstances surrounding the latter's removal at Five Forks, reflecting an 1882 court of inquiry's ruling exonerating Warren of charges raised by Philip H. Sheridan to justify his decision to strip Warren of command. Other corps commanders also fell short of brilliance during the 1864 campaign. Winfield Scott Hancock was never the same after suffering a serious wound at Gettysburg; Horatio Wright took time to rise to the responsibilities of corps command after the death of John Sedgwick. Humphreys, despite his position as chief of staff, chose not to explore the performance of corps commanders in depth.[10]

Humphreys took pains to defend Meade's performance. Meade's failure to prepare for the assault at Cold Harbor—Meade himself bragged to his wife that he exercised command on that bloody field—and his orders to subordinates to

---

*This spelling conforms to Humphreys's own rendering of what is now known as Spotsylvania.

launch uncoordinated attacks are passed over in silence by
Humphreys—who as chief of staff should have made sure of
proper preparations and the coordination of attacking columns. Grant usually receives the blame for what ensued,
and yet ironically Cold Harbor was one battle where he tried
to leave Meade alone. Nor does Humphreys comment about
Meade's less-than-sterling performance at Petersburg in
June 1864, when once more he issued orders for his corps
commanders to attack on their own. These directives reflect
frustration and a bit of desperation, yet Humphreys chose to
keep his opinions to himself. And when Humphreys criticizes
the decision to consolidate the Army of the Potomac into
three corps on the eve of the opening campaign—for the very
sound reason that the result curtailed flexibility—he forgets
to add that it was Meade who made this decision.

Humphreys could offer critical commentary when he chose
to do so. Nor was Badeau his only target. For the first three
weeks of the Wilderness campaign Ambrose E. Burnside and
his Ninth Corps reported directly to Grant, for Burnside
ranked Meade. This arrangement proved awkward, and
Burnside's generalship during the campaign proved at best
uninspired and at worst incompetent. As might be expected,
Humphreys defends Meade and criticizes Burnside in reviewing the battle of the Crater; one should keep in mind
that Humphreys's division suffered serious losses under
Burnside at Fredericksburg. Benjamin F. Butler's fumbling
of his assignment to threaten if not take Richmond from the
James River receives rather cool treatment from Humphreys, although he fails to suggest how Butler's operation
was to contribute to Grant's overall plan or how its collapse
necessitated changes in that plan. Nor does Humphreys

speak kindly of Sheridan's criticisms of the Army of the Potomac in the advance on Spottsylvania or at Five Forks. Much remains unexamined by Humphreys. Although he was cognizant of the political pressures often exerted on the Army of the Potomac from Washington, he says virtually nothing about the political context of the campaign. Nor does he offer much about the changing composition of the Army of the Potomac and the impact of such changes on its ability to fight. Many veterans of the Army of the Potomac decided not to reenlist in 1864, and one strongly suspects that their fighting effectiveness in May and June may have suffered as they looked forward to going home. The high number of slightly wounded men sparked comment from Grant, Charles A. Dana, and others, as much because they were startled at the number of men who took any opportunity to go to the rear as because of their desire to minimize the impact of casualty reports. These soldiers' replacements, including green recruits, bounty hunters, and conscripts, represented a decline in the quality of the common soldier, while Meade proved hesitant to employ black soldiers. Finally, although Humphreys does not probe as deeply as he might into Union command decisions and their implementation, their Confederate counterparts receive even less attention. Humphreys noted in his preface that the records of the War Department were incomplete, and he wrote long before the government issued the volumes of the *Official Records* relevant to his topic. The shortage of records was more obvious and significant in the case of the Army of Northern Virginia, leaving Humphreys to offer rough estimates of numbers and losses while his account of Confederate plans and movements necessarily remains somewhat superficial.

Nevertheless, Humphreys provides a crisp and usually detached narrative of military operations. At points the dispassionate prose tends toward the dry, but the reader, armed with the maps especially prepared for this volume, will find movements easy to follow. There is a good deal of information presented in the compact account, and Humphreys's assessments are usually measured and fair. Especially welcome is his clear-headed dissection of alternative plans of campaign. One comes away wishing for more, especially as Humphreys freely shared his blunt opinions during the war; his restraint in print may suggest one of the reasons why his comrades held him in such high regard. The volume's omissions are telling, but when Humphreys chooses to discuss something, he does so with such assuredness as to remind the reader of Grant's own *Memoirs*. As one especially appreciative reviewer put it, "It is a soldier's book in every sense of the word; none but a thorough soldier could have conceived or written it."[11]

Today visitors to the Gettysburg battlefield can come across a fine statue of Humphreys on the Emmitsburg Road, just south of the Cordori Farm. There he stands, striding forward, eyes intent on finding the enemy. He looks like a soldier; and the statue accurately represents its subject. Hancock may have been more colorful, and Joshua Chamberlain a more prolific writer, but the Army of the Potomac had no abler soldier than Andrew Atkinson Humphreys.

BROOKS D. SIMPSON
Chandler, Arizona
August 1994

NOTES

1. Francis A. Walker, *History of the Second Army Corps* (New York, 1963 [1887]), p. 641; Charles A. Dana, *Recollections of the Civil War* (New York, 1898), p. 173; Joshua L. Chamberlain, *The Passing of the Armies* (New York, 1915), p. 353; Henry H. Humphreys, *Andrew Atkinson Humphreys: A Biography* (Philadelphia, 1924).

2. Harry W. Pfanz, *Gettysburg: The Second Day* (Chapel Hill, 1987), p. 372.

3. Freeman Cleaves, *Meade of Gettysburg* (Norman, OK, 1960), pp. 130, 177.

4. Page quoted in Emerson Gifford Taylor, *Gouverneur Kemble Warren: Life and Letters of an American Soldier* (Boston, 1932), p. 141; Morris Schaff, *The Battle of the Wilderness* (Boston, 1910), pp. 43-44.

5. George Agassiz, ed., *Meade's Headquarters 1863-1865: Letters of Colonel Theodore Lyman from the Wilderness to Appomattox* (1922; reprinted as *With Grant and Meade from the Wilderness to Appomattox* [Lincoln, NE, 1994]), pp. 73, 78.

6. Ibid., pp. 108, 243.

7. Dana, *Recollections*, p. 174.

8. Schaff, *Battle of the Wilderness*, p. 201.

9. Horace Porter, *Campaigning with Grant* (New York, 1897), p. 108.

10. For a contrast, see Theodore Lyman's comments in Agassiz, op. cit.

11. Humphreys, *Humphreys*, p. 226; John Watts DePeyster, *From the Rapidan to Appomattox Court-House* (Philadelphia, 1883), p. 2. In writing his *Memoirs*, Grant failed to draw on Humphreys's volume. Another veteran of the Army of the Potomac critical of Grant, Carswell McClellan (who had served on Humphreys's staff), used Humphreys's volume as the "established record" from which to assail the accounts of Badeau and Grant in *The Personal Memoirs and Military History of U. S. Grant Versus the Record of the Army of the Potomac* (Boston, 1887).

12. There is also a statue of Humphreys at the national cemetery at Marye's Heights next to the Fredericksburg National Battlefield Park Headquarters.

PREFACE.

In preparing this narrative I have met with great and unexpected difficulties from the incomplete condition of the
files of the War Department in the matter of the official
reports of Corps, Division, and Brigade commanders. So
many officers of high command were killed and wounded
during the campaign, the movements by day and night,
the battles, actions, and close contact with the enemy were
so unceasing, that there was but little time for the preparation of reports, and to this day many of them, if prepared,
have not been received at the War Department. The de-.
spatches become therefore the more important, but the files
of these are not complete.

All the Reports, Returns, orders, despatches, and papers
of every kind in the War Department, including the Confederate Archives, have been placed at my disposal by
authority of the Secretary of War, and I am under many
obligations to General Drum, Adjutant-General, and Colonel R. N. Scott, in charge of the preparation of the "Official Records of the Union and Confederate Armies" for
publication.

Major-General Hancock has furnished me with a complete
printed set of the reports made by him during the war.

I am indebted to Colonel George Meade for placing in my
hands the retained copies of all General Meade's despatches

sent and received during the campaign. I have also had my own papers covering the same period.

I am also indebted to Major-General de Peyster for the valuable information contained in his elaborate work, "La Royale," published at his own expense for private circulation, and for the aid I have derived from his correspondence with Confederate officers.

I am also under obligations to General Fitz Lee and General E. P. Alexander for valuable information, and to the Rev. J. William Jones, D.D., Secretary of the Southern Historical Society, for a full set of the publications of that Society from January, 1876, to the present day, and for other information.

The Military Historical Society of Massachusetts placed all its papers in my hands.

Colonel John P. Nicholson, of Philadelphia, offered the volumes of his valuable Military Library for my use.

From the gentlemen having charge of the several sub-offices of the Adjutant-General's Department — Messrs. Joseph W. Kirkley, Henry Ellerbrook, Thomas C. Bourne, A. P. Tasker, F. Jones, and Henry E. Scott—I have had constant aid.

Mr. Fitz Gerald, Librarian of the War Department, has sent me all the volumes of the Library treating of the War. Indeed, wherever I have asked for assistance in any shape it has been given me in the most obliging manner.

To Mr. William J. Warren, Chief Clerk of the Engineer Department, I am under very great obligations for untiring assistance throughout the whole time of the preparation of this narrative. Through him, also, I have had the use of the Journal of Colonel Roebling, of General Warren's staff.

A. A. HUMPHREYS.

CONTENTS.

CHAPTER XI.

CHAPTER XII.

CHAPTER XIII.

CHAPTER XIV.

LIST OF MAPS.

The maps are placed at the end of this volume.

THE

VIRGINIA CAMPAIGN OF '64 AND '65.

CHAPTER I.

THE POSITION OF THE ARMY OF THE POTOMAC AND
OF THE ARMY OF NORTHERN VIRGINIA IN THE
SPRING OF 1864—THE REORGANIZATION OF THE
ARMY OF THE POTOMAC—GENERAL PLAN OF OP-
ERATIONS FOR THE CAMPAIGN—THE MOVEMENT
BY THE LEFT FLANK DECIDED ON—THE COMPO-
SITION AND NUMBERS OF THE TWO ARMIES.

In the Spring of 1864 the Army of the Potomac lay between the Rapidan and the Rappahannock. The infantry
was posted chiefly in the vicinity of Culpeper Court House
covering the roads leading from Lee's position, the First and
Third Corps about two miles in advance of the Court House,
the Second Corps near Stevensburg, the Sixth Corps near
Welford's Ford, on Hazel River, and the Fifth Corps guarding the railroad from the Rappahannock River back to Bris-
toe Station, near Manassas Junction. The Ninth Corps, under
General Burnside, began to relieve the Fifth Corps from
this duty on April 25th, and between the 1st and 3d of May
encamped along the railroad from Manassas Junction to
Rappahannock Station.

The main body of the cavalry of the Army of the Potomac was about two miles in front of the First Corps, the
other part of it near Stevensburg. A chain of infantry

pickets, well in advance, encircled the whole army ; cavalry pickets extended outside of these to give early notice of any serious movement of the enemy. The Rapidan was carefully watched, especially at the fords and at the railroad bridge.

The Army of Northern Virginia lay along its intrenchments on the Rapidan, from Barnett's Ford, about five miles above the railroad crossing of that river, down to the vicinity of Morton's Ford, a distance of eighteen or twenty miles. Ewell's corps held the lower half of these intrenchments, Hill's the upper half. A few brigades guarded the river, the main force being concentrated in the rear ready to advance to the river or to either flank. The fords below and above the intrenchments were watched by small detachments of cavalry, the main force of which lay along the Rappahannock below Fredericksburg, where, in a country scarcely touched by the war, forage was comparatively abundant. Having an intrenched front on the banks of a river, his left partly withdrawn, and the Wilderness on his right flank not far from his return intrenchment on Mine Run, Lee could not use cavalry on his front, and did not need them on his right except in small parties to watch the crossings of the river and the main roads.

The return intrenchment on Lee's right, beginning near Morton's Ford, extended up Mine Run to its source near Antioch Meeting House, south of the plank road running from Orange Court House to Fredericksburg. General Lee's headquarters were at Orange Court House, about seventy miles from Richmond.

General Longstreet with two of the divisions of his Corps returned to the Army of Northern Virginia in the last part of April, and was held in the vicinity of Gordonsville, a position from which he could better meet an advance of the Army of the Potomac by its right flank than by its left. It was known to General Meade that General Longstreet had returned, but it was reported and believed that his three divisions were with him, Pickett's, Field's, and Kershaw's.

On March 4th General Meade recommended to the Secretary of War to consolidate the five infantry corps of the Army of the Potomac and form three corps of them. This consolidation was effected by orders from the War Department dated March 23d, the Second, Fifth, and Sixth Corps being retained, and the divisions of the First and Third Corps transferred to the three retained corps, though preserving their corps and division badges and distinctive marks. This re-organization required brigades and divisions in all the five corps to be consolidated.[1]

The reason given for this reorganization was the reduced strength of nearly all the infantry regiments composing the army ; but it caused some dissatisfaction with both officers and enlisted men, owing to the spirit of rivalry between the several corps, the divisions of a corps, and the brigades of a division. The history and associations of these organizations were different, and when they were merged in other organizations their identity was lost and their pride and *esprit de corps* wounded.

At the opening of the campaign of 1864, in the first week of May, the three infantry corps amounted to 73,390 officers and enlisted men, giving an average strength of nearly 25,000 to each. In a country so heavily wooded as that in which the operations were to be conducted, five infantry corps of about 15,000 each would have been a more judicious organization, owing to the difficulty of communication between the corps commander and the subordinate command-

---

[1] The new Second Corps consisted of the old Second, formed in two divisions, and the old Third Corps, consisting of two divisions. The new Fifth Corps consisted of the old Fifth, formed in two divisions, and the old First Corps, formed in two divisions. A division that had been united with the Third Corps on July 9, 1863, was transferred to the Sixth Corps, and was the third division of that corps.

ers in a battle in such a country, and the consequent difficulty of prompt and efficient control of extensive lines of
battle, especially at critical moments, or when unforeseen
exigencies occurred. The nature of the appointment of a
corps commander, emanating as it did from the President,
conferred a much wider discretion on him than that authorized in a division commander, and that discretion was sometimes needed in the division commanders of corps 25,000
strong.

A marked case exemplifying this difficulty will be found
in the second day's fighting on the left in the Wilderness.
General Hancock's lines were so extended, and his troops on
the right were so separated from those on the left, owing to
the difference in the character of the tasks allotted to each,
that on the second day he assigned General Birney to the
command of his right wing, and General Gibbon to the command of his left wing, in which commands these officers
needed the authority and discretion of corps commanders.
The difficulties were greatly increased when, further on in
the day, General Hancock had, besides his own corps and
Getty's division of the Sixth Corps, two divisions of the
Fifth Corps and one division of the Ninth Corps—divisions
to which General Birney was a stranger, and the character
of whose officers he was unacquainted with. It is well known
that the personal character of a general officer in moments of
difficulty has a powerful influence upon the result.

These criticisms are made in order to a full understanding
of the difficulties of the campaign.

By an act approved on the 29th of February, 1864, Congress
revived the grade of Lieutenant-General in the army, and
authorized the President, during his pleasure, to assign the
officer of that grade to the command of the armies of the
United States.

On the 9th of March following, General Grant received

his commission as Lieutenant-General, and was assigned to the command of the armies.

On the 10th, he visited the Army of the Potomac, the headquarters of which was near Brandy Station, on the Orange and Alexandria Railroad, about seventy miles from Washington, and announced to General Meade his intention of making his headquarters with that army. The reasons for this determination mentioned by Badeau in his " Military History of General Grant" (which are supposed to be those of General Grant himself), were, "the transcendent import- ance of the issues in Virginia upon which the fate of both the national and the rebel capital depended," and the fact that the force opposed to the Army of the Potomac (the Army of Northern Virginia) "was the strongest, the best led, and the best appointed" army in the Confederate service.

Another consideration was, that "the political and per- sonal influences of various sorts and of various individuals which centred at Washington had thwarted some generals, and interfered with all who had commanded the Army of the Potomac since the beginning of the war. It was General Grant's duty himself to encounter these difficulties, and to withstand, if he could not prevent, political interference ; to remain where he could control all the movements of all the armies, absolutely and independently. . . . If he re- mained at the East this was secured, but with the General- in-Chief a thousand miles away, the Government might be unable to resist entreaties or threats of interested or anxious outsiders, and the best concerted schemes might come to naught. . . . Unless he was near the capital, he could not control all the operations of all the armies without in- terruption, and could not carry out the plan that he believed the only one by which the rebellion could be overthrown. In Washington General Grant would not stay in time of war; he must then direct, in person, the campaigns of that renowned Army of the Potomac."

But General Grant says, in his report of July 22, 1865, upon the operations of the armies of the United States from the date of his appointment as Lieutenant-General to the close of the war, " I may here state that commanding all the armies as I did, I tried, as far as possible, to leave General Meade in independent command of the Army of the Potomac. My instructions for that army were all through him, and were general in their nature, leaving all the details and the execution to him."

On the 9th of April, General Meade was instructed that Lee's army would be his objective ; that General Butler with the Army of the James would move against Richmond by the south bank of James River, on the same day that the Army of the Potomac moved against Lee, and that if Lee fell back upon Richmond, the two armies would form a junction on James River, preferably above the city. In the event of Lee's falling back toward Richmond all the lines of supply to that city were to be destroyed as the Army of the Potomac advanced, and if the junction of the two armies took place below the city, the destruction of the lines of supply south of the James would be effected by them.

In co-operation with the movement upon Lee and upon Richmond, General Sigel (succeeded by General Hunter) was directed to move the force under his command in two columns, one under General Crook from the Great Kanawha through Lewisburg to the East Tennessee and Virginia Railroad, and down that railroad (" doing all the damage possible ") and unite with the other column, which was to move up the Shenandoah Valley to Staunton, and, if practicable, to Lynchburg, by way of Lexington or Charlottesville, and then join the Army of the Potomac by way of Gordonsville, destroying, as far as practicable, railroads that could be used as lines of supply to the enemy, and also the James River and Kanawha Canal.

Apart from being the Confederate capital, Richmond was one of the most important military positions in the Southern States. It is at the head of tide-water of James River and of navigation for sea-going steamers of the smaller class, but for over thirty miles below the city the river is so narrow as to be readily defended. It is connected by railroads and by the James River and Kanawha Canal with the most fertile and productive parts of Virginia north of the James, and with East Tennessee. South of the James it is connected by railroads with all the seaports of the South Atlantic and Gulf States as far west as the State of Mississippi, and with all the interior towns and productive districts of those states. Those seaports our blockading squadrons did not succeed in closing against enterprising blockade-runners. It had iron works, workshops, and manufactories in which the materiel of war was prepared.

Its proximity to Washington and the Middle States added to its importance, and being the Confederate capital still further increased it, though this last consideration was not so important as it had been earlier in the war, when it was still doubtful what encouragement or assistance Great Britain and France might afford the Confederate States. The attitude of Great Britain toward Mexico, late in the Spring of 1862, made it evident that she would not take any active part with them, but the invasion of Mexico by French troops rendered it quite probable that the Emperor Louis Napoleon might do so.

The question has been asked why the Army of the Potomac was not withdrawn from the Rapidan in the Spring of 1864, and moved by water to the near vicinity of Richmond, where, by taking possession of the lines of supply of that great military depot, the force defending it would be obliged to assume the offensive and attack the enveloping army in its intrenchments. But it is not to be supposed that Lee would have withdrawn to and remained within the carefully prepared fortifications enclosing Richmond while this transfer was being made, but that, judging from his operations after Gettysburg, and up to the Winter of 1863–64, he would have advanced beyond the city so far that a completely enveloping line by the Army of the Potomac at that distance from the city would not have been practicable and that by his intrenching and continuing to extend and intrench, the Army of the Potomac would have been forced to attack constantly in order to gain possession of those lines of supply at a suitable distance from Richmond, and while extending its enveloping lines would have been subject to attack on the extending flank under unfavorable circumstances.

But suppose the city captured while the Army of Northern Virginia remained strong enough to keep the field and continue the contest with the Army of the Potomac; it would then probably have moved westward toward Lynchburg, or south of west to some similar point, as, for instance, Danville, covering railroads that would have formed its lines of supply. The Army of the Potomac must then have followed, rebuilding railroads and guarding them afterward (which in moving from the Rapidan to Richmond it did not do), and have fought battles corresponding to those it fought on the route to Richmond, but under less favorable circumstances as to the maintenance of its supplies. The face of the country west of Richmond is, however, better adapted to the handling of troops than that of the region near tidal waters, though that would not have rendered the conflicts less bloody.

A direct movement against Lee in the field so distant from Richmond as the Rapidan, would give opportunities of flanking operations by the whole army, and a freer handling of it than the one just referred to, and therefore with more opportunities of success in destroying the power of the Army of Northern Virginia. Until the James River was crossed this movement would cover Washington better than the other.

But move as we might, long-continued, hard fighting under great difficulties was before us, and whatever might be the line of operations adopted, the successful execution of the task of the Army of the Potomac could only be accomplished by the vigorous and untiring efforts of all belonging to that army, and by suffering heavy losses in killed and wounded, and that the whole army well understood.

On the 15th of April, General Benham, of the Engineers, was instructed confidentially to have prepared by the end of April, in such manner as not to attract attention, water transportation for the pontoon bridge materiel for crossing James River, and General Hunt, Chief of Artillery, was ordered to have siege guns and siege materiel ready at Washington for transportation at that time.

Lee's army being the objective, the first question was, by which flank should the Army of the Potomac move.

To move by our right flank would take us through a more open and cultivated country than that we should find in moving by our left; but then we would be obliged to detach a strong force to protect the Alexandria Railroad, and our depot on it, and when the fifteen days' supplies of the wagon train were exhausted, the protecting force must be increased, for the wagon train and for the additional length of railroad we had acquired; or, if the railroad were abandoned, a strong covering force would be required for the wagon train moving to and from navigable waters. The proper care of the wounded, of which we expected to have a large number on hand in a few days, would be greatly facilitated by the easy access to water transportation that a movement by the left would afford. To clear the left of the enemy's intrenchments on the Rapidan at Barnett's Ford, we must cross that river above that point, and advance by the roads from Madison Court House and from Stannardsville to Orange Court House and to Gordonsville, passing over Southwest Mountain, near to which are Orange Court House and Gordonsville. The distance we should be obliged to traverse before reaching Southwest Mountain, more than forty miles, fully exposed to the view of the enemy, would give him ample time to take up and intrench a position covering the roads through Southwest Mountain by which we must advance; and equal difficulties would be encountered should we move still further to his left.

In moving by our left flank we should abandon our line of supply by the Alexandria Railroad, and at once open short routes of communication from our protected flank, the left, to navigable waters connected with Washington and other depôts of supply. No protecting force would be necessary to cover these short land routes.

The objection to moving by our left consisted in the character of the country south of the Rapidan, through which we must pass for the distance of ten or fifteen miles after crossing the river, and in which we might be obliged to fight the first battle. The Army of the Potomac was well acquainted with the chief roads passing through that region, known as the Wilderness, but there were besides these chief roads numerous wood-roads, connecting the farms, mines, etc., and intersecting the main roads. The farms were few in number, the greater part of the country being covered with a forest, usually of dense growth, and over a large part of its extent there was, besides, an almost impenetrable undergrowth, which it was very difficult for even small bodies of men to move in. To handle large bodies of troops in battle in such a field was exceedingly difficult. Except along the main roads and in the open ground of the farms, artillery would be of little use. But that was not the only disadvantage ; for an enemy remaining on the defensive awaiting attack where this undergrowth existed, would be unseen, while the troops advancing to attack would make their presence known, and thus the tangled growth would serve in some measure as an intrenchment, at least for the first and most destructive fire. In the region about Chancellorsville the country was more open and the woods less dense. There was some reason to believe, however, from our experience in the movement against Lee in the preceding November, that by setting the whole army in motion at midnight, with its reserve artillery and great trains of over four thousand wagons, it might move so far beyond the Rapidan the first day that it would be able to pass out of the Wilderness and turn, or partly turn, the right flank of Lee before a general engagement took place. There was no question of the practicability of the troops, with their fighting trains, accomplishing this, as they were quite equal to, and ready for, a continuous march of thirty miles or more in twenty-four hours, by which they would have got substantially clear of the Wilderness ; they had often before made such marches when called on to do so ; but the question was as to the practicability of moving the great trains of the army that distance simultaneously with the troops, so as to keep them under cover of the army.

It was well known that daylight would divulge our movement to Lee's signal officers on Clark's Mountain, and at other points along his lines, and it was believed that he would at once move by the Orange and Fredericksburg pike and plank roads to oppose us.

Superiority in numbers on such a field would be of less value than on any other. Besides, with such intelligent material as the larger part of both armies was composed of, the greater familiarity of the Southern men with the dense forests and wooded swamps of the South would give them an advantage in an encounter in the Wilderness tending to neutralize the disparity of numbers. When lines of battle are broken on such a field, and the troops fall back in disorder, the successful side is thrown into almost equal disorder in attempting to advance quickly, and both sides are obliged to re-form.

In the previous November our movement, begun in the morning, had been observed as soon as the fog rose, but Ewell's corps only succeeded in reaching Locust Grove (Robertson's tavern) on the pike by half past ten o'clock on the morning of the second day, and Hill's corps the corresponding point on the plank road, New Hope Church, at four o'clock in the afternoon of the second day. Robertson's tavern is about five miles west of the old Wilderness tavern, New Hope Church six miles west of the intersection of the Brock road with the plank road, and three miles west of Parker's store.

The movement by the left flank was adopted, and I was requested by General Meade to prepare a project for it. Two were sketched out by me, the one turning Lee's right by the Catharpin and Pamunkey roads in comparatively open country, the other by roads having about the same general direction as the Pamunkey, but from five to eight miles eastward of it, passing two to four miles west of Spottsylvania Court House. The two projects were coincident for the first day and for a part of the second, and both were subject to material modification or entire abandonment on the second day, dependent upon the movements of Lee.

The first project was adopted, and the order of movement was prepared by me in conformity to it. The order for continuing the movement on the 5th of May, issued on the evening of the 4th, also conformed to it, but owing to indications of the enemy's movement on the 4th, the order of march was partial only, and held in view the probability of a general engagement on that day.

Upon the reorganization of the army, Major-General Hancock, who had been absent, owing to wounds received at Gettysburg, resumed command of the Second Corps; Major-General Warren was appointed to the command of the Fifth Corps; Major-General Sedgwick retained command of the Sixth Corps, and Major-General Sheridan was appointed to the command of the Cavalry Corps.[1]

The Ninth Corps, Major-General A. E. Burnside commanding, united with the Army of the Potomac on the morning of the 6th of May, though it was not incorporated

---

[1] On the 30th April the Army of the Potomac was organized as follows, viz.:

Major-General Geo. G. Meade Commanding the Army; Major-General A. A. Humphreys, Chief of Staff; Brigadier-General Henry J. Hunt, Chief of Artillery; Major James C. Duane, Chief Engineer.

Second Corps, Major-General Winfield S. Hancock commanding: First Division (old Second Corps), composed of four brigades, Brigadier-General F. C. Barlow commanding; Second Division (old Second Corps), composed of three brigades, Brigadier-General John Gibbon commanding; Third Division (old Third Corps), composed of two brigades, Major-General D. B. Birney commanding; Fourth Division (old Third Corps), composed of two brigades, Brigadier-General G. Mott commanding.

Fifth Corps, Major-General G. K. Warren commanding: First Division (old Fifth Corps), three brigades, Brigadier-General Charles Griffin commanding; Second Division (old First Corps), three brigades, Brigadier-General J. C. Robinson commanding; Third Division (old Fifth Corps), two brigades, Brigadier-General S. W. Crawford commanding; Fourth Division (old First Corps), three brigades, Brigadier-General J. S. Wadsworth commanding.

Sixth Corps, Major-General John Sedgwick commanding: First Division, four brigades, Brigadier-General H. G. Wright commanding; Second Division, four brigades, Brigadier-General G. W. Getty commanding; Third Division, two brigades, Brigadier-General James B. Ricketts commanding.

Cavalry Corps, Major-General P. H. Sheridan commanding: First Division, three brigades, Brigadier-General A. T. A. Torbert commanding; Second Division, two brigades, Brigadier-General D. McM. Gregg commanding; Third Division, two brigades, Brigadier-General J. H. Wilson commanding.

For further details of the Army of the Potomac, and of the Ninth Corps, see Appendix A.

with it until the 24th of May, when it became a part of Major-General Meade's command.[1]

The consolidated Morning Report of the Army of the Potomac of the 30th April, 1864, gives for its numerical strength on that day [2] "*present for duty equipped:*"

	Officers.	Enlisted Men.	Guns.
Provost Guard......	70	1,048	
Engineers....	50	2,226	
The three Infantry Corps...........	3,506	69,884	
Artillery of the Infantry and Cavalry Corps, and the Reserve Artillery with its Guard....	285	9,945	274
The Cavalry Corps..................	585	11,839	

The total number of officers and enlisted men of the Army of the Potomac of all arms and branches of the service, including Provost Guard, Engineers, Reserve Artillery with its guard, the Infantry Corps and their Artillery, and the Cavalry Corps and its Artillery, "*present for duty equipped*," on the 30th of April amounted to 99,438.

According to the return of the Ninth Corps for the month of April, 1864, the number present for duty was 923 officers and 18,408 enlisted men, with forty-two guns. These numbers include 73 officers and 1,199 enlisted men of cavalry and the officers and enlisted men of artillery.

The Morning Report of this Corps for the 10th of May, 1864, gives for its strength—

	Officers.	Enlisted Men.	Guns.
Infantry.............................	851	18,995	
Artillery..........................	33	1,017	80 [3]
Cavalry.............................	84	1,728	

---

[1] It consisted of four divisions, the First commanded by Brigadier-General Thos. G. Stevenson, the Second by Brigadier-General R. B. Potter, the Third by Brigadier-General O. B. Willcox, and the Fourth, a colored division, by Brigadier-General E. Ferrero. The Third and Fourth Divisions were newly raised, and had not been in the field, and in fact all but 6,000 of the enlisted men of the Corps had just entered the service.

[2] See Appendix B.   [3] Probably a mistake—42 guns.

On the 1st of May, 1864, the Army of Northern Virginia, commanded by General R. E. Lee, was composed of three Infantry Corps, the First Corps commanded by Lieutenant-General James Longstreet, the Second by Lieutenant-General Richard S. Ewell, the Third by Lieutenant-General A. P. Hill. The Cavalry Corps was commanded by Major-General J. E. B. Stewart.[1]

The consolidated Morning Report of the Army of Northern Virginia, of April 20, 1864 (the Morning Report for April 30, 1864, is not in the possession of the War Department, nor is there any information in that Department concerning it) shows that there were that day present for duty :

	Officers.	Enlisted Men.
Second Corps [2]	1,379	15,705
Third Corps	1,551	20,648
Total Infantry	2,930	36,353
Cavalry Corps	467	7,932
Artillery	237	4,617

The last return previous to May 1, 1864, of Longstreet's two divisions that were with him in the Department of East

---

[1] The Chief of Artillery was Brigadier-General William N. Pendleton ; the Adjutant-General, Colonel Walter H. Taylor; the Chief Engineer, Major-General M. L. Smith ; the Chief Quartermaster, Lieutenant-Colonel James L. Corley ; the Chief Medical Director, Surgeon Lafayette Guild.

The First Corps had present with it only two of its divisions, commanded by Major-Generals Field and Kershaw, Pickett's division being absent on the south side of James River. The Second Corps had present its three divisions, commanded by Major-Generals Early, Johnson, and Rodes, and the Third Corps its three divisions, commanded by Major-Generals Anderson, Heth, and Wilcox.

The Cavalry Corps consisted of two divisions commanded by Major-Generals Hampton and Fitzhugh Lee.

For the details of the Army of Northern Virginia, See Appendix C.

[2] Hoke's brigade and two regiments of Rodes's division absent, not counted.

Tennessee (known to the War Department) is that of March 31, 1864, which gives present for duty:[1]

	Officers.	Enlisted Men.
Field's Division	....	3,875
McLaw's Division (Kershaw's before May 1st)	....	4,542
Total	....	8,417

There were probably 1,000 officers with the two divisions. Colonel Taylor, in his "Four Years with General Lee," estimates the effective force of those two divisions when they rejoined the army at 10,000 enlisted men present for duty.[2]

There were, according to our information, four bat-

---

[1] Department of East Tennessee, Lieutenant-General Longstreet commanding, March 31, 1864.

	Officers.	Enlisted Men.
Field's Division	....	3,875
McLaw's "	....	4.542
Buckner's "	....	3,401
Wharton's Brigade	....	838
Jackson's "	....	866
Cavalry two brigades, Generals Jones and Vaughn commanding	....	4,264

Buckner's division, commanded by Brigadier-General B. R. Johnson, consisted of Johnson's brigade of Tennessee regiments and Gracie's and Law's Alabama brigades.

[2] So far as I can make out from the very defective returns in our possession of Pickett's division, its effective force (enlisted men present for duty) at this period, the latter part of April, was about 5,000.

The first return, or Morning Report, in the Confederate archives in the possession of the War Department, in which the numbers of Longstreet's Corps are given after that of March 31, 1864, is the Morning Report of the Army of Northern Virginia of June 30, 1864, in which that corps is reported as having present for duty 1,098 officers and 13,060 enlisted men. That this Corps should have gone into the campaign of 1864 with about the same numbers that it had on the 31st of August, 1863, while the Third Corps (Hill's) increased in that time from 13,601 enlisted men present for duty to 20,648, and the Second Corps (Ewell's) from 15,428 to near 18,000 (including Hoke's brigade, and two regiments of Rodes's, absent), was quite unexpected. Neither General Longstreet nor his division commanders state the strength of their commands in their reports of the opening operations of the campaign.

teries of four guns in each infantry division, which, for the eight divisions, is one hundred and twenty-eight guns, seventy-two guns in the reserve artillery, and twenty-four with the Cavalry—a total of two hundred and twenty-four guns.

Using the figures of the extracts from the Morning Reports of the Army of Northern Virginia, we have for its numbers "present for duty," May 1, 1864, *not less than*—

	Officers.	Enlisted Men.
Infantry	3,930	44,770
Artillery	237	4,617
Cavalry	467	7,932

making a grand aggregate of officers and enlisted men of infantry, artillery, and cavalry of 61,953, with probably two hundred and twenty-four guns.

CHAPTER II.

THE PASSAGE OF THE RAPIDAN—THE BATTLE OF THE WILDERNESS

On the 2d of May the order for the movement of the Army of the Potomac was issued.[1]

The movement began promptly at midnight of the 3d, Major-General Sheridan, with two of his cavalry divisions, leading the two infantry columns, one of his divisions, Torbert's, being left to cover the rear of the army. A canvas and a wooden ponton bridge were laid at Germanna Ford, the same at Ely's Ford, and a wooden ponton bridge at Culpeper Mine Ford, five bridges in all, the river being about two hundred feet wide.

The Second Corps, preceded by Gregg's cavalry division, crossed at Ely's Ford, and moved to Chancellorville, followed by the reserve artillery. The Fifth Corps, preceded by Wilson's cavalry division, and followed by the Sixth Corps, crossed at Germanna Ford, and moved to Wilderness Tavern, at the intersection of the Germanna plank road,[2] by the Orange Court House and Fredericksburg pike. The head of the Sixth Corps halted three miles from Germanna Ford, the rear at the ford.

The trains, except those known as the fighting trains, which accompanied the troops (see the order of movement),

---

[1] See order of May 2, 1864—Appendix D.
[2] This road ran from Germanna Ford to Fredericksburg.

crossed at Culpeper Mine Ford and Ely's Ford. They were covered by the cavalry, and had an infantry guard of 1,200 men from each infantry corps.

Gregg's cavalry moved to the vicinity of Piney Branch Church, throwing out reconnoissances on the Pamunkey road and toward Spottsylvania Court House, Fredericksburg, and Hamilton's crossing. Wilson's cavalry moved to Parker's store, on the Fredericksburg and Orange Court House plank road, throwing out reconnoissances to the right on the Orange pike and plank roads, and on the Catharpin and Pamunkey roads.

The head of the Second Corps arrived at Chancellorville at 10 A.M. of the 4th, and the whole corps, with the trains moving with the troops, were at the halting-place designated about 1 o'clock. The whole of the Fifth Corps was up to its position by 2 o'clock. Each of these corps had marched more than twenty miles, and both had assisted in laying the wooden ponton bridges at their crossings of the Rapidan, and had improved the roads leading up the steep river-banks. The Sixth Corps had marched more than sixteen miles, but following the Fifth Corps was later in getting to its halting-ground for the night.

The canvas bridges were taken up on the 4th, and joined the corps to which they belonged. The wooden bridges were left for the trains and the Ninth Corps.

Respecting this operation General Grant says, " This I regarded as a great success, and it removed from my mind the most serious apprehensions I had entertained, that of crossing the river in the face of an active, large, well-appointed, and ably-commanded army, and how so large a train was to be carried through a hostile country and protected." And he might well be gratified at the result, for it was a good day's work in such a country for so large an army with its artillery and fighting trains to march twenty miles, crossing a river on five bridges of its own building, without a single mishap, interruption, or delay.

It was not practicable, however, to get over all the great trains on the 4th, nor was it expected, as the order of movement shows. In fact it was two o'clock in the afternoon of the 5th of May before they had ceased crossing at Ely's Ford, when the wooden bridge there was taken up and moved to Chancellorville ; and it was five o'clock in the afternoon of the 5th of May before they had ceased crossing at Culpeper Mine Ford, when the bridge there was taken up and the ponton train moved one and a half miles from the river. It was in consideration of the fact that it was not practicable in this region to move the great trains along the protected flank of the army simultaneously with the troops, that led to fixing the halting-places of the heads of the infantry columns at Chancellorville and Wilderness tavern, points which they reached early in the day. The troops might have easily continued their march five miles further, the Second Corps to Todd's tavern, the head of the Fifth Corps to Parker's store, and the head of the Sixth Corps to Wilderness tavern ; but even that would have left the right too open during the forenoon of the 5th, and it was more judicious to let the troops remain for the night where they had halted, as it made the passage of the trains secure, and the troops would be fresher when meeting the enemy next day, of which there was much probability.

At 1.15 P.M. of the 4th, General Grant telegraphed from Germanna Ford to General Burnside to make a forced march until he reached there. His First Division, General Stevenson, had then arrived at Brandy Station, and his Fourth, the colored division, had marched that morning from Manassas Junction, more than forty miles distant from Germanna Ford. General Stevenson's division crossed the Rapidan at Germanna Ford on the morning of the 5th, and by the night of the 5th Potter's and Willcox's divisions, coming from Bealeton and from Rappahannock Station, had likewise crossed there and advanced some three miles. General Ferrero's division (Fourth) crossed on the morning of the 6th.

Indications concerning the movements of the enemy were noted before one o'clock in the afternoon of the 4th ; some few shots were fired toward Robertson's tavern, and they were observed moving in some force from Orange Court House on the plank road toward New Verdiersville.

Major-General Sheridan having received some information during the day to the effect that the main body of the enemy's cavalry was near Hamilton's crossing, and suggesting that he should proceed against them, the order for movement on the 5th directed him to do so with Gregg's and Torbert's divisions. The army was to move at five o'clock in the morning, General Wilson to proceed to Craig's Meeting House on the Catharpin road, and to keep out parties on the Orange Court House pike and plank road, the Catharpin and Pamunkey roads, and in the direction of Twyman's store and Andrew's tavern or Good Hope Church ; General Hancock to move to Shady Grove Church, on the Catharpin road, and extend his right toward the Fifth Corps at Parker's store ; General Warren to move to Parker's store and extend his right toward the Sixth Corps at Old Wilderness tavern ; General Sedgwick to move to Old Wilderness tavern, leaving a division to cover the bridge at Germanna Ford, until General Burnside's command arrived. After reaching the points designated the army was to be held ready to move forward. The movement began promptly as ordered.[1]

Let us see what the Army of Northern Virginia was doing to meet this advance of the Army of the Potomac.

---

[1] See order of May 4th—Appendix E.

General Ewell states that the corps and division commanders of the Army of Northern Virginia met General Lee
on the 2d of May at the signal station on Clark's Mountain,
when he expressed the opinion that the Army of the Potomac would cross by some of the fords below them ; that the
movement of that army being observed on the morning of
the 4th, he, General Ewell, moved, under orders, toward
Locust Grove (Robertson's tavern) on the Orange pike,
where the head of his corps, Early's division, halted for the
night about five miles from Old Wilderness tavern, Rodes's
and Johnson's divisions closing up on him.[1]

General Hill with Heth's and Wilcox's divisions of his
corps moved about midday of the 4th along the Orange
Court House plank road, halting for the night, Heth at Mine
Run and Wilcox at Verdiersville, the former about seven
miles from Parker's store and about ten from the intersection of the Brock road with the Orange Court House plank
road. Anderson's division remained on the Rapidan and
did not unite with the corps until the morning of the 6th.

It will be observed that General Lee moved more
promptly toward the Army of the Potomac than he had
done in the preceding November when that army crossed
the Rapidan, though the reports from General Wilson's parties indicated that these corps were no further advanced
than they had been on that occasion.

General Longstreet moved from the vicinity of Gordonsville at four o'clock in the afternoon of the 4th, halting for
the night at Brock's bridge, and on the night of the 5th at
Richards's shop on the Catharpin road, not far from Craig's
Meeting House. He was probably retained on the Catharpin road until it was ascertained what disposition was made
of Hancock. Stewart's cavalry, which had been drawn in,

---

[1] R. D. Johnson's brigade of Rodes's division joined it on the morning of the 6th.

was to operate on the Confederate right flank, on the Catharpin and other roads.

On the morning of the 5th, General Ewell moved down the pike, Johnson's division leading, followed by Rodes's and Early's. He was instructed by General Lee to regulate his march by that of General Hill on the plank road, and was informed that it was preferred not to bring on a general engagement before General Longstreet came up. General Ewell, being three or four miles further advanced than Hill, halted his command when the head of it was two miles distant from the Wilderness tavern or Germanna road. Just before halting he sent Walker's brigade of Johnson's division down the road leading, on his left, from the pike to Spottswood on the Germanna plank road.

General Crawford's division led the column of the Fifth Corps, General Wadsworth's followed, then General Robinson's ; General Griffin's forming the rear—his division having lain during the night across the pike, about a mile out from the Germanna road.

At a quarter past seven General Meade, while on his way to General Warren's headquarters near the Old Wilderness tavern, received a despatch from that officer informing him that the enemy's infantry was on the pike in some force about two miles from the Wilderness tavern. A few minutes later General Meade was with General Warren, and at once directed him to halt his column and attack the enemy with his whole force. This would soon develop what part of Lee's army was there. At the same time, 7.30 A.M., a despatch was sent to General Hancock informing him that the enemy was on the pike in some force, and directing him to halt at Todd's tavern until further developments were made. This despatch was received by him at 9 o'clock, at which time his advance was two miles beyond Todd's tavern.

General Sedgwick was directed to move out on the road

that leaves the Germanna plank road at Spottswood and enters the pike some two and a half miles from Wilderness
tavern, attack the enemy and connect with the Fifth Corps
on the pike.   His force was Wright's division and Neill's
brigade of Getty's division, to which the second brigade of
Ricketts's division, General Seymour commanding, was
added in the afternoon.   General Ricketts's division covered
the Germanna bridge until General Burnside's troops relieved him toward noon.

General Grant had been at once informed by General
Meade of what was transpiring and soon joined him.   After
brief conference the two rode forward a short distance, and
took position on a knoll in the open ground around Wilderness tavern and the Lacy farm, and on this knoll General
Grant and General Meade remained during the battle, with
only an occasional brief absence to the nearest troops.

When the head of Crawford's column reached the high
open ground of Chewning's farm, about a mile from Parker's
store (and three miles from Wilderness tavern), he found
Colonel Hammond, commanding the cavalry detachment left
there by General Wilson until the infantry should arrive,
skirmishing with what General Crawford, at 8 A.M., reported to be the enemy's cavalry.

At 5 A.M. General Wilson had reported his command moving toward the Catharpin road, and that his pickets reported nothing new from the enemy that morning.

At 8 A.M. General Crawford had received the order to halt,
and had taken up a good position in high open ground at
Chewning's, from which a good road ran to Parker's store,
and another to Tapp's farm on the plank road, about two
miles east of Parker's store.   Finding that our cavalry at
Parker's store needed assistance, General Crawford threw
forward a skirmish line that became engaged with the
flankers of an infantry force moving on the plank road, the

advance guard of Hill, Kirkland's brigade, but by that time the cavalry had been forced back, retiring slowly on the plank road before the skirmishers of Hill's advance.

Some time after eight o'clock General Crawford was informed by General Warren that Griffin and Wadsworth would attack Ewell on the pike, and he was ordered to join in it with one of his brigades.

Between nine and ten o'clock, the development of the enemy's force was such that a despatch was sent to General Hancock, directing him to move up the Brock road to the Orange Court House plank road, and be prepared to move out that road toward Parker's store.

When Sedgwick was ordered out against Ewell's left, Getty's division of the Sixth Corps, except Neill's brigade, was brought to the Wilderness tavern, and as soon as it was ascertained that the enemy's infantry were on the plank road at Parker's store in force, between nine and ten o'clock, Getty was sent on the Brock road to its intersection with the Orange plank road, about two miles from the Wilderness tavern, and directed to move out the latter road and attack the enemy, and, if he could, drive them back beyond Parker's store. The order to General Getty was sent at the same time as that to General Hancock to come up.

The Brock road begins on the Orange pike about a mile east of the Old Wilderness tavern, and runs in a southeast direction to Spottsylvania Court House, intersecting the Germanna plank, the Orange plank, the Furnace, the Catharpin and other roads running in a southwest and south direction.

General Ewell, seeing our force on the pike, supported Jones's brigade of Johnson's division (which had led the advance prepared for action) with Battle's and Doles's brigades of Rodes's division. The other brigades of Johnson's division (Steuart's, Stafford's, and Walker's) were formed on their left of the pike in the order stated, or were forming, when, about noon, General Griffin, advancing with great difficulty through the woods—Ayres's brigade on the right of the pike, Bartlett's and Barnes's on the left—suddenly struck Jones's brigade, broke it and drove it back through the supporting line, disordering Battle's brigade, which, with Doles's, was then hard pressed. General Jones, a gallant officer, was killed in a desperate effort to rally his brigade.[1] Ayres's brigade at the same time attacked the part of Johnson's division in his front. Daniel's brigade of Rodes's division was at once sent forward to the assistance of Doles and Battle. Early's division was brought up and formed across the pike, Gordon's brigade being ordered forward to the right of Rodes's line (the contest still going on), where it took an active and important part in repelling the attack.

Wright's division of the Sixth Corps was to have attacked in connection with the Fifth Corps, but met with such delay and difficulty in forcing its way through the dense scrubby pine and tangled undergrowth, that it could not connect with the Fifth, and did not get in contact with the enemy until much later in the day. General Griffin stated that, not being supported on his right, Ayres's brigade was forced back across the pike, and that entailed the falling back of the other brigades of his division, the enemy following and forming on the line first occupied by them, where they at once intrenched. Two of Griffin's guns on the pike were lost. They remained between the two lines until night, when they were taken away by the enemy.

In the meantime Wadsworth's division, followed and supported on the left by Dennison's Maryland brigade of Robinson's division, had advanced through thick woods and

---

[1] General Early, in his Memoir, says these two brigades, Jones's and Battle's "were driven back in some confusion."

dense thicket, passing through which had probably changed the direction of his movement, so as to bring him, about the time that Daniel's and Gordon's brigades got on the ground, in front of the enemy's right, with his left flank toward them, of which they took instant advantage to attack, and his front line being so entangled in the wood as not to admit of ready handling, its left fell back quickly, and in some confusion, and the enemy, passing through the opening thus made, took Dennison's brigade in flank, as well as the two brigades of the right, and, after a short, sharp engagement, forced them also to retire.

Wadsworth's division had moved before McCandless's brigade of Crawford's division could unite with it, and this brigade had to take such direction as, it was thought, would bring it to Wadsworth's left, but it did not. Passing through the same kind of entangled wood found everywhere, it came in contact with Ewell's right, a part of it became enveloped by Gordon's brigade, had many killed and wounded, lost several hundred prisoners, and fell back. Crawford's division, being now somewhat isolated, was, toward two o'clock, drawn in, and posted about a mile southwest from the Lacy house, facing toward Chewning's.

The line of the Fifth Corps was established with its right on the pike, about three hundred yards from the enemy's line, thence gradually diverging further from it to Crawford. The enemy had reformed his line on the ground occupied when attacked, Rodes's division (Daniel's, Doles's, and Battle's brigades) on the right (their right) of the pike, Johnson's division on the left of it (Steuart's, Walker's, and Stafford's brigades), then Hays's and Pegram's brigades of Early's division, Gordon's brigade remaining on the right of Rodes until night, when it was placed on Pegram's left. The whole line was intrenched as soon as occupied.

It was between two and three o'clock, perhaps even later,

when Wright's division of the Sixth Corps got up to the
enemy's front north of the pike and formed about three
hundred yards from Johnson's and Early's line. Upton's
brigade resting its left on the pike, connected with the Fifth
Corps ; the brigades of Penrose and Russell came next,
Neill's brigade of Getty's division being on the right. The
ground between Upton and the enemy had been fought over,
and many killed and wounded of both sides lay on it. The
woods were on fire on his entire front. Soon after arriving
on the ground Russell's and Neill's brigades were attacked
by Stafford's and Walker's brigades, which, after a sharp
encounter, were repulsed, Neill capturing some prisoners.
General Stafford was mortally wounded. The enemy had
artillery on their left in the open ground of a farm, which
partly enfiladed Neill's line, and the ground on his right and
left. Shortly after this attack, while the firing was still
heavy, Seymour's brigade of Ricketts's division arrived and
was posted on the right of Neill.

Turning now to our left we find that General Getty arrived
at the crossing of the Brock and Orange plank roads not
long after eleven o'clock, and threw out his skirmish line
across the Orange plank road. Half a mile out it encountered the skirmishers of the enemy's advance, forcing back
Colonel Hammond's cavalry. These skirmishers fell back
before Getty's. Learning, about noon, from the prisoners
taken, that Hill's corps was on the road, Heth's division
leading, General Getty disposed his troops for attack, extending his right toward the left of the Fifth Corps, but
finding the enemy in force, deemed it best to await the
arrival of part of the Second Corps before attacking, and
while thus waiting intrenched slightly.

General Hill had undoubtedly received the same instructions as General Ewell, that " General Lee preferred not to
bring on a general engagement before Longstreet came up."

Heth's division of Hill's corps led on the morning of the 5th on the Orange plank road, and a little after midday, when near the Brock road, the head of his column was met by Getty's division, as already stated, in front of which Heth took up a position crossing the plank road on some comparatively elevated ground, having in its front and on its right and left the swampy heads of affluents of the Ny on the right and of Wilderness Run on the left.

General Davis's (Colonel Stone commanding), General Cook's, and General Walker's brigades were on the right of the road, General Kirkland's on the left. Heth's artillery was posted in the rear on an eminence in the open ground of Tapp's farm on the Confederate left of the road, and was covered by epaulments. The same close underbrush was found in this part of the Wilderness, as in almost every other portion of it occupied by our troops, aggravated in the swampy parts. General Lee and General Hill accompanied Heth's division and remained near the artillery on this and the following day.

Wilcox's division followed Heth's, and at about two o'clock, when at Tapp's farm, turned to the left in order to connect with Ewell, and moved beyond Chewning's; it then formed line of battle (its skirmishers engaged) looking toward Ewell's right, which was in sight, in the open ground of Hagerson's farm; toward five o'clock however, Wilcox was called back to Heth's support, a movement that was observed by General Warren.

Hill had moved with caution, and when Heth came in front of Getty showed no disposition to attack, for instead of forming Wilcox to support Heth, he sent him to the left to unite with Ewell.

As already stated, when it became apparent that the enemy in full force were moving against us on the Orange plank and pike roads, General Hancock was directed to

move up the Brock road to the intersection of the Orange
plank road and be prepared to move out toward Parker's
store. Toward noon he was advised that Hill's corps, or
part of it, had driven our cavalry from Parker's store, and
were moving down the plank road ; that Getty had been
sent to drive them back, but might not be able to do so,
and he was directed to support Getty, and drive the enemy
beyond Parker's store, occupy that place and unite with
Warren's left, then about a mile from the store. At half
past one P.M. he was advised that the enemy had the plank
road near to the Brock road; that Getty was not strong
enough to attack, but would aid him; that Griffin had been
pushed back somewhat; that Warren's left was within a
mile of Parker's store, but might be drawn in or driven in ;
that he must push out the plank road and connect with
Warren. An hour later he was informed of the result of
Warren's attack, and that Crawford had been drawn in a
mile. At quarter past three P.M. General Getty was ordered
to attack at once, General Hancock informed of it and directed to support him with his whole corps, that the attack
up the plank road must be made at once, for it was believed
that Longstreet could not be up before the next morning.
General Sedgwick and General Warren were advised of this
and ordered to be prepared to renew the attack as soon as
they were informed that Hancock and Getty had begun it.
General Ricketts's First Brigade, General Morris commanding, was placed to support the left of the Sixth Corps or the
right of the Fifth as might be needed; the part of the
Ninth Corps that had got up covered the Germanna bridge
and the road which led from the enemy's left to the Germanna road near the bridge. As soon as General Hancock
received the despatch directing him to move his command
up the Brock road to its intersection with the plank road
(about 11 A.M.), he at once set his corps in motion toward

that point, and, riding in advance of the corps, met General Getty there, whose division he found in line of battle along the Brock road, the Second Brigade, General Grant's, on the left of the plank road, the First and Fourth Brigades, General Wheaton's and General Eustis's, on the right of the road. Lieutenant-Colonel Morgan, General Hancock's Chief of Staff, was sent to inform General Meade of General Hancock's arrival, and of the condition of affairs. At 2 P.M. the head of his command, General Birney's division, arrived and was formed on Getty's left in two lines of battle along the Brock road. It will be noted that at the same hour General Wilcox's division came up to General Heth's, but moved off toward Ewell. Mott's and Gibbon's divisions coming up rapidly, took their position on Birney's left in the same formation. Barlow's division, except Frank's brigade, held the left of the line, and was thrown forward on high clear ground in front of the Brock road, which commanded the country for some distance to the right and left, and covered the bed of the Fredericksburg and Orange Court House unfinished railroad in front. As this was the only point on the line where artillery could have an effective range, the artillery of the corps, except one battery and a section, was put in position here. It was supported by Barlow's division. Dow's battery was placed in the second line near Mott's left; the section of Ricketts's battery was placed on the Orange plank road. Frank's brigade covered the junction of the Brock road with a road leading northerly to the Catharpin furnaces, and thence to Chancellorville and to the Catharpin and other roads. At this point (where Frank's brigade was posted) a road came in also from the south, leaving the Catharpin road about a mile west of Shady Grove Church, and near the junction of the road from Parker's store with the Catharpin road.

The division commanders were directed to throw up

breastworks (of logs and earth) upon going into position, a work which was accomplished without delay, the line beginning at Getty's left and extending along the whole position occupied by the corps, being refused on the left so as to include the junction of the road leading to the Furnaces where Frank's brigade was posted. The second line also threw up breastworks, and a third line was subsequently constructed in rear of the Third and Fourth Divisions.

General Hancock states that when the despatches heretofore mentioned (except that of 3.15 P.M.) reached him, the greater portion of his troops were coming up to join General Getty. Birney's division had already taken position on Getty's left. The remaining divisions were forming as they arrived on the ground. The Brock road was very narrow and heavily wooded on both sides, and hence the formation of the infantry in line of battle was impeded; their march had been greatly retarded by the artillery occupying the road. General Getty had informed General Hancock when he came up that there were two divisions of Hill in his front and that he momentarily expected an attack. For that reason General Hancock directed the breastworks to be completed in order to receive the attack.

At quarter past four, General Getty, in compliance with his orders from General Meade, advanced to the attack through thick undergrowth, and some four hundred yards from the Brock road became hotly engaged with Heth's division, part of which was lying down behind the crest of a small elevation.[1]

Finding that General Getty had met the enemy in force, General Hancock ordered General Birney to advance his command (his own division and Mott's) to the support of Getty, although the formation he, General Hancock, had

---

[1] See the report of General Grant, commanding the Vermont brigade. He states his loss to have been 1,000, about one-half of his brigade.

directed to be made before carrying out his instructions to advance was not yet completed. General Birney at once moved forward his own division on the right and Mott's on the left of Getty, with a section of artillery on the plank road, which did good service in the course of the action. General Hancock says the fight became "very fierce at once, the lines of battle were exceedingly close, the musketry continuous and deadly along the entire line." General Alexander Hays, commanding the Second Brigade of Birney's division, an officer of distinguished gallantry, was killed at the head of his brigade. Carroll's brigade of Gibbon's division was sent to the support of Getty's right, and Owen's brigade of the same division to the support of Getty on the plank road. Colonel Carroll was wounded, but remained on the field. The battle continued with great severity until near eight o'clock, when darkness and the dense forest put an end to it, fortunately for Hill, whose troops were shattered and his lines disjointed; an hour more of daylight, and he would have been driven from the field, for Longstreet and Anderson were many miles distant.[1]

Before the close of the action Colonel Smyth's Irish bri-

---

[1] General McAllister, commanding First Brigade, Mott's division, states that soon after they went into action, the brigade on his left, Mott's second, suddenly gave way from the left, without any apparent cause, rolling away to the rear, and carrying his own brigade in the same way after it. He imputes it to the fact that the time of many of the regiments would soon be out; but I find that Colonel Burns of the Seventy-third New York, belonging to the Second Brigade, an intrepid soldier, attributes it to the falling back of troops in their front, followed quickly by the outflanking of their brigade by the enemy. There is no report from the commander of the Second Brigade, nor do I find General Mott's report on the files of the War Department.

These two brigades, forming Mott's Fourth Division of the Second Corps, were the remnant of the old Second Division, Third Corps. They were good troops, with three years' experience in fighting, and I think the explanation of Colonel Burns is the right one, viz.: that they were struck in flank and, as they were sometimes apt to do, acted on their own judgment without waiting for that of their commander. I commanded the division at Gettysburg, having been assigned to it about the middle of May, and I knew the troops well.

gade, and Colonel Brooke's brigade, both of Barlow's division, attacked the enemy's right and forced it back.

General Wadsworth, with his division, and Baxter's brigade of the Second Division, was ordered to move between four and five o'clock in a southeast direction so as to strike the force engaged with Hancock and Getty on its left flank and rear.

Moving in the direction stated, General Wadsworth found his progress greatly impeded by the thick woods and underbrush. He met only the skirmish line of the enemy, which he drove before him until it was too dark to see, when the troops halted for the night in line of battle, facing southeast, his left about half a mile from the Brock road.

Soon after the attack on Heth began, Wilcox's division was recalled to his support, McGowan's brigade forming across the road, Thomas's on the left, parallel with the road, Scales's and lastly Lane's on the right. The brigades on the right passed through Heth's lines and advanced at different times as far as the swamps, in and near which they encountered Hancock's and Getty's men with varying success, but were finally forced back to Heth's position, their right and left flanks pressed back. Hill's lines were very irregular and much broken, and his troops in some disorder.

In one of the narratives of the battle it is stated, in order to show how close the lines were, and how bewildering the dense forest growth was, that many men from both armies, in looking for water during the night, found themselves within the opposing lines, and were made prisoners. This probably refers to the left of Hill, opposite to which Wadsworth's troops had halted.

At midnight of the 5th, General Longstreet received a message from General Lee, informing him of the results of the day, and directing him to come up to Parker's store. Marching at once, he arrived there at dawn of the 6th, and was directed to move his column down the plank road, and relieve the divisions of Heth and Wilcox. Anderson's division, of Hill's corps, which had reached Verdiersville in the night of the 5th, was also ordered up, and arrived the next morning soon after Longstreet's divisions.

During the afternoon of the 5th, heavy skirmishing went on on our right, and at about five o'clock, under orders from General Meade for the right to attack, General Seymour's brigade, Colonel Keifer commanding the first line, and Neill's brigade, with part of Penrose's, attacked Pegram's and Hays's brigades, both intrenched ; Pegram's was strongly posted on rising ground, and had artillery in the open ground on his left, which enfiladed our lines. General Neill, finding that he could not carry the enemy's intrenched line, and that his loss was severe, withdrew, but Seymour's troops maintained the contest until dark, losing heavily in killed and wounded, Colonel Keifer among the latter. On the other side General Pegram was severely wounded.

Artillery was placed in the lines of the Fifth Corps wherever it could be used to aid in carrying the enemy's intrenched line, but the attempts were unsuccessful.

Turn now to the cavalry. At daylight of the 5th, General Wilson, leaving Colonel Hammond with 500 men at Parker's store to remain until the infantry came up, moved toward Craig's Meeting House, posting his First Brigade at the junction of the Parker's store road with the Catharpin road, and sending the Second Brigade, Colonel Chapman commanding, to Craig's Meeting House, where, at 8 A.M., it encountered Rosser's brigade of Hampton's division, and, General Wilson states, drove him back two miles. Here Rosser was, it is stated, strongly reinforced in the afternoon, and, it was believed, by Longstreet's infantry—in part, at least. The enemy now assumed the offensive, and drove Chapman back upon the First Brigade, and General Wilson, having in the meantime found that the enemy's infantry had possession of the Parker's store road, fell back rapidly to Todd's tavern, pressed by the enemy. Here he found Gregg's division, sent by General Sheridan to his support, which in its turn drove the enemy's cavalry beyond Corbin's Bridge.

A reconnoissance on the morning of the 5th by a part of Gregg's division, from Piney Branch Church to Fredericksburg, found no enemy there, and one sent toward Hamilton's crossing came upon the rear of two brigades of cavalry moving from that place toward Lee's right. The enemy's cavalry had been drawn in.

General Torbert, delayed by the trains, reached Chancellorville at midday, and was held in front of that place to cover the trains and support Gregg. General Sheridan found the defensive enforced on him by the necesssity of protecting the trains and their immense amount of materiel.

As soon as the fighting ceased in the evening of the 5th, General Hancock, General Warren, and General Sedgwick were ordered to attack punctually at five o'clock the next morning.

General Burnside was ordered to start at two o'clock in the morning of the 6th, with General Willcox's, General Potter's, and General Stevenson's divisions, and be in position with the first two between General Warren and General Hancock, so as to advance against the enemy with the rest of the army at five o'clock. His movement was to be so directed as to get possession of the high open ground at Chewning's and then attack Hill's left and rear; for so far as could be ascertained the gap between Hill and Ewell was not yet closed; neither was that between Hancock and Warren. Stevenson's division was to be retained at Old Wilderness tavern as a reserve.

Each corps commander was advised of the instructions given to the others. Ewell's corps strengthened their in trenchments during the night, and put artillery in position. Ramseur's brigade came up, and early in the morning of the 6th was sent to the extreme right in the vicinity of Chewning's. Hill's corps also intrenched at some time, for on the morning of the 6th Hancock's troops found an earth intrenchment three or four hundred yards back of the Confederate log intrenchment.[1]

The first shots on the morning of the 6th were fired by the enemy on the right and left a few minutes before five o'clock. Punctually at five our attack began. Two vigorous assaults were made by Wright from the right of his division against the intrenched lines of the enemy, but they were repelled with severe loss. General Warren's attacks on Ewell's right were also unsuccessful; for Ewell's lines were much stronger than on the day before, and were still further strengthened by artillery. The attacks of both corps were frequent and persistent throughout the morning.

An examination of prisoners during the night of the 5th, drew from them the statement that Longstreet was expected to be up in the morning to attack our left, and that his force was about 12,000. General Hancock was notified of this and advised to look out for his left. Preparations were at once made by him to meet the enemy at this point. Barlow's division was posted for that purpose, and artillery was placed to cover the road by which Longstreet was expected to advance, the road heretofore mentioned leading from the Catharpin road to the Brock road at Trigg's. A strong skirmish line was thrown out to cover the Brock road. General Gibbon was placed in command of the left, composed of his own and Barlow's divisions and the artillery. General Birney was put in command of the right, composed

---

[1] It is evident from the reports of some of Longstreet's subordinate command-ers that they supposed these intrenchments had been thrown up by our troops.

of his own, Mott's, and Getty's divisions. At five o'clock
General Birney's command advanced along the Orange
plank road, his own and Mott's divisions in the first line,
Getty's in the second, supported by Carroll's and Owen's
brigades of Gibbon's division. Wadsworth's command advanced at the same time on the right of Birney. All attacked the enemy with great vigor, and after a desperate
contest the enemy's line was broken at all points, and he
was driven in confusion through the forest, suffering severe
loss in killed, wounded, and prisoners. Just before Hill's
troops gave way, the head of Longstreet's corps arrived on
the ground, Kershaw leading, and had begun to form on his
right of the road ; Birney's left was farther forward than his
centre on the plank road, and probably farther forward than
his right, opposite which the Confederate artillery in the
open ground of Tapp's farm with some of Heth's division
still held. Indeed, some of the musketry fire of Birney's
left is stated to have come in on the rear of the batteries.
The advance through the forest, undergrowth, and swamps
for more than a mile, in a hot contest, had separated and
disordered Hancock's troops, and Birney's left, met in this
condition by Kershaw's division, was not only brought to a
standstill, but at some points swayed back and forward,
until at length Kershaw, himself leading his division, forced
Birney's left back as far as his centre. Wadsworth's advance
had crowded many of Birney's troops to the south side of
the plank road, so that the greater part of his, Birney's,
command was on his left of that road. Field's division of
Longstreet's corps, following close on Kershaw's division,
some of it coming on the ground at double-quick, was formed
on the Confederate left of the plank road, and, advancing, at
once became hotly engaged with Birney's right and Wadsworth's troops, Gregg's Texans and Benning's Georgians, in
the lead, bearing the brunt of the fight and losing heavily

in killed and wounded, General Benning among the latter.[1] Anderson's division of Hill's corps, following Field's division, formed on the same part of the line, one portion uniting with Field's troops in the attack, the other portion supporting. It was when Hancock's troops were partially checked by the fresh troops of Longstreet's corps, that the necessity of readjusting his formation became imperative. Regiments were separated from their brigades and mixed with others, and the line of battle was very irregular, and commanders were in this way losing the control of their troops. This was about half-past six o'clock.

General Hancock informed General Meade of the arrival of some of Longstreet's command, and was notified in reply (7 A.M.) that Stevenson's division of the Ninth Corps was held at Wilderness tavern in reserve, and would be sent him if absolutely required. Generals Sedgwick and Warren were ordered to press their attacks. General Sheridan was directed to attack with a division of cavalry on Longstreet's flank and rear by the Brock road, and Hancock was subsequently informed that Sheridan had received the order at eight o'clock at Chancellorville. General Sheridan had been previously (on the 5th) advised that it was left to his discretion to take the offensive against the enemy's cavalry so far as he could do so without endangering the safety of the trains.

General Webb's brigade of Gibbon's division was now ordered to Birney, and Getty's division, which had suffered severely again to-day, General Getty himself severely wounded, was withdrawn to the Brock road.

---

[1] As Gregg's brigade were hastening forward in double-quick they passed General Lee in Tapp's field, and as they had not seen him in several months, greeted him with cheers. Under the impulse of the moment, knowing the urgent need of Hill's troops for help, Lee dashed forward to the head of the brigade to lead it into the fight, when with one voice they cried out to him to go back, and at this moment Longstreet (whom Lee wished to confer with) coming upon the ground, he was constrained to yield to their demand and turn to other duties.

At half-past six o'clock, General Hancock, not hearing any fire from the direction of Burnside's intended attack, sent a request to General Meade that he, Burnside, should attack as soon as possible, as many of the regiments of Birney's command were tired and shattered, and just held their own against Longstreet; but reiterated orders to General Burnside to push forward and attack did not bring about his expected co-operation. As late as 11.45 A.M. General Rawlins wrote him, "Push in and drive the enemy from Hancock's front and get on the Orange plank road. Hancock has expected you for the last three hours, and has been making his attack and dispositions with a view to your assistance."

At 7 A.M., General Hancock sent a staff officer to General Gibbon, commanding the left wing, informing him of the success of his right wing and directing him to attack the enemy's right with Barlow's division, and to press to the right, toward the Orange plank road. This order, General Hancock says, was only partially carried out, Frank's brigade of Barlow's division being the only one sent to feel the enemy's right, which after an obstinate contest connected with Mott's left; but had Barlow's division advanced, as directed by him in several orders, he felt confident that the enemy's force he was in contact with would have been defeated; at all events an attack on the enemy's right by Barlow's division would have prevented the turning of the left of Mott's division which occurred later in the day. The cause of the failure to carry out his orders more fully General Hancock states that he does not know, but that it was probably owing to the expected approach of Longstreet on his left about that time. The report of General Gibbon throws no further light upon the subject. General Hancock's Chief of Staff, Colonel Morgan, who was then, between 7 and 8 A.M., on the extreme left with General Gibbon, sent word that infantry, supposed to be Longstreet's, was moving toward the left on the Brock road from the direction of Todd's tavern, and again preparations were made to meet him by sending out Brooke's brigade and constructing an intrenchment across the road. After these preparations were made, it turned out that the troops advancing were a body of several hundred convalescents returning to the army, and mistakenly following the route of march of the Second Corps.

It must be remembered that according to our information Pickett's division was with Longstreet, and only Field's and Kershaw's divisions had as yet been encountered; and that Anderson's division of Hill's corps had not then been felt by our troops, nor its presence become known to them. These two divisions, with perhaps some of the brigades of the other divisions of Longstreet, might well be the force which, later, about 9 o'clock, threatened Hancock's left flank at Trigg's, though, in point of fact, it turned out to be Confederate cavalry dismounted, with some artillery.

About 8 A.M. General Stevenson's division of the Ninth Corps reported to General Hancock at the intersection of the Brock and plank roads, and about the same hour General Wadsworth was formally placed under his command, and he was informed by General Meade that Burnside had pushed forward nearly to Parker's store, and would attack across his front, information that turned out to be erroneous. Subsequently, at nine o'clock, a despatch was sent to General Hancock, informing him that Colonel Comstock, aide-de-camp of General Grant, had been sent to point out to General Burnside where to attack the enemy on the plank road; but this attack did not take place until two o'clock.

At 8.50 A.M. the divisions of Birney, Mott, and Wadsworth and part of Stevenson's division resumed their attack along the plank road, with Webb's, Carroll's, and Owen's brigades of Gibbon's division—all his division, indeed—and became furiously engaged with the enemy.[1] The firing had hardly commenced when Hancock was informed that his left flank at Trigg's was so seriously threatened as to fully occupy Barlow's division, and Eustis's brigade of Getty's division and Leasure's brigade of Stevenson's division were sent to support him. The enemy's dismounted cavalry opened upon him with artillery, and pressed forward their skirmish line. The rapid firing of Sheridan's attack on Stewart's cavalry near Todd's tavern helped to confirm the impression that this was a serious flank attack by the enemy. These repeated reports of an advance by Longstreet on his left prevented General Hancock from throwing his full strength into the attack along the plank road.

About half-past nine Cutler's brigade of Wadsworth's division was driven back into the open ground around the Lacy house in some disorder, and with heavy loss. Under Hancock's order General Birney with two brigades re-established the line. The contest continued without material change of position on either side. At about half-past ten, Generals Sedgwick and Warren were directed to suspend further attack, to strengthen their intrenchments and to throw up new works, in order that a part of their troops might be available for an attacking force to move from the vicinity of Hancock's right. Engineer troops to the number of about 1,200 had been sent to General Warren the night of the 5th, and had been placed in his second line. They were now used for constructing intrenchments and bridges, and were not at any time afterward used as infantry, for it was difficult to replace

---

[1] General Webb says that upon reporting to General Birney he was ordered by him to move out along the plank road and relieve Getty; that in doing so he saw nothing of Getty's troops, but when about three-quarters of a mile out, he suddenly found himself in close contact with the enemy, who opened a destructive fire upon him, and his brigade at once entered into a hot contest, in the course of which it became mixed with regiments of Stevenson's and Wadsworth's divisions. He lost 23 officers and 957 enlisted men killed and wounded.

such well-instructed, experienced engineer troops. Kitching's brigade, guard of the reserve artillery, had also been ordered to General Warren at the same time, and was now sent to the support of General Wadsworth.

Toward eleven o'clock the firing on Hancock's front died away. As yet Burnside had not engaged the enemy.

General Longstreet says that about ten o'clock Major-General M. L. Smith and others, who had been sent out to examine the position of the enemy in his front, returned and reported that their left extended but a short distance from the plank road, and that upon this report Wofford's brigade of Kershaw's division, which brigade had just come up, Anderson's brigade of Field's division, and Mahone's of Anderson's division, Hill's corps (to which Davis's brigade of Heth's division, Colonel Stone commanding, was afterward added), were sent to attack the enemy's left and rear, the flank movement to be followed by a general advance of all his, Longstreet's, troops. The brigades mentioned moved by the right flank until they reached the bed of the unfinished Fredericksburg Railroad. There they formed, facing north, and at about eleven o'clock advanced until they encountered the flank and rear of Birney's command, which with Wadsworth's was engaged with Kershaw's, Field's, and Anderson's divisions. This movement, concealed from view by the dense wood, was completely successful. Frank's brigade, on the left of Mott, was the first encountered. It had been heavily engaged, and had nearly exhausted its ammunition, and was at once driven before the enemy's vehement attack. Passing over Frank's brigade, they struck McAllister's, which, at the firing of the first shots against Frank's, had changed front to meet the attack, for General McAllister had in person ascertained the position of the flanking force a short time before, but not in time to communicate with General Mott. He soon found himself with a fire on his front, flank, and rear, under which his line broke and fell back in confusion to the intrenchments on the Brock road. The confusion extended to the adjoining troops. General Hancock, whose bearing on the field had so powerful an influence on his command, endeavored to restore order and reform his line of battle along the Orange plank road, retaining his right, as it was then, in front of Field and Anderson, but was unable to do so, owing to the great difficulty of adjusting lines under fire in such a dense forest, and to the partial disorganization of the troops, the most of whom had been engaged since five o'clock in the morning under heavy musketry fire. Consulting with General Birney, it was deemed advisable to withdraw to the breastworks on the Brock road, which was accomplished, and the troops reformed in two lines of battle on the ground from which they had advanced to the attack in the morning. The enemy pushed forward to within a few hundred yards of the breastworks, but did not attempt to assault them.

General Wadsworth, an officer of distinguished intrepidity, was mortally wounded in front of his command during this attack and fell into the hands of the enemy. General Baxter was wounded.[1]

As soon as the success of the flank attack was established, General Longstreet made arrangements to follow it up, and ordered an advance of all his troops for that purpose. While riding at the head of his column, moving by the flank down

---

[1] General Hancock says of the field of battle in the Wilderness:

"It was covered by a dense forest, almost impenetrable by troops in line of battle, where manœuvring was an operation of extreme difficulty and uncertainty. The undergrowth was so heavy that it was scarcely possible to see more than one hundred paces in any direction. The movements of the enemy could not be observed until the lines were almost in collision. Only the roar of the musketry disclosed the position of the combatants to those who were at any distance, and my knowledge of what was transpiring on the field, except in my immediate presence, was limited, and was necessarily derived from reports of subordinate commanders."

the plank road, when opposite the brigades that had made the flank movement, which were drawn up parallel with the road, about sixty yards from it, a portion of them fired a volley, which killed, among others, General Jenkins, commanding the leading brigade of Field's division, and severely wounded General Longstreet. General Kershaw was riding with General Jenkins, arranging the details of the attack to be made, when the firing took place, and he says that General Lee soon came upon the ground, postponed the attack to a later hour, and ordered him to take position with his right resting on the unfinished Orange Railroad.

Colonel Leasure's brigade of the Ninth Corps, which had been posted on the left under Gibbon, was now ordered by General Hancock to sweep along his whole front from left to right, holding his own right about one hundred yards from the breastworks and attack any enemy he should find. This order was promptly and thoroughly executed ; some of the enemy were encountered, who fell back without engaging him.

About 2 P.M. General Robinson with his First Brigade, Colonel Lyle commanding, and two regiments of heavy artillery, reported to General Hancock. They were massed near the plank road in reserve.[1]

To return to an earlier hour of the day. As soon as Heth's

---

[1] A description of the route of the Fredericksburg and Orange Court House unfinished railroad, where it runs through the battlefield, will serve to explain the manner in which Longstreet's flank attack was made. The road runs from Trigg's, Hancock's extreme left, in a northwest direction about parallel with the Brock road, and at a distance of about half a mile from it. At the end of a mile it turns, and runs a little south of west, until, at Parker's store, it is about three hundred yards from the plank road. The part of it parallel with the Brock road was opposite the position of Barlow's division and the artillery of the Second Corps. Longstreet's troops formed for the flank attack on this railroad bed near the bend. It was a good enough road for troops to move on. Had Barlow's division gone forward at the time mentioned by General Hancock, when Frank's brigade was sent to feel the enemy's right, whether by the unfinished railroad, which was much the best route, or by any other route, its line would have extended across the railroad-bed west of the bend, and none of the enemy's troops could have entered or crossed that bed without its being known to our troops, and

and Wilcox's divisions were reformed, after Longstreet and Anderson came upon the field, they were placed on the left of Anderson's division, reaching Ewell's right, and at once intrenched. Willcox's left extended beyond the open ground of Chewning's farm.

General Burnside's two divisions had moved out in the morning toward Chewning's, near which place it was found that the enemy had put some artillery in position supported by infantry. Receiving the fire of this force, dispositions were made for its attack, but in accordance with more recent orders the command moved toward Tapp's, where the firing still continued heavy. The advance in this direction was through woods with matted undergrowth, and the progress was very slow. Willcox's division was composed entirely of raw troops, inexperienced in every way. Finally, about two o'clock, Potter's division came upon the enemy intrenched on the opposite side of a swampy ravine, and, attacking, gained some advantage. This appears to have been the line held by Perry's brigade of Anderson's division, and Law's brigade of Field's division, commanded by General W. F. Perry. Willcox's division of the Ninth Corps was now brought up, and, to relieve the attack on Hancock, about half-past five a further attack was made, which broke Law's and Perry's brigades, and drove them back in disorder. General Perry was severely wounded. But General Wofford came to their assistance, and attacked successfully the somewhat disordered troops of Willcox. General Heth arriving with a part of his division, the Confederate brigades that had been forced back advanced with it, passing over the ground on

Longstreet's flanking attack could not have been made without due preparation to meet it. Its success depended upon its being concealed. Frank's advance should have been made along this road, and the road should have been watched as far as the bend. But these considerations as to the action of others did not relieve General Birney from the necessity of taking precautions to guard the left flank of his command from surprise. Its right flank was not exposed to it.

which the contest had taken place. Apparently those contending forces recovered the position they had held before their fighting began, for General Burnside says that he formed his command for the night immediately in front of the enemy's intrenchments and connected with Hancock on his left.

The chief object of General Burnside's movement was not accomplished. His presence near the left of Longstreet's corps and Anderson's division in the afternoon probably kept some of those troops from joining in the attack on Hancock at 4.15 P.M. Could his attack have been made early in the day, and followed up with vigor, it would have had important consequences. Hancock, expecting his co-operation, made his dispositions with a view to it.

About three o'clock General Hancock was directed to attack at six, and General Burnside advised of it and ordered to attack at the same hour, aiding Hancock. Hearing the firing on General Hancock's front at a quarter past four, General Burnside attacked as soon as Willcox was in position, with the result already stated.

At a quarter past four o'clock the enemy advanced in force against Hancock's line until they came within a hundred paces of it, when they opened a heavy musketry fire, which was not, however, very destructive. The attack was heaviest on Hancock's left of the plank road. At the end of half an hour a portion of Mott's division and of Ward's brigade of Birney's division gave way, retiring in disorder; but through the exertion of General Hancock, his staff, and other officers, many of them returned to the line of battle. The moment the break began the enemy pushed forward, and Anderson's brigade of Field's division [1] took possession of that part of the first line of intrenchments and planted their colors there.

---

[1] General Hancock says Anderson's brigade, but in the Lee Memorial volume it is stated to have been Jenkins's brigade led by Bratton. See also the report of Colonel James R. Hagood, commanding First South Carolina Regiment, Jenkins's brigade, whose regiment formed part of the force that got possession of our in·

Colonel Carroll of Gibbon's division had his brigade near at hand, and was ordered by General Birney to drive them out, which he did, moving forward at double-quick. General Hancock's despatch referring to this says both the attack and counter-attack were of the handsomest kind. By five o'clock the enemy was completely repulsed, and fell back with heavy loss in killed and wounded.

During this attack Dow's battery, Sixth Maine, rendered effective service, one section on the plank road, the other near Mott's left, in the second line. It was served with great steadiness and gallantry.

As Hancock's troops were nearly out of ammunition, and the ammunition wagons were at some distance in the rear, and there was not time to replenish and organize a formidable attack by six o'clock, that attack was given up.[1]

It should be mentioned that just before the attack the front line of breastworks near the point where the line was broken through, which was entirely of logs, took fire from the forest in front (the battleground of the morning), which had been burning for some hours. The heat and smoke were driven into the faces of the men, preventing them on portions of the line from firing over the parapet, and at some points obliged them to abandon it.[2]

---

trenchment, in which he says they received a terrific musketry and artillery fire from our second line, and that the troops on his left giving way he abandoned the intrenchments; he lost something more than one-third of his command, killed and wounded, in this attack.

[1] Colonel Theodore Lyman, an accomplished gentleman from Boston, a volunteer aide on the staff of General Meade from the Summer of 1863 to the close of the war, serving without pay or allowances, passed the 5th and 6th of May with General Hancock, sending constantly brief notes with small diagrams to General Meade, showing the progress of the operations and giving the latest information. It was General Meade's habit to intrust this service to Colonel Lyman, sending him to the different corps commanders. These little despatches are on file in the War Department and furnish valuable information.

[2] General McAllister, who was in the second line, says that he opened upon the enemy when they got into the first line, and that a part of his brigade advanced upon them also. He was wounded and obliged to leave the field.

The attacking force, so far as I can make out, was Field's and Anderson's divisions, excepting Law's and Perry's brigades, with probably some part of Heth's division.

To return to the Sixth Corps. Shaler's brigade reported back to it from the trains some time in the day and was placed on the right of Seymour. Owing to the close proximity of the enemy, intrenching here was difficult, but the brigade engaged in it.

General Johnston's brigade of Rodes's division having arrived from Hanover Junction, was sent to General Early, who posted it to watch his left. General Gordon having ascertained where the right flank of the Sixth Corps rested in the woods, and that it was without support, proposed attacking it in flank with his brigade, which was to be formed in open ground four or five hundred yards distant. But at that time it was deemed best not to do so, as there were, in General Early's opinion, indications of an attempt to turn their left by Burnside's corps or part of it. Later in the day this objection no longer existed, and preparations were made in the afternoon for the attack, with Gordon's brigade, supported by Johnston's, to be followed up by a front attack with the rest of Early's division. Gordon's brigade was formed in some open ground near the edge of the woods, and Johnston's in rear of it. The advance was then made a short time before sunset. Shaler's brigade was partly engaged building breastworks when the attack came, and was struck in flank, rolled up and thrown into confusion, and several hundred prisoners captured from it, including General Shaler. Seymour's brigade was also disordered, and toward the end of the attack he was captured, though not many prisoners were taken from his brigade. But the advance of Gordon's brigade through the dense thicket disordered his troops, and his right, striking that part of Shaler's line that was refused, gave way. The disorder of his troops

and the darkness in the forest of approaching night put a
stop to Gordon's further progress. Johnston's brigade
passed Gordon's left, and got in rear of Wright's line, encountered some part of it, and took some prisoners. Pegram's brigade attacked in front very soon after Gordon
struck Shaler. Darkness coming on found the opposing
troops in some disorder, and in very close proximity, but
General Wright promptly restored order among his troops.
General Early drew back his brigades and formed a new
line in front of his old.[1] During the night an entirely new
line was taken up by the Sixth Corps, its front and right
thrown back, a change which the right of the Fifth Corps
conformed to.

I have recently learnt that the facilities which the open
ground on which Gordon formed offered for making a flank
attack on Sedgwick's right, and also on Early's left, had
been noted during the day by General Wright, and only the
want of troops prevented him from making the flank attack
on Early. Morris's and Upton's brigades, the only disposable troops the Sixth Corps had, were held available, under
orders from General Meade, for Warren's left, or Hancock's
right. Had General Sedgwick suggested this flank attack
for those brigades or the support of his own flank by them
it would have been acceded to. There must have been some
neglect in the vedettes or skirmish line in keeping a lookout on that ground, otherwise timely notice would have
been given of the presence of Gordon there.[2]

---

[1] General Early, in his Memoir, after describing this affair, says of it: "It was
fortunate, however, that darkness came to close this affair, as the enemy, if he
had been able to discover the disorder on our side, might have brought up fresh
troops and availed himself of our condition. As it was, doubtless the lateness of
the hour caused him to be surprised and the approaching darkness increased the
confusion in his ranks, as he could not see the strength of the attacking force,
and probably imagined it to be much more formidable than it really was."

[2] Soon after this flank attack began, staff officers of the Sixth Corps rode in to
General Meade's headquarters and informed me (General Meade was at General

The operations of the cavalry on the 6th must now be stated. On the morning of that day General Sheridan directed General Custer with his own brigade and Devin's to move down the Furnace road to the Brock road, connect with Hancock's left, and attack the enemy there. At the intersection of the Furnace and Brock roads Custer encountered Hampton's division, while Gregg met Fitzhugh Lee's division at Todd's tavern, both repulsing the enemy's attacks handsomely. General Sheridan was restrained from following up any advantage gained, as the cavalry was very far out from the trains, the care of which he was especially entrusted with.

Upon the receipt of General Sheridan's despatch informing him of these encounters, General Meade at 1 P.M. replied, that as Hancock's line had been heavily pressed, and his left turned, he, General Meade, thought it best to draw in the cavalry so as to secure the protection of the trains. Exactly what had taken place on Hancock's left flank was not then thoroughly known at headquarters. Before this direction was executed the enemy's cavalry again attacked and were repulsed, leaving their dead and wounded on the field. In reporting this at 2.35 P.M., General Sheridan stated that they,

---

Grant's headquarters near by) that in endeavoring to carry a despatch to the right of their line they found that it had just been broken and rolled up ; that the enemy occupied the position, and that part of them were advancing down the Germanna plank road on our right and rear, following the fugitives from Shaler's and Seymour's brigades ; and they added that probably both Sedgwick and Wright were captured. I at once made dispositions to meet this with the Provost Guard and some troops that General Warren sent me, and the reserve artillery near by, and then sent notice of the affair to General Meade, who at once came over with General Grant. Soon the staff officers whom I had sent up the Germanna road to rally the fugitives returned, reporting there was no enemy on it ; reports from a brigade of Warren's corps sent in the same direction confirmed their report, and then information was received from General Sedgwick and General Wright showing the actual condition of the corps.

I have mentioned these details because exaggerated statements concerning this affair, which quickly spread through the army, gave rise, I think, to unfounded rumors.

the enemy's cavalry, were then working to his left, and that
he had made new dispositions in accordance with the orders
received.   The cavalry were accordingly drawn in from
Todd's tavern and the Brock road in front of the Furnaces,
and the enemy's cavalry followed them.   In the morning of
the 7th, Custer drove such of the enemy's cavalry force as
were at the Furnaces to Todd's tavern, where General Sheridan with Gregg's and Merritt's divisions attacked Stewart's
whole cavalry force, Hampton's and Fitzhugh Lee's divisions,
and drove them along the Spottsylvania road and also back
upon the Shady Grove Church road (Catharpin road), Fitzhugh Lee's division along the Brock road, and Hampton's
along the Catharpin.   They had constructed barricades and
rifle-pits, which were charged and captured.   The drawing
in of the cavalry the day before did not oblige them to fight
on disadvantageous ground on the 7th, nor under any other
adverse condition.

   To return to the infantry corps of the army.   On the
morning of the 7th, reconnoissances were made of the
enemy's position, which was found to be well intrenched :
part of it ran along the open ground of the Hagerson, Chewning, and Tapp farms ; artillery was placed not only where
the ground was open, but at other portions of the line.   The
average distance apart of the lines of the two armies was
about three-quarters of a mile.   To attack a position of such
character, situated as this was, covered by a tangled forest
that inevitably disordered the attacking forces as they advanced, was not judicious ; it promised no success.   General
Grant therefore decided to continue the movement by the
left flank, with a view to a general engagement in the more
open country.

   Early in the morning of the 7th, the bridge at Germanna
Ford was taken up, and relaid at Ely's Ford, for the passage
of the ambulance train containing the wounded, who were to

be sent to Washington by the Orange and Alexandria Railroad. In the course of the day their destination was changed, and they were subsequently sent to Washington by way of Fredericksburg.

According to the reports of the Medical Director of the Army of the Potomac, Surgeon Thomas A. McParlin, from May 4 to December 31, 1864 (see pages 148–178, Appendix to First Part of the "Medical and Surgical History of the War," and also the tables of killed, wounded, and missing in Part First, Surgical Volume), the number of wounded of the Army of the Potomac in the battle of the Wilderness was 9,102, not including the Ninth Corps (see pages 151 and 152, Appendix). This I believe to be more correct than any other statement we have of the number of wounded in that battle. In the same report it is stated that the number of wounded according to the regimental reports was 10,805, but that subsequent reports rendered it probable that that number was erroneous. The number of killed, according to the regimental reports, was 2,009, which number is undoubtedly very nearly accurate. The number of missing according to the regimental records was 2,902. This is the number furnished by the Adjutant-General of the army to General Badeau, and includes the missing of the Ninth Corps.

The casualties in General Burnside's Ninth Corps were, according to his report, 256 killed and 1,118 wounded. These added to the regimental reports of killed and the medical reports of wounded, we have for the casualties of the Army of the Potomac and the Ninth Corps in the battle of the Wilderness 2,265 killed, 10,220 wounded, and 2,902 missing. Total, 15,387. Killed and wounded, 12,485. General Burnside's missing numbered 145.[1]

---

[1] For a notice of the errors in Badeau's tabular statement of the killed, wounded, and missing in the Army of the Potomac and James, from May 5, 1864, to April 9, 1865, found on page 713, vol. iii., of his Military Life of General Grant,

The woods took fire in many places, and it is estimated that 200 of our wounded perished in the flames and smoke.

According to the tabular statement, Part First, "Medical and Surgical History of the War," the casualties in the Army of Northern Virginia were 2,000 killed, 6,000 wounded, and 3,400 missing. The authority for this statement is not given, and I do not find anywhere records of the loss of that army in the Wilderness.[1]

Concerning the difference of loss between the two armies, it must be recollected that the Army of the Potomac was the attacking party on the right and left, and that these attacks were continued and repeatedly renewed after Ewell and Hill had intrenched. It is true that some counter-attacks were made by the Army of Northern Virginia, or parts of it, upon Sedgwick, Warren, and Hancock, but it was when the positions of those corps in the woods were well defined, though, with two exceptions, not intrenched, and when there was no

---

see Appendix F. See, also, the same Appendix for the correction of the errors of a statement of the losses of the Army of the Potomac in the battle of the Wilderness, by Major-General C. M. Wilcox, which errors arose from his misapprehension of the tabular statement in the Medical and Surgical History of the War.

[1] General Ewell, in his report of March 20, 1865, states that his killed and wounded in the Wilderness numbered 1,250. General McGowan in his report states that the casualties of his brigade (Wilcox's division) amounted to 438 killed and wounded, and 43 missing. General Lane states the loss of his brigade (Wilcox's division) at 272 killed and wounded and 143 missing. In General Kershaw's brigade (see General Kershaw's report of his division) the loss was 296 killed and wounded and 26 missing. In General Goode Bryan's brigade (Kershaw's division) the killed and wounded were 133. In Mahone's brigade the number was 146. It is stated that the losses in Gregg's and Benning's brigades of Field's division were very heavy. The heaviest losses were probably in Hill's corps and part of Longstreet's. But I can find no sufficient data to serve as a test of the correctness of the numbers of the table of the Medical and Surgical History of the War.

General Early, who took command of Hill's corps on the morning of May 8th, says that when he took command of it "the infantry numbered about 13,000 muskets for duty." By the return of April 20th, the number of enlisted men of infantry of Hill's corps present for duty was 20,648. This contrast of numbers may afford some indication of the loss of that corps by killed, wounded, and missing in the Wilderness. It is true there are other sources of reduction of numbers than the casualties of battle, such as expiration of terms of service.

uncertainty as to where and how they were posted. The chief exceptional attack made against our troops intrenched was that against Hancock in the afternoon of May 6th, when his loss was small, that of the enemy severe. The other was the front attack of Early, late in the afternoon, and in the evening, when Gordon's flank attack was made.

Besides the general officers named, both sides lost many valuable officers in this battle, and of those in the Army of the Potomac none were held in higher esteem for soldierly qualities than Major H. L. Abbott, of the Twentieth Massachusetts, a brilliant young officer.[1]

I have gone into more detail in the account of this battle than I shall undertake to give of those that are to follow, chiefly because it may serve to show what difficulties were encountered by the forces engaged in it, owing to the character of the field on which it took place. Some of its features were found in other of the battle-grounds of the two armies; but, so far as I know, no great battle ever took place before on such ground.[2] But little of the combatants could be seen, and its progress was known to the senses chiefly by the rising and falling sounds of a vast musketry fire that continually swept along the lines of battle, many

---

[1] Colonel Theodore Lyman informs me that on a visit he made to the battlefield of the Wilderness after the war, in going over the ground where the Twentieth Massachusetts, one of the very best regiments in the service, lost a third of its number in killed and wounded, he found the line occupied by the enemy to be just behind the crest of a slight elevation, where they had placed a row of logs, and, lying down behind it, were effectually screened from the bullets and sight of our troops, for in front of and around them was a dense thicket of saplings; and in that thicket, not more than twenty or thirty yards distant, was the Twentieth Massachusetts and other of our troops, whose presence was made known by their thrusting through the brush, and whose return fire, aimed, as they supposed, at the Confederate troops, had cut off the saplings three, four, and five feet above the ground as regularly as if they had been cut by a machine. Many of the partially cut off tops were still hanging when Colonel Lyman visited the ground.

[2] The ground occupied by the Army of the Potomac in the vicinity of Chancellorville in the Spring of 1863 was either open or in woods chiefly of ordinary character with but little undergrowth.

miles in length, sounds which at times approached to the sublime.

General Badeau, in his "Military Life of General Grant," appears to intimate that General Grant intended to bring on a general engagement on the 5th of May, in the preliminary position directed to be taken up in the order of march issued on the 4th. But that view is not consistent with the orders issued nor with what was best to do. Had he really wished to fight a battle on the 5th, the Second Corps, after crossing at Ely's Ford on the 4th, should have moved out the Orange plank road to New Hope Church; the Fifth Corps out the pike to Robertson's tavern; the Sixth Corps to Old Wilderness tavern; and, on the morning of the 5th, to position between the Second and Fifth Corps; Wilson's cavalry out the Orange plank road in advance of the Second Corps, and moving to the left at New Hope Church. That would have brought on a battle in more open and better ground for the Army of the Potomac than that of the Wilderness. Had Lee gone into the strong, intrenched position of Mine Run, or had he withdrawn to it after the battle, we could have moved to turn his right as soon as the trains were sufficiently advanced to admit of it, and in doing so should have found still more open country. I do not perceive that there is anything to induce the belief that General Grant intended or wished to fight a battle in the Wilderness. His doing so was, under the circumstances, unavoidable, not a matter of choice. Further, it would have been strange if the Chief-of-Staff of the Army of the Potomac, whose special occupation concerned the operations of that army, its movements and battles and their object, should not have known of this intention if it had any existence.

CHAPTER III.

SPOTTSYLVANIA COURT HOUSE.

As before stated, General Grant had determined to continue the movement by the left, and in that view directed
General Meade to take position, by a night march, at Spottsylvania Court House with one corps, at Todd's tavern with
another, and with a third at the intersection of the road from
Piney Branch Church to Spottsylvania Court House, with
the road from Alsop's to the Old Court House; Burnside to
move to Piney Branch Church. These positions were merely
preliminary to further movement in a more southerly direction, dependent partly upon the course that General Lee
should take.

This movement required the trains to be set in motion
about three o'clock in the afternoon of the 7th, so as to
clear the road for the troops, though it was apprehended
that the people of the country would inform General Lee of
it, and that he would readily surmise its object.

In accordance with the project of General Grant, the army
began to move at half-past eight in the evening; General
Warren by the Brock road toward Spottsylvania Court
House, General Sedgwick by the pike and plank roads to
Chancellorville, and thence by way of Aldrich's and Piney
Branch Church toward the point designated in the order of
march, the intersection of the two roads named; but early
in the morning of the 8th he was directed to hold one division at that point, another at Piney Branch Church, and the

third midway between the two. Burnside followed Sedgwick, but early on the 8th he was directed to halt at Aldrich's, where the Piney Branch Church road leaves the Fredericksburg plank road (about two miles from the church), in order to cover the trains. Ferrero's division went to the trains, with which it remained several weeks. Hancock followed Warren as far as Todd's tavern. The reserve artillery went to Piney Branch Church, the trains to that vicinity. General Sheridan was directed to have a sufficient force on the approaches from the right to keep the corps commanders advised in time of the appearance of the enemy.[1]

After overlooking, for a time, the commencement of the movement, General Meade, with General Grant, rode to General Hancock's headquarters on the Brock road, near the left of his line, to await there the arrival of the head of Warren's column, and about eleven o'clock set out for Todd's tavern, in advance of the Fifth Corps, reaching there about midnight.[2]

Arrived at Todd's tavern General Meade found Gregg's cavalry division there, Merritt's being further forward on the

---

[1] See Appendix G for the orders of General Grant and General Meade.

[2] While at General Hancock's headquarters it was learnt, about eleven o'clock, that the head of Warren's column was near by, halted and seriously delayed by the mounted troops of the Provost-Marshal-General, which, following the headquarters, had occupied the road instead of drawing out of it. General Warren had remained in the vicinity of the Lacy house to oversee the withdrawal of his troops, the most important part of his duty. Had he been at the head of his column the delay would not have occurred, since he would at once have notified General Meade of the obstruction, and it would have been removed immediately. The headquarters at once set out as the speediest way of removing the obstacle, and rode rapidly to Todd's tavern, reaching there about midnight. The narrow road lay through woods all the way, and made the night appear very dark; for some distance after passing the Second Corps the woods were still on fire, and at one time obliged us to turn off to the right, and there was a little uncertainty afterward whether we had returned to the right road, a matter of some concern, as the enemy were probably within a mile of us on the right. As we shall see further on, Longstreet's corps was at that time moving toward Spottsylvania Court House, along a road parallel with the Brock road, and about a mile from it.

road to Spottsylvania Court House. They had not yet received their orders, and General Meade at one A.M. directed Merritt to move his command at once beyond Spottsylvania Court House, placing one brigade at the Block House, which is at the intersection of the Shady Grove Church road with the old Court House road, a mile and a half west of the Court House, and a mile east of the Shady Grove road bridge over the Po River. He was to picket the roads approaching the Court House, and to dispose of the other two brigades to cover the trains. He was to open the Brock road beyond the Court House for the infantry corps, closely following him on its way to occupy that place. Gregg he directed to move immediately to the vicinity of Corbin's bridge and watch the roads approaching from Parker's store, and when the Second Corps reached Todd's tavern, to send a force on the Brock road to watch it in the direction of the Wilderness. General Sheridan was notified at the same hour of these orders.

At five A.M. General Warren informed General Meade that the head of his column reached General Merritt's headquarters (about a mile east of Todd's tavern) at half-past three A.M., that Merritt's troops had then already moved to clear the road, and that he, General Warren, had massed his troops there as they came up to rest, for the march on a dark night by a narrow road running through woods had much fatigued them; that at the hour of his writing General Merritt had been engaged some time.

General Fitzhugh Lee's cavalry division was on the road, which they had barricaded by felling trees across it, and disputed every foot of ground, and in the darkness of night General Merritt found it exceedingly difficult to make any progress. At six A.M. General Warren, upon an intimation from General Merritt that his infantry could push the enemy faster than he could, ordered an advance of his corps,

General Robinson's division now leading. In reporting this General Warren added, "It is difficult to do much with troops in an expeditious manner in these dense woods." The same obstacles continued until about half-past eight o'clock, when Robinson's division emerged from the woods into the open ground of Alsop's, about two and a half miles from the Court House. Here the Brock road forks, uniting again at the end of a mile. Robinson advanced along the left hand fork to the junction of the two, Lyle's brigade on the left, Dennison's on the right, Coulter's, formerly Baxter's, brigade on the left rear. At the junction of the forks the line was reformed in column of regiments, and advanced along the road in open ground, a strong line of skirmishers in front, to within two or three hundred yards of the wood which the road entered, when suddenly a severe musketry and artillery fire was opened upon their front and right from an intrench-ment just inside the edge of the wood. This staggered them, and in a short time they fell back to the shelter of the woods in their rear. The Maryland brigade took up a position in the edge of the wood and checked the further advance of the enemy, who followed them after turning the left of Lyle's brigade, which had held on close to the enemy's intrenchment under the shelter of a steep crest. General Robinson was severely wounded at the first fire, while lead-ing his men. Prisoners taken showed this force of the enemy to be Kershaw's and Humphreys's brigades of Ker-shaw's division. Their intrenchments were slight, but gave sufficient cover to the men. They were at the intersection of the Brock road by the old Court House road, and about a mile and a half from Spottsylvania Court House and the same distance from the Shady Grove Church road bridge over the Po.

In the meantime Griffin took the right fork, Bartlett in line of battle in advance, Ayres and Sweitzer marching on the road. When Bartlett got half way across the open ground of Alsop, he also came under the fire of the enemy's infantry and artillery soon after Robinson, and with nearly similar results, but by the personal exertions of General Griffin, who led his division in person, and of Generals Bartlett and Ayres, the men reformed quickly under cover of Ayres's brigade, who were in a sunken part of the road; and Griffin again advanced, taking up the line afterward held for several days. Crawford came up on his left, driving the enemy out of the woods there. Field's division of Longstreet's corps had been coming up all this time, and taking part in the fight; they began now to push through the pines on Griffin's right, threatening that flank. But Cutler came up : his division had had several hours' rest and were in good condition. Forming in a ravine, they advanced in fine style, drove the enemy out of the woods on Griffin's right, and established their line so as to connect with his. The position now held by the corps was intrenched. It was from two to four hundred yards distant from that of the enemy. At half-past twelve P.M. General Warren reported that he had pushed back the enemy, but had not quite gained the junction of the Brock and Catharpin roads (Shady Grove Church road he meant, not the Catharpin); that General Wright had, at his request, come up to his support; that the straggling had been heavy, the men, wounded and tired, falling out of the ranks into the woods; that he had encountered a division of cavalry (Fitzhugh Lee's) and two divisions of Longstreet's corps, from whom he had taken prisoners; that Longstreet's men stated that they had left their trenches the night before at eleven o'clock.

Turning now to the Second Corps, we find that the troops in front of Hancock occupied the road all night, and for that reason the head of his column did not march until after daylight, reaching Todd's tavern about nine o'clock in the morning, and relieving Gregg's division of cavalry, which was holding that point, *his skirmishers engaged with the enemy's cavalry in front of the tavern.* The Second Corps was placed in position and intrenched here.

About 11 A.M. Colonel Miles was sent to make a reconnoissance on the Catharpin road toward Corbin's bridge (about two miles distant) with his own brigade and one of Gregg's cavalry brigades and a battery. Upon his occupying a wooded crest facing the river and half a mile from it, the enemy, Hampton's cavalry division, on the high ground on the opposite bank of the river, opened upon him with artillery. He remained here until ordered to return later in the day.

We have now to trace the movement of the Army of Northern Virginia during the night of the 7th and on the 8th.

On the afternoon of the 7th, General Lee, informed of the movement of our trains, and partly surmising its object, directed General R. H. Anderson, now in command of Longstreet's corps, to move to Spottsylvania Court House, and in the official diary of the First Corps it is stated that the corps took up the line of march for the Court House at eleven o'clock that night. General Bratton, commanding a brigade in Field's division, says in his report that orders to move were received at nine o'clock in the evening. The right of the corps rested opposite Hancock's left, and from that point a road running south, at the end of two miles entered the Catharpin road between Todd's tavern and Corbin's bridge. This road the corps followed, and after crossing Corbin's bridge, took the Shady Grove Church road to Spottsylvania Court House, crossing the Po a second time on the bridge a mile west of the Block House and two and a half miles west of the Court House. This bridge the head of the column reached about daylight of the 8th.[1] Their route was about three miles shorter than General Warren's, who, when he arrived at General Merritt's headquarters, at half-past three in the morning, had marched as far as they had when arriving at the point where their leading troops met those of General Warren between nine and ten o'clock in the morning. They had the additional advantage of not encountering on their route an enemy's barricades and other obstructions in a thick wood, and of resting an hour at daylight where they could find water and fuel, and get something to eat and drink ; small matters, those not familiar with campaigning may perhaps think, but nevertheless important, as every soldier knows.[2]

Kershaw was in advance after the rest, and finding Fitzhugh Lee engaged, turned off rapidly to the left with his leading brigades, Kershaw's and Humphreys's, after they had crossed the Block House bridge, and occupied some cover made by the cavalry. They were followed quickly by Field's division, and with the result already told. The other two brigades of Kershaw's division, Wofford's and Bryan's, were sent to the Court House, and with some of Fitzhugh Lee's cavalry drove off General Wilson's cavalry division. This division leaving Aldrich's on the Fredericksburg road at 5 A M. had, at an early hour, encountered Wickham's brigade of Fitzhugh Lee's division in Spottsylvania Court House, and driving it from the town had held the place two hours when General Wilson was recalled by General Sheridan. The force already mentioned was moving against him at the same time.

---

[1] See authorities already mentioned, and a Paper of Colonel William Wallace, Second·South Carolina, Kershaw's brigade (Southern Historical Society Papers, March, 1879).

[2] Medical officers have noted that the amount of shock and depression of vital power with the wounded who have gone into action early in the morning without the usual meal is much greater than with those who have had the meal (see Report of the Medical Director of the Army of the Potomac, Surgeon McParlin).

On the night of the 7th General Ewell was ordered to ex·
tend his right, and if at daylight he found no large force in
his front to follow General Anderson to Spottsylvania Court
House. This was done, the corps moving past Parker's
store, and on the longest route taken by Lee's troops. On
the march General Early was assigned to the command of
Hill's corps, Gordon to the command of Early's division, and
some transfers of brigades were made among Ewell's divisions.
Mahone had succeeded to the command of Anderson's division of Hill's corps. General Ewell says the march was dis-
tressing from the intense heat, the thick dust, and the smoke
from burning woods ; and that his troops reached Spottsylvania Court House about 5 P.M., just in time for Rodes's division to repel (he says) an attempt to turn Anderson's right,
which rested on the ——— road : the Brock road is meant.

General Early states that General Lee's orders to him were
to move by Todd's tavern along the Brock road to Spottsylvania Court House as soon as his front was clear of the
enemy : that in order to get into that road he was obliged to
reopen an old one leading from Hill's right, by which he
was enabled to take a cross-road leading into the road from
Todd's tavern to Shady Grove Church (the Catharpin road),[1]
his trains and artillery, except one battalion, going around
by Shady Grove ; that when about a mile from the Catharpin
road the enemy's cavalry vedettes were encountered by him,
and Mahone's division was thrown forward to develop the
enemy's force and position ; that Mahone encountered a body
of infantry on that road, about a mile from Todd's tavern,
and had a brisk engagement with it, causing it to fall back
rapidly toward Todd's tavern, and at the same time General
Hampton moved with his cavalry on his, Early's, right, and
struck the enemy on the flank and rear, but on account of

---

[1] I suppose from this description that General Early took a route lying between
those followed by Longstreet's and Ewell's corps.

their (the Confederates') want of knowledge of the country, and the approach of darkness, the enemy was enabled to make his escape. This affair showed him that the Army of the Potomac held Todd's tavern and the Brock road, and that his march as ordered could not be continued. He halted for the night on the Catharpin road a mile from the tavern.

Let us see what General Hancock says of this. He states that at half-past one o'clock he sent Gibbon half way to Spottsylvania Court House to support Warren and Sedgwick ; that when General Miles was returning from his reconnoissance at 5.30 P. M., he was attacked by Mahone's brigade (division), which was marching toward Spottsylvania Court House. A brigade from Barlow's division was sent to his support, and the corps held ready to move. At this time he was informed that the enemy's infantry was also advancing along the Brock road against his right, information which he afterward ascertained by reconnoissance to be erroneous, and he directed General Miles to retire slowly to the main line of battle at Todd's tavern. This movement, he says, was executed with great skill and success by that officer, who, while accomplishing it, repelled two spirited attacks of the enemy, inflicting severe loss upon him. After the second repulse of the enemy, he withdrew Miles to Todd's tavern.

To resume the general narrative. At one o'clock General Meade ordered General Sedgwick to move to Spottsylvania Court House and unite with General Warren in an immediate and vigorous attack upon the enemy. Of this General Hancock was notified. The arrangements for the attack of the Fifth and Sixth Corps were not completed until late in the afternoon, and it was then only partial, and not determined and vigorous. The ground was new to everyone, and the troops were tired. It was also made too late in the day to be followed up advantageously if successful. Some advance was made by a part of the Sixth Corps, and Penrose's New Jersey brigade of Wright's division, leading the advance in open ground, was repulsed by a sharp fire from the wood in their front. A little later, toward dusk, General Crawford passed over the open ground into the woods beyond—he had, it appears, passed the right of Longstreet's corps, and had come upon Rodes's division of Ewell's corps unexpectedly to them, while they were moving by a flank, and forced them back three-quarters of a mile, it is stated, taking some prisoners. After nightfall Crawford fell back to the line of the corps. Ewell, after stating that his troops reached Spottsylvania Court House just in time for Rodes to repel an attempt to turn Anderson's right, adds that Rodes advanced nearly half a mile, when his left coming upon strong works was checked, and he was forced to halt; that Johnson's division formed on his right and Gordon remained in reserve. Both sides now continued to intrench.

At 1 P.M., by order of General Grant, General Sheridan was directed to concentrate his available mounted force and move against the enemy's cavalry, and when his supplies were exhausted to proceed to James River, communicate with General Butler, procure supplies, and return to the army.

At the same hour an order of movement southward was prepared by direction of General Grant, the Second and Fifth Corps to move *via* Block House, Peany's tavern, Mount Pleasant, Three Cornered Handkerchief, and Waller's Church to Dabney's mills on the North Anna; the Sixth Corps and reserve artillery to move *via* Spottswood Court House, Mattapony Church, Green Branch, and New Market to Davenport's Ford on the North Anna, near Dabney's mills; the main trains, followed by the Ninth Corps, to move *via* Alsop's, Gates's, Anderson's, Smith's mill, Stannard's mill, Mud tavern, and Round Oak Church to Childsburg—the time of movement to be determined afterward. This order was not issued, as, later in the day, it was found that Lee was concentrating his whole army at Spottsylvania Court House.

General Badeau, in describing the movement to Spottsylvania Court House, in his "Military Life of General Grant," dwells somewhat upon what he calls Meade's blunders, by which, according to him, Spottsylvania Court House was lost to us. Describing the three bridges across the Po connected with this movement, Corbin's bridge, the bridge a mile west of the Block House (and two and a half miles west of the Court House), and Snell's bridge (two and a half miles south of the Court House), he says:

"These bridges were of the first importance, for they commanded Lee's only approaches to Spottsylvania, and Sheridan, who had been ordered to keep a good lookout toward the enemy, disposed his force so as to secure all three positions. Wilson was ordered to advance on the left, by the Fredericksburg road, to take possession of the Court House, and then move into position at Snell's bridge; while Gregg and Merritt on the right were directed to proceed to the same point, crossing the Po at Corbyn's bridge and then advance by Shady Grove and the Block House road.

"Had these orders been carried out," he goes on, "every avenue to Spottsylvania would have been closed to the rebel army." He continues: "But Meade arrived at Todd's tavern at midnight, where Gregg and Merritt were bivouacked. Sheridan's orders had not yet arrived, and Meade at once issued new and different ones, Gregg being simply instructed to move to the vicinity of Corbyn's bridge and watch the roads from Parker's store, while Merritt was ordered to open the Brock road to Spottsylvania; Snell's bridge and that on the Block House, the most important points of all, being utterly ignored. Meade, indeed, directed Merritt to place a brigade at the Block House, and to picket the roads leading to the Court House; but the Block House was a mile from the bridge, which was not mentioned in the order, and one brigade could hardly withstand the rebel army. Sheridan had ordered two divisions to hold these points."

Let us see what the orders of General Sheridan say (Badeau does not give a copy of them), the time when they were issued, the hour at which the three cavalry divisions were to move, and whether the roads they were directed to take were open to them at that time, or at the time when General Sheridan's orders were received by them, or, indeed, written. As to Snell's bridge, it was rather too far out of the way to be used by Lee in approaching the vicinity of the Court House and he did not use it. There was another bridge nearer, close to the Old Court House, which Lee did use for his trains, but which General Badeau does not mention and apparently knows nothing about.

The instructions of General Sheridan, issued at 1 A.M. of the 8th, are comprised in those to Gregg, which are as follows :

"May 8th, 1 A.M.

"Move with your command at 5 A.M., on the Catharpin road, crossing at Corbin's bridge, and taking position at Shady Grove Church. General Merritt will follow you, and at Shady Grove Church will take the left hand, or Block House road, moving forward and taking up position at that point [viz., Block House]. Immediately after he has passed, you will move forward with your division, on the same road, to the crossing of Po River, where you will take up position supporting General Merritt. General Wilson with his division will march from Alsop's by way of Spottsylvania Court House and the Gate to Snell's bridge, where he will take up position. . . . The infantry march to Spottsylvania to-night."

The first point to note in this order in connection with Badeau's criticisms is that Merritt is directed to take position at *the Block House*, not at the bridge, and that Gregg is to take up position at the bridge *and support Merritt*—that is, he was to look east, not west.

The next point to note in the same connection is that the cavalry were to move at daylight, 5 A.M., of the 8th. But the Fifth Corps was expected to be in its position at Spott·

sylvania Court House by daylight of the 8th, and would
have been but for the presence of Fitzhugh Lee on the
Brock road. Next, had Gregg and Merritt moved from
Todd's tavern on the road to Corbin's bridge at any time on
the night of the 7th, or on the morning of the 8th, they
would have found themselves opposed by Hampton's cavalry
division (just as Merritt was opposed by Fitzhugh Lee's on
the Brock road), for Hampton fell back on that road after
the engagement at Todd's tavern on the 7th, and held it.
Moreover, by one o'clock in the morning of the 8th Longstreet's corps also occupied the roads on which Gregg and
Merritt were ordered to move to the Block House, and to
the Shady Grove road bridge over the Po. Had they attempted to carry out their orders to move that way, and had
they succeeded in getting rid of Hampton, they would have
found Longstreet's corps between them and the points they
were ordered to occupy. "Had these orders been carried
out,' Badeau says, meaning that Meade prevented them from
being carried out by issuing others, "every avenue to Spottsylvania would have been closed to the rebel army," while,
in fact, before the orders were issued the Confederate troops
held every avenue to Spottsylvania that they desired to close
against us and to occupy themselves.[1]

It has been already stated that there was reason to apprehend that Lee would surmise the object of the movement of
our trains in the afternoon of the 7th, and the two armies
were so close to each other that the fact of our being in motion early in the night could scarcely be concealed from
him. That Lee would use the Shady Grove road to make
corresponding movements was anticipated.

The orders of General Meade to General Merritt directed
him, while retaining one brigade at the Block House, to

---

[1] I am not criticising General Sheridan's orders, but Badeau's statements.

open the road *beyond the Court House* with two of his brigades; the brigade at the Block House was expected to
have some force at the Block House bridge on the watch;
it was with that view that it was ordered there. All these
roads were to be picketed so as to give early intelligence to
the Fifth Corps of the approach of Lee's troops. As to
Meade's not having knowledge of the existence of the Block
House (Shady Grove road) bridge and of Snell's bridge,
those and other bridges were marked on our maps, the
name of Snell's bridge being written in red ink on some of
the earlier editions which General Meade and myself used,
and printed on the later editions. He could not have failed
to know of them, and as to the Block House bridge, I have
a distinct recollection of my referring, when he had written
Merritt's order, to the necessity of having some force at that
bridge; and of his replying that the object of the order was
so plain that Merritt would certainly have such force there.
General Meade himself wrote and signed the orders to Merritt and Gregg and the notification to General Sheridan.

Fitzhugh Lee's presence on the Brock road prevented our
gaining Spottsylvania Court House. So long as it was dark
General Warren's infantry could have made but little more
progress against Fitzhugh Lee than Merritt's cavalry did,
and the final result would have been the same whether he
or Merritt had the advance. The presence of Fitzhugh
Lee's cavalry on the Brock road, and Hampton's cavalry
and Longstreet's corps on the Shady Grove road, settled the
question as to who should first hold the Court House with
infantry, whatever might have been the disposition of our
cavalry. The distance from the Wilderness to Spottsylvania
Court House was about the same, by the routes followed,
for both armies, though Hancock's left was nearer to it by
two or three miles than Longstreet's right, measured by the
shortest route the latter could follow.

There was nothing in the site of Spottsylvania Court House that gave it special military strength. Its military importance was derived from its proximity to the Richmond and Fredericksburg Railroad and the stage and telegraph roads between these towns. Roads also radiated from it in all directions, including a good wagon-road to Richmond. But sufficiently good roads southward lay open to us on either side of it, by which, if we did not attack in front, we could have moved to turn either flank.

Very early in the morning of the 9th General Early was ordered to Spottsylvania Court House by way of the Shady Grove road, and took position in the afternoon close to and east of the Court House, covering the road to Fredericksburg, where he intrenched. During the day Lee rectified his lines, intrenched carefully, and put artillery in position.

General Hancock was directed to move up to the right of the Fifth Corps, where he took position and intrenched on high ground overlooking the Po and the Shady Grove road south of it. In the afternoon Mott's division was sent to the left of the Sixth Corps.

No active operations were undertaken against the enemy on the 9th; the army was allowed to rest. The Fifth and Sixth Corps readjusted their lines, threw up intrenchments, strengthened those already made, and put artillery in position. The skirmishers and sharpshooters were very active on both sides, and in the morning General Sedgwick was killed close to the intrenchments at the right of his corps, but not under cover, at the point where the forks of the road in Alsop's field unite. He was highly esteemed, being a modest, courageous, honest-hearted man. General Wright succeeded to the command of the corps.

The skirmishers of the Fifth and Sixth Corps were pushed forward so as to develop the position and character of the enemy's works, and ascertain where they were probably vulnerable. This work was continued by both those corps on the 10th.[1]

Early in the morning of the 9th, General Burnside moved with the Ninth Corps from Aldrich's, on the Orange and Fredericksburg plank road, to Gate's house, on the road from Spottsylvania Court House to Fredericksburg, and then toward the Court House, crossing the Ny at Gate's house (a mile and a half from the Court House) with Willcox's division, and encountering a force of dismounted cavalry and a brigade of Longstreet's corps, according to General Burnside's report. About midday Stevenson's division arrived, a portion of which was also thrown across the river, while Potter's division following was held near Alsop's, about a mile back from the Ny.

Some description of Lee's intrenched position may be necessary to the comprehension of the operations that followed. The principal roads leading to the Court House have been already noted, as well as the general position of Longstreet's, Ewell's, and Hill's corps.

Longstreet's corps occupied a line running from the river Po in a general direction, a little north of east, and about a mile and a quarter long in a straight line, not following the

---

[1] From an examination of the Report of the Medical Director of the Army of the Potomac, Surgeon McParlin, pp. 153–178, Appendix to Part First, Medical and Surgical History of the War, I find that the number of wounded of the cavalry on the morning of the 8th of May was 250 ; the number of the wounded of the Fifth Corps on the 8th and 9th of May, nearly all on the 8th, was 1,419. The wounded of the Second and Sixth Corps on those days was about 150 each, making a total of 1,969 wounded. Taking the mean between one-fourth and one-fifth of this number, for the number of killed, a proportion which I have found to be very nearly correct, we have about 443 killed, and a total loss of killed and wounded on those days of about 2,412. The number of missing was small.

Of the General officers, General Robinson, Fifth Corps, was severely wounded on the 8th ; General Sedgwick killed, and General Morris, Sixth Corps, wounded on the 9th. On the Confederate side, Brigadier-General Hays, Johnson's division, was wounded on the 9th.

I have not found a statement of the killed, wounded, and missing of the Confederate force.

varying directions and sinuosities of the intrenchments. Its left rested on the Po, opposite the right of the Fifth Corps, in high, open ground, about one-third of a mile, in a straight line, above the Shady Grove road bridge, which its artillery covered. The intrenchments here lay for one-third of a mile on the elevated, open ground of Perry's farm, having in front of them, at varying distances, in no place exceeding two hundred yards, a belt of wood, chiefly on the descending slope of the plateau, which wood intervened between them and the intrenchments of the right of the Fifth Corps, though not extending to those intrenchments. The line then ran through this belt of wood and along its outer edge on the Spindler farm to the junction of the Brock and Block House roads, around which was the open ground of Spindler's farm. This part of the line, from the Po to the Brock road, was occupied by Field's division of Longstreet's corps. On the right of the Brock road the intrenchment ran through woods (which were slashed in part) in a northeast direction for the space of half a mile, entering then the open ground of Harrison's farm. This part was occupied by Kershaw's division, whose right extended beyond the left of the Fifth Corps. The line now ran nearly north for half a mile, chiefly through wood, which was slashed, some part being in open ground, where there were abatis. Rodes's division of Ewell's corps occupied this part of the line, his right (Doles's brigade) resting at what was afterward known as the bloody angle. From this angle the line ran along the outer edge of a wood in a nearly east direction (a little north of east) for about four hundred yards, having in front of it for a long distance the open ground of Landron's and Brown's farms; it terminated at a high, open point, which, General Ewell says, if held by the enemy, would have enabled their artillery to command our line. Six or eight guns were in position at this angle. This east and west line

is usually termed the salient, but should be called its **apex.**
The intrenchments turned here at this high, open point,
making a second angle which has been sometimes con-
founded with the west angle, and ran nearly south six
or seven hundred yards, having fairly open ground in
front and the wood about the McCool house in rear. General Johnson's division of Ewell's corps held the intrenchments from Rodes's right along the apex of the salient, and
along a part of its east face for the distance of six or
seven hundred yards. Walker's (Stonewall) brigade was
on the left of Johnson's division, then York's (formerly Stafford's), then Terry's (formerly Jones's), whose right was at
the east angle, the high open point which he held. Stewart's brigade held from the east angle south toward Hill.
Gordon's division was held in reserve.

Hill's corps, on Ewell's right, occupied a line running
nearly south, and terminating south of the road from Spottsylvania Court House to Fredericksburg. The interval between Ewell and Hill was occupied by skirmishers. The
ground in front of Hill was broken and wooded over the
third of its length adjoining Ewell's line ; for the remaining
distance the ground was open. In a straight line the distance from the left to the right of Hill's corps was, at this
time, about a mile and a half—by the line of intrenchments
more. From Rodes's left centre to Hill's left an intrenchment cutting off the northerly part of the salient (or the
" two angles," as General Ewell terms it) was built and occupied by Gordon's division, but some batteries of the Sixth
Corps enfilading this line, his division was placed near the
junction of Kershaw's and Rodes's divisions in order to support either. Artillery, giving flank as well as direct fire,
was placed in position throughout these intrenchments, and
wherever they were subject to the enfilade fire of our artil-
erly they were well traversed. Where there was wood in

front of them it was slashed, where the ground was open there was abatis.

On the 10th the intrenchments on the enemy's left were extended a mile west of the Po, on the high, open ground of Graves's farm, in order to cover the Shady Grove road, and an additional intrenchment was thrown up early in the morning of the 10th in similar ground on the east bank of the Po, to hold the Shady Grove crossing of that stream. Later on, the intrenchments east of the Court House were extended about two miles south of it, the extreme right resting on the Po at Snell's bridge.

It will be perceived from this brief sketch of Lee's intrenchments, that, from the vicinity of the intersection of the Brock and Block House roads, where the advanced infantry troops of the armies first came in contact, his line formed a salient projecting a mile to the north, with a width of half a mile from the west to the east face. The eastern half or more of the salient was covered by wood ; in the western part was the open ground of Harrison's and McCool's farms. West of the salient these intrenchments extended in a direction a little south of west about two miles, as already described, covering the chief road leading west from the Court House and the crossing of the Po by that road, while on the right of the salient its easterly face was extended a mile south, and subsequently two miles further, to Snell's bridge over the Po.

With such intrenchments as these, having artillery throughout, with flank fire along their lines wherever practicable, and with the rifled muskets then in use, which were as effective at three hundred yards as the smooth-bore muskets at sixty yards,[1] the strength of an army sustaining attack was more than quadrupled, provided they had force

---

[1] Accuracy of fire is meant, not *range*.

enough to man the intrenchments well. In fact there is scarcely any measure by which to gauge the increased strength thereby gained. Much the greater part of this intrenchment was concealed by wood, which in some places was scrubby and dense. The enemy's skirmish lines and sharpshooters were very active in trying to keep off all our attempts to examine them closely. Our own skirmishers were pressed against them, and in many places forcing them back into, or close to their works, gave the opportunity for quick examination, and furnished the information upon which our assaults were made.

The report of General Burnside to General Grant on the 9th, of the force he had encountered on the Fredericksburg road, seeming to indicate that Lee was moving in the direction of Fredericksburg, General Hancock was directed to examine the Po with a view to crossing it. From Corbin's bridge to the left of Hancock's corps the course of the Po is about east; it then turns and runs south about two and a half miles, when it again runs easterly. In front of Hancock its course was east, having the Shady Grove road running parallel to it at the distance of a mile. It was determined that Hancock should cross the river in his front and make a reconnoissance in force along the Shady Grove road on the enemy's left, crossing the river again by the Shady Grove road bridge or below it, with a view to turning and attacking the enemy's left.

Hancock says that at six o'clock in the morning, in accordance with instructions from the Commanding General, he directed Birney, Barlow, and Gibbon to cross the stream, which they did at three different points, Gibbon being the furthest down and opposite the left of the position of the Second Corps. The passage was difficult, owing to the depth of the water and the thick undergrowth of the banks. The resistance to Birney was stubborn, but not so to Barlow, and to Gibbon there was none. After the crossing, three pontoon bridges were laid by General Hancock, one at Barlow's crossing and two near Gibbon's. The river was fifty feet wide and not fordable. The troops were pushed forward toward the Block House bridge, but night coming on, it was impracticable to keep the skirmish line moving through the dense woods in the darkness, though a portion of it reached the stream and ascertained that it was too deep to ford. General Hancock was compelled to wait until morning, though anxious to secure the Block House bridge and cross before halting.

Late in the night orders were issued from the headquarters of the Army of the Potomac for the operations of the next day. General Hancock was to endeavor to ascertain the position and force of the enemy in his front and the *location* of his left flank, and hold his corps ready to advance against the enemy; the Sixth Corps to feel in like manner for the enemy's intrenchments in his front, General Mott to hold his division ready to move to General Burnside upon hearing heavy firing in that direction.

At early dawn on the 10th, a close examination was made by Hancock of the Block House bridge, with the design of forcing a passage over it, but the enemy was found in strong force on the opposite bank in intrenchments which commanded the bridge and its approaches, and General Hancock concluded not to attempt to carry the bridge, but sent Brooke's brigade of Barlow's division down the river to ascertain what could be effected there.[1] General Birney was directed to send a small force out on the Andrews's tavern road to cover Brooke's movement. Brooke crossed the Po about half a mile below the bridge, and pushing forward a

---

[1] It is stated in the Official Diary of Longstreet's Corps, May 9th, "At night Mahone's division is sent to the left of Field to hold the Shady Grove road." The intrenchments mentioned were thrown up by Mahone.

detachment a short distance, discovered the enemy's line of strong earthworks occupied by artillery and infantry.

At this time General Hancock received a despatch from General Meade, dated 10 A.M., directing him to transfer two divisions to General Warren's position, and arrange with General Warren to make a vigorous attack on the enemy's line at five o clock, the remaining division to be so disposed as to keep up his threatening attitude on the enemy's left, but in such manner that it could be promptly withdrawn to him if needed. General Wright and General Mott were ordered to attack at the same hour. General Warren was correspondingly instructed, and informed that General Hancock, in virtue of seniority, would command the combined operations of the two corps.

Accordingly Gibbon's division recrossed at once and formed on Warren's right; Birney's division followed, and was massed in rear of Warren, leaving Barlow to hold the ground on the south side of the Po ; General Hancock proceeded at once to examine the ground where the assault was to be made. When General Birney began to withdraw, the regiments he had ordered toward Andrews's tavern were attacked near Glady Run and driven in, and it soon became evident that the enemy were advancing in force on Barlow's position. When General Meade was informed of this, he directed Barlow's division to be withdrawn to the north side of the Po, as he did not wish to bring on a battle at that time on the south side. General Hancock accordingly joined General Barlow and directed him to recross the river. This withdrawal commenced about two o'clock. Brooke's and Brown's brigades were in front (south) of the Shady Grove road ; Miles's and Smyth's brigades along the road, the left resting on a crest a few hundred paces from the Block House bridge. In rear of this line a broad open plain extended to the ponton bridges ; it was swept by the artillery of Field's left and of the intrenchments at the Block House bridge. Brooke's and Brown's brigades were withdrawn to the right and rear of Miles's and Smyth's brigades to a wooded crest, and Miles and Smyth retired to a crest in front of the ponton bridges. The enemy, Heth's division of Hill's corps, now advanced and attacked Brooke and Brown with great vigor, but were met by a destructive fire that forced them to fall back at once with severe loss. They reformed and again attacked, pressing forward close up to our line, but were again met by so deadly a fire that they again fell back with heavy loss. During this contest the woods took fire on the right and rear of these two brigades, and approached so close that upon the second repulse of the enemy, Brooke and Brown were ordered to retire across the river, which they did in admirable order, under the artillery fire of the enemy already referred to, which swept the plain. The enemy seeing these troops retiring, again advanced, but were checked by their fire. The horses of one of Captain Arnold's guns became terrified and unmanageable by the fire of the woods, and wedged the gun so firmly between two trees that it could not be extricated, and was lost—the first gun, General Hancock says, lost by the Second Corps. The loss of these two brigades in killed and wounded was heavy. Some of the wounded perished in the fire of the woods. A heavy artillery fire between the guns of the Second Corps and of the enemy closed the operation.

General Early says of this operation of the Second Corps, that " early on the morning of the 10th he was ordered to move one of his divisions back to cover the crossing of the Po on the Shady Grove road ; and to move with another to the rear and left by the way of Spottsylvania Old Court House, and drive back a column of the enemy which had crossed the Po and taken possession of the Shady Grove road," thus threatening their rear and endangering their trains, which were on the road leading from Louisa Court House past the Old Court House. Mahone's division, he says, was sent to occupy the banks of the Po on Field's left, while with Heth's division and a battalion of artillery he moved to the rear, crossing the Po on the Louisa Court House road, and then following that road until he reached one coming in from Waite's shop on the Shady Grove road. After moving about a mile on Waite's shop road, he continues, he met Hampton gradually falling back before the enemy, who had pushed out a column of infantry considerably to the rear of the Confederate line. (This column was the regiments sent by Birney to cover Brooke's right.) "This column was, in turn," he says, "forced back to the position of the Shady Grove road, which was occupied by what was reported to be Hancock's corps. Following up and crossing a small stream (Glady Run) just below a mill-pond, we succeeded in reaching Waite's shop (on the Shady Grove road), from whence an attack was made on the enemy, and the entire force which had crossed the Po was driven back with the loss of one piece of artillery, which fell into our hands, and a considerable number in killed and wounded." "This," he says, "relieved us from a very threatening danger, as the position the enemy had attained would have enabled him to completely enfilade Field's position, and get possession of the line of our communications to the rear, within a very short distance of which he was, when met by the force which drove him back. In this affair Heth's division behaved very handsomely, all of the brigades (Cook's, Davis's, and Walker's) being engaged in the attack. General H. H. Walker had the misfortune to receive a severe wound in the foot, which rendered amputation necessary, but otherwise our loss was slight."

Intrenchments were thrown up from Field's left on the

Po, covering the Shady Grove road for the space of a mile, in addition to those on the east bank, covering the Block House bridge. General Hancock says, "The enemy regarded this as a considerable victory, and General Heth published a congratulatory order to his troops, etc. Had not Barlow's fine division, then in full strength, received imperative orders to withdraw, Heth's division would have had no cause for congratulation."

Throughout the morning of the 10th there was sharp skirmish and artillery fire going on, part of it preliminary to the attacks directed for the afternoon. At 3.30 P.M. General Hancock was informed by General Meade that General Warren reported the opportunity for immediate attack to be so favorable that he was ordered to attack at once, and Gibbon directed to co-operate with him; that Wright was ordered to be ready to attack at once. At a quarter before four o'clock General Wright with Mott was ordered to attack immediately.

General Warren, wearing his full uniform, proceeded to assault the enemy's position at once with Crawford's and Cutler's divisions, and Webb's and Carroll's brigades of Gibbon's division under Gibbon's orders.[1] Opposite the right of this attacking force the wood in front of the enemy's intrenchments was dense, and filled with a low growth of dead cedar trees, whose hard, sharp-pointed branches, interlaced and pointed in all directions, made it very difficult for the troops to advance under the heavy artillery and musketry fire they met at the outset. They emerged into the open ground near the intrenchments with disordered ranks and under a heavy artillery and musketry fire, part direct, part flanking, that swept the whole ground, but went for-

---

[1] Robinson's division had been broken up and its troops distributed to the other divisions, excepting Dennison's Maryland brigade, the term of whose service expired before the close of May.

ward, some to the abatis, others to the crest of the parapet, but were all driven back with heavy loss. General Carroll says that the right of his line gained the enemy's breast-works, and his whole line reached the abatis. It is claimed that some of Crawford's men did the same, or it may be Cutler's. The Official Diary of Longstreet's Corps says, "Some of the enemy succeed in gaining the works but are killed in them." Brigadier-General Rice, commanding a brigade in Cutler's division, a very gallant officer, was mortally wounded in this assault.

General Hancock returned to the ground at about half-past five P.M., just before the close of the assault. He was ordered to renew it at half-past six P.M., but, under orders, deferred it until seven P.M , when he attacked with Birney's and Gibbon's divisions, part of the Fifth Corps uniting with him, but with no more success than the preceding attempt. In this second attack the wood was on fire in some places.

It is to be regretted that Hancock had not been directed to cross the Po at daylight of the 10th, instead of being ordered to cross late in the afternoon of the 9th. Had he been, there appears to be every reason to conclude that the Confederate left would have been turned and taken in rear, while the Fifth Corps attacked it in front.

As it was, Hancock's crossing in the evening of the 9th put Lee on his guard, and enabled him to bring troops to the threatened flank by daylight of the 10th and throw up in-trenchments.[1] It was a mistake, too, as Hancock had crossed, to abandon the turning movement on the morning of the

---

[1] Hancock says that *at early dawn of the* 10*th* the enemy was in strong force at the bridge, in intrenchments which commanded the bridge and its approaches.

The Official Diary of Longstreet's Corps, May 9th, says: "*At night* Mahone's division is sent to the left of Field to hold the Shady Grove road." General Early, however, says: "Early in the morning of the 10th, I was ordered to move one of my divisions back to cover the crossing of the Po, on the Shady Grove road."

10th, and make, instead of it, a front attack on the strong intrenchments of Longstreet's left. It would have been better to have continued the turning movement, the Fifth Corps aiding by sending one of its divisions to Hancock and making a front attack with the other two at the critical moment.[1]

The examination of the enemy's works under cover of the skirmishers of the Sixth Corps developed a part of them which General Wright deemed to be vulnerable to a systematic, resolute attack. The other portions in his front were covered by a wide slashing and had a flanking artillery fire. The vulnerable part was the right of Rodes's front held by Doles's brigade, whose right rested at the west angle of what I have called the apex of the salient, and the part of the apex itself held by the left of Johnson's division. The intrenchment held by Doles was in open ground, two hundred yards from a pine wood with abatis in front and traverses at intervals. In the re-entrant of the line there was a battery with traverses. One hundred yards in rear was a second line partly finished, occupied by a line of battle. A wood-road led from the open ground of the Scott or Shelton house, where the column of attack was formed, directly to the point of attack. Colonel Upton, commanding Second Brigade, First Division, Sixth Corps, was designated to make the attack on Doles. General Russell now commanded the First Division. Colonel Upton's command was composed of his own brigade, the Third Brigade, formerly Russell's, and four regiments of Neill's brigade of the Sec-

---

[1] There were two officers commanding the same army. Such a mixed command was not calculated to produce the best results that either singly was capable of bringing about. It naturally caused some vagueness and uncertainty as to the exact sphere of each, and sometimes took away from the positiveness, fulness, and earnestness of the consideration of an intended operation or tactical movement that, had there been but one commander, would have had the most earnest attention and corresponding action.

ond Division.   General Russell, Colonel Upton, and all the
regimental commanders examined the ground.

In conjunction with Upton's attack, Mott early in the day
moved to the open ground of the Brown house, which is
three-quarters of a mile north of what I have called the apex
of the salient; open ground connected Brown's farm with
Landron's, on the south end of which lay the apex; but
there was wood on each side of that open connecting space
that came up to within four or five hundred yards of the
apex.   At 2 p.m. General Mott was instructed by General
Wright, under whose orders he had been placed, to be ready
to assault the works in his front at five o'clock.   These
works, like those of Doles's, had abatis and were well traversed and well supplied with artillery.

Upton's column was formed in four lines.   They were led
quietly to near the edge of the wood, two hundred yards
from the enemy.   A heavy battery of the Sixth Corps had
been put in position to give a direct fire on Doles's front
and to enfilade the apex line of the salient, which, as before
said, adjoined Doles's brigade.   This battery kept up a constant fire until the moment of Upton's charge arrived.   Its
cessation was the signal to charge.   The column had been
led up silently to the edge of the wood, and upon the signal
being given, rushed forward with a hurrah under a terrible
front and flank fire, gained the parapet, had a hand-to-hand
desperate struggle, which lasted but a few seconds, and the
column poured over the works, capturing a large number of
prisoners.   Pressing forward and extending right and left,
the second line of intrenchments with its battery fell into
Upton's hands.   The enemy's line was completely broken
and, Colonel Upton says, an opening made for the division,
Mott's, which was to have supported the left, but it did not
arrive.   Colonel Upton says further, that reinforcements to
the enemy arrived and assailed him in front and on both

flanks, the impulse of the charge was over and it remained for them to hold the intrenchments won, which they did until General Russell ordered them to withdraw, which they effected under the cover of darkness. Their loss in the assault Colonel Upton states to have been about 1,000 in killed, wounded, and missing. The enemy, he says, lost at least 100 killed at the first intrenchment, and met with a much heavier loss in trying to regain their works ; that he captured between 1,000 and 1,200 prisoners, and several stand of colors. He mentions that Captain Burham, of the Forty-third New York, had two colors in his hands when he was killed in coming back from the second line.

It appears from General Ewell's report, made in Richmond on March 20, 1865, that the right of Daniel's brigade was involved in the breaking of Doles's works, and fell back to the second line.   Gordon at once brought up his division, and with it Battle's brigade, the remnant of Doles's brigade, and the right of Daniel's, and at once attacked Upton in front and on his right flank, while Walker's brigade of Johnson's division attacked his left flank.[1] In a short time he (General Ewell) says, the enemy was driven from our works, leaving 100 dead within them, and a large number in front. Our loss, as near as I can tell, was 650, of whom 350 were prisoners.

Upton's report was prepared soon after the affair occurred, while everything was fresh in his memory. He was, besides, an active participant in everything that took place, and saw and knew exactly all that occurred. General Ewell's report was not made until long after, and is not accompanied by detailed reports of subordinates. He says the attack took

---

[1] In a paper prepared by Captain McHenry Howard, on the staff of General Steuart, Steuart's brigade of Johnson's division, or part of it, promptly took part in the attack on Upton. This paper is on the files of the Military Historical Society of Massachusetts.

place at four o'clock, whereas Colonel Upton states that it took place at ten minutes past six o'clock, which is undoubtedly accurate. The report of Colonel Upton is an admirable paper upon the manner of conducting such attacks. He was, immediately after this, promoted to the rank of Brigadier-General. Colonel Carroll of the Second Corps was also promoted to the same rank at the same time.

There is no report on the files of the War Department from General Mott of his attack, nor is there any from General Wright of that or any other operation of that part of the campaign. The only report upon it that I found in the War Department is that of Colonel McAllister who commanded the First Brigade of Mott's division; Colonel William R. Brewster, commanded the Second Brigade. The division consisted of two brigades. Colonel McAllister says that his brigade formed the first line, Colonel Campbell, with two regiments of the Sixth Corps, being on his right; that the Second Brigade formed the second line, and that the command moved forward to the attack punctually at five o'clock; but he must be mistaken in the hour, since it is evident that the attack of Mott was intended to be simultaneous with that of Upton, and must have been set in motion by the same signal, the cessation of our artillery fire in that quarter. On entering the fields, McAllister says, the enemy opened his batteries upon them, enfilading their lines, and the men fell back in confusion, except a small part of the front line, and that, after consulting with his Colonels, he fell back to the foot of the hill, where he massed his command. He says nothing of General Mott, who was well known as a gallant officer. Colonel McAllister was also well known to myself and many others as a man of courage and coolness.

Mott formed his division for attack in view of the enemy, who made every preparation to meet it. Upton's attack was concealed from their view and was a surprise, and the plan of assault being well arranged and carried out, was a success. The plan and manner of Mott's assault, on the contrary, did not admit of its being a surprise. The formation of his troops probably kept the attention of the enemy upon him, and in that way helped more effectually to conceal Upton's preparations.

The failure of Mott's division did more than neutralize the success of Upton. Had Mott joined him, the two pressing forward, taking the enemy on the right and left in flank and rear, and receiving further reinforcements from the Sixth Corps as they progressed, the probabilities were that we should have gained possession of Lee's intrenchments. One difficulty in the way of entire success was, however, the lateness of the hour at which the attack was made, but the arrangement of the attacking columns could not be completed before. It is disheartening to troops to be obliged to abandon intrenchments won so gallantly and with such severe loss.

On the morning of the 10th, General Burnside was ordered to make a reconnoissance upon the Court House, in the course of which General Stevenson was killed, an officer, General Burnside says, who commenced his services in the war with him in the expedition to North Carolina, and on all occasions proved himself a brave and efficient soldier.[1]

The reconnoissance was pushed close to the enemy on the Fredericksburg road, and a position taken up there and intrenched.[2]

On the 11th the Ninth Corps was ordered to withdraw to the north side of the Ny, take up a position with its left on the main road (to Fredericksburg) near the Harris house, its

---

[1] The following day Major-General Crittenden arrived and took command of the First Division.

[2] It was in a despatch to General Halleck on the 11th of May that General Grant, referring to the fighting up to that time, made use of the noted phrase, " I . . . propose to fight it out on this line if it takes all summer."

right connecting with Mott's division near the Brown house, but before this order could be carried out, General Burnside was ordered to recross the Ny, and reoccupy his position near the Court House, which was done without any serious opposition. Corps commanders were directed to ascertain the least force sufficient to hold their positions securely, and the number of troops that would be available for offensive movements, and what additional works, if any, were necessary to reduce the holding-force to a minimum. They were also directed to keep their skirmishers pressed well up against the enemy, and ascertain what changes, if any, had been made by them in their works or troops. The object of these instructions was to ascertain where a concentrated attack could best be made.

At 11.30 A.M. General Hancock was directed to send Birney to unite with Mott, and to form connection between Wright and Burnside, but this was subsequently recalled.

On the Confederate side, Heth was moved back to Spottsylvania Court House on the morning of the 11th and connected his left with Wilcox, who was on the left of Hill's corps. Mahone remained to cover the Shady Grove road. "On the afternoon of the 11th," Early says, "the enemy was demonstrating to our left, up the Po [Miles's brigade sent to Todd's tavern], as if to get possession of Shady Grove and the road thence to Louisa Court House," and he "was ordered by General Lee to take possession of Shady Grove by light the next morning and hold it. To aid in that purpose two brigades of Wilcox's division (Thomas's and Scales's) were moved from the right, and Mahone was ordered to move before light to Shady Grove; but during the night it was discovered that the movement to our left was a feint [it was not] and that there was a real movement of the enemy toward our right. Before daybreak on the morning of the 12th, Wilcox's brigades were returned to him and at dawn Mahone's division was moved to the right, leaving Wright's brigade to cover the crossing of the Po on Field's left."

On the 10th of May, the wounded, according to Surgeon McParlin, including the 700 brought to the hospitals on the 11th were, of the

Second Corps	1,680
Fifth Corps	767
Sixth Corps	900
Making a total of	3,347 wounded.

Taking the same proportion as that used for the 8th and 9th for the killed, we have 753, and a total of killed and wounded of 4,100. The missing were not many. Brigadier-General Rice, Fifth Corps, was mortally wounded on the 10th. Brigadier-General Stevenson, Ninth Corps, was killed. On the Confederate side Brigadier-General W. W. Walker, Heth's division, was severely wounded.

The Confederate loss in killed and wounded must have been severe in Heth's division, and also in the troops of Ewell's corps that were engaged, particularly in Rodes's division. The loss in Longstreet's corps was probably small. The total Confederate loss in killed and wounded may have been 2,000.

In the afternoon of the 11th General Meade received the following despatch from General Grant, dated 3 P.M.

" Move three divisions of the Second Corps by the rear of the Fifth and Sixth Corps under cover of night, so as to join the Ninth Corps in a vigorous assault on the enemy at four o'clock A.M. to-morrow. I will send one or two staff officers over to-night to stay with Burnside, and impress him with the importance of a prompt and vigorous attack. Warren and Wright should hold their corps as close to the enemy as possible to take advantage of any diversion caused by this attack and to break in if the opportunity presents itself. There is but little doubt in my mind that the assault last evening would have proved entirely successful if it had commenced an hour earlier, and had been heartily entered into by Mott's division and the Ninth Corps."

Personal conferences with the three corps commanders were had by General Meade concerning this attack, and General Hancock sent two staff officers with Colonel Comstock of General Grant's staff to examine the ground in the vicinity of the intended point of attack. It was intended that General Hancock should form his command in the open ground of Brown's farm, and assault the apex of the salient. It was a repetition of Mott's attack on the 10th, on a much larger scale in every way. Mott's division had been on the Brown farm and in that vicinity for two days. The details of the enemy's works were not known, but it was known that open ground, four hundred yards wide in its narrowest part, led from Brown's fields nearly due south to the apex of the salient, and that a line from Brown's house to McCool's house, which was just inside the enemy's intrenchment, ran along the middle of this open ground. This open ground, four hundred yards wide, connected Brown's fields with the wide fields of Landron, in the southwest corner of which was the apex of the salient.

During the day General Wright, commanding the Sixth Corps, had been examining carefully the ground on his left, including as much of the ground just mentioned as could be got at, and all roads and ways leading to them. Meeting afterward General Hancock at General Meade's headquarters, and learning what was going on, he mentioned having found a much shorter road than that which it was intended General Hancock's column should take, and having had Captain Mendell of the U. S. Engineers with him, suggested that he should accompany General Hancock's leading troops, a suggestion that was adopted, and Captain Mendell accompanied them.

General Hancock was directed to move his three divisions at dark to the vicinity of the Brown house, near Mott's division, and assault the enemy's line at four o'clock in the morning.

General Warren was directed to hold the position vacated by the Second Corps, in addition to the position held by him, and Colonel Kitching's heavy artillery brigade was assigned to him for this purpose ; he was further directed, in this connection, to shorten his lines wherever, in his judgment, it was advisable. It was not designed to change the concentrated formation of the Fifth Corps. General Warren and General Wright already held their corps as close to the enemy as was judicious, whether with a view to assaulting in their fronts, or to withdrawing to attack elsewhere. General Wright was directed to hold two of his divisions, General Russell's and General Wheaton's (Getty's), ready in rear of his intrenchments to move wherever required, holding his intrenchments with his remaining division, Ricketts's. Both these corps commanders were directed to have their troops in readiness at the hour named for the combined attack of Burnside and Hancock, when, it was understood, they might be required, according to the developments of the day, either to attack in their fronts, or move elsewhere and attack.[1]

---

[1] From the hour of our arrival before Spottsylvania Court House, the greater part of my time was passed with the troops ; the ground occupied by them, and between them and the enemy, was therefore well known to me.

Badeau, not acquainted with it or the enemy's works, and because the direction of General Grant that Warren and Wright should hold their corps as close as possible to the enemy was not repeated by Meade in his order (their corps being already as close to the enemy as was judicious), descants upon the loss of Grant's spirit and force by his orders percolating through three brains before they reached a corps commander. But he does not attempt to point out in what manner the dispositions ordered by Meade were inapplicable, nor how, with any reference to the ground and the enemy's works, they could have been bettered, nor where, nor how they caused any failure in promptitude or efficiency to meet the necessities of the day. On the contrary, it is very evident from what took place that they met in the best possible manner the requirements of the day. Badeau

Hancock's troops moved after it became dark, under the guidance of Captain Mendell, over a narrow, difficult road and in a heavy rain. The head of the column arrived at the Brown house about half an hour after midnight, the night still dark and rainy, and as soon as practicable were formed for attack, about twelve hundred yards from the enemy's intrenchments. The direction by which the troops were to advance was ascertained by the compass bearing of the McCool house (inside the Confederate intrenchments) from the Brown house. This line, as before mentioned, ran midway of the open ground four hundred yards wide connecting the Brown and Landron farms. Barlow's division was formed opposite this opening in two lines of masses, each regiment in close column of attack, Brooke's and Miles's brigades in the first line, Smyth's and Brown's in the second, Birney's division formed in two deployed lines on Barlow's right, Mott's in Birney's rear in one line. In Birney's front there was a marsh, and then a thick wood of low pines. Half way up to the enemy's intrenchments Birney's left came upon the open ground of Landron's farm; his right continued in wood until very near the enemy.

General Gibbon was held in reserve in rear of Barlow and Birney.

Owing to a heavy fog, General Hancock postponed the hour of attack until there should be sufficient light to see dimly, and at 4.35 A.M. gave the order to advance. The ground sloped up to the Confederate intrenchments. The

---

does not seem to have known, even when he wrote his account of the operations of the 12th of May, that Longstreet's troops remained that day in their intrenchments as strong as they were on the 10th of May, when the repeated assaults on their position proved it to be too strong to be carried by assault, *if well manned.* It was of the utmost importance to the enemy to maintain that part of their works, for if it had been carried the troops in the salient would have been taken in rear and flank. It was their point of support and the hinge upon which Lee was to swing back from the salient, and its giving way would have proved disastrous to him.

troops in column and in line kept even pace, and when about half way up, and in the open ground of Landron, burst into a cheer, and ran forward, disregarding the sharp musketry fire they received, passed through the abatis and over the intrenchments, capturing, General Hancock says, nearly 4,000 prisoners of Ewell's corps, twenty pieces of artillery, with their caissons, horses, etc., several thousand stands of small arms, and upward of thirty colors. Major-General Edward Johnson, and Brigadier-General George H. Steuart were among the prisoners. General Hancock says the loss of the enemy in killed and wounded was unusually great, the most of the dead having been killed with the bayonet. Our troops, he continues, after the capture of the intrenchments pursued the enemy through the forest in the direction of Spottsylvania Court House until they encountered a second formidable line of earth works (the works built by Gordon and heretofore mentioned).

General Barlow says in a paper upon the capture of the salient, prepared for the Military Historical Society of Massachusetts, that soon after his division began to move to the attack, the intervals between the lines and the brigades were lost, and the division became a solid mass; that when the works came in sight, the troops, seeing the east angle to their left, instinctively swayed toward it. This division appears to have entered the east angle held by York's brigade and the intrenchments running south from it six or seven hundred yards, held by Steuart's brigade. General Owen's and Colonel Carroll's brigades of Gibbon's division ran forward and entered the works with them, on their left, capturing the two guns on Steuart's centre, and turning them on the enemy. General Birney's and General Mott's troops appear to have entered the enemy's intrenchments just west of the east angle, extending from that point to the west angle and down the west face of the salient some four hundred yards, encountering Terry's and Walker's (Stonewall) brigades on the apex of the salient and, I think, Battle's brigade of Rodes's division on the west face. The two commands and McAllister's brigade of Mott's division appear to have entered the works at about the same time. In the capture of the intrenchments the troops became disordered and mixed, and it was exceedingly difficult to restore order. It was particularly difficult in Barlow's division, where the men must have been twenty deep and had mingled in one common mass.[1] Immediate efforts were made, however, by the commanders to re-form the troops, and General Hancock ordered his reserves to move up at once and occupy the captured works. Of these mention has been already made of Owen's and Carroll's brigades of Gibbon's division. Webb's brigade soon followed them on their right, he severely wounded in the head when close up. General Gibbon says his division held the line they had gained. The prompt movement of McAllister's brigade has been already noted ; the other, Colonel Brewster's, soon followed. The condition of the command does not appear to have admitted of a sufficient force sweeping down the interior of the salient along its east and west faces, taking the troops of Hill's corps and of Rodes's division in flank.

According to the statements of several Confederate officers the withdrawal of General Burnside to the north side of the Ny on the 11th, together with the throwing back of Mott's division and the reconnoissance of Miles's brigade to Todd's tavern on that day, had satisfied General Lee that we were about to turn his left, and he therefore, about sunset, ordered the withdrawal of General Ewell's artillery, which was

---

[1] It is apparent from this experience of Barlow's division, and from that of Upton's command of the 10th of May, that the first line in columns of attack would have been sufficiently massive to have carried the intrenchments, and that it would have been better to have had the second line in more open formation, following the first carefully at a distance of several hundred yards.

done along Johnson's front; but during the night General Johnson learnt from scouts, his pickets, and brigade commanders that we were massing in his front, evidently to assault in the morning. This he reported, and asked that his artillery might be sent back at once. When this report reached General Lee he is said to have remarked that General Johnson's despatch informed him the enemy were massing in his front, at the same time General Early informed him that they were moving around his left. The order was, however, given for the artillery " *to be back at daylight.*" [1]

Johnson's division was put on the alert, the whole of Ewell's corps, indeed, and General Gordon was ordered to be ready to support Johnson. Johnson's division was in the trenches, ready an hour before day. Daylight, Captain McHenry Howard says, was late in coming, and there was no indication of the assault. Presently a distant cheer was heard just off the salient (east angle) followed by silence. Then a few shots from the picket line off the (east) angle, and presently a blue line appeared, and at the same moment the returning artillery was coming up at a gallop, but Hancock's assaulting column and lines swarmed over the works and captured it before a shot could be fired, excepting only from two guns on the centre of Steuart's line, which fired two rounds. Johnson's infantry, however, delivered a brief, heavy musketry fire upon the assaulting forces, but with no apparent effect. General Johnson states emphatically that he was not surprised, that his division was ready in the trenches before the assaulting force made its appearance, and Captain Howard says that the cheering of that force would have given ample time to be ready for it if their troops had not been ready at that time; he further says that their own line, that of Steuart's brigade, was first broken on the left,

---

[1] Paper of Captain McHenry Howard, Staff of General George H. Steuart, Military Historical Society of Massachusetts.

at the angle, and that Steuart's brigade was taken in flank and rear as well as in front.

General Gordon, whose instructions were to support both Johnson and Rodes, had placed Evans's brigade in front of the McCool house, in rear of Rodes's right and Johnson's left; his other two brigades, Pegram's and R. D. Johnston's, he had posted about six hundred yards in rear, near the Harris house; but during the night, being informed by General Johnson that the enemy were massing in front of his division, he sent Pegram's brigade to him, which was placed in the trenches near Johnson's left. At daylight, hearing the musketry firing in the direction of the east angle, held by Terry, he ordered Johnston forward, who, moving up, was met in the woods between the McCool house and the east angle by Hancock's troops, Barlow's right, Birney's left (both in the disorder consequent on the assault), who broke his brigade and drove it back, he wounded. Withdrawing Pegram's and Evans's brigades at double-quick to the vicinity of the Harris house, in rear of the intrenchment constructed by himself across the salient, Gordon formed them there and then advanced against the troops of Hancock's left, driving them, he says, with heavy loss from the captured works from the left of Wilcox's division (the right of Johnson's division) to the salient (east angle) and a quarter of a mile further, retaking some of the captured guns, which, by some blunder, he says, were lost in the night again. The loss in these two brigades, he says, was not heavy. The loss of Johnston's brigade he does not mention. With this account we shall presently contrast what General Barlow says, since it was his troops chiefly, and those of Birney's left, that Gordon's troops met. The right of Birney's and Mott's troops, although disordered from the capture of the works, also entered the salient, moving down it some distance. General Rodes met this by sending Daniel's and Ramseur's brigades from their works to the attack, which, Ramseur says, was made in the most gallant manner, driving the troops (of Birney and Mott) that had entered the salient, out of it and from a part of that portion of its west face which they had captured. The outer face of the west angle, however, remained in the possession of its captors, as well as the outer face of the apex of the salient. General Daniel was killed ; General Ramseur was severely wounded, but refused to leave the field.

The success of Hancock's assault had been at once communicated to General Meade, and at 6 A.M. such intelligence was received by him from General Hancock of the attempts of the enemy to assume the offensive, that General Wright was ordered to move toward Hancock and attack at once on his, Hancock's, right. Taking Russell's and Wheaton's divisions, which were held ready to move, he marched with them quickly to the west angle of the salient, and relieved the troops of the Second Corps in that vicinity. He was wounded soon after coming up, but retained the command of his corps. At the time the Sixth Corps had begun to arrive, the enemy had compelled such of the Second Corps as had advanced into the interior of the salient in this part of the field to retire to the outer face of the captured intrenchments. In fact, it appears that by this time all the troops of the Second Corps were on the outer face of these intrenchments, except a skirmish or picket line of Barlow's division.

General Barlow says that his division remained during the day in about the same position that it was in an hour after the assault, except that it was extended considerably to the left in order to guard against any attack on our flank (Owen's and Carroll's brigades of Gibbon's division, both of which had taken part in the assault of the intrenchments, were on his left, Webb's brigade also), that the enemy gradually pushed forward (on his front) until in some places they actually reached their first line, on the outer side of which our

men were lying.   Brigadier-General Grant, commanding the
Vermont brigade of the Second Division of the Sixth Corps,
as soon as he arrived on the ground was ordered to relieve
General Barlow's division, and states that at the time he
reached there, about eight o'clock, there was some skirmishing going on in the woods beyond the captured intrenchments, and that there was an evident attempt on the part of
the enemy to recover lost ground, and that our skirmishers
were being pressed back.   These skirmishers he relieved,
but soon returned with his brigade to the Sixth Corps, on
the right.   It is apparent from these statements that the
outer face of the captured intrenchments in this part of the
field were held by our troops, as they were from there
around to the apex of the west angle and some distance on
the west face of the salient.

As soon as he came upon the ground General Wright began a heavy attack from the apex of the west angle and the
thick pine wood and morass west of the angle but close up to
the west face of the salient.   It was in this vicinity that the
close deadly fighting of " *the Angle* " took place, continuing
with undiminished fury until near dark, when it began to
abate, but lasting until three o'clock the next morning, when
the enemy were withdrawn to a new line of intrenchment
across the base of the salient, which had been built during
the night.

But I am anticipating.   When Ramseur got into the
trenches on the right of Daniel, the west angle and some
part of the intrenchment south of it were still held wholly by
us, and a deadly fire was poured on Ramseur's right flank.
Perrin's and Harris's brigades of Mahone's division, Hill's
corps, now came up to Ewell's assistance, and under a heavy
artillery and musketry fire regained some further part of the
inner face of the intrenchments on Ramseur's right, where
they captured, General Harris says, between 200 and 300

prisoners. McGowan's brigade of Wilcox's division followed, passing through a heavy fire in getting to the trenches. The right of his brigade extended some distance up the left or west side of the angle, and was enfiladed from the point of the angle and the apex of the salient. We held the apex of the salient and the west angle in strong force, as well as the woods and ravine on the right, from all of which an incessant, powerful fire was kept up. General Perrin was killed, General McGowan severely wounded.

General Hancock had directed a portion of his artillery to be posted on some high ground about three hundred yards from the apex of the salient, which maintained an incessant fire over our line on the enemy. Some guns were run up close against the breastworks of the west angle, and kept up an enfilade fire of canister along the west face of the salient, but lost heavily in men and horses. Other guns also were brought close to the intrenchments nearer the east angle. It must be remembered that all these parts of the enemy's intrenchments were thickly traversed. The contest continued incessantly throughout the day along the whole line, from the right of the Sixth Corps to the left of the Second Corps : occasionally changes in troops were made where it was practicable, in order to replenish ammunition. At the west angle the fighting was literally murderous. One of the participants, Brigadier-General Grant, commanding the Vermont brigade of the Second Division of the Sixth Corps, says of it :

" It was not only a desperate struggle but it was literally a hand-to-hand fight. Nothing but the piled up logs or breastworks separated the combatants. Our men would reach over the logs and fire into the faces of the enemy, would stab over with their bayonets ; many where shot and stabbed through the crevices and holes between the logs ; men mounted the works, and with muskets rapidly handed them, kept up a continuous fire until they were shot down, when others would take their place and continue the deadly work. . . . Several times during the day the rebels would show a white flag about the works, and when our fire slackened jump over and surrender, and others were crowded down to fill their places. . . . It was there that the somewhat celebrated tree was cut off by bullets, there that the brush and logs were cut to pieces and whipped into basket-stuff; . . . there that the rebel ditches and cross-sections were filled with dead men several deep. . . . I was at the angle the next day. The sight was terrible and sickening, much worse than at Bloody Lane (Antietam). There a great many dead men were lying in the road and across the rails of the torn down fences, and out in the cornfield; but they were not piled up several deep and their flesh was not so torn and mangled as at the 'angle.'"

As an indication of the sanguinary character of the conflict of the 10th and 12th, Colonel Upton remarks that Captain Lamont of the Fifth Maine, the only one of seven captains who escaped in the assault of the 10th, was among the killed on the 12th.

General Mc Gowan, of Wilcox's division, Hill's corps, says : "Our men lay on one side of the breastwork, the enemy on the other, and in many instances men were pulled over." He believed that he captured as many prisoners as he lost. "The trenches," he says, "on the right in the bloody angle had to be cleared of the dead more than once. An oak tree, twenty-two inches in diameter, in rear of the brigade was cut down by musket-balls and fell about twelve o'clock Thursday night, injuring several men in the First South Carolina regiment."

Many others give the same account of the character of the contest at and in the vicinity of the west angle. All the brigades engaged in it lost heavily. Rain fell during the day and heavily toward night.

What occurred on our right has not yet been mentioned.

Early in the morning of the 12th, General Warren opened with all his artillery, and pressed forward his skirmish line. The intrenchments of the enemy gave no sign of having been stripped of any of their troops to meet Hancock's and

Wright's attacks on the salient, but the manner in which the contest there was carried on and the reinforcements the enemy received, together with the fact that Burnside was attacking on the east face of the salient, led to the conclusion that the enemy could not be very strong in Warren's front, and at 9.15 A.M. he was ordered to attack at once at all hazards, with his whole force if necessary.[1] He accordingly prepared to do so, and assaulted, but was repulsed, for Longstreet's corps was holding its intrenchments in force, the only change made in his line being the extension of his right to fill the place from which Ramseur's brigade had been taken.[2] Ricketts's division had followed Wright as soon as he could be withdrawn, and at 11.30 A.M. was forming in rear of Wright's other divisions. Immediately upon the failure of Warren's attack he was directed to send General Cutler's division to General Wright and be prepared to follow with his whole corps.[3] Cutler's division went into action as soon as it reached the ground. It appearing probable that the enemy's intrenchments in the vicinity of the west angle could be carried if assaulted by the whole Fifth

---

[1] At 9.20 A.M. General Warren reported : " My left cannot advance without a most destructive enfilade until the Sixth Corps has cleared its front." [By attack at the west angle of the salient is meant.—A. A. H.] "My right is close up to the enemy's works and ordered to assault. The enemy's line appears to be strongly held. It is his *point d'appui* if he throws back his right."

Immediately after this despatch he reports : " I cannot advance my men farther at present."

[2] In the Official Diary of Longstreet's Corps this attack of Warren is designated as " two violent assaults " between nine and ten o'clock on a part of General Field's line. That part of the attack against the intrenchments held by Bratton's brigade, where the works crossed the Brock road, was made over open ground which extended from one intrenchment to the other. General Bratton says of Warren's troops that they advanced beautifully in two lines of battle to within fifty yards of the intrenchments, when the musketry and artillery fire was opened that broke them.

[3] I was overlooking the right of the army, and gave the order for the assaults there to cease, as soon as I was satisfied they could not succeed ; and directed the transfer of the troops to the centre for attack there.—A. A. H.

Corps, General Warren was directed to withdraw from his front and move with his whole corps to the designated point and attack. Griffin's division followed Cutler's closely. The other troops of the Fifth Corps were following, except Crawford's division, when the project of further assault was given up, as it did not appear to promise a complete success. Our line on the right was very much shortened, Crawford remaining in the old intrenchments of the Fifth Corps, and of the Sixth Corps in part.

Turn now to our left; at four o'clock in the morning of the 12th, General Potter's division of Burnside's corps advanced against the enemy's intrenchments held by Lane's brigade, the left of Hill's corps. These he carried about five o'clock, capturing some prisoners and two guns. But General Lane, reforming his brigade in some old intrenchments that enfiladed those he had been dispossessed of, forced General Potter out of the intrenchments he had taken, and, reinforced by Scales's and Thomas's brigades, sent by General Wilcox as soon as he heard the firing, they followed up Potter for a short distance, but were recalled. The captured guns were retaken. General Lane mentions General Doles's brigade of Ewell's corps coming to him at about the same time as the others, and joining in the advance.

Urgent orders, General Burnside says, were received from the Lieutenant-General to establish connection with the Second Corps at all hazards, and " General Crittenden's and General Potter's divisions were ordered forward to repeated attacks, which resulted in severe loss, but did not succeed in driving the enemy from his main line." General Potter established connection with General Hancock at 9.15 A M. General Willcox was now ordered to attack with his whole force on the left of General Crittenden. Considerable delay occurred in arranging his artillery to cover his left against attack in the event of his being repulsed. He was on the left of the whole army. His attack was made against a salient held by Walker's brigade (Colonel Mayo commanding) of Heth's division. There was a pine thicket in front of the salient, under cover of which General Willcox got close up to the works, but was met with a heavy fire of musketry from Mayo's brigade, and Thomas's on Mayo's left, and the fire of Heth's artillery on the right of the salient. At the same time Lane's brigade, supported by Mahone's (under Colonel Weisiger), attacked him on the left flank, Lane charging close up to his artillery, but, according to General Willcox, his charge was splendidly repulsed, the Second Michigan Infantry, commanded by Colonel William Humphrey, which supported the artillery, manning the guns when the artillerists were killed. Lieutenant Benjamin, Chief of Artillery of the corps, who was severely wounded, was highly commended for the manner in which he handled his artillery.

The assault of Willcox's first line was repulsed with severe loss in killed, wounded, and missing, the latter, he says, swept off by Lane's brigade when retreating. His second line, he says, was brought forward, and held its ground until ordered to withdraw to the edge of the wood, where they threw up breastworks. General Lane says he captured a battery of six guns, but was unable to bring them off; that he then directed his attack against the assaulting troops, and that some part of his brigade became mixed with the enemy and had fighting at close quarters, and that he finally fell back upon the close approach of two lines of the enemy.

Lane's and Weisiger's brigades, General Early says, had been thrown to the front for the purpose of moving to the left and attacking the flank of the column which had broken Ewell's line, to relieve the pressure on him and, if possible, recover the part of the line which had been lost.

Another attempt was made in the afternoon, he says, to carry out the flank movement with Weisiger's brigade and

Cook's brigade of Heth's division, but it was discovered that the flanking column would have been exposed to the fire of one or more intrenched lines, and the attempt was not made. Skirmishing and heavy artillery firing were kept up by General Burnside until late in the day. Late in the afternoon Humphreys's and Bratton's brigades of Longstreet's corps were sent to General Ewell.

Early on the morning of the 13th it was found that the enemy had withdrawn from the salient, and the several corps were ordered to press up as close to them as possible, to ascertain their position. Colonel Carroll, of Gibbon's division, advancing through the woods, driving back the enemy's skirmishers, found them three-quarters of a mile in rear of the apex of the salient in a strongly-intrenched line occupied by infantry and artillery. Pushing forward in his usual intrepid manner, Colonel Carroll was severely wounded and compelled to quit the field.

It has been said that the continuance of this desperate contest at the apex of the salient on the part of General Lee was an unnecessary sacrifice of troops he could ill afford to spare; but in fact he could not withdraw them during daylight without the risk of serious disaster, and Meade continued to press against him there with the hope of bringing about that withdrawal and disaster.

For the losses of the day, the same authority as that heretofore used gives for the wounded on the 12th :

The Second Corps	2,043
The Fifth Corps	970
The Sixth Corps	840
Making a total of	3,853

For the killed we have 880, and for the killed and wounded 4,733. The prisoners lost did not probably exceed 500.

General Burnside states his losses in his three divisions, from the 8th to the 20th of May, to have been 2,454 killed and wounded and 590 missing, one-half of which loss he assigns to the 12th of May. The number of killed and wounded he gives is probably in excess of the actual number, but I have no means of correcting it. The Ninth Corps did not at that time form part of the Army of the Potomac, and I have not been able to find the report of its Medical Director for that period. The killed and wounded of the Ninth Corps between the 8th and 12th was very small.

The total killed and wounded on the 12th, including the Ninth Corps, is, therefore, 6,020. The total missing, 800. The killed, wounded, and missing, 6,820.

I have not found any exact statement of the Confederate loss in killed and wounded. At the salient it must have been equal to that of our troops engaged there; in Burnside's and Warren's attacks much less than ours. Altogether their killed and wounded must have been between 4,000 and 5,000.

Respecting the number of prisoners lost by the Confederates, General Ewell says of his corps, that after the loss of Johnson's division (before sunrise) his force barely numbered 8,000. This was before the losses by fighting, after the capture of the salient, occurred. He says previously that when Hancock broke through the lines he captured about 2,000 men. His killed, wounded, and prisoners on the 10th he states to have been 650; his killed and wounded in the Wilderness, 1,250. The sum of these figures is 11,900, or say 12,000. But the number of enlisted men of Ewell's corps present for duty on the 20th of April, 1864 (Hoke's brigade and two regiments of Rodes's division absent and not counted), was 15,705, leaving about 3,700 men not accounted for by General Ewell's figures. His report, as before stated, was made in March, 1865, from Richmond, where the exact data may not have been accessible to him. If General Ewell's estimate, that after the loss of Johnson's division before sunrise of the 12th his force barely numbered 8,000, be correct, then the greater part of the 3,700 men not accounted for may be attributed to an underestimate of his losses on the 10th, and an underestimate of Hancock's captures at daylight on the 12th.

The Confederate loss on the 12th in killed, wounded, and prisoners, appears from the preceding discussion to have been between 9,000 and 10,000, officers and enlisted men.

In General officers the Confederates suffered severely, Brigadier-Generals Daniel and Perrin being killed, and Brigadier-Generals Walker (commanding the Stonewall Brigade, Johnson's division), Ramseur, R. D. Johnston, and McGowan being severely wounded, and Major-General Edward Johnson and Brigadier-General. Geo. H. Steuart captured.

On the part of the United States, Major-General Wright was wounded, and Brigadier-Generals Webb and Carroll were severely wounded.

A movement by our right flank would probably have resulted in Lee's abandoning his intrenchments at once and taking position behind the North Anna. That was not desired, and as a movement by the left promised an opportunity of attacking Lee's right before it could be reinforced from his left or his intrenchments extended, and as at the same time it would cover our hospitals and communication with our depots in Washington, the movement by the left was adopted.

General Warren was directed to move his corps immediately after dark on the 13th, by way of Scott's (Shelton's), Landron's, and thence by a farm-road to a ford of the Ny, half a mile distant, then crossing the Ny, to move across the country, chiefly through fields, to the Fredericksburg and

Spottsylvania Court House road, and, advancing along that road, recross the Ny, form on the left of the Ninth Corps, and attack on the Fredericksburg road at four A.M. of the 14th. The artillery of the Fifth Corps was directed to move by roads further to the rear and join the corps on the Fredericksburg road. The Sixth Corps was directed to follow the Fifth and attack on its left on the Massaponax Church road. Guides were sent to the two corps.

General Hancock was directed to be prepared to attack at four A.M. on his front, but not to attack until ordered. General Burnside was instructed similarly to General Hancock.

The night set in dark and rainy. Every precaution was taken by General Warren to mark out the line of his march; men were posted at short intervals, and fires built along the line; but the rain and heavy mist obscured and extinguished them. The mud was deep over a large part of the route; the darkness intense, so that literally you could not see your hand held before your face.

The march was necessarily very slow. The fatigue of floundering along in such a sea of mud but few can apprehend. In spite of all the care taken to prevent it, men lost their way and lay down exhausted, until daylight enabled them to go on.

At six o'clock in the morning the head of General Warren's column arrived at the point where they were to form for attack, but the column was broken and scattered, and it was not practicable to get the command in condition for offensive operations that day. The attack was therefore abandoned.

The Sixth Corps followed the Fifth, the head of the column starting at three o'clock in the morning of the 14th, and was massed out of sight on the Massaponax Church road, on the north side of the Ny. A high point on this road at Gayle's, on the south side of the river and about half a mile from it, commanded the country around it (which was open) and the

Fredericksburg road also. It was therefore occupied by Upton's brigade, now only 800 strong. But shortly after he took possession he was attacked by Chambliss's cavalry brigade and Mahone's infantry, and forced to abandon the position. Under orders from General Meade, General Warren sent General Ayres to recover it, which was done, the enemy drawing off. General Wright at the same time sent two brigades, who relieved Ayres, and followed with his corps.

General Wright's brigade of Mahone's division, which had been holding the intrenchments on the Confederate left covering the Shady Grove road bridge, was brought over to Early's position at the Court House on the 14th, and the reconnoissance made by it and by Mahone disclosed our movement and presence on their right.

It was not until the afternoon of the 14th that our withdrawal from the right was discovered by Longstreet's skirmishers, who then entered the breastworks abandoned by the Fifth Corps ; nor was it until the night of the 14th that Field's division was brought over to the Court House and posted on the right of Hill's corps. Kershaw remained on the left until midnight of the 15th, and then moved to the Confederate right, where he was held in reserve.

Fortune evidently did not favor us on the night of the 13th, for the intrenchments on the Confederate right did not extend much south of the Court House, and only Hill's corps was on that front. With ordinary weather the Fifth and Sixth Corps would have been able to attack there early in the morning, before reinforcements could have been brought from the Confederate left.

At four o'clock on the morning of the 15th, General Hancock, by direction of General Meade, moved Barlow's and Gibbon's divisions to the Spottsylvania and Fredericksburg road in the vicinity of the Ny River, leaving Birney's division to cover Burnside's right flank.

During the 15th, 16th, and 17th, the Fifth and Sixth Corps advanced their intrenched lines, established batteries, opened roads, examined the country and roads leading southward, and on the 17th the Fifth Corps prepared an intrenchment to be held in connection with an operation to be undertaken on the morning of the 18th. Communication was being opened with Aquia Creek by railroad, which was completed the 22d of May, and the wounded sent to the general hospitals at Washington. Supplies for the army and some additional troops were received during this time.

Brigadier-General Grant, commanding Vermont brigade, Second Division, Sixth Corps, reports that Colonel Warner's regiment, 1,500 strong, joined his brigade on the 15th of May.

On the 17th of May Brigadier-General R. O. Tyler, with a temporary division of heavy artillery regiments serving as infantry, and the Corcoran Legion, joined the Second Corps, making an addition to it, General Hancock says, of 8,000 men. The Corcoran Legion was assigned to General Gibbon's division. These troops were distributed to the army soon after their arrival, and General Tyler was assigned to the command of one of Gibbon's brigades.

Owing to the losses in action and the expiration of the terms of service of many regiments of Mott's division (the 4th), it had become so reduced in numbers that it was consolidated into a brigade on the 13th of May, and assigned to Birney's division.[1]

---

[1] According to Badeau (foot-note, page 198, Vol. II.), some 1,800 drafted men, recruits, and convalescents were also received at this time, in addition to the reinforcements already mentioned, making a total of 11,300. I have not been able to obtain any detailed statement from the War Department of additional troops sent to the Army of the Potomac during this campaign. The statement of the Department gives the whole number sent from May 4, 1864, to June 12, 1864, and from June 12, 1864, to April of 1865; and when the reinforcement was by organization—that is, by regiments—the numbers of the statement comprise the absent as well as the present, the extra duty men, etc.

The statement of the War Department is that the reinforcements sent to the

On the 19th of May the organization of the Reserve Artillery was broken up. Its guns, ninety-two in number, were sent to the Washington dépôt. Its caissons were retained, and took the place of the army wagons carrying the reserve ammunition. The artillerymen were transferred to the Corps Artillery. Upon arriving before Petersburg, the guns were returned to the Army of the Potomac. They had accompanied the army chiefly with a view to their use before Richmond. The brigade guard of Colonel Kitching remained with the Fifth Corps, with which it had been serving from an early day after the campaign began.

It had been suggested by Major-General Wright, and also by myself, that after the lapse of a few days a return by night to the enemy's left, which would probably be abandoned, or very much weakened by our concentration on his right, might afford a good opportunity to attack there. General Wright's suggestion was for his corps only to undertake it; but it was concluded to send both the Second and Sixth Corps, and on the 17th, Generals Hancock and Wright were ordered to move their troops in the night to the works captured on the 12th, and attack the enemy's new intrenchments there at daylight on the 18th, the Sixth Corps on the right of the Second. General Burnside was directed to attack in conjunction with them, and General Warren to open his artillery at the same time and be prepared for the offensive. The Second Corps, being nearest to the point of attack, led, the Sixth Corps following. The troops were in the

---

Army of the Potomac (including Burnside's corps) from May 4 to June 12, 1864, was by organizations 1,031 officers and 26,780 enlisted men, making a total of 27,811. But these numbers, as already remarked, included the absent as well as the present, and of the present, those on extra duty, etc. During the same period it, the Army of the Potomac, received, by recruits to regiments, 2,453 enlisted men. The effective force sent between May 4 and June 12 was probably about 12,000. But during this same period the term of service of many regiments expired, and they were mustered out of service. From May 2d to July 4th, thirty-six regiments were in this way discharged from the service.

position designated before daylight, and at four A.M. Gibbon and Barlow moved forward to assault, their troops in lines of brigades. Birney and Tyler were held in reserve. The artillery was posted in the first line of works at the apex of the salient, firing over the troops. The Sixth Corps advanced on the right of the Second. But the enemy was on the alert, and the new intrenchments across the base of the salient were of the most formidable character, being concealed on their right by woods and having on that part of their front a heavy slashing, and on their left front, which was in the open ground of the Harrison farm, lines of abatis. As the troops approached they were met with a heavy musketry and artillery fire which completely swept the ground in front; but, notwithstanding, they pressed forward to the slashing and abatis, and made several gallant attempts to carry the enemy's lines, but without success.

Upon its being reported to General Meade that there was but little probability of the enemy's lines being carried, he directed the attack to be discontinued, and the troops were accordingly withdrawn. The Sixth Corps returned at once to the left of the Fifth Corps, resuming its position there.

During the night of the 18th, Barlow's, Gibbon's, and Birney's divisions moved to the vicinity of Anderson's mill, on the east side of the Ny River, below the left of the Sixth Corps. Tyler's division was posted on the Court House and Fredericksburg road near the Harris house, in the vicinity of which Colonel Kitching's brigade, now of the Fifth Corps, was also posted, on the left of Tyler.

General Burnside made the attack directed on the morning of the 18th with the divisions of Crittenden and Potter, and all his artillery, uniting on the right with Hancock, but could not carry the enemy's intrenchments. The artillery of the Fifth Corps also opened and continued its fire for several hours.

During the night of the 18th the Ninth Corps was moved to the left of the Sixth Corps, its left resting near the Po at Quesenberry's. The enemy's right at this time rested on the Po, covering the road crossing that stream at Snell's bridge. The Sixth and Ninth Corps were pressed up as close to the enemy's intrenchments as practicable without assaulting, and intrenched. During the 20th the Ninth Corps made reconnoissances in the direction of Smith's and Stannard's mills, on the Ny and Po crossings of the Telegraph road.

The Fifth Corps now formed the right of the army, and had an intrenchment running across the Ny above the Fredericksburg road crossing, with Kitching's brigade and Tyler's division, as before stated, near the Harris house on the east side of the Ny, covering the right of the army and the road to Fredericksburg, now in full use by our trains of all kinds. The Second Corps was held ready to move southward, reconnoissances in that direction going on. In the afternoon of the 19th instructions were sent to General Hancock to move that night, but an encounter with the enemy late in the afternoon on our right flank, held by Tyler's division and Kitching's brigade, led to its being deferred until the night of the 20th.

General Ewell was directed by General Lee on the 19th to demonstrate in his front to ascertain whether the Army of the Potomac was moving to his, Lee's, right, as he believed it to be. General Ewell says that to accomplish this he moved with his corps around on our right by a detour of several miles, on roads impassable for artillery, when he came upon us prepared to receive him—his force 6,000. Our position being developed, and his object attained, he was about to retire, he says, when he was attacked. Part of his line, he continues, was shaken, but Pegram's and Ramseur's brigades held their ground so firmly that he maintained his position till nightfall, when he withdrew unmolested; that his loss was about 900 killed, wounded, and missing.

Ramseur (whose account is the only one I find besides that of General Ewell) says that his brigade was in front, that their movement was discovered, and that he then attacked with his brigade and drove the enemy rapidly, and with severe loss, until his flanks were enveloped, when he retired two hundred yards and formed, Grimes's brigade on his left, Battle's on his right; but that Gordon's division on their left being flanked, retreated, and the whole line was compelled to fall back, when it was repeatedly attacked by a heavy force until night, when it quietly and safely withdrew.

Kershaw's division held Ewell's intrenchments while he was absent.

The force encountered by Ewell was Kitching's brigade and General Tyler's division, posted on the Fredericksburg road in the vicinity of the Harris house. Colonel Kitching, on the left of Tyler, perceived indications of the movement in the course of the afternoon, and precautions were taken to meet it. The firing began about half-past five o'clock, and it being heavy, General Hancock was at once directed by General Meade to send a division in double-quick to Tyler, and to hold his corps ready to move up. General Warren, being the nearest at hand, was directed to send some troops over, and the Maryland brigade sent by him got to the ground in time to take an active and effective part in the fight. The First Maryland regiment, returning from Fredericksburg, had at once, without waiting for orders, joined in the attack on Tyler's right.

General Hancock ordered up Birney's division in double-quick, directed Barlow and Gibbon to be ready to follow, and went himself to the ground, where he found Tyler's division " fiercely engaged " with the enemy in front of the Fredericksburg road. As soon as General Birney's troops arrived two of his brigades were thrown into action on Tyler's right, but the severity of the action was already over. General Crawford, of the Fifth Corps, arrived shortly after Birney, about dark, and was formed in support of Kitching and the Maryland brigade on the left.

The fighting, General Hancock says, continued obstinate until about nine o'clock, when the enemy gave way, retreating rapidly across the Ny. The loss of the enemy in killed and wounded was severe, and about 400 prisoners fell into our hands. This was the first engagement Tyler's troops had taken part in, and they acquitted themselves handsomely, he says.

General Early says that his whole corps was held ready to co-operate with Ewell, should his *attack* prove successful, and that, to create a diversion in his favor, Thomas's brigade was thrown forward. It made a demonstration on General Cutler's front so far as to drive in the pickets on his right flank.

Russell's division of the Sixth Corps was massed near the Harris house during the night of the 19th, and on the morning of the 20th relieved Birney's and Tyler's divisions, which joined the other two divisions of the Second Corps near Anderson's or Clark's mill. Crawford and Kitching with Russell now protected the right flank of the army.[1]

---

[1] I was surprised to find in Badeau's account of this affair the following statement :

"Warren had participated in the battle on the left of the Second Corps, and when the rebels were seen to be repelled, he was ordered to fall upon their flank and rear with the view of cutting off and capturing Ewell's entire column, but he failed to carry out his instructions and under cover of night the enemy retired."

The troops from both corps engaged received the same orders from General Meade, and continued the action together, both equally close to the enemy until its close. Nothing took place on the field nor is there anything on record to support the statement of Badeau. Ewell was close to the ford near Landron's when the fighting terminated, two miles from Warren, who was with Griffin's and Catlin's divisions close up to the Spottsylvania intrenchments, under orders to attack them if there was promise of success.

Badeau further states :

"Ferrero with his colored division was on the road to Fredericksburg in rear and on the right of Tyler and near the point where Ewell struck the National

The number wounded on the 18th of May, almost entirely of the Second Corps, was, according to Medical Director McParlin, 552, and on the 19th, chiefly from the Second Corps, 1,100, making a total wounded of 1,652. Estimating by the rule adopted, we have for killed, 371, and for killed and wounded 2,023. Colonel Coulter, commanding brigade in Crawford's division, was severely wounded on the 18th.

Adding the number of wounded of the Army of the Poto-

line. This road formed Grant's direct communication with his base and he sent word at once to Ferrero: ' The enemy have crossed the Ny on the right of our lines in considerable force, and may possibly detach a force to move on Fredericksburg. Keep your cavalry pickets well out on the plank road and all other roads leading west and south of you,' " etc., etc.

Badeau continues:

" The rebels did indeed push on as far as the Fredericksburg road, but Ferrero and his colored division handled them severely. Twenty-seven wagons were captured in the first surprise, but all retaken ; and on the soil of Virginia men who had once been slaves, beat back the forces of those who had held them in slavery. It was the first time at the East when colored troops had been engaged in any important battle, and the display of soldierly qualities obtained a frank acknowledgment from both troops and commanders, not all of whom had before been willing to look upon negroes as comrades. But after that time, white soldiers in the Army of the Potomac were not displeased to receive the support of black ones. They had found the support worth having."

Ferrero's division of colored troops was not in rear and on the right of Tyler, nor near the point where Ewell struck the National line, nor was he on the road forming Grant's direct communication with his base (the Fredericksburg and Spottsylvania Court House road) but on the plank road from Orange Court House to Fredericksburg, not far from Salem Church, and over five miles north of the Harris farm where Ewell was encountered as narrated by me. General Ferrero had with him besides his division, the Second Ohio and the Third New Jersey (both white veteran cavalry regiments) thrown out in advance of his infantry, and this cavalry had an outpost on the road from Alsop's to Silver's on the Orange plank road. This outpost was driven in about half-past five in the afternoon by some cavalry and artillery force of the enemy. This force the Second Ohio and the Third New Jersey engaged, and Ferrero formed his division in line to support them. The enemy fell back with slight loss, our two cavalry regiments losing 2 enlisted men killed, 7 wounded, and 2 missing. The colored division had not a casualty of any kind whatever, handled nobody, severely or otherwise ; in fact, were not engaged.

The wagons captured were taken near the Harris farm, and were retaken by the troops there, not by Ferrero's troops.

This affair is in itself insignificant, but I have found it to be characteristic of the spirit of Badeau's volumes in much that concerns the Army of the Potomac.

mac heretofore stated as occurring at Spottsylvania Court House, from the morning of the 8th to the night of the 19th, we have a total wounded of 10,821. Medical Director McParlin states it to have been 10,531, but I find he omits the 300 wounded left in the hands of the Confederates in the afternoon of the 10th of May.

The number of killed, according to the regimental reports, he states to have been 1,781; and of missing, according to the same authority, 2,077; making a total, by his numbers, of 14,389.

But many of those counted among the missing were killed. Using the numbers I have given, we have :

Wounded	10,821
Killed	2,447
Killed and wounded	13,268
Missing	1,411
Total	14,679

The sum of the killed and missing, according to the regimental records, is probably correct, and I have used that sum, apportioning its parts differently.

General Burnside states his losses to have been 2,454 killed and wounded, and 590 missing. These numbers, added to those of the Army of the Potomac, give killed and wounded, 15,722; missing, 2,001; total casualties, 17,723.

Medical officers were directed to retain in the field-hospital all cases of slight wounds, but it was difficult to execute the order ; men would slip off in the night, and find their way to the steamers. Several hundred were, however, retained, accompanying the army in ambulances.

Medical Director McParlin states that the total number of wounded *received in Washington* from Fredericksburg (the wounded of the Wilderness and Spottsylvania Court House) was 21,966, of which 19,766 belonged to the Army of the Potomac, and 2,200 to the Ninth Corps. The number I have given for the Army of the Potomac in those two battles is 19,923. The number reported by General Burnside for the Ninth Corps is, 3,123 ; total, 23,046, an excess of Surgeon McParlin's numbers of 1,080. But that excess is more than made up by the number of slightly wounded accompanying the army, and those left in the hands of the Confederates on the 10th of May.

The number of killed and wounded in the two battles of the Wilderness and Spottsylvania Court House is therefore 28,207. The number of missing 4,903, making a total of killed, wounded, and missing, of 33,110.

Surgeon McParlin further states that the number of sick sent to Washington from Fredericksburg at this period was 4,225. This would make a total of losses in this period of sixteen days of 37,335, the men discharged by expiration of their term of service not included.

The casualties at Spottsylvania Court House, according to Badeau, were 2,271 killed, 9,360 wounded, 1,970 missing ; total, 13,601. The source of error in his figures has been already pointed out ; his number of wounded is too small.

I have no means of presenting an accurate account of the casualties in the Army of Northern Virginia at Spottsylvania Court House. Excepting on those days and at those parts of the field noted in the narrative, they must have been much fewer in number than our own, since they remained on the defensive under the cover of intrenchments, entangled in their front in a manner unknown to European warfare, and, indeed, in a manner new to warfare in this country. Their losses were, however, severe.

This account of the operations shows in what manner the contest between the two armies was carried on. The marching was done chiefly at night, and the contact was so close as to require constant vigilance day and night, and allow but little time for sleep.   The firing was incessant.   The fatigue, the loss of sleep, the watchfulness, taxed severely the powers of endurance of both officers and men.   Usually, in military operations, the opposing armies come together, fight a battle and separate again, the strain lasting only a few days.   In a siege it is only a small part of the opposing troops that are close together.   But with these two armies it was different. From the 5th of May, 1864, to the 9th of April, 1865, they were in constant close contact, with rare intervals of brief comparative repose.

CHAPTER IV.

MOVEMENT TO THE NORTH ANNA RIVER—THE CAV-
ALRY CORPS SENT AGAINST THE CONFEDERATE
CAVALRY, AND TO HAXALL'S LANDING ON JAMES
RIVER.

It was supposed that, if one of the corps of the Army of
the Potomac was sent some twenty miles distant on the road
to Richmond, keeping the rest of the army ready to follow,
Lee might endeavor to attack the corps, thus separated before it could be reinforced, and upon the first indication of
such intention (or even before it, after allowing full time
for the intention to disclose itself, if it should exist) the rest
of the army following the corps might be able to attack before Lee could intrench.   If Lee did not make this attempt
on the isolated corps, then the movement would become
simply a turning or flank operation.

With this view, General Grant, on the 18th, directed General Meade to move Hancock on the night of the 19th, with
all his force, and as much cavalry as could be got together
for him under General Torbert, as far toward Richmond on
the line of the Fredericksburg Railroad as he could make, he
fighting the enemy in whatever force he might find him.   If
the enemy made a general move to meet this, the three
other corps of the army would follow and attack, if possible,
before Lee had time to intrench.

The order for this was issued early in the afternoon of the
19th, but the encounter with Ewell caused the movement to
be postponed.   On the 20th, Hancock was directed by Gen-

eral Meade to move as soon after dark as practicable, by way of Guinea Station and Bowling Green to Milford Station, about twenty miles distant by the route named, and take position on the right bank of the Mattapony, if practicable, and attack the enemy wherever found ; he was to report progress constantly to headquarters.

General Warren was directed to make all preparations to move in the morning of the 21st to Massaponax Church, and thence south by the Telegraph road, crossing the Ny at Smith's mill, the Po at Stannard's mill, and thence southward by Mud tavern, Thornburg, Nancy Wright's, etc. Burnside was to follow Warren, and Wright, who was to concentrate in the vicinity of the commanding position of the Gayle house, was to withdraw on the night of the 21st, and follow Hancock's route.

General Hancock moved on the night of the 20th, arrived at Guinea Station (eight miles on the way), at daybreak of the 21st, where there was experienced a little opposition. About ten o'clock in the morning, Torbert, with the cavalry in advance, came upon some of Kemper's infantry brigade (Pickett's division) intrenched at Milford Station, and drove them out of their pits and across the Mattapony, captured some prisoners, and secured the wagon-road bridge as well as the railroad bridge there.   By midday Barlow's division was across the river, in position and intrenched, the rest of the corps following.

Very early in the morning of the 21st, Burnside's, Warren's, and Wright's skirmishers were pressed close up against the enemy's intrenchments to ascertain if any part of their force had been withdrawn. A movement of troops toward their right was noted, for Lee, learning from his cavalry detachment at Guinea Station, and through his signal stations, that infantry and cavalry of our army had passed there at daybreak, brought Ewell at a very early hour to his right, and posted him along the south bank of the Po, a part of his force holding the crossing of the Telegraph road at Stannard's mills.[1]

At ten o'clock General Warren began to withdraw. His instructions were modified so as to bring him to Guinea Station where he crossed the river (below the junction of the Po and the Ny) and moved out the road running southwest to Madison's store, halting for the night at Catlett's where the road from Mud tavern comes in, and sending forward detachments toward Mud tavern and to Madison's store ; the latter place is about a mile from the telegraph road at Nancy Wright's. Detachments of the enemy's cavalry were at Guinea bridge when General Warren crossed and kept in front of his detachments on both roads. The modification of General Warren's route was made to bring him several miles nearer General Hancock. Wright's route was also modified, he to follow Burnside.

General Burnside, in accordance with his instructions, set his corps in motion as soon as the road was clear of the Fifth Corps, sending a brigade of Potter's division in advance to secure the crossing of the Po at Stannard's mill. The enemy's pickets were found on the north side of the river a mile in advance of it, and were driven to the south side, and dispositions were made by General Potter to carry the ford

---

[1] " SPOTTSYLVANIA COURT HOUSE, 8.40 A.M., May 21, 1864.

" HON. J. A. SEDDON, *Secretary of War :*

" The enemy is apparently again changing his base. Three (3) gunboats came up to Port Royal two days since. This morning an infantry force appeared at Guinea's. His cavalry advance at Downer's bridge on Bowling Green road. He is apparently placing the Mattapony between us, and will probably open communication with Port Royal. *I am extending on the Telegraph road, and will regulate my movements by the information . . . . of his route.* I fear will secure him from attack till he crosses Pamunkey. R. E. LEE."

This telegram was in cypher. The part apparently confidential is omitted in the translation. The last sentence should probably read, " I fear it will secure him," etc., etc. The underlining is mine. A. A. H.

by assault.   But under the orders he had received General
Burnside did not deem it advisable to attempt this, but took
the alternative in his instructions, and moved by the road to
Guinea Station, the head of his column arriving there at
2 A.M. of the 22d, on their way to Downer's bridge by the
Bowling Green road.   The corps was halted as soon as it
cleared Guinea Station.

The withdrawal of so much force from contact with the
enemy led to General Wilcox of Hill's corps being sent out
late in the afternoon with two of his brigades to ascertain
what force of our army still remained before Spottsylvania
Court House.   As soon as General Warren abandoned his intrenchments General Wright withdrew to his new lines at
the Gayle house ; about six o'clock Wilcox's brigades made a
brisk attack upon Wright's picket lines, but were repulsed by
it except at one point where the skirmishers were driven
back a short distance, when some artillery intervened and restored their line.

As soon as General Burnside was out of the way General
Wright withdrew without further molestation, and arrived at
Guinea Station early the next morning.

During the day the enemy's cavalry detachments had
been busy picking up information of our movement, and
one of General Hancock's despatches was captured.   General
Hampton had some of his cavalry in front of Hancock on the
road from Milford to Hanover Junction, and some of Pickett's infantry on the same road.   Other of Hampton's cavalry
were on the roads between the Mattapony and the Telegraph
road.   General Breckinridge was at Hanover Junction.

The withdrawal of the Fifth Corps, which could not be concealed from the enemy, set Lee's army in motion, but not to
attack the Second Corps, as it was hoped he would, but to
interpose between the Army of the Potomac and Richmond,
and to cover the Virginia Central Railroad, one of those

roads that connected Richmond with the most fertile parts of Virginia.

This road coming from the west intersects the Fredericksburg and Richmond Railroad between the North and South Anna rivers, a few miles above the confluence of those streams, and there turns and runs south to Richmond, keeping east of the Fredericksburg road and five or six miles distant from it. The point of crossing of these roads is called Hanover Junction, after the county of that name.

Hanover Junction is twenty-four or twenty-five miles north of Richmond, and twenty-eight miles south by the Telegraph road from the right of Lee's Spottsylvania Court House intrenchments at Snell's bridge on the Po.

About the time when Lee began to move, Hancock's leading division had just crossed the Mattapony at Milford and taken position there, but this fact could not then have been known to Lee, who must still have been under the belief that we were moving east of the Mattapony to cross it at a point much lower down than Milford, and then avoiding the North and South Anna rivers to cross the river formed by their junction, the Pamunkey, at Littlepage's bridge on the stage road to Richmond, or at other convenient points below. Lee's shortest route to meet this movement was by the Telegraph road through Hanover Junction; and about midday of the 21st, Ewell set out on that road for the Junction, followed by Longstreet's corps on the same road. Ewell arrived at the Junction some time in the forenoon of the 22d; the head of Longstreet's corps reached the North Anna at the Telegraph road bridge about midday. The bridge is two miles north of the Junction. General Lee accompanied Ewell's corps. Hill's corps moved in the night of the 21st, taking a route west of the Telegraph road, probably passing through Childsburg and crossing the North Anna at Anderson's bridge, near Beaver Dam Station. It united with the other corps at Hanover Junction evidently not later than the morning of the 23d.

On the afternoon of the 21st General Hill returned to the command of his corps ; and General Early resumed command of his division on the morning of the 22d.

General Gordon was assigned to the command of Johnson's division, to which his own brigade, now commanded by Brigadier-General Evans, was transferred.   Hoke's brigade, now commanded by Colonel Lewis, joined General Early's division at the Junction on the 22d, coming from Petersburg.   Its effective force is put down by Colonel Taylor, Adjutant-General of Lee's army, at 1,200.

The effective total of infantry with General Breckinridge was, most probably, 2,500.   Having defeated General Sigel on the 15th of May at New Market, in the Shenandoah Valley, with severe loss, and that officer having retreated behind Cedar Creek, General Breckinridge, by General Lee's direction, after sending off his temporary force and leaving General Imboden with his mounted infantry to look after the Valley, brought his two infantry brigades by railroad from Staunton to Hanover Junction, arriving there on the 20th of May.

General Pickett, with his division, had also arrived at the Junction, his effective total being, according to the best information, 5,000.[1]

---

[1] Respecting the strength of Pickett's division when it rejoined Longstreet's corps at this time, Badeau states that Pickett's Division Return for November 27, 1863, shows his present for duty at that time to have been 9,162, and then adds some information concerning the division subsequent to that time, indicating the probability of its not being materially less than that number when it rejoined the Army of Northern Virginia at Hanover Junction.   I can find no Return of Pickett's division of the 27th of November, 1863, or for any day of November of that year, in the Confederate Archives Office, nor for any date subsequent to November, indicating such strength.   His Return of his division for September, 1863, gives for its effective total 4,419.   There is, however, in the Confederate Archives Office, a Return by General Pickett of the Department of North Carolina for November 27, 1863, in which the present for duty of all arms,

General Butler having at this time withdrawn to his in-trenchments at Bermuda Hundred, in the forks of the James and Appomattox rivers, General Beauregard having a short line of intrenchments in Butler's front, running from river to river, was able to send General Pickett's division to General Lee. Lee's reinforcements at Hanover Junction, according to this statement, amounted to 8,700 muskets and probably 600 officers.

Shortly after sending General Pickett to General Lee, General Beauregard sent General Hoke's division to him. It joined General Lee at Cold Harbor with an effective total of infantry (enlisted men) a little less than 6,000, according to Colonel Walter H. Taylor.

Warren's cavalry outpost at Lebanon Church, near Madison's store, or ordinary, had heard the noise of troops passing along the Telegraph road all night, and some part of the trains that accompany troops were in view from Lebanon Church early in the morning of the 22d. Information was received from the detachment sent by General Warren toward Mud tavern that Ewell's and Longstreet's corps had passed over the road in the night.

Early in the morning of the 22d General Warren was directed to move as soon as the Sixth Corps was up to him, by way of Madison's ordinary and Nancy Wright's to Harris's store, and halt there for the night. Harris's store is near the Telegraph road and on the cross-road from Childsburg to Milford. General Wright was directed to move to Madison's ordinary as soon as his corps rested; General Burnside to resume his march at ten o'clock, cross the Mattapony at Downer's bridge, and take the road running from that bridge

---

officers and enlisted men, is 9,192. General Pickett commanded the Department at that time. Only one of his brigades was included in the Return of that Department. Can Badeau have mistaken this Return for a Return of Pickett's Division?

to Hanover Junction, halting at New Bethel Church, where there is a cross-road running past Madison's ordinary to Bowling Green.

General Hancock was directed to remain at Milford during the 22d. By this arrangement, on the night of the 22d the four corps were at points three or four miles distant from each other. Communication was kept up between them during the day.

Upon arriving at Madison's ordinary General Warren transferred part of his corps to the Telegraph road, the other part taking a road one mile east of and parallel with it. Stragglers of the enemy's infantry were picked up. The rear of Longstreet's corps was reported to be but three miles distant. At one o'clock P.M. Rosser's cavalry brigade was encountered at the crossing of the Mat River near Dr. Flipper's.

The enemy's cavalry pickets hung about Hancock during the day, and one body of them was at Athens, about three miles distant.

Upon leaving Spottsylvania Court House the character of the country in great part changed. It was now open and well cultivated, but there were still extensive woods, with thick undergrowth and swamps.

The chief object of Hancock's circuitous movement was not accomplished.[1] There would probably have been more chance of success had Hancock moved by the Telegraph

---

[1] It has been already stated that the distance from the right of Lee's intrench-ments on the Po to Hanover Junction by the Telegraph road is twenty-eight miles, measured on the map.

From the position of the Second Corps at Anderson's mill on the Ny by the Telegraph road to Hanover Junction is, by the map, twenty-five miles; by Hancock's route through Bowling Green to Hanover Junction, the distance is thirty-four miles.

From the positions of the Fifth and Sixth Corps at Spottsylvania Court House, by way of Guinea Station and then by the Telegraph road to Hanover Junction, the distance is thirty miles.

road on the night of the 20th, followed by Warren ; the Sixth and Ninth Corps to be moved subsequently in accordance with the developments of the Second and Fifth Corps : that would perhaps have brought on a collision before Lee could intrench on new ground.

At 9.30 A.M. of the 22d General Lee telegraphed from Hanover Junction to Richmond : " I have arrived at this place with the head of Ewell's corps.   Longstreet is close up.   Hill I expect to come on my right, but I have not heard from him since I left him last night.   I have learned as yet nothing of the movements of the enemy east ·of the Mattapony."   But it could not have been much after midday of the 22d when General Lee received information from his cavalry of our advance toward the North Anna by the Telegraph and other roads west of the Mattapony,[1] and began to dispose his force to meet our attempt to cross it.

On the night of the 22d Lee was at Hanover Junction with two of his corps (the third joining him the next morning), while the leading corps of Meade's army were fifteen miles distant from it, the other two nineteen miles.

On the night of the 22d General Grant directed General Meade to hold the army in readiness to move at 5 A.M. on the 23d, each corps to send at that hour the cavalry detachments serving with it, with some infantry, on all the roads in the front leading south, and ascertain, if possible, where the enemy was.   Similar instructions were given to the Ninth Corps.   The corps were to follow their reconnoitering parties.   If it was found that the enemy had crossed the North Anna, the army would follow ; the Second Corps would move to Chesterfield ford (near the Fredericksburg and Richmond Railroad bridge) ; the Ninth Corps to Jericho

---

[1] General Bratton, whose brigade was the rear guard of Longstreet's corps, states that he crossed the North Anna (by the Telegraph road bridge) at sunset of the 22d.

bridge ; the Fifth Corps to a point on the river west of Jericho bridge. There were but two roads leading south marked on our maps, and corps commanders were directed to seek for plantation or other roads so as to facilitate our movements. Our maps were erroneous in many places, but especially so in the vicinity of the North Anna. What was marked as Jericho bridge was really Jericho mills. The bridge across the North Anna was where the Telegraph road crossed it, four miles below Jericho mills and about half a mile above the Fredericksburg Railroad bridge. Chesterfield ford was at the site of the Telegraph road bridge. These map-errors led to but little delay or embarrassment. The general intention of the order was apparent, and the corps commanders arranged their troops in accordance with that. The Sixth Corps followed the Fifth on the Telegraph road, that being found the better arrangement. The Ninth Corps used in part plantation roads between those followed by the Second and Fifth Corps.

Rosser's cavalry kept in front of the Fifth Corps up to the vicinity of the North Anna.

General Warren arrived at Mount Carmel Church about eleven A.M., and from that point moved to Jericho mills, about three miles distant, so as to give place for the Second Corps in its movement to Chesterfield ford (bridge over the North Anna). At Jericho mills no enemy was visible on the opposite bank, and to secure the crossing-place Bartlett's brigade waded over and formed on the opposite bank, encountering only a few of the enemy's pickets. The banks of the river were high and precipitous and the road on both sides very rough, consisting of a series of rocky steps. The laying of a ponton bridge was at once commenced. Upon receiving this information, General Meade, with the sanction of General Grant, directed General Warren to cross the river with his whole corps. By 4.30 P.M. all the infantry was over,

Crawford's division wading across while Cutler's was passing on the ponton bridge. Artillery followed the infantry. It was learnt that Hill's corps was near at hand, partially intrenched on the Central Railroad. Line of battle was formed about half a mile from the river, on the edge of a wood next to the river, the front being covered by the wood. On the right there was open ground, and here artillery was posted. Crawford was on the left, resting near the river; Griffin in the centre; and Cutler on the right. Cutler was still going into position when, at about six o'clock, Hill attacked the centre and right of Warren's line; the attack was heaviest on Cutler, whose troops on the right not having formed, broke and were followed by the enemy, but the artillery drove them back, and being repulsed on Griffin's front they fell back to the railroad, having suffered considerable loss, especially in prisoners. The loss in killed and wounded was probably equal on both sides.

The head of the Sixth Corps was at Mount Carmel Church when the action began, and the corps moved at once to the support of General Warren, but did not cross the river until the morning of the 24th, as it was not deemed necessary. The Fifth Corps intrenched during the night.

At eleven A.M. of the 23d General Hancock reported from Old Chesterfield (about four miles from the North Anna, at the railroad and Telegraph road bridges) that part of his infantry had passed that point, moving toward those bridges, his First Division massed at Old Chesterfield and the rest coming up. In accordance with his instructions, advancing, he took position on the north bank about a mile from the river, his right across the Telegraph road, his left across the Fredericksburg Railroad; Birney on the right, Barlow in the centre, and Gibbon on the left. The enemy were seen in force on the south side of the river, moving in column. They had batteries in position on the high southern bank of the river, as well as infantry intrenchments. On the north side they had intrenchments covering the Telegraph road bridge, and on the south side, close to both bridges, similar works. The bridge-head works were held in force by a part of Kershaw's division. After examining them General Birney was of opinion they could be taken, and about six o'clock General Hancock directed him to make the attempt. The force sent, Egan's and Pierce's brigade of Birney's division, had to advance several hundred yards over open ground ascending to the river bank under artillery and infantry fire, which they did in a spirited manner carrying the works and capturing some of the enemy, the rest being driven over the river. The bridge was taken possession of, and the attempts of the enemy to burn it during the night were frustrated. The south end of the railroad bridge was, however, held by them throughout the night, and that end was burnt.

General Burnside had been directed to take position on the right of Hancock, seize Ox ford, which was about a mile above the Telegraph road bridge, and hold it if practicable. But on his approach to the ford it was found to be in the possession of the enemy, who at this point were strongly intrenched on the south bank of the river, and in heavy force.

On the morning of the 24th it was found that the enemy in front of the Second Corps had abandoned his advanced works on the south bank of the river, and General Hancock crossed and occupied them. Upon examining the enemy's position it was seen that in this part of the field he held a strongly intrenched line, having slashing and abatis ; his left rested on the river half a mile above the bridge, then extended up it to Ox ford ; his right was several miles below and near the site of Morris's bridge, the line being about three miles long and running in a southeast direction along the chord of a bend in the river. He had artillery in position, and traverses were being added where the line was ex-

posed to enfilade or reverse fire. Ewell's corps was on the
right, Longstreet's on the left.   The Second Corps advanced
and intrenched within six or eight hundred yards of this
line.   About six o'clock in the evening Smyth's brigade of
Gibbon's division, which was on his left, became briskly engaged, the enemy pressing Gibbon's outposts but gaining no
material advantage.   Barlow's division was got ready to attack, but the enemy's intrenchments were found to be so
strong that the design was abandoned.   Potter's division of
the Ninth Corps was sent to Hancock and occupied the right
of his line.

General Burnside was ordered on the morning of the 24th
to carry Ox ford and cross with his corps to the south side
of the river, but found the enemy so strongly intrenched on
the south bank at this point that he did not attack.   Crittenden's division crossed the river at Quarles's mill (about a
mile and a half above Ox ford), where he found General
Crawford with his division.   These two advanced toward
the enemy's position at Ox ford, with a view to carrying it
and enabling General Willcox to cross there; but the
enemy were found too strongly posted and in too strong
force, and these two divisions, after a brief encounter, withdrew.   Part of Griffin's division and part of the Sixth Corps
were thrown forward to the railroad.

The next morning, the 25th, the Fifth Corps (with Crittenden's division, which was placed under General Warren's
orders) and the Sixth Corps were thrown forward to within
six or eight hundred yards of the enemy's line, which was
found to run south from Ox ford to Anderson's mill on
Little River, a distance of about a mile and a half.   It had
been partially developed the day before by Crawford.   It
was well intrenched and traversed throughout, as it was exposed to enfilade and reverse fire from the high ground on
the north bank of the North Anna, upon which General

Willcox established some batteries.   This part of Lee's line
was held by Hill's corps and Pickett's division.

The position of Lee's army, we now see, was well chosen.
With its left resting on Little River, the line ran north in
open ground to the North Anna at Ox ford, extended along
the river three-quarters of a mile, and then ran in a southeast direction to the river at the site of Morris's bridge.
His army was concentrated.   The two parts of the Army of
the Potomac were not only widely separated, with only a
division between them, but the river had to be crossed
twice to reinforce one part from the other.   Lee could reinforce a point attacked in one-third of the time that Meade
could reinforce at the same point.   Some persons, indeed,
have thought that Lee should have left a small part of his
force to hold the intrenchments of his left and attacked
Hancock with the rest of his army.   But Hancock was intrenched, and Lee knew well the advantage that gave, and
he could not afford the loss that he would have inevitably
suffered in such an attack.   It was only by surprise at some
exposed point that he could afford to attack.   Hancock's
force, including Potter's division, did not probably exceed
24,000 officers and enlisted men of infantry.   Leaving 7,000
to hold the west face of his intrenchments and the apex on
the river, Lee might have attacked Hancock with about
36,000 officers and enlisted men of infantry ; but intrenchments make up for greater differences than that in numbers.[1]

---

[1] Colonel Venable, an officer of General Lee's staff, in his address at the Lee
Memorial Meeting in Richmond on the 3d of November, 1870, said that at this
period General Lee was constantly seeking an opportunity to attack the Army of
the Potomac ; that he hoped to strike the blow at the North Anna, or between the
Annas and the Chickahominy ; that he hoped much from the attack on Warren's
corps at Jericho ford, where it was in a hazardous position, separated from the
rest of the army ; that General Hill also was sanguine of success in this attack ;
but that the main plan miscarried through some mishap, though one or two minor
successes on the left flank, notably the one by Mahone's division, were effected.

Colonel Walter H. Taylor, Adjutant-General of the Army of Northern Virginia,

The strength of Lee's position was such that it was determined to continue the movement by the left flank, a movement in that direction being considered, under the existing conditions, preferable to that by the right flank.

During the 25th and 26th portions of the Central and Fredericksburg railroads were broken up, and on the 26th General Wilson, with his cavalry division, was sent across the North Anna to demonstrate on our right, and also to aid in the destruction of the Central Railroad. The movements of his division gave General Lee the impression, as it was designed it should, that it was contemplated to move the Army of the Potomac by its right flank.

According to the report of Medical Director McParlin, the wounded of the Army of the Potomac from the 21st to the 26th of May, both days included, numbered 2,100, that being the number sent from Port Royal on the Rappahannock River to the hospitals in Washington.[1]

General Benham, at Washington, was directed on the 26th of May to proceed to Fort Monroe with all his bridge-equipage and materiel and be ready to move up the James River.

General Sheridan returned with the Cavalry Corps to the Army of the Potomac on the 24th of May.

In compliance with his instructions of the 8th of May to concentrate his available mounted force and proceed against

---

also says of this period that if General Lee's army had been of even reasonable proportion in comparison with that of his adversary, his movement would have been of another character than that of moving parallel with the Army of the Potomac, and one of the two wings of the Federal Army would have been assailed while on the south side of the river.

[1] The tabular statement, however, of the losses of the Army of the Potomac and Ninth Corps during that time, in Part First, Medical and Surgical History of the War, does not altogether agree with McParlin's report, though he mentions this tabular statement. The dates are also different. Surgeon McParlin's report is, I believe, correct. The tabular statement is, from the 23d to the 27th of May, 223 killed, 1,460 wounded, 290 missing.

the enemy's cavalry, replenish his supplies at Haxall's Landing from General Butler's stores, and return to the army, he concentrated in the vicinity of Aldrich's, on the Orange and Fredericksburg plank road, and, on the morning of the 9th, moved on the Telegraph road past the right of Lee's army to cross the North Anna, and get out of the reach of Lee's infantry before encountering Stewart's cavalry. Passing through Childsburg, his leading division, Merritt's, crossed the North Anna at Anderson's ford by dark. Gordon's (James B.) brigade of W. H. F. Lee's cavalry division overtook his rear guard, Davies' brigade, Gregg's division, south of the Ta River, and continued in contact with Gregg's and Wilson's divisions until a late hour, these divisions halting for the night on the north side of the North Anna.

Custer's brigade was sent to Beaver Dam Station, on the Virginia Central Railroad, where, on the 10th, it destroyed ten miles of the road, locomotives, cars, and a large amount of army supplies, and recaptured 375 prisoners taken from us at the Wilderness, who were on their way to Richmond.

On the 10th Sheridan crossed the South Anna at Ground Squirrel bridge, halting for the night on the south bank.

Gordon's brigade of Stewart's cavalry clung to Gregg's and Wilson's divisions while they were crossing the North Anna in the morning, and until they entered the Negro Foot road, about five miles before reaching Ground Squirrel bridge. General Fitzhugh Lee's cavalry division, composed of Wickham's and Lomax's brigades, had, during all this time, been moving by a circuitous route to interpose between Sheridan and Richmond.

On the night of the 10th Davies' brigade was sent to Ashland, on the Fredericksburg Railroad, where it arrived at daylight before the Confederate cavalry, drove out some force there, destroyed the dépôt, several miles of the road, a train and a large amount of stores, and rejoined the main body at Allen's Station. There it was ascertained that Stewart was concentrating at the Yellow tavern on the Brook pike, six miles from Richmond, and Sheridan's whole force moved on that point, Merritt in advance, Wilson next, then Gregg. Sheridan was advancing in a southeast direction on the Mountain road, which intersects the Brook pike at Yellow tavern, and, upon arriving at the intersection, formed between that road and the Fredericksburg Railroad. Stewart was formed at the intersection of the Brook pike and Mountain road, facing west or north of west. Merritt attacked and gained the Brook pike, but Stewart got a position on his flank and enfiladed his line with artillery. Then Custer charged this flanking force, Wilson supporting him, and captured their artillery, two guns, with their gunners, and broke their line. Stewart's detached force under Gordon now attacked Sheridan in rear, but Gregg drove it toward Ashland and across the north fork of the Chickahominy; Fitzhugh Lee's division fell back toward Richmond.

The casualties on both sides were severe, and especially on the Confederate side, their brilliant cavalry commander, General Stewart, being mortally wounded, and Brigadier-General James B. Gordon killed.

Following up the part of Stewart's force that fell back toward Richmond, General Sheridan crossed Brook Run aad entered the most advanced line of intrenchments. Intending to keep south of the Chickahominy, and passing by Fair Oaks, to make a demonstration in favor of General Butler, who, he was informed, was on the south side of the James four miles from Richmond, he massed his force at daylight of the 12th on the plateau at Meadow bridge. Some force of the enemy's cavalry held the north bank at the bridge, which had been so injured as to be impassable. Merritt's division repaired it, crossed and followed up the other side to Gaines's mill.

On the Mechanicsville road the defensive works of Richmond extended out close to the Chickahominy, and Wilson found that he could not pass them. Two brigades of infantry, Barton's and Gracie's, with some dismounted cavalry, advanced from these works, and in conjunction with their artillery attacked Wilson and Gregg, and at first with success, but finally they were forced to withdraw within their lines, and Wilson and Gregg crossed the Chickahominy above the Mechanicsville bridge. The corps encamped for the night between Walnut Grove and Gaines's mill. Crossing to the south side of the Chickahominy at Bottom bridge the next day, General Sheridan reached the vicinity of Haxall's Landing on the 14th of May, and remained there until the 17th.

The casualties on our part in this operation were 425 killed, wounded, and missing. I have not been able to find any Confederate report or account of it or of their losses. In returning to the Army of the Potomac by way of the White House,[1] Custer was sent to destroy the railroad bridges over the South Anna and Gregg to Cold Harbor to cover Custer's operations. But on the way to Hanover Court House Custer encountered so large a force of infantry, apparently on the march to join the Army of Northern Virginia, that he was unable to accomplish the task, and they both returned to General Sheridan, who, as before stated, rejoined the army on the 24th of May.

---

[1] The White House is on the north bank of the Pamunkey River, where the Richmond and York River Railroad crosses it.

CHAPTER V.

THE CO-OPERATIVE MOVEMENT OF THE ARMY OF THE JAMES.—THE BATTLE OF DRURY'S BLUFF.

The Army of the James was composed of the Tenth and Eighteenth Corps, commanded respectively by Major-Generals Q. A. Gillmore and Wm. F. Smith, and a cavalry division commanded by Brigadier-General A. V. Kautz. The Tenth Corps, drawn from the troops in South Carolina, consisted of three divisions commanded by Brigadier-Generals Terry, Turner, and Ames, and numbered, present for duty, 684 officers and 16,128 enlisted men of infantry, and 36 officers and 1,078 enlisted men of artillery, with 44 guns and 2 siege howitzers.

The Eighteenth Corps consisted of three divisions commanded by Brigadier-Generals Brooks, Weitzel, and Hinks, and numbered, present for duty, 653 officers and 14,325 enlisted men of infantry, and 25 officers and 987 enlisted men of artillery, with 36 guns. Hinks's division was composed of colored troops. Butler's infantry force was therefore 1,329 officers and 30,543 enlisted men of infantry, with 82 guns served by 61 officers and 2,065 enlisted men of artillery.

Kautz's cavalry numbered 97 officers and 2,804 enlisted men, with 6 guns. There was also a brigade of colored cavalry under Colonel West, some 1,800 strong.

General Butler had been instructed by Lieutenant-General Grant that Richmond was his objective point; that he was to move at the same time as the Army of the Potomac, take City Point and that vicinity ; intrench, concentrate all his troops for the field there as rapidly as possible, and operate on the south side of the James against Richmond, holding close to the south bank of the river as he advanced, and using every exertion to secure a footing as far up the river as possible ; that his army and the Army of the Potomac were to co-operate. Should General Lee fall back upon Richmond, the Army of the Potomac would unite with the Army of the James. If he, Butler, should be able to invest Richmond on the south side so as to rest his left upon the James above the city, the junction of the two armies would preferably take place there. Under any circumstances it might be advisable to make the junction there, and if he, General Butler, should hear that the Army of the Potomac was advancing in that direction, or have reason to believe from the action of the enemy that they apprehended danger from that quarter, then he was to attack vigorously, and if he could not carry the city he would, at least, be able to detain a considerable force of the enemy there.

On the 28th of April Butler was directed to move on the night of the 4th of May, so as to be far up the James River by daylight of the 5th ; and to push from that time with all his might for the accomplishment of the object before him.

The two infantry corps of Butler's army were concentrated at Yorktown and Gloucester, on the York River, when the time for movement was near at hand, in order to give the impression that he was to advance upon Richmond on the line taken by General McClellan in 1862.

On the night of the 4th of May they embarked on transports, and descending the York River moved up the James early on the 5th, convoyed by Rear-Admiral S. P. Lee's fleet of five armored ships and a large number of gunboats. On the afternoon of the 5th the fleet of transports reached Bermuda Hundred Neck, at the confluence of the James and Appomattox rivers, and by morning of the 6th of May the troops had disembarked.

Brigadier-General Wilde's brigade of colored troops had landed at Fort Powhatan, on the south bank of the James, and at Wilson's wharf, some five miles below, on the north bank. General Hink's division of colored troops (of which General Wilde's brigade was a part) landed at City Point, at the mouth of the Appomattox, on the south side. His division was about 5,000 strong.

On the morning of the 5th of May Colonel West, with his colored brigade, moved up the Peninsula to cross the Chickahominy and unite with General Butler, which he accomplished.

On the same morning General Kautz set out from Suffolk to cut the Petersburg and Weldon Railroad at the crossings of the Nottoway River, Stony Creek, and Rowanty Creek, with a view to delay the arrival at Richmond of troops on their way from the South, as well as to seriously impair the roads as lines of supply to the Army of Northern Virginia.

On the morning of the 6th the troops on Bermuda Hundred Neck advanced some six miles from their landing-place, and taking up a position at a narrow part of the neck, three miles across, with their right on the James, at Trent's reach, and their left on the Appomattox, near Port Walthall, intrenched there, Smith on the right, Gillmore on the left. About two and a half miles in front of this line was the Richmond and Petersburg Railroad, and running near it the pike between those towns. A brigade was sent out to these roads, which returned to the main body after having encountered some force of the enemy at Port Walthall Junction, about six miles from Petersburg and sixteen from Richmond. This force was a part of Brigadier-General Hagood's South Carolina brigade, which had just arrived from South

Carolina, having been halted at that point by General Pickett, who still remained in command at Petersburg.

The defensive works of Richmond consisted of a series of field forts encircling the city at a distance from it varying from a mile to a mile and a half. Outside of these, on the north side of the James, there was a connected enveloping line of batteries and infantry intrenchments, in most places a mile beyond the forts, in others one and a half or two miles beyond them. This line crossed the James two and a half miles below Richmond, and then extended westerly to within a mile and a half of the river above the city. Beyond this again there was, on the north side of the river, a disconnected line of intrenchments, part of which was occupied in 1862, varying in distance from the line already described from half a mile to three miles. It abutted on the James at Chapin's Bluff, some seven miles by the road below the city.

At Chapin's Bluff and the bluff a little higher up on the opposite side of the James (Drury's) were the batteries, with sea-coast guns, to oppose the passage of the river.

There were also several gunboats and torpedo boats assembled for the defence of the river, which above the mouth of the Appomattox was very narrow, and as high up as Drury's Bluff very winding; the width above the Appomattox varied from six hundred to one thousand feet, in some places being even still narrower. The armored vessels of Rear-Admiral Lee's fleet could not ascend above Trent's Reach, the depth on its bar not admitting their passage. The right of Butler's army, intrenched on Bermuda Hundred Neck, rested on the James just below the bar, which was some five miles below Drury's Bluff by land and nine by water.

Torpedoes had been planted on the bars of the James, some of them to be exploded from the land, others by contact with the vessel. Notwithstanding the great care used in dragging for them as Admiral Lee's fleet ascended the river, the gunboat Commodore Jones was destroyed by a torpedo, one-half the crew being killed and wounded.

From Drury's Bluff a line of intrenchments extended westward two and a half miles, so as to inclose both the Richmond and Petersburg pike and railroad, and then ran northerly. This line of intrenchments was, to use General Gillmore's language, judiciously located, and of great strength naturally and artificially, with deep ditches, and arranged for both artillery and infantry. An advanced line of intrenchments, equally strong as the one just described, left the interior line near Drury's Bluff and ran in a southwest direction, crossing Proctor's Creek at the railroad crossing about a mile in front of the interior line and resting its right on Wooldridge's Hill.

For the defence of Petersburg, as early as 1862, a circle of strong redans or batteries, connected by infantry parapets of high profile had been erected some two miles outside of the city.

The troops for the defence of these two cities were few in number on the 1st of May. Besides the artillery for the heavy guns at Chapin's and Drury's bluffs, and the field artillery of the intrenchments of Richmond, the effective force of infantry there (enlisted men present for duty) did not probably exceed 6,000, and in this number is included Hunton's brigade at Chapin's Bluff, and Bushrod Johnson's and Gracie's brigades, which I suppose to have been there by that time. They were there, certainly, on the 7th of May, but the information concerning the force there on the 1st of May is very defective. The number 6,000 does not include the clerks and employes and others in Richmond, who had been organized as military companies to be used in exigencies. At Petersburg General Pickett had a Virginia regiment with some artillery, and, under his command, a part of Clingman's North Carolina brigade posted along the Blackwater to look after any force approaching from Norfolk or Suffolk. General Pickett had been in command of the Department of Southern Virginia and North Carolina, but had been relieved of that command by General Beauregard about the 1st of May. The latter officer had commanded the Department of South Carolina, Georgia, and Florida, and had been relieved from the charge of that Department in April by General Sam Jones, to enable him to take command of the force for the defence of Richmond against the approach by James River. He was directed to bring or send forward all the disposable force in both Departments for the defence of Richmond.

So far as I can ascertain, the troops to be brought or sent forward by General Beauregard were Barton's, Terry's, and Corse's brigades of Pickett's division, which had been serving in North Carolina ; Wise's Virginia brigade, Hoke's, Ransom's, Clingman's and Martin's North Carolina brigades ; Hagood's South Carolina, and Colquitt's Georgia brigades ; General W. S. Walker's Georgia brigade appears also to have been brought from South Carolina. There were, besides, several battalions of artillery, and Dearing's North Carolina and Walker's or Butler's South Carolina brigades of cavalry. These infantry brigades, not including Walker's, gave an effective force of infantry (enlisted men present for duty) of 19,000. Dearing's brigade was about 2,000 strong.

But the leading troops of this force, excepting a part of Clingman's brigade, had only begun to arrive at Petersburg by the Weldon Railroad on the 5th of May. These (part of Hagood's brigade) General Pickett was authorized by General Beauregard, in a telegraphic despatch from Weldon, to retain in Petersburg, and also to take command of all troops arriving there.

When Butler's fleet of transports was seen moving up the
James, General Pickett called in Clingman's troops from the
Blackwater, hastily collected such citizens as could be
found, armed them, and posting the artillery he had in the
intrenchments, moved out on the road to City Point with his
infantry, numbering about a brigade. The next morning,
the 6th, he sent Hagood's troops forward to Port Walthall
Junction to protect the Richmond Railroad from the force
sent out by General Butler. The order and time of arrival
in Petersburg and movement to Richmond of Beauregard's
troops I do not find stated anywhere. On the 7th, Wise's
brigade, or a part of it, arrived and joined the troops on the
City Point road. Near midday of the 7th, General Beauregard, at Weldon, telegraphed to Richmond that Hoke (division) would begin to arrive at Kingston that night, that
most of the cavalry was with him; that half of Wise's brigade was expected at Weldon in a few hours; that Hagood's
last detachment had passed there the night before.

Kautz, who made long and rapid marches, was at Wake-
field on the Norfolk and Petersburg Railroad on the evening of the 6th, and cut the road and telegraph there. The
next day, the 7th, he destroyed the Weldon Railroad bridge
over Stony Creek, where he learned that three trains with
Beauregard's troops had passed there at twelve o'clock, and
that five more trains with troops were due there between
five and six o'clock that evening. The next day, the 8th,
Kautz was unable to destroy the railroad bridge over Rowanty Creek, it being well defended, but succeeded in destroying the bridge over the Nottoway River, though it was
well defended by Colonel Tabb with the Fifty-ninth Virginia. Having accomplished all that he deemed practicable,
he then marched to City Point, arriving there on the morning of the 10th.

The destruction of the bridges over Stony Creek and Not-

toway River caused some delay in the transportation of
Beauregard's troops. On the 12th of May all of them had
not yet reached Petersburg, for on that day he telegraphed
from Petersburg to Richmond that he had ordered Hoke at
Drury's Bluff to obey the orders of the Secretary of War,
that he, Beauregard, would join him (Hoke) with the remainder of troops as soon as they arrived. The evening of
the 11th he had telegraphed that the equivalent of two brigades was still to arrive. His telegrams to Richmond on the
11th say that the division of his force was temporary and
made to meet an emergency; that the movement was in
progress ; and that he would unite with Ransom (at Drury's
Bluff) as soon as possible ; that the troops at Petersburg
and arriving there were pushed forward as rapidly as possible ; that they had to make a flank march of nine miles
across a country occupied by a powerful enemy.

It is inferred from these despatches to the Secretary of
War that while Beauregard had sent forward the larger part
of his troops to the defence of Richmond as rapidly as possible, he had retained a part of his force in Petersburg to
secure that place.

By the 15th of May, or it may be a day or two earlier,
General Beauregard had collected and organized an active
army in the field to oppose Butler's operations against
Richmond and Petersburg, of 22,000 enlisted men of infantry, and 2,000 cavalry,[1] with a due proportion of artillery.
This force does not include Hunton's brigade of infantry at
Chapin's Bluff, nor the Richmond defences, nor the artillery
force, heavy and field, of the forts, batteries, and intrenchments of Richmond.

On the 7th of May General Butler sent some force from

---

[1] More than double that number of cavalry, if Butler's brigade is counted. It
was probably there, for it does not appear with Lee's army before the 28th of May.

his two corps to the railroad, which encountered the enemy without any important result either way, except that every day that passed without an attack in full force upon the slender strength of the enemy was an important gain to them.

On the 9th General Butler moved out of his intrenchments with a large part of his command under General Gillmore and General Smith, and destroyed the railroad between Swift Creek on the south and Chester Station on the north, a length of about six miles. The enemy in some force held the south bank of Swift Creek, a stream that was not fordable and the bridges of which were defended.

On the evening of the 9th, Generals Gillmore and Smith proposed to General Butler to lay a ponton bridge that night over the Appomattox, and cross it with the greater part of their corps, which they could do before daylight (leaving sufficient force to hold their intrenched line), and destroy the railroads entering Petersburg, and take that city. This General Butler disapproved, stating that General Kautz was destroying those roads so that they would be useless, and that the Danville Railroad must be destroyed near Richmond.

General Robert Ransom occupied the advanced intrenchments of Drury's Bluff on the 9th of May, with Barton's and Gracie's brigades, and at daylight of the 10th advanced toward the portion of Butler's force covering the destruction of the railroad in that vicinity ; but only some skirmishing ensued.

Butler's troops returned to their intrenchments on the 10th.

On the morning of the 12th, General Butler moved along the pike toward Richmond, Smith's corps on the right, Gillmore's on the left, meeting with only slight opposition, and halting for the night on Proctor's Creek, the right resting near James River. A force sufficient to hold the Bermuda Hundred intrenchments was left there. Ames, with his division, was posted at Walthall Junction to cover the rear from the direction of Petersburg. General Kautz set out on a raid from Chester Station against the Richmond and Danville, and the Petersburg and Lynchburg railroads, as soon as Smith and Gillmore were so posted as to mask his movement. Hinks's division of colored troops remained at City Point.

The object of the movement, besides covering Kautz's raid, is stated to have been to develop the full strength of the enemy in and about Richmond, and force him into his intrenchments or turn them.

On the morning of the 13th, Smith crossed Proctor's Creek, and advanced along the pike, Brooks on its left, Weitzel on its right, to within eight hundred yards of the enemy's outer line of intrenchments, which were here in open ground, and were held by infantry and artillery. So strong was the line that General Smith reported to General Butler that if held in force it could not be carried by assault. General Gillmore in the meantime had, as directed by General Butler, moved to the left to turn the right of the intrenchments on the head of Proctor's Creek. The enemy was in force there, their right on Wooldridge's Hill, a commanding position half a mile west of the railroad. Terry attacked, unsuccessfully, and while preparing for a second attack, the enemy abandoned their line, passing down toward Drury's Bluff, Gillmore pressing them until dark, and getting a mile of their works.

General Butler now requested Admiral Lee to move the monitors above Trent's Reach, so as to keep pace with the Army. But this Admiral Lee was unable to do, as there was but thirteen feet of water at high tide on the bar of Trent's

Reach,[1] a fact that the Coast Survey maps showed, and the armored ships drew fifteen or sixteen feet. For the gun-boats there was ample depth of water, but the enemy held the left bank of the river, from which they controlled torpedoes and commanded the decks of the ships. On the 17th of May, however, Admiral Lee's advance division (not the monitors) searched for torpedoes until they came under the fire of the guns at Chapin's Bluff.

On the morning of the 14th, Brook's division of Smith's corps occupied a part of the enemy's intrenchments on the left of the pike. Gillmore's two divisions, Turner's and Terry's, occupied them on Smith's left. About two and a half miles of the enemy's outer line of works were thus held by our troops. The Confederates occupied their second line, the right of which was well refused.

Weitzel's division was on the right of the pike. The outer and the inner line of the enemy's intrenchments united in his, Weitzel's, front, near Drury's Bluff, at a bastion salient situated on an eminence which completely commanded Weitzel's position. He did not occupy any part of the enemy's intrenchments, but constructed a breastwork of logs along his line, just inside the edge of a wood, and stretched a telegraph wire a short distance in front of it. General Heckman's brigade was on the right of the division. From some cause not known the order for stretching the wire entanglement, unfortunately for himself and his brigade, was not carried out on his front.

---

[1] Once above the shoal of Trent's Reach, the monitors could have ascended to the mouth of Kingsland Creek, one mile below Chapin's Bluff. There a shoal having but twelve feet water at high tide would have obstructed their passage. Beyond that there was water enough for them as high up as three miles above Drury's Bluff.

The request of General Butler appears to indicate that there was not a thorough understanding in advance between him and Admiral Lee as to the highest point on the river that the fleet could reach.

An assault of the intrenchments was ordered for the morning of the 15th, but was abandoned for the want of disposable troops to form the column of attack. During the 15th, Gillmore's skirmishers were constantly engaged; his artillery frequently. General Smith, examining the ground on his right as far as the river, found it offered every facility for the movement of a heavy force on his right and rear. He threw back the right of Heckman's brigade so as to cover a road leading to the Bermuda Hundred intrenchments by a route shorter than that by the pike or by the river road. He notified General Butler that he had a thin line of battle, with no reserves to repair a break or strengthen his right. Upon this three regiments of Ames's division, posted at the Half-way House, were placed at his disposal.

The means now at hand for the defence of Richmond and Petersburg, and for the protection of their lines of supply south of the James, were very different from what they had been nine days before. General Beauregard now had, in the strong intrenchments resting on the river at Drury's Bluff, a movable force of infantry of not less than 17,000 enlisted men, formed in three divisions, commanded by Generals Ransom, Hoke, and Colquitt, with a battalion of artillery, and a regiment of cavalry with each division.[1] In addition to these troops there were Hunton's brigade at Chapin's Bluff, the troops known as the Defences of Richmond, and the artillery in the forts and batteries. At Petersburg, General Whiting had the brigades of Wise and Martin, numbering not less than 4,600 muskets, with a battalion of artillery and Dearing's brigade of cavalry, about 2,000 strong. There was besides some other force of infantry and artillery in Petersburg, but their strength I am unable to state.

---

[1] The battalion of artillery usually consisted of four batteries of four guns each.

The number of General Butler's infantry before the Drury's Bluff intrenchments did not exceed that of the enemy, Ames being at Walthall Junction with his division, about 5,000 strong, Hinks with his division of 5,000 at City Point, and about 3,000 having been left in the Bermuda Hundred intrenchments. Beauregard, indeed, was in a better position now than Butler, for his troops occupied an unassailable line, with open ground in front, upon which they could form and attack Butler's weaker line. The right of Butler's line was especially weak ; it had no naturally strong ground to rest on, and was a mile from the river.

Thus, while General Butler had made no material advance toward the accomplishment of the object of his campaign during the nine days that had elapsed since he landed, General Beauregard, who, at the time of General Butler's landing, had substantially no force available adequate to withstand or even delay him, had in those eight or nine days got together an army sufficiently strong to take the offensive and had so posted it as to control the situation. General Butler could not assault the Drury's Bluff intrenchments, he could not move to turn them, and he could not fall back to his Bermuda Hundred lines, or to a new position on the river without abandoning his campaign against Richmond with the Army of the James. In other words, he was completely paralyzed so far as concerned offensive operations.

General Butler's true policy upon landing at the mouth of the Appomattox would have been to disregard Richmond for a time and turn his attention to attacking Beauregard's forces in detail as they arrived from the South, first taking Petersburg, which was then nearly defenceless.

The Richmond Cabinet was urgent for an immediate attack by Beauregard, especially as they apprehended that General Sheridan might return to co-operate with Butler and attempt to enter the city north of the James at the same time that Butler moved to turn and attack Beauregard's right. They had probably received exaggerated statements of the numbers of the Army of the James, as its fleets of transports made a very formidable appearance in ascending the river.

Beauregard's army was composed of four divisions, commanded by Major-General Robert Ransom, Major-General Hoke, Brigadier-General Colquitt, and Major-General Whiting.[1]

On the 15th of May General Beauregard issued his instructions for the battle of the next day, the object of which, he stated, was to cut off the enemy from his base of operations, Bermuda Hundred, and capture or destroy him in the position he then held. With this object, Major-General Ransom, whose division constituted Beauregard's left wing, was directed to form his command outside the intrenchments, near the river, during the night, and at daybreak to attack and turn Butler's right by the river road.

Major-General Hoke was directed to form his division during the night outside of the intrenchments on his right of the turnpike, and at daylight to attack with a heavy skirmish line sufficiently to prevent reinforcements being sent to Butler's right, and when the enemy's right was evidently turned and beaten, to attack with full force.

General Colquitt's division constituted the reserve, and was formed in the centre across the pike in rear of the line of Ransom and Hoke.

---

[1] General Ransom's division consisted of Barton's (Colonel Fry commanding), Gracie's, Kemper's (Colonel Terry commanding), and Hoke's (Colonel Lewis commanding) brigades. Its effective force was about 5,400. General Hoke's division consisted of Corse's, Clingman's, Bushrod Johnson's, and Hagood's brigades. Its effective force was about 7,000. General Colquitt's division consisted of Colquitt's and Ransom's brigades. Its effective force was about 4,900. General Whiting's division consisted of Wise's and Martin's brigades. Its effective force was about 4,600.

Each division had its battalion of artillery. A regiment of cavalry was placed on Ransom's left flank, one on Hoke's right flank, and one with the reserve.

Major-General Whiting at Petersburg was directed to take position that night (the 15th) on Swift Creek with Wise's, Martin's, and Dearing's brigades and two regiments of Colquitt's, with about twenty piece of artillery, and at daybreak to march to Walthall Junction, and when he heard the engagement in his front (the plan of the battle was sent to all the division commanders) he was to advance in the direction of the heaviest firing and attack the enemy in rear or flank.

The Confederate gunboats were to unite in the attack on Butler's army, but on neither side did the gunboats take any part in the battle.

This plan of battle was submitted to President Davis in a personal conference with General Beauregard at his head-quarters on the 14th of May, and was approved except that part relating to General Whiting's operation, which Mr. Davis objected to, "because of the hazard during a battle of attempting to make a junction of troops moving from opposite sides of the enemy"; and he proposed "that Whiting's command should move at night (on the 14th) by the Chesterfield road, where they would not probably be observed by Butler's advance." Whiting's division could, in this way, unite with the troops in the Drury's Bluff intrenchments on the morning of the 15th. This modification of the plan was not, however, carried out, though Mr. Davis expected it would be.[1]

The night was sufficiently clear (there being moonlight), until just before day, when a dense fog suddenly enveloped both armies so that a horseman could not be seen at the distance of fifteen paces. During the night repeated attacks

---

[1] See The Rise and Fall of the Confederate Government, by Jefferson Davis, Vol. II., pp. 511-513.

were made on the reserve of Weitzel's pickets posted on a hill which had a good view clear up to the Confederate intrenchments, but no report of it was made to General Weitzel, who mentions this in his report, and adds that it was stated to him after the battle that word had been sent in from this post that the enemy were forming in their front.

General Ransom began to move out of the trenches at two A.M., and a little after daylight had formed two lines of battle in the position indicated to him across the river road, Gracie's brigade on the left of his first line, Lewis's on the right; Terry's on the left of the second line, Fry's on the right. Hoke's and Colquitt's divisions were also formed as directed, though General Hoke was delayed by the fog.

At a quarter before five o'clock Ransom advanced in the dense fog, drove in Smith's skirmishers across open ground, and completely surprised Heckman's brigade; Gracie's brigade attacked it in front and rear but met with a stubborn resistance. At the end of an hour, however, the breastworks were carried and Heckman's brigade driven in confusion to the rear, General Heckman and several hundred of his men, and five stands of colors being captured.

The attack on Smith's right and right rear was quickly followed by repeated attacks on his front, Weitzel's and Brooks's divisions, all of which were repulsed. General Smith, who had been up a short time before daybreak, when it was clear and moonlight, was roused soon after by heavy musketry and artillery fire on the right of his line. Perceiving that a heavy fog had suddenly fallen, he ordered his artillery, which was far advanced, to be withdrawn, as the fog rendered it useless, but the attack in his front followed that on his right so quickly that the order did not reach the more advanced guns, five in number, which were captured, the sergeant carrying the order being killed when near the guns. Two of the regiments from the Half-way House were sent at once to Weitzel, who posted them at a cross-roads in the rear of the right, which they held against the efforts of the enemy.

At half-past six o'clock General Hoke, who had been delayed by the fog, began his attacks upon General Gillmore's position, which were repeated twice in quick succession. A few minutes before the first was made, General Gillmore was notified by General Butler of the attack on Smith, and was ordered to carry the enemy's line in his front. Notifying General Butler of the attack on him, and that his judgment was against trying to carry the enemy's intrenchments, General Gillmore was authorized to use his discretion in the matter, and finding that General Smith needed support, sent him what he could spare, four regiments. The whole line was now heavily engaged.

General Ransom found his troops scattered by the fog, his line confused and requiring readjusting, and his ammunition nearly exhausted. His two leading brigades, Gracie's and Terry's, had suffered severe loss. To reform his lines and replenish ammunition he withdrew to the position from which he had assaulted Smith's intrenchments. As soon as his line was readjusted, he moved forward again, and then by his left flank to take position just in front of Heckman's captured breastworks. This flank movement was reported to General Smith, and as it appeared to threaten directly Butler's communications and Smith's artillery and ammunition-train, that had been withdrawn a short distance and were without supports, and also the Bermuda Hundred lines left feebly defended, General Smith immediately ordered a retirement of his whole line, notifying General Gillmore's adjoining troops to conform to it. While falling back the fog lifted and enabled General Smith to observe his right, when he ordered the line forward again, but the changes that had already taken place obliged him to recall the order and move by his right flank to cover the roads east of the pike leading to the rear. His new position crossed the pike near Half-way House, about three-quarters of a mile from the outer line of Confederate intrenchments. Here it remained during the rest of the day. A partial advance was made to bring off the wounded of Heckman's brigade, but the ground was found to be held in force by the enemy, and the attempt was given up.

General Gillmore, finding General Smith's troops moving to the right, and being informed by General Butler that the enemy were attempting to turn Smith's right, and that Smith was moving to meet the attempt, and being ordered to move by his right flank to keep up the connection, moved along the intrenchments in that direction and ordered Terry's and Turner's divisions to attack the flank of the enemy pressing back Smith. These divisions were in motion to carry out this order, when General Gillmore was instructed to press his reinforcements to the right, that Brooks and Weitzel were falling back. The fog cleared away about nine o'clock. Moving in accordance with the several instructions received, his troops were hotly engaged with the enemy and gaining ground, when, at about ten o'clock, he was ordered by General Butler to fall back, press to the right, and get in the rear of Smith's corps, near the Half-way House, and clear the way back to the intrenchments at Bermuda Hundred. This was followed, General Gillmore says, by several verbal and written orders of the same purport. General Gillmore accordingly began at once to withdraw his troops, and by twelve o'clock reached the position on the pike in rear of the Half-way House.

General Ransom, after re-establishing his line close in front of the breastworks that he had recently taken, reported in person to General Beauregard, and was directed to halt for further arrangements.

Rumors during the day of the approach of gunboats to take part in the contest, of reinforcements arriving, and other unfounded statements of movements on both sides, led to misapprehensions and mistakes.

General Beauregard says that at ten A.M. his right was still heavily engaged and that all his reserves had been sent to the right and left. Nothing had been heard from Whiting; his (Whiting's) guns had been heard at eight o'clock, but not since. Between nine and ten o'clock he sent an order to him to press forward, and the day would be complete. General Ransom, he says, not only reported the enemy strong in his front, but was of opinion that the safety of his command would be compromised by an advance.

Hoke, with Johnson's and Hagood's brigades, had been hotly engaged on the pike. They it was who captured the five guns. Johnson's brigade lost heavily—one-fourth of its numbers. Then Clingman and Corse were thrown forward, but both were obliged to draw back. At about ten o'clock the fighting in front of Hagood and Johnson was stubborn and prolonged. In the language of their reports, the enemy slowly retiring from Johnson's right, took a strong position on the ridge in front of Proctor's Creek, massing near the turnpike and occupying advantageous ground at Charles Friend's.[1] At length Johnson rested in the Confederate line of outer works ; but his skirmishers continued engaged some hours longer, the enemy, he says, having fallen back.

General Beauregard states that he now suspended further movement to hear from Whiting, and to reform his troops, which were more or less disorganized. General Whiting was at Swift Creek by daylight of the 16th, and moved forward along the railroad to Walthall Junction, where he met a stubborn resistance from Ames, and formed line of battle.

---

[1] This was the position to which Smith and Gillmore fell back.

No sounds of Beauregard's battle were heard; no despatch, no information was received. General Dearing was directed to move on the left and communicate with General Beauregard. The day wore on without tidings or sound of battle, though it was but six miles distant. The wooded country, aided, perhaps, by the wind, had deflected all sounds of the contest from them. Receiving information (erroneous) of an advance of General Hinks's force from City Point toward Petersburg and also of the advance against him on his left of a heavy force, Whiting fell back to Swift Creek. There General Dearing reported to him the occurrences of the day with Beauregard, he, Dearing, having succeeded in communicating with Beauregard by sending a small detachment on a very circuitous route. At 7.15 P.M. General Whiting received General Beauregard's despatch of 4.15 P.M., saying: "The enemy has been driven back on our right. Corse's and Clingman's forces are moved to the line of works on hill west of railroad. We are about making a general advance with all our forces. Can you not aid in the movement at once?" General Whiting replied: "Too late for action on my part."

General Beauregard says that at four P.M. he abandoned all hope of effective co-operation from Whiting, and resumed his original formation in order to pursue Butler vigorously, and drive him within his intrenchments. A heavy and long-continued rain-storm ensued, and it was dark before they were ready to advance; the advance was therefore deferred until the following morning.

Toward evening General Butler fell back toward his Bermuda Hundred intrenchments, which he occupied that night.

At 1.15 P.M. General Beauregard sent a telegraphic despatch to Richmond, saying: "We occupy the outer lines; the enemy is still in our front with open ground between us. Am preparing for a combined attack, reorganizing commands which are somewhat scattered. Some of the brigades are much cut up. Nothing from Whiting."

On the morning of the 17th General Beauregard took up a position in front of General Butler's lines, and intrenched it. "The enemy," he says, "is now hemmed in by our lines, which completely cover the southern communications of the capital, one of the principal objects of our attack." "The complete success," he adds, "was lost by the hesitation of the left wing, and the premature halt of the Petersburg column before obstacles in neither case sufficient to have deterred from the execution of the movements prescribed."

In the case of the Petersburg column, General Ames's division was sufficient to hold that in check, though its presence at Walthall Junction did not justify General Whiting's feeble course. As to the left wing, the fog, the resistance of Heckman's brigade, and the dispositions of Generals Smith and Weitzel, account, in great part, for the failure of its entire success. The attacks by the left wing on all other parts of Weitzel's front were unsuccessful.

The fog was equally detrimental to Smith's troops as to Ransom's.

General Beauregard reported his casualties on the 16th as 354 officers and enlisted men killed, 1,610 wounded, and 220 missing—a total of 2,184. He says the enemy left in his hands 1,400 prisoners, five pieces of artillery, and five stands of colors.

The statements of losses in the reports and accompanying papers of Generals Smith and Gillmore are incomplete, and it is apparent that the Tabular Statement of the "Medical and Surgical History of the War" is not correct. I do not find the report of the Medical Director. Badeau's Tabular Statement furnishes the best data. According to it, Butler's loss on the 16th was 390 officers and enlisted men killed, 1,721 wounded, and 1,390 missing—total, 3,500. The losses in the encounters previous to the 16th are not in-cluded.

General Kautz in his raid upon the Richmond and Dan-ville Railroad destroyed the stations, tracks, some trains, and large stores of subsistence and other supplies at Coal-field, Powhatan, and Chula, the last, south of the Appomat-tox River. He then crossed over to the South Side Railroad (Petersburg and Lynchburg Railroad), and after destroying the roads and stations at Black's and White's, Wilson's and Wellsville, returned to City Point, reaching there on the evening of the 17th. On the 16th he found the railroad bridge over the Nottoway, which he had destroyed on the 8th, replaced by a new structure.

On the 20th, the advanced rifle-pits on Butler's right, General Ames's front, and a part of General Terry's were captured, and a sharp fight ensued to regain them, unsuc-cessfully on Ames's front; but on Terry's front, Colonel Howell's brigade, after a severe contest, conducted with skill and gallantry, retook the pits. The loss was severe, 702 killed and wounded. The loss of the enemy was equally great, and among their severely wounded was their Brigade Commander, Brigadier-General W. S. Walker, who was cap-tured.

On the 22d of May, while the movement from Spottsylva-nia Court House was going on, General Grant learnt the result of General Butler's operations, and at once directed him to send all his troops under the command of General Smith to join the Army of the Potomac, except a number sufficient to keep a foothold at City Point. On the 25th the order was repeated, and the forces sent were directed to land at the White House, at the head of navigation on the Pa-munkey. They were embarked during the night of the 28th and the morning of the 29th.

General Smith took with him Brooks's division of his own

corps, and the Second and Third divisions of the Tenth Corps, commanded by General Devens and General Ames. His force consisted, according to his report, of very nearly 16,000 infantry (enlisted men), sixteen guns, and a squadron (100) of cavalry.

General Butler retained about 10,000 enlisted men of infantry; Kautz's cavalry, 2,600; and Hinks's colored cavalry, about 2,000.

Before General Butler sent off any part of his force, General Beauregard was instructed to strengthen his line, retain sufficient force to hold it, and send forward the remainder to General Lee. Under this order Pickett's division and Hoke's brigade (Colonel Lewis commanding) of Early's division joined General Lee at Hanover Junction, and Hoke's division, consisting of Martin's, Clingman's, Hagood's, and Colquitt's brigades, joined him later at Cold Harbor.

General Beauregard retained Bushrod R. Johnson's division, about 5,000 strong, consisting of Ransom's, Gracie's, and B. R. Johnson's brigades, the last now commanded by Colonel Fulton, Wise's brigade, about 2,400 strong, and probably General W. S. Walker's South Carolina brigade, afterward commanded by General N. G. Evans, making a force of about 9,000 infantry. Dearing's brigade of cavalry also remained with him.

CHAPTER VI.

PASSAGE OF THE PAMUNKEY RIVER—TOTOPOTOMOY AND COLD HARBOR.

In accordance with instructions received from General Grant, General Meade set the Army of the Potomac in motion as soon as it was dark, on the evening of the 26th of May, to cross the Pamunkey River at and in the vicinity of Hanover Town, some thirty-two or thirty-three miles, by the shortest route, below the position then occupied by the Army of the Potomac.

General Sheridan, with Torbert's and Gregg's divisions of cavalry, preceded the infantry, taking the river road in the afternoon of the 26th, and leaving some force at Little Page's bridge and Taylor's ford to deceive the enemy and watch those crossings until the army had passed. He was followed by Russell's division of the Sixth Corps, which was to make a forced march to Hanover Town. As soon as it was dark the withdrawal of the Army of the Potomac to the north bank of the North Anna began, and by three o'clock in the morning of the 27th was completed, the ponton bridges taken up, the other bridges destroyed, and the army on the march, following the advanced force. General Wilson's cavalry took the place of the infantry at the river crossings, and brought up the rear. The night was intensely dark, and the withdrawal was effected apparently without the knowledge of the enemy.

General Wright with Getty's and Ricketts' divisions followed Russell. The Fifth Corps, followed by the Ninth, which now formed a part of the Army of the Potomac, marched on a road more distant from the river, and were to cross the Pamunkey at New Castle Ferry, four miles below Hanover Town. The Second Corps followed the route of the Sixth Corps. The roads were not cleared for the Second and Ninth Corps until half-past ten in the morning.

At nine A.M. of the 27th, General Sheridan reported that he then occupied Hanover Town; that the crossing was taken with but little opposition; that two ponton bridges were laid and in use; that his first division had crossed, and that the second was about crossing.

In the vicinity of Hanover Town, on the Hanover Court House road, General Barringer's (formerly Gordon's) cavalry brigade of W. H. F. Lee's division was encountered and forced back toward the Court House as far as Crump's Creek, five miles northwest from Hanover Town. Our cavalry also occupied the road from Hanover Town to Atlee's Station and Richmond. A strong force of the enemy's cavalry was reported to be at Hanover Court House. At noon of the 27th, General Russell reported from the south side of the Pamunkey that his division had reached that point an hour before.

On the afternoon of the 27th the routes of the army were changed; the Sixth and Second Corps were directed to cross the Pamunkey at Huntley's, four miles above Hanover Town, and the Fifth and Ninth Corps to cross at Hanover Town.

Some brief description of the streams and roads in the section of country in which the operations now about to be described, took place, seems to be necessary.

About two miles below Hanover Town, Totopotomoy Creek, after a course nearly due east of twelve miles, empties into the Pamunkey. It rises near Atlee's Station on the

Virginia Central Railroad, about ten miles north of Richmond. Three or four miles south of the Totopotomoy is Matadequin Creek, which also empties into the Pamunkey. Both these streams have many swampy heads and affluents.

The Chickahominy rises some fourteen miles northwest of Richmond, and running in a southeast direction, passing four miles east of Richmond, empties into the James about ten miles west of Williamsburg.

The Chickahominy, the Totopotomoy, the Matadequin, and other streams in this section of country, have but little slope, have low swampy banks or bottom lands, usually wooded, and quickly become impassable swamps in the heavy, early summer rains.

From Hanover Junction, the central point of Lee's position on the North Anna, a road runs down the south bank of the North Anna and Pamunkey rivers, at no great distance from them, passing through Hanover Court House, Hanover Town, near New Castle Ferry, the White House at the head of navigation, etc. There are many roads from the Pamunkey to Richmond, crossing this river-road. The old stage-road from Fredericksburg to Richmond crosses the Pamunkey at Little Page's bridge, and passes through Hanover Court House, which is about seventeen miles from Richmond. From Hanover Town (also seventeen miles from Richmond) there is a direct road to Richmond, passing through Hawes's Shop (four miles from Hanover Town), Pole Green Church on the Totopotomoy, Huntley's Corners, and Shady Grove Church, crossing the Chickahominy at the Meadow bridges, and also from Huntley's Corners to Richmond by way of Mechanicsville. A branch from the Shady Grove Church road runs to Atlee's Station. A road comes in at Huntley's Corners from White House by way of Old Church. Again a road leads from New Castle Ferry on the Pamunkey to Richmond, passing through Old Church, and

by the Old Church road past Bethesda Church and through
Mechanicsville on the Chickahominy.   From Old Church
another road leads to Richmond by way of Cold Harbor and
New Bridge.   Several other roads lead from points lower
down on the Pamunkey to Richmond, crossing the Chickahominy below New Bridge.

All these roads from the Pamunkey to Richmond communicate with each other by numerous small cross-roads.

From Hanover Junction several roads lead to the points
where the Army of the Potomac was to cross the Pamunkey,
and to the roads by which it would advance after crossing.
The first and shortest was the river-road already mentioned,
passing through Hanover Court House.   At the Court House,
besides the river-road and the Richmond stage-road, there is
one that leads due south to Atlee's Station; another that leads
in a southeast direction past Hawes's Shop, and, after crossing
the Totopotomoy, enters the Old Church road.   This last described road from the Court House has a branch before crossing Crump's Creek that leads direct to Pole Green Church.

Another of the routes from Hanover Junction passes
through Ashland and Atlee's to Shady Grove Church and
Huntley's Corners on the Hanover Town road to Richmond.

Another route from Hanover Junction south, midway between Hanover Court House and Ashland, passes through
Merry Oaks and leads to Atlee's Station, at which point the
roads from the Pamunkey to Richmond south of Atlee's Station are near at hand.

Not long after midday of the 28th, the Sixth Corps had
crossed the Pamunkey and was in position across the Hanover Court House or river-road, at Crump's Creek.   The
Second Corps followed the Sixth closely, and formed on its
left, completing the cover of the road from Crump's Creek
to Hawes's Shop.

The Fifth Corps crossed the Pamunkey before midday of

the 28th, and was posted with its right on the road to Richmond, two miles in front of Hanover Town, and its left near
the Totopotomoy, where it is crossed by the road from
Hawes's Shop to Old Church.

It was midnight before the Ninth Corps crossed the river.
General Wilson remained on the north bank, covering the
crossing of the trains until the morning of the 30th of May.

On the morning of the 28th General Sheridan was directed
to make a demonstration on the road from Hanover Town to
Richmond to ascertain where the enemy was posted; and
about a mile beyond Hawes's Shop Gregg's division encountered the enemy's cavalry, dismounted and occupying temporary breastworks of rails. This force, General Sheridan
says, appeared to be the Confederate cavalry corps and a
brigade of South Carolina troops armed with long-range
rifles, reported to be 4,000 strong, and commanded by Colonel Butler.

But I learn from General Fitzhugh Lee that the Confederate cavalry force there on the 28th consisted of his own
division of two brigades, Hampton's division of two brigades,
and a brigade under the command of Colonel, afterward
General, Butler, which had recently arrived from South Carolina.[1] Fitzhugh Lee was on the right of their line, Hampton
on the left.

A long, hard contest ensued, and continued until late in
the evening, when Custer's brigade (of Torbert's division)
and Gregg's division carried the intrenchments and drove

---

[1] This brigade consisted of the Fourth, Fifth, and Sixth South Carolina regiments and the Twentieth Georgia battalion. Part were armed with long-range
rifles. Butler was, or had been, Colonel of the Sixth South Carolina. Although
this brigade had never been in action, yet, General Sheridan says, it did good
service in this encounter.

General Dunovant succeeded General Butler in the command of the brigade
when General Butler succeeded General Hampton in command of his division,
then composed of Young's, Rosser's, and Dunovant's brigades.

back the enemy. Torbert, with Devin's and Merritt's brigades, was also brought in from Crump's Creek in the afternoon, and formed on Gregg's right, but was not, General Sheridan says, seriously engaged.

At six P.M. General Sheridan reported that his prisoners stated that General Longstreet's and General Ewell's corps were four miles from Hawes's shop.

Let us see what the Army of Northern Virginia had been doing since the evening of the 26th.

At seven o'clock on the morning of the 27th, General Lee telegraphed to Richmond that the enemy had retired to the north bank of the North Anna during the night; that a portion of his force was still visible, but that some of his cavalry and infantry had crossed the Pamunkey River at Hanover Town, and that he had sent his cavalry in that direction to check the movement, and that he would move his army to Ashland. Ashland is a station on the Fredericksburg Railroad, ten miles south of the position then held by the Army of Northern Virginia, and fourteen miles north of Richmond. Roads radiate from it in all directions.

Ewell's corps, on the Confederate right at Hanover Junction, under the command of General Early, General Ewell being ill, crossed the South Anna at the Central Railroad bridge, and moved by way of Merry Oaks and Atlee's Station to Huntley's Corners at the intersection of the road from Hanover Town to Richmond by way of Hawes's shop with the road from White House to Richmond by way of Old Church and Shady Grove Church. Here he placed his troops in position on the afternoon of the 28th of May (after a march of twenty-four miles from Hanover Junction), covering the roads mentioned, his right resting near Beaver Dam Creek, which empties into the Chickahominy near Mechanicsville, his left on the Totopotomoy, near Pole Green Church, about four miles from Hawes's shop.

Longstreet's corps, under the command of General An-derson, crossed the South Anna by the Fredericksburg Railroad bridge, and, moving by Ashland and Atlee's, halted in the afternoon of the 28th on Early's right, between Hunt-ley's Corners and Walnut Grove Church, covering the road from White House by Old Church, Bethesda Church, and Mechanicsville to Richmond.

Breckinridge's command and Hill's corps formed along the Totopotomoy, and extended from Early's left to the vicinity of Atlee's Station, crossing the railroad a mile north of it. The Confederate cavalry was at Hawes's shop and Hanover Court House.

It will be perceived that while we were securing the roads from the Pamunkey to Richmond, upon which to advance against Lee, Lee was endeavoring to cover those roads.

On the morning of the 29th, the commanders of the Sixth, Second, and Fifth Corps were directed to make reconnois-sances in their front, supported by their whole force. Gen-eral Wright toward Hanover Court House, General Hancock on the roads from Hawes's shop to Atlee's and to Richmond, General Warren on the Shady Grove road. General Burn-side was held in reserve near Hawes's shop. General Sher-idan, with Torbert's and Gregg's divisions, was on the left of the army on the Old Church road, watching the roads to Mechanicsville, Cold Harbor, and White House. General Wright's leading division, Russell's, proceeded to Hanover Court House, meeting with no opposition, and encountering only small parties of cavalry. There was no infantry force of the enemy in that vicinity. General Hancock's leading division, Barlow's, met only the enemy's vedettes, until it arrived at the crossing of the Totopotomoy by the Richmond road, when the enemy was found in force intrenched on the south side, and a brisk skirmish ensued. General Birney and General Gibbon were ordered up, the former placed on

Barlow's right, the latter, on the morning of the 30th, on Barlow's left, and on the left of the Richmond road. General Hancock had before him the left of Early's corps, Breckinridge's command and Hill's corps, the Confederate left. General Griffin's division of General Warren's corps crossed the Totopotomoy, and moved along the Shady Grove Church road, encountering only the enemy's infantry pickets, which fell back before it. The enemy being in force on this road, Cutler's division moved over to Griffin. The Ninth Corps was in reserve between the Fifth and Second Corps.

It was apparent that we were close upon Lee's whole army, which was, in fact, well intrenched in the position it had taken on the evening of the 28th, as already described.

The infantry were directed to move close up to the enemy's position the next morning—General Wright to move at daylight of the 30th, form on Hancock's right, and endeavor to place his corps across the enemy's left flank. Unfortunately, the heads of Crump's Creek lay in the country through which the Sixth Corps moved on the morning of the 30th, after leaving the road from Hanover Court House to Richmond, and formed a swamp and tangle of the worst character, which delayed the arrival of the corps on Hancock's right, until it was too late for it to effect anything against the enemy that afternoon. On Hancock's front batteries were put up, and the enemy's artillery fire silenced. The skirmishing here was incessant, and resulted in the capture of most of the enemy's strongly intrenched skirmish line.

Burnside's corps formed, with sharp skirmishing, on Hancock's left, and at the close of the day had crossed the Totopotomoy, and had its right resting on that stream near the Whitlock House, and its left near the Shady Grove Church road.

Warren's corps moved along the Shady Grove Church

road, Griffin leading, Cutler and Crawford following. The
enemy's infantry and skirmishers fell back, Warren's following them until they entered thickly wooded, swampy ground,
formed by several small affluents of the Totopotomoy, which
here crossed the road.   On the opposite side of this swampy
ravine was Huntley's Corners, occupied by Early, well intrenched.   Warren's skirmishers on the Old Church and
Mechanicsville pike, three-quarters of a mile south of the
Shady Grove Church road, had encountered all day small
parties of the enemy's cavalry, and now the skirmishing increased.   It was still thought to be with cavalry, but on
the afternoon of the 30th General Early, in accordance with
orders from General Lee, moved to his right across Beaver
Dam Creek to the Mechanicsville and Old Church pike, and
out the pike to Bethesda Church, and was then across Warren's left.   Supposing this increased skirmishing to be with
cavalry parties, General Crawford sent a brigade over to look
after them, and Cutler moved up to the support of Griffin.
The brigade sent by Crawford had scarcely arrived in the
vicinity of Bethesda Church, when Rodes's division, of
Early's corps, moved down the road to attack them.   The
contest was brief ; the brigade was driven back to the Shady
Grove Church road, the enemy following.   A battery had been
well posted where the cross-road from Bethesda Church enters the Shady Grove Church road, and by its effective fire
delayed the enemy until Crawford's remaining brigade and
the scattered brigades of Cutler's division could be brought
up and put in position.   The enemy made a resolute attack,
but was repulsed and forced to retire, losing, among others,
Colonel Willis, Twelfth Georgia, commanding Pegram's brigade, mortally wounded, and Colonel Terrill, Thirteenth
Virginia, and Lieutenant-Colonel Watkins, Fifty-second Virginia, killed.   General Early says this last attacking force
was Pegram's brigade, and one of Rodes's which he had

sent forward to feel the enemy and ascertain his strength, and as this movement showed that the enemy was moving to the Confederate right flank, he withdrew at night a short distance on the Mechanicsville pike, covering it.

General Warren says that toward evening the Maryland brigade swung around on our left over to the pike, driving back the enemy's pickets to Bethesda Church, and that by ten o'clock the enemy had abandoned the field, moving back on the pike, leaving some of their wounded and dead in our hands.

To relieve the attack on General Warren, if it should prove to be serious, General Hancock was directed to attack as soon as he could find a suitable place. This despatch he received a little after seven P.M. There was no place on his line where an assault could be made with success at short notice, but to relieve General Warren, he gave the order for General Barlow's division to attack. Barlow, he says, moved, as usual, with most commendable promptness, and Brooke's brigade of his division advanced just at dark over obstacles which would have stopped a less energetic commander, and carried the enemy's advanced line of rifle-pits. At 7.40 General Meade ordered the attack to cease.

When Early moved from Huntley's Corners, General Anderson took his place there, Pickett on his right, Field in the centre, Kershaw on the left.

General Sheridan, with Torbert's and Gregg's divisions, covered the left of the army. Some cavalry force of the enemy being in position on the road from Old Church to Cold Harbor, at the crossing of the Matadequin Creek, near Old Church, General Sheridan attacked it about one o'clock in the afternoon with Torbert's division and drove it to Cold Harbor,[1]

---

[1] *Cold Harbor.* Probably so named after the former home of an early settler. I find on the Ordnance maps of England, Cold Harbor Point, on the Thames, ten miles below London, and a cluster of buildings at the Point called Great Cold

Torbert taking up position within a mile and a half of that place.

Wilson's cavalry division was on the right at Crump's Creek, under orders to cover that flank and destroy the bridges of the two railroads across the South Anna, and as much of the railroads south of the river as practicable.

At midday of the 30th, General Smith's transports began to arrive at the White House, and General Grant, upon learning it that evening, informed General Meade that Smith would probably debark his troops during the night, and move up the south bank of the Pamunkey, starting early on the 31st, and that it was not improbable that the enemy, being aware of Smith's movement, might feel to get on our left flank, to cut Smith off, or, by a dash, to crush him, and get back before we were aware of it ; that Sheridan should therefore be notified to watch the enemy's movements well out toward Cold Harbor and also on the Mechanicsville road, and send a brigade early in the morning of the 31st to Smith, the brigade to return with him.

But Lee did not learn of the arrival of Smith's command at the White House until the afternoon of the 1st of June, at which time it had already been engaged at Cold Harbor.[1]

On the 31st the infantry corps were pressed up against the enemy as close as practicable without assaulting, but the position was so strong naturally, and so well intrenched, and the intrenchments so strongly held that an assault was not

---

Harbor, apparently a farm or country place. A mile above Great Cold Harbor is another cluster of buildings called Little Cold Harbor, and about seven miles southwest of London another cluster called Cold Harbor.

[1] The first notice to be found in General Lee's despatches of the arrival of Smith's troops at the White House is in his despatch to Richmond in the evening of the 1st of June, in which he says, among other things : " A force of infantry is reported to have arrived at Tunstall's Station from the White House and to be extending up the York River Railroad. They state that they belong to Butler's force." Tunstall's railroad station is five miles from the White House, on the road up the south bank of the Pamunkey.

attempted ; the skirmish lines, however, were kept up against the enemy's, and an attack threatened.

On the same day General Sheridan, in pursuance of his instructions, finding the enemy at Cold Harbor, Fitzhugh Lee's division, apparently meditating an attack on Torbert's division, anticipated them, and, with Torbert, attacked Lee in the afternoon and gained possession of the position of Cold Harbor. Gregg followed Torbert. But Clingman's brigade of Hoke's division came up to Lee's support about dusk, and General Sheridan deeming he could not hold the position against the force accumulating against him (Hoke's division was not far off), directed Torbert to withdraw, but receiving an order from General Meade to hold Cold Harbor at all hazards, returned, and during the night modified the breastworks.

Cold Harbor [1] was an important point to us, as it was on the line of our extension to the left, and roads concentrated there from Bethesda Church, from Old Church, from White House direct, from New Bridge, and, directly or indirectly, from all the bridges across the Chickahominy above and below New Bridge. Some of these roads, and others connected with them, furnished great facilities to us in the movements and operations that took place here and those that followed.

On the right, General Wilson, in pursuance of his orders, had, on the 31st, a sharp encounter with General Young's cavalry brigade near Hanover Court House, and got possession of that place.

The detachment General Sheridan sent to the White House returned and reported the road clear; that they could get no information of the enemy being anywhere in the section of country passed over, and that Smith's troops were still debarking.

---

[1] Sometimes called Old Cold Harbor to distinguish it from New Cold Harbor, a mile west of it.

On the 31st Anderson's corps (Longstreet's) was placed on the right of Early's, and Early moved somewhat to the left, having Rodes's division west of Beaver Dam Creek. Hoke's division, which had joined Lee on the night of the 28th, was on the extreme right of the Confederate line near Cold Harbor; Kershaw's division near Beulah Church (Woody's), about a mile north of Cold Harbor, Pickett's division on his left, reaching to or toward Walnut Grove Church road, and Field on the left of the corps, his left on the Mechanicsville pike. This general line was partly intrenched. It was the intention, General Anderson says, to make a strong movement from his right, with Hoke and Kershaw, toward Cold Harbor and Beulah Church, on the morning of the 1st of June.

The presence of General Hoke near Cold Harbor was known to General Meade from Sheridan's reports, but it was not known that Kershaw was near him, or that Anderson's (Longstreet's) corps was on the right of Early, between Bethesda Church and Cold Harbor.

An attack of the enemy's position on the Totopotomoy, and covering the Shady Grove Church road and Mechanicsville pike, giving no promise of success, it was determined to send two infantry corps to maintain possession of Cold Harbor, and attack the enemy there before they and the troops sent to their support could intrench. General Wright was directed to move that night, and make every effort to get to Cold Harbor by daylight of the 1st of June, for it was believed that Sheridan would be attacked heavily at daybreak. But Wright's only practicable route was through Hawes's shop and across to the road from Old Church to Cold Harbor, a night march of more than fifteen miles, through a strange country covered with an intricate network of narrow, ill-defined roads.

General W. F. Smith had landed about 12,500 men at the White House by three o'clock in the afternoon of the 31st, and leaving General Ames there with 2,500 men to guard the landing-place, marched with 10,000 men and all his artillery, sixteen guns, toward New Castle on the Pamunkey, to which place he had been directed to proceed by despatches of the 28th from General Rawlins, General Grant's Chief-of-Staff. All his troops had not arrived, nor had any of his wagons or ammunition. About ten o'clock at night he halted at Bassett's, near Old Church, his troops suffering from the heat of the day, and from being unaccustomed to heavy marching. Reporting by despatch for orders, the next morning at daylight he received an order from General Grant's Headquarters to proceed at once to New Castle Ferry, and take position between the Fifth and Sixth Corps. Cold Harbor was intended. Marching at once, General Smith perceived, upon arriving at New Castle Ferry, that there must be some mistake in his order, and sent word to General Grant, who, in the meantime, hearing of the mistake that had been made, had sent Colonel Babcock to correct it. Some four or five hours were lost in this way, and the march of the troops increased several miles.

On the morning of the 1st of June Hoke did not become engaged, but took position on the right. Kershaw, however, attacked Sheridan with two of his brigades, one of them his own, but was repulsed by the fire of repeating-carbines and artillery. He repeated the attack with the same result, Colonel Keitt's regiment, the Twentieth South Carolina,[1] giving way, and Colonel Keitt himself being mortally wounded in the effort to rally it. The attack was not renewed, and at nine o'clock General Wright arrived, the head of his column near at hand. As soon as it was up, the cavalry were relieved, and moved toward the Chickahominy, covering the left of the army.

---

[1] This is called a big regiment in the Official Diary, First Corps. It was apparently a newly-raised regiment.

The arrival of the Sixth Corps was observed by the enemy, and Kershaw at once closed in to the right on Hoke, Pickett on Kershaw, and Field on Pickett.

This closing in to the right by Longstreet's corps, which occupied about an hour, and was made under cover of intrenchments in Warren's front and beyond his left, was observed by him at half-past ten, and under General Meade's order to attack, he deployed Lockwood's and Cutler's divisions, but these troops were embarrassed and delayed in forming by the wooded swamps of the Totopotomoy and Matadequin, and by the time they were in line in open ground the enemy's movement to the right had ceased. Their intrenchments were too formidable to attack.

By two o'clock in the afternoon the Sixth Corps was all up, and covered the roads to Cold Harbor from Bethesda Church, New Bridge, and Despatch Station on the York River Railroad near the Chickahominy.

In the course of the morning General Smith had been placed under the orders of General Meade, and was directed to take position on the right of General Wright, and endeavor to hold the road from Cold Harbor to Bethesda Church, and co-operate with General Wright in his attack. By six o'clock he was in position on the right, ready to advance to the attack.

The main line of the enemy's intrenchments was about fourteen hundred yards distant from the preliminary position of Generals Wright and Smith, the interval between being mostly open ground. On Smith's right the open ground was of less width. The intrenchments of the enemy's picket or skirmish line were from three to four hundred yards in advance of their main line; much of it was in a narrow strip of pine wood.

The intrenchments ran across, and were at right angles with the road from Old Cold Harbor to New Cold Harbor

(Richmond road). The right of the Sixth Corps, General Ricketts's division, was to move along this road, having Russell's division on its left, Getty's (General Neill commanding) next, Neill's brigade being refused to protect the left flank.

General Smith's line was formed with General Devens on the left, connecting with the Sixth Corps, General Brooks next on the right of Devens, and General Martindale on the right of the corps, his division refused. General Martindale was to hold the roads leading to Bethesda Church and toward Mechanicsville.

Hoke's division formed[1] the Confederate right, his left resting near the road upon which Ricketts's division was to advance. Kershaw's division was on Hoke's left, then Pickett's, Field's division forming the left.

At six o'clock Wright and Smith advanced to the attack, under heavy artillery and musketry fire. Ricketts's division struck the main line of intrenchments at Hoke's left and Kershaw's right, and carried them,[2] Clingman's brigade giving way; Wofford's on his left, being flanked, did the same, together with the right of Bryan's brigade. Kershaw recovered the ground lost by Bryan, and captured some prisoners and a stand of colors.[3] Hunton's brigade was sent to Hoke's assistance, and Gregg's to Wofford, and a new line was formed in rear of the part captured.

General Ricketts took over 500 prisoners. The loss of his division in killed and wounded was severe. The right of Russell's division, Upton's brigade, took part with Ricketts in the capture of the intrenchments, the leading regiment, the Second Connecticut Artillery, losing 53 killed, 187

---

[1] General Fitz Lee's cavalry was on their extreme right.

[2] It is stated in the Official Diary of Longstreet's Corps that the enemy penetrated an interval between Hoke and Kershaw.

[3] Official Diary, First Corps, Army of Northern Virginia.

wounded, and 146 missing; their colonel, Kellogg, was killed at the head of his command.

The right of Getty's division (Neill commanding) kept pace with the left of Russell's, but the left of the division was not heavily engaged.

The Sixth Corps lost in this engagement about 1,200 killed and wounded.

Devens's division of the Eighteenth Corps passed over the wide space of open ground under heavy fire, and captured the enemy's advanced intrenchments in the pine wood, with 250 prisoners, and, passing through the wood, came close upon the main line of intrenchments, which being too strong to attack, the division held the line of woods. General Devens's leading brigade lost heavily in officers and men, among them its gallant commander, Colonel Drake, of the One Hundred and Twelfth New York.

The leading brigade of General Brooks's division pushed through the open ground in their front, driving the enemy before them, and through the pine wood, until they came upon the main line, when they received so heavy a fire that they fell back to the woods.

The loss of the Eighteenth Corps was about 1,000 killed and wounded.

Both corps at once intrenched the positions they had gained. The right of Smith crossed the Bethesda Church road at Woody's near Beulah Church. During the day the skirmish lines of the army were incessantly engaged, as well as the artillery.

In the afternoon General Hancock was ordered to with-draw early in the night, and make every effort to reach Cold Harbor by early morning to reinforce Wright's left. General Wright was advised of it, and directed to attack as early as possible in the morning, Smith to attack in conjunction with him, Warren also, supported by Burnside. But Smith was nearly out of ammunition, and this, with the well-known exhausting effect of a night march upon troops in hot weather, on dusty roads, especially when they had been actively engaged all day in close contact with the enemy, caused a postponement of the hour of attack to five in the afternoon.

During the 1st, Sheridan, after being relieved by Wright at Cold Harbor, moved to the left with Gregg's and Torbert's divisions.

Wilson, on the right of the army, sent Chapman's brigade to destroy the two railroad bridges over the South Anna, while McIntosh's brigade proceeded to Ashland Station to cover the operation and destroy as much of the railroad as practicable. McIntosh, at Ashland, was attacked in rear from the direction of Hanover Court House by Hampton, with Rosser's brigade [1] (Wilson says Young's brigade and other troops), and then from the direction of Richmond, part of General W. H. F. Lee's division joining Rosser in this attack. A hot engagement ensued, during which Wilson sent the First Maine from Chapman's brigade to attack the enemy's rear. But the enemy's force was too strong for him, and McIntosh was obliged to fall back rapidly toward Hanover Court House, Hampton following him closely until dark. Wilson halted his division for the night near the Court House on the river-road. Both railroad bridges were destroyed, and the roads otherwise injured.

On the morning of the 2d, General Warren was directed to extend his left so as to unite with Smith at Woody's, and to contract his right to such extent as to make one-half his force available for attack. This, it was expected, would bring his right to the vicinity of Bethesda Church. General Burnside was directed to withdraw his force and mass it in

---

[1] Lee's despatch to Secretary of War, Richmond.

rear of Warren's right, to protect that flank and support Warren. But this gave General Warren a line about three miles long, the left of which he held chiefly with artillery. It was interrupted here and there by the swamps of the Matadequin, which virtually shortened his lines, as he could command the swamps without occupying them. General Wilson was directed to cover the right of the army from the vicinity of Bethesda Church to the Pamunkey. The main body of the Confederate cavalry was on Lee's left, Fitz Lee's division on his right.

Early on the night of the 1st, General Hancock began to withdraw; his route was necessarily circuitous; every effort possible was made to reach Cold Harbor early the next morning, but the night was dark, the heat and dust oppressive, and the roads unknown. An attempt to take a short cut with one of the divisions, where artillery could not follow, turned out to be a cause of delay. Notwithstanding these difficulties, the head of the column was at Cold Harbor at half-past six in the morning, but in such an exhausted condition, that a little time was required to close up and cook rations (the attack ordered for the morning had been postponed until five in the afternoon).

At 7.30 A.M. the corps was placed in position on the left of Wright, brisk skirmishing going on during and after the formation. Gibbon was put across the road from Cold Harbor to Despatch Station by way of Barker's mill, Barlow on his left; Birney went to Smith until the afternoon. This allowed the Second Division of the Sixth Corps (Neill) to be transferred from the left to the right of the Sixth Corps, and take Devens's place. Devens was then transferred to the right of Smith's corps, the Eighteenth. Brisk skirmishing went on during and after the formation.

In view of the movement of troops during the night and the morning, the heat of the day, and the short time had for preparation, the attack was postponed until half-past four in the morning of the 3d, and the corps commanders were directed to make all the required preparations.

Perceiving the withdrawal from our right, General Lee, on the morning of the 2d, sent General Breckinridge and General Hill, with Wilcox's and Mahone's divisions, to his right, Breckinridge forming on the high ground on Hoke's right, Hill on Breckinridge's right, Fitz Lee moving across the Chickahominy and picketing down toward the James.

Kershaw was supported by Anderson's, Law's, and Gregg's brigades of Field's division. Early remained on the left with his own corps and Heth's division. Intrenching went on all day, with heavy skirmishing and artillery fire.

But General Lee directed General Early to get upon our right flank and drive down in front of the Confederate line. To carry out this order Rodes's division moved out the Shady Grove Church road in the afternoon, Gordon swung around to keep pace with Rodes, and Heth, following Rodes, took position on his left. This movement brought on sharp fighting, which lasted until night, but did not accomplish what was designed. It found General Burnside's withdrawal unfinished, and his skirmish line, occupying the corps intrenchments, was driven from them by Rodes's division, and a large number of prisoners taken from it. In this way Rodes's troops got in rear of the Fifth Corps skirmishers unperceived, and captured a number of them.

Cutler and Crawford held the long line from Bethesda Church to Smith's right. Griffin's division was massed at Bethesda Church, but as soon as Early's movement was discovered it was formed in line, Ayres on the left, Bartlett in the centre, Sweitzer on the right, and moved forward under musketry and artillery fire, to the attack of Rodes's division, which had advanced from the Shady Grove Church road. Rodes was forced back to the road, and in this encounter lost a gallant officer, Brigadier-General Doles, who was killed.

General Crittenden's division brought up the rear in the withdrawal of Burnside, and was attacked with some vigor in doing so, but held Heth in check until Willcox and Potter got into position and stopped his further advance.

Early's troops remained on the Shady Grove Church road, and intrenched during the night, while Ramseur's division held the intrenchments on the left of Anderson's (Longstreet's) corps.

The whole army was now ordered to attack at half-past four in the morning of the 3d, except the cavalry on the left. Wilson, reinforced by 3,000 infantry and 2,000 cavalry from Port Royal, was ordered to move from Hanover Court House to Hawes's shop and attack the enemy's left flank and rear.[1]

Lee's position was naturally strong on the right, and was made strong throughout by intrenchments, which everywhere had open ground in front except for a short distance through the swamp on the right and parts of General Early's front. It had artillery in position with direct and flanking fire. The right rested on the Chickahominy in swampy ground, but soon rose to high ground, and ran in a direction a little west of north to the right of Early's position, the line of which was about northeast. The road from Despatch Station past Barker's mill to Cold Harbor ran along the foot of the high ground on Lee's right until it diverged to the right toward Cold Harbor, near and in front of the point where Gibbon's division crossed the road. Along this part of the road, near the foot of the high ground, was an advanced line of Confederate intrenchment. Hill and Breckinridge with

---

[1] General Wilson, reporting at 8.10 A.M., June 3d, says of the reinforcement: "Colonel Cesnola's command has been marching all night, all day yesterday, and is still on the road," etc.; he had only about 1,400 efficient infantry and 1,000 good cavalry, the rest being 1,200 or 1,500 disarmed stragglers, and "an indifferent force of dismounted cavalry regiments."

probably a part of Hoke's division held here in front of the Second Corps ; then followed Hoke, Longstreet's corps, and Early's as before noted.

Lee's position was about six miles from the main line of the Richmond exterior intrenchments, his right only about half that distance from the most advanced intrenchments.

The Chickahominy was in its lowest stage of water, and could be crossed anywhere by infantry above Lee's right.

This proximity to the defences of Richmond, together with the condition of the Chickahominy, appeared to bring turning movements to an end, though from what took place subsequently, when the Army of the Potomac was crossing the James, it appears probable that such a movement by our left would have brought on an engagement somewhere between the Chickahominy and Malvern Hill, though on conditions similar to those that had attended previous encounters. Lee's right was secure. His left being among the wooded swamps of the heads of the Totopotomoy and Matadequin, made it difficult of attack. The front was the assailable part, though it had not been reported that it was practicable to carry it by assault ; and the question was whether to take the chances of an assault there, which, if successful, would give the opportunity of inflicting severe loss upon Lee when falling back over the Chickahominy, as that must necessarily be attended with some disorder of his troops. General Grant decided to make the attack. As already stated, the order was issued fixing half-past four in the morning for the hour.

It will be perceived that from Smith's right near Woody's to Bethesda Church, a distance by the line occupied of nearly three miles, no effective attack could be made upon the enemy; the Fifth Corps not only occupied this line, but extended nearly a mile to the right of it, uniting then with Burnside. From Field's division, which occupied a large part of the Confederate intrenchments opposite this long thin line from Bethesda Church to Woody's, Law's, Gregg's, and Anderson's brigades had been sent to strengthen Kershaw, and Hunton's brigade of Pickett's division, on the right of Field, had been sent to reinforce Hoke.

The 2d of June was a hot, sultry day, as those preceding it had been, and wherever troops and wagons moved the dust hung in dense clouds. About five o'clock in the afternoon it began to rain, and the rain continued, with slight intermissions, all night, proving to be of great comfort to the men.

The assaulting was to be done by the Second, Sixth, and Eighteenth Corps. Promptly at the hour these corps advanced to the attack, under heavy artillery and musketry fire, and carried the enemy's advanced rifle-pits. But then the fire became still hotter and cross-fires of artillery swept through the ranks, from the right of Smith to the left of Hancock. Notwithstanding this destructive fire the troops went forward close up to the main line of intrenchments, but not being able to carry them, quickly put themselves under cover, and maintained the positions they had gained, which in some places were but thirty, forty, and fifty yards from the enemy's works. The loss in officers and men was heavy, and especially so in brigade and regimental commanders, who are the leaders in action. The greater part of the fighting was over in an hour or less, though attacks were renewed after that time. The killed and wounded of these three corps in that time exceeded 4,000. Including the Fifth and Ninth Corps, the total number killed and wounded was over 5,600. It is probable, indeed, that the numbers were considerably larger than those I have given.

The attack of the Second Corps was made by Barlow's division on the left, Gibbon's on the right, Birney supporting them. Barlow formed in two lines of battle, the brigades of

Miles and Brooke in the front line, those of Byrnes and McDougall in the second line. Gibbon formed in two lines, the first in line of battle consisting of Tyler's and Smith's brigades, the second consisting of McKeon's and Owen's brigades, in close columns of regiments.

Barlow advancing came against the salient work along the road from Despatch Station, which, after a severe struggle, he carried, captured two or three hundred prisoners, a color, and three guns, turning the guns upon the enemy, and following them as they retreated from that portion of the line into their main works. But his second line did not get up in time to support the first, which under the close musketry and artillery fire of the main works and a sweeping enfilade artillery fire which now opened on them, followed by an attack made by Breckinridge's troops, reinforced by Hill's, was forced out of the captured works ; but taking advantage of a slight crest some thirty to seventy-five yards distant from them, maintained a position there, putting themselves under cover in a short time. The gallant Colonel Brooke was severely wounded in the assault, falling at the moment his troops entered the enemy's works. Colonel Byrnes, Twenty-eighth Massachusetts, and Colonel Morris, Sixty-sixth New York, tried and excellent officers, were killed.

Gibbon had ordered his second line to follow the first promptly, push rapidly forward and pass over the front line in column, and effect a lodgment if possible in the enemy's works, and then deploy. His line was cut in two by an impassable swamp, which widened as he advanced toward the enemy. The troops pushed gallantly forward close up to the enemy's works, under, General Gibbon says, a terrific fire of artillery and musketry. General Tyler fell early in the action, severely wounded. McKeon, following on the right of Tyler's brigade, struggled against the heavy fire of the enemy until he and many of his command were killed, and his ranks thinned and scattered. Colonel Haskell, Thirty-sixth Wisconsin, succeeding to McKeon's command, was soon carried from the field mortally wounded in a second attempt to carry the enemy's works. Colonel McMahon, One Hundred and Sixty-fourth New York, forming the left of McKeon's brigade, but separated from it by the swamps, gained the breastworks with a portion of his regiment, and whilst alongside of his colors, cheering on his men, fell, with many wounds, dying in the enemy's hands, they capturing his colors and the men with them. A portion of Smith's brigade also gained the enemy's intrenchments, but, General Gibbon says, being unsupported were unable to hold them, for, he adds, General Owen, instead of pushing forward in column through Smith's line, deployed on his left as soon as the latter became fully engaged, and thus lost the opportunity of supporting the lodgment made by Smith and McMahon. To the names of the officers already mentioned must be added that of Colonel Porter, Eighth New York Heavy Artillery, who was killed a few yards from the enemy's works.

The division, General Gibbon says, lost in this assault 65 officers and 1,032 men killed and wounded ; and from the 3d to the 12th of June, when it was occupied in perfecting its position and pushing forward works toward the enemy, constantly under fire, both artillery and musketry, day and night, it lost besides, 280 officers and enlisted men killed and wounded.

The loss of the two divisions on this day, and until the army moved from Cold Harbor, was 2,217 officers and men killed and wounded.

The assault of the Second Corps could not be renewed unless the enemy's enfilading artillery fire could be silenced, and there were no good artillery positions available for that purpose, though guns were, as soon as practicable, put in covered positions for the purpose. But, anxious as both

General Grant and General Meade were that the attempt to carry the works should be renewed, if practicable, General Hancock did not consider it wise to make another assault.

The Sixth Corps advanced to the attack, with Russell's division on the left, Ricketts's in the centre, Neill's (Getty's) on the right. The advanced rifle-pits were carried on the right, and then the assault on the main line was made, but was repulsed with heavy loss. Yet positions were gained and held close to the works, at some points only thirty or forty yards from them.[1]

During all the time, besides the direct fire, there was an enfilade artillery fire that swept through the ranks from the right and from the left.

The casualties of the corps were some 800 killed and wounded, among the number valuable officers.

General Smith, in his report of this battle, gives a clear and brief account of the part taken in it by his command. He says : " In front of my right was an open plain swept by the fire of the enemy, both direct and from our right; on my left the open space was narrower, but equally covered by the artillery of the enemy. Near the centre was a ravine, in which the troops would be sheltered from the cross-fire, and through this ravine I determined that the main assault should be made. General Devens's division had been placed on the right to protect our flank, and hold as much as possible of the lines vacated by the troops moving forward. General Martindale, with his division, was ordered to move down the ravine, while General Brooks, with his division, was to advance on the left, taking care to keep up the connection between Martindale and the Sixth Corps ; and if, in the advance, those two commands should join, he (Brooks) was ordered to throw his command behind General Martin-

---

[1] The only reports on file are those of five brigade commanders. There are none from the corps and division commanders.

dale, ready to operate on the right flank, if necessary. The troops moved promptly at the time ordered, and, driving in the skirmishers of the enemy, carried his first line of works, or rifle-pits.   Here the command was halted, under a severe fire, to readjust the lines." Inspecting General Martindale's front, General Smith found that he had to form a line of battle faced to the right to protect the right flank of the moving column (the enemy's intrenchments making a partial re-entrant here), and that he could not advance farther unless the Sixth Corps covered his left from a cross-fire—a cross-fire, however, from which we have seen the Sixth Corps was also suffering.   General Martindale was ordered to keep his column covered as much as possible, and to move only when General Brooks moved.   General Martindale, hearing the firing in front of the Sixth Corps, mistook it for Brooks's, and made three gallant assaults with Stannard's brigade, but was repulsed each time.   This brought so severe a cross-fire upon Brooks, who was forming his column of attack, that he was ordered to keep his men under shelter until it was over. The fire from the right came from a part of the enemy's works against which no part of our attack was directed, and General Smith was unable to keep it down with his artillery. Reporting the condition in his front, General Smith said that his troops were very much cut up, and that he had no hope of being able to carry the works in his front unless the Sixth Corps could relieve him from the galling fire on his left flank.   To this General Meade replied (eight A.M.) that General Wright had been ordered to assault without reference to his, General Smith's, advance, and that he, General Smith, must continue his assaults without reference to General Wright, who but a short time before had reported that his assault was waiting for General Smith's.

To this General Smith says, General Devens's command, which held his right, had been so much cut up in officers and men during the two days previous, that he did not deem it in condition to do more than act on the defensive. Of the two brigades of General Martindale's division, General Stannard's had been too much reduced by the assault to be sent in again, and Colonel Stedman's brigade, in addition to having been repulsed, was holding a line he could not neglect. Of the three brigades of General Brooks, two had suffered severely during the first advance and the holding of the ground gained under a terrible cross-fire; and there was left of fresh troops only the brigade of General Burnham, which was ordered to the front to form a column of attack. But the severe flank fire from the right, which General Smith says went through his line into the right of the Sixth Corps, must first be silenced; and later in the day additional artillery was sent him for the purpose; but at half-past one o'clock General Meade suspended all further offensive operations, and directed corps commanders to intrench the positions they held, and make reconnoissances with a view to moving against the enemy's works by regular approaches from the advanced positions they held.

The killed and wounded of the Eighteenth Corps numbered about a thousand. The loss in leading officers on this day, as well as on the 1st of June, was severe. Among the killed on the two days were Colonel Meade and Lieutenant-Colonels Perry, Anderson, and Marshall, all commanding regiments.

The order of General Meade suspending the attacks was issued upon receiving a despatch from General Grant, stating that as the corps commanders were not sanguine of success in case an assault was made, that further advance might be suspended for the present; that advances to advantageous positions should be made by regular approaches, after due reconnoissance; that to aid the expedition under General Hunter it was necessary to detain all the army then with

Lee until Hunter got well on his way to Lynchburg. This would be more effectually done by keeping the enemy out of the intrenchments of Richmond than by forcing him into them.   It should be mentioned that as early as seven o'clock General Grant had directed General Meade to suspend the offensive the moment it became certain that an assault could not succeed.

General Burnside threw forward Generals Potter and Willcox early on the morning of the 3d, and took the advanced rifle-pits of Early's left (those taken by Willcox having been captured from him the evening before) and established these divisions close up to the enemy's main line.   One o'clock was fixed upon by him for an attack upon the main works by the three divisions, as by that hour it was expected that the artillery put in position would silence the severe enfilading fire of the enemy.   General Wilson was to co-operate by an attack on Early's rear.

The order suspending further offensive operations, however, was received just as the skirmishers were about to move, but not long after Early attacked vigorously and was repulsed.

The fighting was sharp during the day, the killed and wounded of the corps numbering about 800, and including, General Burnside says, some of their best officers and men.

General Warren, co-operating with General Burnside, had General Griffin's division, moving and attacking Rodes's and Heth's divisions in concert with Burnside's troops and pushing Early off from the Shady Grove Church road.   While Warren was thus attacking from his right, Gordon attacked his right centre, but was repulsed.   The Fifth Corps line was too extended for offensive operations, and about noon Birney's division of the Second Corps was sent to hold its left.   But the order suspending offensive operations was received by the time this division was in position.   The losses of the Fifth Corps were some 400 killed and wounded.

General Wilson, after establishing Cesnola's force on Burnside's right, moved across the Totopotomoy to Hawes's shop, attacked the enemy there, Barringer's brigade, W. H. F. Lee's division, and drove them from the rifle-pits, losing several valuable officers, Lieutenant-Colonel Preston killed, and Colonel Benjamin severely wounded. The enemy withdrew on the road to Enon Church in the direction of their former infantry intrenchments on the Totopotomoy. General Wilson then attacked Heth's left rear near Via's, on the road running south from Hawes's shop, engaging a brigade of three regiments, and got possession of their rifle-pits, which he held for an hour. Failing to connect with Burnside's infantry, he withdrew to Hawes's shop.

General Lee, in reporting the operations of the day to the Secretary of War at Richmond, says of this: "General Hampton encountered the enemy's cavalry near Hawes's shop, and a part of General Wm. H. F. Lee's division drove them from their intrenchments."

General Early says: "There were repeated attacks on Rodes's and Heth's fronts on the 3d, those on Cook's brigade of Heth's division being especially heavy, but all of them were repulsed. There was also heavy skirmishing on Gordon's front. During the day Heth's left was threatened by the enemy's cavalry, but it was kept off by Walker's brigade under Colonel Fry, which covered that flank, and also repulsed an effort of the enemy's infantry to get to our rear. As it was necessary that Heth's division should join its corps on the right, and my flank in this position was very much exposed, I withdrew at the close of the day to the line previously occupied, and next morning Heth moved to the right." General Early does not mention his losses.

About eight o'clock in the evening, the right of Barlow and the left of Gibbon were sharply attacked, but the enemy was repulsed. The Diary of Longstreet's Corps says of this:

"At dark a final and furious assault is made on Martin, the right brigade of Hoke.   Hunton also severely engaged."

General Lee, in reporting to the Secretary of War on the 4th of June, says: "Last night, after the date of my despatch, Generals Breckinridge and Finnegan were attacked by the enemy as they were preparing to re-establish their skirmish line.   The enemy was soon repulsed.   Immediately afterward an attack was made upon General Hoke's front, with a like result."

The lines were so close that an attempt to establish a picket line brought on a sharp contest, in which each side thought the other the attacking party.

Although the lines were advanced by regular approaches (they were so close to the enemy's intrenchments, and the ground was so open, they could not be advanced in any other way), yet an assault gave no promise of success.   The army remained in position here until the night of the 12th, when it withdrew to cross the James River.   The daily skirmishing during that time was sharp, and caused severe loss in some divisions; during the nights there was heavy artillery firing, and sometimes heavy musketry.   The labor in making the approaches and strengthening the intrenchments was hard.   The men in the advanced part of the lines, which were some miles in length, had to lie close in narrow trenches with no water, except a little to drink, and that of the worst kind, being from surface drainage; they were exposed to great heat during the day; they had but little sleep; their cooking was of the rudest character.   For over a month the army had had no vegetables, and the beef used was from cattle which were exhausted by a long march through a country scantily provided with forage.   Dead horses and mules and offal were scattered over the country, and between the lines were many dead bodies of both parties lying unburied in a burning sun.   The country was low and marshy in character. The exhausting effect of all this began to show itself, and sickness of malarial character increased largely. Every effort was made to correct this; large quantities of vegetables were brought up to the army, and a more stringent police enforced. So much was every one absorbed in the offensive operations against the enemy that, for a brief time, the police duties for the maintenance of cleanliness and health had not been as closely looked after as usual. The good effect of these efforts was soon apparent.

According to the report of the Medical Director, Surgeon McParlin, the wounded brought to the hospitals from the battle of the 3d of June numbered 4,517. The killed were at least 1,100. The wounded brought to the hospitals from the battle of the 1st of June were 2,125; the killed were not less than 500. The wounded on the 1st and 3d of June were, therefore, 6,642, and the killed not less than 1,600; but adopting the number of killed and missing furnished General Badeau from the Adjutant-General's Office, 1,769 killed, 1,537 missing (many—most, indeed—of them, no doubt, killed), we have 8,411 for the killed and wounded, and for the total casualties, 9,948. Previous to June 1, and after crossing the Pamunkey, we have 1,622 wounded,[1] 400 killed, and about 1,000 missing, making a total of 10,433 killed and wounded, and a total of casualties of 12,970.[2]

---

[1] Received at the hospitals from—

Second Corps	732	wounded.
Fifth Corps	500	"
Sixth Corps	14	"
Ninth Corps	76	"
Cavalry Corps	300	"
Total	1,622	"

[2] Surgeon McParlin further states in his report that the number killed, wounded, and missing from the time of crossing the Pamunkey to the evening of the 12th of June, may be estimated as follows, excluding the Eighteenth Corps. Number of wounded, according to the classified returns, 7,545; number of wounded, straggling, and unrecorded (slightly wounded, A. A. H.), 900; total, 8,445. Number killed, according to regimental reports, 1,420; number missing, 1,864. Total of

At the close of the day on the 3d of June there were many of our wounded lying between the lines and very near the enemy's intrenchments, completely covered by the fire of his pickets and sharpshooters.   But our men made extraordinary efforts by night to get in their wounded comrades, and so far succeeded that very few were left.   There were many dead of both sides lying there unburied, and General Grant proposed an arrangement with General Lee for bringing in the wounded and burying the dead.   This proposition was made on the afternoon of the 5th, but no cessation of hostilities for the purpose took place until the afternoon of the 7th, when a truce was agreed upon from six to eight in the evening.   Very few wounded were collected.   Of those not brought in at night by their comrades, as before mentioned, the greater number had died of their wounds and exposure. The dead were buried where they lay.

The number of casualties in the Army of Northern Virginia during this period, from the 27th of May to the 12th of June, are nowhere stated.   General Lee reported to the Secretary of War, on the 3d of June, that his loss that day was small. Up to, and including, the morning of the 1st of June, they were probably nearly equal to our own; in the afternoon of the 1st of June, less than ours, but still severe; on the 3d of June, very much less than ours.   According to the Tabular Statement of the " Medical and Surgical History of the War," the number of its wounded, from the 1st to the 12th of June, was 1,200; its missing, 500.   This would make its killed and wounded about 1,500.   The authority for the statement is not given.   The actual number was probably much greater. But even that number, when added to the probable number of killed and wounded between the 27th of May and midday

---

casualties, 11,729.   The losses in the Eighteenth Corps he estimates at 1,900 wounded, 500 killed and missing; total, 2,400.   Grand total, 14,129.   The number of sick sent to general hospitals North, 3,000.   Total loss, 17,129.

of the 1st of June, would give between three and four thousand killed and wounded for the whole period we are considering, and, including the missing, not less than between four and five thousand.   Besides the Confederate general officers already mentioned as killed or wounded, it is noted in the Tabular Statement of Casualties that General Kirkland of Heth's division, General Lane of Wilcox's, General Finnegan of Mahone's, and General Law of Field's divisions were wounded.   In the Diary of Longstreet's Corps it is mentioned that General Law was wounded.

On the 5th General Birney was returned to the Second Corps, and extended its left to the Chickahominy.   General Warren was withdrawn to the rear of Cold Harbor, and General Burnside, with his left on Smith's right, was extended along the Matadequin toward Allen's mill-pond.

On the 7th Griffin's and Cutler's divisions moved to the Chickahominy, and held from the left of Hancock to Despatch Station.

Two attempts were made by Lee to attack the right flank and rear of our army—one on the 6th, the other on the 7th. On the 6th General Early moved out on the north side of the Matadequin, getting as far as Bosher's on Burnside's right flank, but becoming entangled in the swamps of that stream, and troops from Anderson's corps failing to cooperate in time, probably owing to the same cause, he could effect nothing, and retired to his intrenchments.   On the 7th he made a similar effort on the south side of the Matadequin, which failed from the same cause.

CHAPTER VII.

PASSAGE OF JAMES RIVER—ASSAULTS UPON THE IN-
TRENCHMENTS OF PETERSBURG.

A FEW days after the Battle of Cold Harbor, General Halleck proposed to General Grant that the Army of the Potomac should invest Richmond on the north bank of the James. This would have given greater security to Washington, but it would have left open to Richmond not only all the lines of supply on the south bank of the James, but, through railroad connections with Lynchburg, the supplies of the Valley of Virginia and of West Virginia would have also been available for it. The original plan of campaign was therefore adhered to. The Central and Fredericksburg railroads had not been sufficiently damaged, and, on the 5th of June, General Sheridan was directed to move to Charlottesville with two of his divisions, starting on the morning of the 7th, destroy the railroad bridge over the Rivanna near that town, and the Central Railroad from that point to Hanover Junction, if practicable, which being effected, he would rejoin the army. General Sheridan carried instructions to General Hunter (whom he was expected to meet at Charlottesville) to unite his forces with Sheridan's, and, after thoroughly destroying the Central Railroad, to join the Army of the Potomac.

General Hunter, moving up the Valley of the Shenandoah, had, on the 5th of June, encountered a force, consisting of Jones's, Vaughn's, and Imboden's brigades, under Brigadier-General Jones, at Piedmont, about ten miles northeast from

Staunton, defeated it, and captured 1,500 men, with three guns. On the 8th of June he formed a junction with Crook and Averill at Staunton, and moved by way of Lexington upon Lynchburg, the possession of which, with its manufacturing establishments and stores, was important to the Confederates. General Vaughn, who succeeded to Jones's command, fell back to Waynesboro' at Rockfish Gap, on the railroad to Charlottesville.

As soon as General Lee received information of Jones's defeat, General Breckinridge was sent back to the Valley with the force he had brought with him from it, and on the 11th of June General Early moved his corps to the rear, near Gaines's mill. In the evening of the 12th, he was directed to move at three o'clock the next morning for the Shenandoah Valley, by way of Louisa Court House and Charlottesville ; to strike Hunter's force in rear, and, if possible, to destroy it ; then to move down the Valley, cross the Potomac near Leesburg or Harper's Ferry, and threaten Washington. General Breckinridge was directed to unite with him.

General Hunter was supposed by General Lee to be at that time at Staunton, and Breckinridge at Waynesboro'. General Early marched on the morning of the 13th, at two o'clock.[1]

The object in threatening Washington appears to have been the protection of Lynchburg and the upper part of the Valley of Virginia. It could hardly have been made with

---

[1] General Early, mentioning the condition of the Second Corps, refers to its heavy loss at Spottsylvania Court House, "where it lost nearly an entire division, including its commander, Major-General Johnson, who was made prisoner." Of the brigadier-generals with it at the commencement of the campaign, he says : "Only one remained in command of his brigade. Two (Gordon and Ramseur) had been made major-generals ; one (G. H. Stewart) had been captured ; four (Pegram, Hays, J. A. Walker, and R. D. Johnston) had been severely wounded ; and four (Stafford, J. M. Jones, Daniel, and Doles) had been killed in action. Constant exposure to the weather, a limited supply of provisions, and two weeks' service in the swamps north of the Chickahominy, had told on the health of the men. Divisions were not stronger than brigades ought to have been, nor brigades than regiments."

the expectation of drawing off from around Richmond any very large part of our forces operating against it.

On the morning of the 8th of June, General Lee learnt from Major-General Hampton that General Sheridan had crossed the Pamunkey the day before, and had encamped that night between Aylett's and Dunkirk on the Mattapony ; and that he had with him artillery, ambulances, wagons, and beef cattle.   General Hampton was directed to follow him with two divisions, and he at once set out for Gordonsville and Charlottesville with his own division, directing General Fitz Lee to follow as speedily as possible with his division.

On the 9th of June General Meade directed Major Duane, Chief-Engineer of the Army of the Potomac, to select and intrench a line in the rear of the position at Cold Harbor, to be held while the army was withdrawing.   The intrenchment extended from Elder Swamp to Allen's mill-pond, passing by Cold Harbor, and was finished on the morning of the 11th of June.

On the 10th, General Warren was directed to move his two divisions held in reserve near Leary's, on the 11th to Moody's on the New Kent Court House road, four miles from Bottom Bridge, keeping them out of the observation of the enemy.   He was advised confidentially of the part his corps would take in the march to the James, and directed to be prepared to move as soon as it was dark on the evening of the 12th.

On the 9th of June, General Butler sent General Gillmore and General Kautz on an expedition against Petersburg, the object being to capture the city and destroy the railroad bridge across the Appomattox.   General Gillmore had with him 1,800 infantry of his own troops, under the command of Colonel Hawley, and 1,200 of General Hinks's, which were to move up from City Point and join him.   General Kautz had about 1,500 cavalry.   General Gillmore says that the ponton

bridge over the Appomattox at Port Walthall was not muf-
fled as it was promised it should be, and that the crossing of
Kautz's cavalry could be heard for miles, and, no doubt, put
the enemy on his guard. General Wise, with his brigade,
2,400 strong, and such local troops as could be got together
under exigencies, had charge of the defences of Petersburg.
General Gillmore arrived before the works on the City Point
road at seven o'clock in the morning ; General Hinks at the
same hour before those on a road a mile from Gillmore's left.
General Kautz moved on the Jerusalem plank road four or
five miles on the left of Gillmore, and was expected to attack at nine o'clock. Wise's command held the intrenchments in front of Gillmore and Hinks. Manned as strongly
as they were, General Gillmore was satisfied, after careful
examination (in which opinion General Hinks and Colonel
Hawley both concurred), that he could not carry them. He
did not, therefore, make the attempt. Receiving no communication from General Kautz during the day, he withdrew
at half-past one from the front of the intrenchments, and at
three o'clock began his return march.

Kautz attacked the intrenchments on the Jerusalem plank
road with Colonel Spear's brigade at half-past eleven. The
force defending them was small, for no part of Wise's brigade
was posted there, but it was sufficient to repel three front attacks. The works were then turned with a part of the brigade, and Kautz advanced close to the water-works of the
town. But here he found an earth intrenchment and stock-
ade on Reservoir Hill, which had infantry and artillery in it.
General Dearing's brigade, sent over by General Beauregard,
now came up, and the artillery opened. Kautz, satisfied
that he could not capture the town, withdrew, followed by
Dearing.[1]

---

[1] I could not find any report of this affair from General Kautz on the files of the
War Department.

In the course of the day General Beauregard sent all the force he could spare from his intrenchments to Petersburg, and telegraphed to Richmond that, without the troops he had sent to General Lee, he should be obliged to abandon the lines of Bermuda Hundred or those of Petersburg.

To return to the Army of the Potomac. There was some delay in the arrival at Fort Monroe of the bridge materiel for crossing the James. Some of it had been sent to Harper's Ferry for General Hunter's use. Steamers and steamboats of different kinds had been collected at Fort Monroe to ferry troops over and thus expedite the crossing of the army.

The object of crossing the James was, as already stated, to carry out the plan with which the Army of the Potomac began the campaign, that is, to destroy the lines of supply to the Confederate depot, Richmond, on the south side of the James as close to that city as practicable, after those on the north side of the river had been rendered useless.

The capture of Petersburg would leave but one railroad in the hands of the Confederates, though, with that and its connections, they would still retain access to a large region of supply. Following the possession of Petersburg would be the turning of Beauregard's intrenchments in front of Butler and an advance toward Richmond. Finally, but not immediately, the remaining railroad would be severed, or, in anticipation of it, Richmond would be abandoned, and the Army of Northern Virginia would retreat toward Danville or Lynchburg.

The place of crossing the James, the vicinity of Wilcox's Landing, was judiciously chosen, both in its general and local features. Herring Creek covered it on the west, and the river on the east. Positions for protecting the rear were selected by the Engineers of the Army of the Potomac in advance of the arrival of troops there, the right of the line, looking north, crossing Weynook Neck, and resting on the river.

To cross so wide and deep a river with so large an army with all its artillery, together with its ammunition, subsistence, quartermaster, ambulance, and hospital trains, was a difficult operation, and exposed the army to attack under disadvantages while crossing. Should General Lee attempt to interrupt the crossing at the point selected, he must advance a long distance from Richmond, and thus expose himself in turn to attack.

The vicinity of Malvern Hill would have afforded better bridging places of the James than that at Wilcox's Landing, and the routes to Butler's intrenchments, and to Petersburg from Cold Harbor, would have been ten or fifteen miles shorter than those by way of Wilcox's Landing (which exceeded fifty miles in length to Petersburg), but the crossing near Malvern, as well as the preparations for it, would have been under the observation of the enemy, and exposed to interruption. Lee, at Cold Harbor, was about twenty-four miles from Butler's intrenchments at Bermuda Hundred, by way of Drury's Bluff, and about thirty-four from Petersburg.

In the movement of the army from Cold Harbor to James River, the Chickahominy must be crossed. Obviously, the crossings should be at points so far below Cold Harbor that a sufficient force could be over that stream and in position to cover the crossing of the remainder of the army by the time Lee should learn that the movement had taken place.

The chief road-crossings of the Chickahominy below Lee's position were Bottom Bridge, eight miles below Cold Harbor, Long Bridge, fifteen miles, Jones's Bridge, twenty miles, and Window or Windsor Shades, the head of navigation, twenty-four miles below Cold Harbor. The bridges at these places had been destroyed.

Two miles below Bottom Bridge, the White Oak Swamp empties into the Chickahominy. The head of the swamp is about a mile northwest of Seven Pines. The general course of the stream is east, bending first toward the south, then, for the last three miles, to the north.   It is about ten miles long, and is similar in character to the streams of this section of country already described, and is, therefore, difficult to cross.   Three miles above its mouth it is crossed on a bridge by a road running due south from the vicinity of Bottom Bridge, which road, at a mile south of the bridge, intersects the Long Bridge road.   No main road crosses the White Oak Swamp above this point, though some plantation roads do.

Between White Oak Swamp and James River there are three roads leading to Richmond, the Charles City road, the most northerly, the Central road, and New Market or river-road.   The general direction of the Long Bridge road, after crossing the Chickahominy, is southwesterly.   Five miles from Long Bridge it is entered by the road from White Oak Bridge; a mile further on it is entered by the Charles City road and by the Quaker road from the south, coming from the River road at Malvern Hill.   At this point of meeting of the three roads is Riddell's shop.   Three miles farther on, the Long Bridge road is entered by the Central road, and a mile farther it is merged in the river-road.

It was determined that Warren and Hancock should cross the Chickahominy at Long Bridge, Wright and Burnside at Jones's Bridge, and the great trains moving from White House, at Windsor Shades and Coles's Ferry.   Wilson had one of his cavalry brigades on the right of the army, and the other on the left, picketing the Chickahominy.   The brigade on the left was to precede Warren.   The one on the right was to withdraw at the same time as the Second and Sixth Corps, and cover the rear of the army and the trains during the movement.   Ponton bridges accompanied each of the columns.   Smith was to move with the Eighteenth Corps to White House, having the right of way over everything, embark his command, and proceed with all possible despatch to Bermuda Hundred and report to General Butler. His artillery and trains were to join the main trains of the army at Tunstall's Station.

The army was to commence withdrawing from Cold Harbor as soon as it was dark on the evening of the 12th, Hancock and Wright to occupy the intrenched line in rear from Elder Swamp to Allen's mill-pond, until the roads for their corps were cleared, when they were to move. The order for the movement will be found in Appendix H.

The routes for the movement of the corps and trains, and directions as to precedence where routes joined, were carefully prescribed. Upon crossing the Chickahominy, General Warren was to cover the passage of the army toward James River, and then follow the Second Corps, which was to move toward Charles City Court House by way of St. Mary's Church, Walker's, etc. The Sixth Corps was to take the route from Jones's Bridge to Charles City Court House, by way of Vandorn's, and the Ninth Corps a route passing east of Charles City Court House, by Vandorn's, Clapton, and Tyler's mill. The depot at White House was to be maintained with its garrison until the arrival of General Hunter and General Sheridan.

In preparing the programme of movement, it appeared to me important that General Warren should move out the Long Bridge road, not only far enough to cover the crossing of the Chickahominy by the army, but so far as to hold the bridge over the White Oak Swamp, and to look toward the three roads to Richmond already mentioned, which substantially met at Riddell's shop, about a mile in advance of the position General Warren was directed to take. He could not well advance to Riddell's shop, since that would have exposed him to attack in rear from White Oak Bridge. It was expected that such a movement by General Warren would deceive Lee, and give him the impression that the Army of the Potomac was advancing upon Richmond, or, if intending to cross the James, that it would do so near Malvern Hill, at City Point, or above. The movement made the desired impression upon him, and to a greater extent than was contemplated, for, as we shall see farther on, he was uncertain what the Army of the Potomac was doing until the afternoon of the 17th of June.

The movement to James River took place as ordered, without interruptions or delays. The ponton bridge at Long Bridge was laid at one A.M. of the 13th, and Wilson's cavalry at once crossed, and moved out to White Oak Bridge and to Riddell's shop, meeting with sharp opposition from Barringer's cavalry brigade and some mounted force under General Geary. Wilson was followed by two divisions of the Fifth Corps to the position General Warren was directed to take, the other two divisions of the corps being held in support. As soon as the Fifth Corps relieved Wilson at White Oak Bridge, where there was some force of the enemy, he pushed parties out the Charles City and Central roads, which had sharp skirmishing. His losses and those of Crawford during the day were some 300 killed and wounded.

The Second Corps followed the Fifth in crossing at Jones's Bridge, and reached the vicinity of Wilcox's Landing at half-past five on the 13th. The Sixth and Ninth Corps reached there on the 14th. The Fifth Corps withdrew to St. Mary's Church on the night of the 13th, and arrived at Charles City Court House at noon of the 14th.

The marches were very long and exhaustive, being from twenty-five to thirty-five or forty-five miles in length.

General Butler turned over all his bridge materiel and vessels of every kind, not in use, to the Army of the Potomac to aid in crossing the river. General Weitzel, his Chief Engineer, was charged with constructing roads through the swamps at the two ends of the bridge and at the landing-places for the ferrying vessels. The approaches to the bridge being completed, and everything ready for its construction, the battalion of engineers, under Major Mendell (Major Duane, Chief Engineer), commenced laying it at four o'clock in the afternoon of the 14th, and finished it by midnight.[1]

The artillery and trains of the Ninth, Fifth, and Sixth Corps began at once to cross upon it, in the order stated, that being the order in which the corps were to cross the river. By midnight of the 16th the army, with all its artillery and trains, was over the James, General Wright covering the operation, and being the last to reach the right bank.

General Wilson's cavalry held their advanced positions toward the White Oak Swamp and Malvern Hill, until they were drawn in by General Wright to precede him over the bridge.

The navy also assisted with its armored ships and gunboats in covering the passage of the river.

General Butler had, in the latter part of May, procured several vessels to sink upon Trent's Reach bar, at the right of his line of intrenchments, if, he stated in his correspondence with Admiral Lee, in the judgment of the Naval Commander this obstruction would add to the security of the fleet. Upon those terms Admiral Lee declined to sink them. But General Grant, upon learning, on the 13th of June, that his order to General Butler to obstruct the navigation in this way had not been carried out, again directed him to sink

---

[1] The site of the bridge was between Windmill Point and Fort Powhatan, where the river was 2,100 feet wide. The depth in mid-channel was from twelve to fifteen fathoms. The tidal current was strong; the rise and fall of the tide four feet. The number of pontons was one hundred and one. In the channel the pontons were anchored to vessels above and below, moored for the purpose. Here there was a draw for the passage of vessels. The bridge was commenced from each end and built by successive pontons and by rafts. After considerable progress was made under Major Duane, General Benham arrived and took charge of the operation.

them, as it was deemed a military necessity, essential to the success of the campaign.   Upon learning this from General Grant, Admiral Lee rendered every aid required in obstructing the channel, which was now accomplished.

On the morning of the 13th General Lee discovered that the Army of the Potomac had withdrawn from Cold Harbor, and learned that it was advancing toward Richmond on the Long Bridge road.   His army was at once set in motion, General Anderson moving with his corps past Fair Oaks and Seven Pines over White Oak Swamp to the Charles City road, and down that road a few miles to Williams's, when, turning from it, he halted for the night near the battlefield of Frazier's farm, between Malvern Hill and Riddell's shop. General Hill crossed White Oak Swamp lower down, and moving out the Charles City road, took up a position at Riddell's shop, where he intrenched, having some skirmishing with Wilson's cavalry.   Lee was thus holding from Malvern Hill to White Oak Swamp.

In the night of the 13th Wilson withdrew to St. Mary's Church, where he established McIntosh's brigade, which by that time had joined him.   On the afternoon of the 14th and morning of the 15th, McIntosh advanced toward White Oak Swamp, and Chapman toward Malvern Hill, the latter to ascertain if it was held by the enemy, and in what force.   He was also to ascertain whether a crossing could be secured from Shirley to Bermuda Hundred or City Point.   Colonel Chapman reached Turkey Creek bridge at the foot of Malvern Hill, and ascertained that the enemy's cavalry occupied the hill in force. These cavalry reconnoissances caused the retention of Anderson and Hill in the positions they took on the evening of the 13th.

As soon on the 14th as any boats were available, General Hancock began crossing his troops from Wilcox's Landing to Windmill Point, and by four o'clock on the morning of the 15th all his infantry and four batteries of artillery had landed on the south bank. The means of crossing were very limited, and the landing-places, wharfs, and roads were incomplete. At half-past six in the morning of the 15th three ferry-boats were added to his means of crossing and greatly facilitated the passage of his artillery and wagons.

On the evening of the 14th he was directed by General Meade to hold his troops in readiness to move, and was informed that it was probable he would be instructed to march toward Petersburg, and that rations for his command would be sent him from City Point. At ten o'clock that night the following despatch was sent him by General Meade: "General Butler has been ordered to send to you at Windmill Point 60,000 rations.[1] So soon as these are received and issued, you will move your corps by the most direct route to Petersburg, taking up a position where the City Point Railroad crosses Harrison's Creek, where we now have a work. After Barlow has crossed you will cross as much of your artillery and ammunition train as possible up to the moment you are ready to move, and if all is quiet at that time the ferriage of the rest can be continued and they can join you." But the rations did not arrive, as expected, that night or the next morning, and the corps marched without them at half-past ten on the 15th.[2]

---

[1] Three days' rations. The Second Corps had 20,000 enlisted men, not 28,000, as has been stated.

[2] At 7.30 A.M. of the 15th, after receiving several despatches from General Hancock concerning the rations, and the readiness of the corps for movement, General Meade sent a despatch to him saying: "You will not wait for the rations, but move immediately to the position assigned you last evening," etc., etc. Then, continuing, "Your despatch just received" [concerning the reported arrival of rations, which turned out to be erroneous]. "It is important you should move. Exercise your judgment as to which will be best, to issue rations now, or send them as directed in the foregoing." At nine o'clock, finding that the rations had not arrived, General Hancock ordered the corps to move, but the Signal officer by whom the order was sent failed in some way to communicate it; and the boat in which Colonel Morgan, who carried the same order, crossed the river grounded, so that the column did not begin to move until half-past ten.

General Smith withdrew from the intrenchments of Cold Harbor shortly after dark on the night of the 12th of June, and at daylight had arrived at the White House, when the embarkation began, but delay occurred from the want of transportation. By sunset of the 14th he had reported in person to General Butler at Bermuda Hundred and received orders to move at daylight on Petersburg.[1]

General Butler had a ponton bridge over the Appomattox near the left of his line, at Point of Rocks or Broadway Landing, about two miles below Port Walthall. Near this landing General Smith's transports continued to arrive all through the night. General Butler's cavalry under Brigadier-General Kautz, 2,400 strong, and the available part of the division of colored troops under Brigadier-General Hinks[2] (3,700 officers and enlisted men, infantry and artillery) were assigned to General Smith, in addition to his own infantry, 10,000 enlisted men. General Kautz was ordered to cross the river at one o'clock in the morning, and threaten the intrenchments near the Norfolk and Petersburg Railroad, and at the same time protect the left flank of the infantry ; Hinks to follow Kautz, and take a position across the Jordan's Point road as near as possible to the enemy's works ; Brooks to follow Hinks and form on his right, and General Martindale to proceed on the river-road to a point near the City Point Railroad and await orders. It will be recollected that the Petersburg intrenchments encircled the city at the distance of two miles from it, and consisted of a series of strong redans or batteries connected by infantry parapets with high profiles, all with ditches. General Smith's in-

---

[1] In the latter part of May, just before embarking to join the Army of the Potomac, General Smith had proposed to capture Petersburg, as he regarded it to be of great importance to us from its railroad connections and its giving us the line of the Appomattox.

[2] The remainder of the division was at Wilson's Landing, Fort Powhatan, City Point, and Bermuda Hundred.

fantry would have a march of six or seven miles to come up to them. General Kautz, General Smith says, was unavoidably delayed in his march, so that the movement from Broadway did not take place until after daylight. He soon met the enemy's skirmishers, and came upon a rifle-pit near the railroad, about two miles in front of the enemy's intrenchments, which was held by some dismounted cavalry and a light battery. Some time was required to take this isolated intrenchment, which Hinks's troops accomplished, capturing one of the guns. General Hinks moved to his assigned position by the flank, while General Brooks deployed and moved forward along the City Point Railroad and wagonroad. A mile-and-a-half's march brought them under the fire of the enemy's artillery, and General Smith began to reconnoitre the position and form the troops for assault. General Martindale had come up on the right of the railroad. In his front, extending to the Appomattox, was a broad, low valley, cut up by ditches and ravines, completely swept by the fire of the enemy's artillery, the intrenchments here being withdrawn some six hundred yards from the salient at and about Jordan's Hill (where the City Point Railroad entered), in front of which was Brooks's division. The line of works in front of Hinks's division was similarly withdrawn, though not to the same extent. Deep ravines were found all along these fronts also. The enemy had a cross-fire of artillery upon the front threatened.

The reconnoissances were necessarily slow. Very little infantry could be seen in the works, but, General Smith says, that was not positive proof that it was not there, and it did not seem probable to him that the number of guns at work against him would be there without support. But in fact the whole force in the intrenchments at that time, besides the artillery, consisted of Wise's brigade, 2,400 strong, the militia, and Dearing's brigade of cavalry. Heavy artillery firing was going on against Kautz.   About five o'clock, after completing a careful reconnoissance, General Smith concluded not to assault in column under such a heavy artillery fire, but to mass his artillery upon the salient near General Brooks's centre, and try to carry the works with a very strong skirmish line, which he could do if they were thinly held by infantry.   The troops were formed accordingly, but his chief of artillery had, without authority, taken everything to the rear to water the horses, and this caused a further delay of an hour.   About seven o'clock the skirmishers advanced, and the artillery opened upon the salient (Redans 5 and 6), which made no reply.   The skirmishers met a sharp infantry fire, but carried the works, taking between 200 and 300 prisoners and four guns.   The lines of battle followed and occupied the intrenchments.   General Brooks was formed to resist an attack, while General Martindale on the right, and General Hinks on the left, were following up the advantage gained.   Five of the redans on the left, from No. 7 to 11, both inclusive, which commanded the position at the centre, were captured by Hinks's division, the last, No. 11, at the Dunn house, about nine o'clock in the evening.   Artillery was captured in each.[1]   A mile and a half of the intrenchments, with sixteen guns, were thus captured, and this showed that the infantry force defending Petersburg was very small.

The four redans from the river to the City Point Railroad remained in the hands of the enemy, as did those on our left of No. 11.

About four o'clock in the afternoon, General Smith was informed by a staff officer sent by General Grant, that the

---

[1] General Hinks reported the loss of his division to be 507 killed and wounded, among the latter Colonel H. S. Russell, Fifth Massachusetts Cavalry, and Lieutenant-Colonel Nathan Goff, Jr., Twenty-second Regiment United States Colored Troops.   The loss of Brooks and Martindale I do not find mentioned.   It is included in the general statement of the loss of the army during this period.

Second Corps was marching toward him on the road from Windmill Point. Upon receiving this intelligence General Smith at once sent a despatch to General Hancock, requesting him to come up as rapidly as possible. This despatch General Hancock received at half-past five, about a mile from Old Court House, and about four miles from Smith's left. A few minutes before, General Hancock had received a despatch from General Grant at City Point, directing all haste to be made in getting up to the assistance of General Smith, who, it stated, had attacked Petersburg, and carried the outer works in front of that city.[1] The head of Birney's division was just passing a country road that led directly to Petersburg when these despatches were received, and was at once turned in that direction, Gibbon's division following, and orders were sent to General Barlow to march toward the same point from Old Court House, on the road to which he was moving.

As soon as he received General Grant's despatch, General Hancock sent Colonel Morgan to inform General Smith where his column was, and that he was marching to his support with all despatch. This information General Smith probably received shortly after six o'clock.

General Beauregard, apprehensive that the Army of the Potomac, in withdrawing from Cold Harbor, would move directly upon Petersburg, had urged General Lee to send him troops sufficient to defend it, while he held his lines in front of Butler. But Lee, not satisfied that Richmond was not the object of the movement of the Army of the Potomac, would not withdraw Hill and Anderson from their position at Riddell's shop. He directed Hoke's division, however, to return to Beauregard. It left Drury's Bluff early in the morning of the 15th, having eighteen miles to march to the

---

[1] This evidently referred to the rifle-pit captured by General Hinks early in the day.

Petersburg intrenchments where threatened.   General Beau·
regard says that the leading brigade, Hagood's, arrived by
rail about sunset, and was placed on Wise's left, his, Hagood's, left extending to the Appomattox. The rest of
Hokes's division, he says, arrived during the night, and was
put on Hagood's right.   All the division was probably put
in position before nine o'clock, and intrenchments were
thrown up in rear of the captured part of the defences during the night.

General Smith says that he had heard some hours before
the last works were captured, that Lee's army was rapidly
crossing at Drury's Bluff, and that he deemed it wiser to
hold what he had, than, by attempting to reach the bridges,
to lose what he had gained, and have the troops meet with a
disaster.   He knew also, he says, that some portion of the
Army of the Potomac was coming to aid him ; and therefore
the troops were placed so as to occupy the commanding positions and wait for daylight.   Upon the arrival of General
Hancock he requested him to relieve his troops and allow
them to rest, which request General Hancock complied with.

It is probable that an immediate advance of the whole of
Smith's force when the salient was carried, or at nine o'clock,
when it would have been supported by two divisions of the
Second Corps, would have resulted in the capture of Petersburg and the possession of the north bank of the Appomattox.[1]

It was a march of at least sixteen miles by the direct road
from Windmill Point (through Prince George Court House)
to the Petersburg intrenchments where intersected by the
City Point Railroad.   Had General Hancock's instructions
merely directed him to move his corps by the most direct

---

[1] General Hinks says it was about seven o'clock when General Birney's arrival
was reported to him by Colonel Livermore of his (Hinks's) staff (see Paper
Massachusetts Military Historical Society).

route to the intrenchments of Petersburg, as soon as the rations were issued, it would, in his judgment, notwithstanding the delay caused by the matter of rations, have arrived there by four o'clock in the afternoon. Certainly it would have been there by six o'clock, and in time to attack with Smith's force. It would have found no infantry and but little artillery in the intrenchments on Smith's left, and continuing to advance, would have secured the possession of Petersburg. Why General Hancock was not ordered to march at daylight of the 15th, I have been unable to ascertain. He could have done so as readily as at half-past ten, and it would have brought him up to Smith at midday.

He was to "take up a position where the City Point Railroad crossed Harrison's Creek, where we now have a work," and this condition did not admit of his continuing on the most direct road, but obliged him to leave it; and, turning to the right, take one several miles longer, after much delay in seeking in vain to ascertain from the people of the country where Harrison's Creek was, and what roads led to it, for the maps in use were, for this section of country, so erroneous as to be not only useless but misleading. Harrison's Creek was, in fact, inside the enemy's intrenchments, and was such an insignificant rivulet as probably not to be known by any name much beyond the limits of Petersburg. There was a run marked on the map as Harrison's Creek, but erroneously laid down. This stream, according to the map, was crossed by the railroad about three and a half miles from Petersburg. There was actually a diminutive stream crossed by the City Point Railroad half way between City Point and Petersburg, about five miles from each, and this rivulet emptied into the Appomattox near the ponton bridge of General Butler at Broadway Landing, where there was a bridge-head, as there was at the site of the ponton bridge, a mile and a half above. These works appear to be referred to in the despatch by the phrase *"where we now have a work,"* for we had no work where the railroad crossed the run.[1]

Apparently it was designed that the Second Corps should be in position at the railroad crossing of Harrison's Creek to support General Smith, the erroneous map misleading as to its distance from the Petersburg works. General Hancock states in his report that the messages from Lieutenant-General Grant and from General Smith were the first and only intimations he had that Petersburg was to be attacked that day, and that up to that hour he had not been notified from any source that he was expected to assist General Smith in assaulting that city. The artillery firing which he had heard he attributed to a raid or a reconnoissance which the people of the country informed him Kautz was making.[2]

The head of Birney's division, General Hancock says, arrived at the Bryant house, about a mile in rear of Hinks's position, at half-past six o'clock. Leaving instructions for Birney and Gibbon to move forward as soon as they could ascertain where they were needed, General Hancock rode to General Smith and informed him that two of his divisions were close at hand, ready for any movements which in his judgment should be made. General Smith, informing him that the enemy had been reinforced during the evening, requested him to relieve his troops in the front line of the captured works. This relief was completed by eleven o'clock, by which time, General Hancock says, it was too late and too dark for an immediate advance. About midnight General Hancock was informed by General Grant that the enemy

---

[1] " Taking up a position where the City Point Railroad crosses Harrison's Creek, *where we now have a work*." I cannot recall where this information " *where we now have a work* " came from. Evidently the information and instruction had its origin at General Butler's Headquarters. The order was written and signed by General Meade. I was not at the headquarters at the time.—A. A. H.

[2] No such information was sent him through me, nor did General Meade communicate such information to me if he possessed it.

were throwing reinforcements into Petersburg, and he was directed, if Petersburg should not be taken in the night, to take up a defensive position, and maintain it until all our forces were up.[1]

At six o'clock in the afternoon of the 15th General Burnside was informed of what was transpiring at Petersburg, and directed to cross the river at once on the ponton bridge, and move up to Harrison's Creek and form on Hancock's left. His advance reached the vicinity of Petersburg on the left of the Second Corps at ten A.M. of the 16th. General Warren at the same time was directed to cross his artillery and trains after Burnside and to begin to cross his troops by ferrying, at daylight of the 16th, and to push forward his corps to Petersburg by divisions as soon as each crossed. By midnight of the 16th the corps halted a few miles from Petersburg.

General Beauregard, during the evening of the 15th, determined to withdraw Johnson's division from the Bermuda

---

[1] It appears to me that General Grant's plan for capturing Petersburg was something like the following, though I am without positive information on the subject. The force holding that town was known to General Butler to be very small, merely the artillery of the works, Wise's brigade, 2,400, with some local militia, to be called from their daily vocations at need, and Dearing's cavalry, 2,000. In the Bermuda Hundred lines there was Johnson's division, which, without Evans's or Elliott's brigade, was 4,500, with it probably 6,800, making a total of 9,000 infantry, or without Evans about 7,000 infantry.

With the return of General Smith's command, General Butler would have 23,000 or 24,000 infantry, and with 3,000 cavalry and 14,000 infantry, with due proportion of artillery, sent with Smith against Petersburg early in the day, and some 10,000 infantry and sufficient artillery at the Bermuda Hundred lines, the capture of Petersburg seemed to be certain. The undertaking might very properly be considered to belong to Butler's command, and apparently it was designed that the Second Corps and such of the troops of the Army of the Potomac as might need to follow, should not take part in the capture, which was most amply provided for, but go into position as a support, where the City Point road crossed Harrison's Creek, so called, which even by the erroneous maps was a mile and a half distant from the Petersburg intrenchments. With this support at hand and such other force as might be needed from the Army of the Potomac, which could be got up quicker than Lee's army, not only the retention of Petersburg seemed to be secured, but more than that.

Hundred lines, leaving at first General Gracie's brigade, about 1,000 strong, to do what he could to hold them until General Lee could reoccupy or retake them. This he telegraphed to General Lee, who received the notice at two A.M. of the 16th, Anderson's corps being then at Malvern Hill, Hill's at Riddell's shop. At four A.M. General Lee had arrived at Drury's Bluff with Pickett's division on its way to the Bermuda Hundred lines, of which he gave notice to Beauregard and to Richmond. Pickett was followed closely by Field, Kershaw remaining at Malvern and Hill at Riddell's shop. At half-past ten A.M. he telegraphed Beauregard that he did not know the position of Grant's army and could not strip the north bank. At three P.M. he telegraphed he had not heard of Grant's crossing James River. At that hour only the Sixth Corps and Wilson's cavalry remained on the north bank.

About ten o'clock in the night of the 15th, Lieutenant-Colonel Greely, Tenth Connecticut, in command of the picket line on the right of Butler's intrenchments, discovered that the enemy were moving in their works, and crawling forward upon his hands and knees close up to their pickets at different points, ascertained, between two and three o'clock in the morning of the 16th, that a large number had withdrawn, and that the movement was still going on. This he reported to General Terry about three o'clock in the morning, and with his sanction advanced at daylight, captured many of the pickets, and finally, though with some resistance, the enemy's main line, taking a large number of prisoners, among them several officers. General Terry at once moved out and took possession of the works.

About six P.M. Pickett's division came upon the ground, driving in our skirmishers, and advanced upon the works, when (General F. A. Osborn says [1]) orders were received from

---

[1] Papers, Massachusetts Military Historical Society.

headquarters to retire, and the command abandoned the works, and withdrew to the line of rifle-pits formerly occupied by their advanced pickets. Pickett assaulted this line about dusk, but was repulsed. The despatches of General Lee to Richmond and to General Beauregard, together with the Diary of General Anderson's Corps, indicate that the whole of the enemy's Bermuda Hundred intrenchments were not retaken on the 16th, but General Osborn is positive that they were, and he was on the ground.

General Johnson's division, whose effective strength, without Gracie's brigade, was 3,500,[1] ought, from the preceding account, to have been in position in the Petersburg intrenchments early on the morning of the 16th. Upon arriving it was placed on the right of Hoke's division, Wise being on the extreme right of the Confederate infantry force, his right not reaching the Jerusalem plank-road by half a mile. From his right westwardly, four and a half miles,[2] to the Appomattox River, the intrenchments, General Beauregard states,[3] were entirely unoccupied, except by a few cavalry pickets stationed there to give him timely notice of danger in that direction. General Dearing's cavalry, he says, were principally occupied outside of the lines on the enemy's (our) left flank, watching his movements to give timely notice of his approach from that direction, which would, he thought, have endangered his command, and compelled him to abandon Petersburg with but little resistance. But with this disposition of Dearing's cavalry he would have had notice of our approach in time to have transferred troops to the unoccupied intrenchments before we could have got up to them. Our attack made in that manner would, however,

---

[1] This number does not include Colonel Elliott's South Carolina brigade, which, from the best information I have been able to get, was 2,300 strong. Both Generals Walker and Evans were wounded on the 20th of May, and were now absent.

[2] Our maps make it five miles.

[3] Papers, Massachusetts Military Historical Society.

have been more likely to succeed than attacking connectedly as we did, though our attacks were now directed against intrenchments thrown up in a night, whereas the works beyond our left were the original, carefully built intrenchments, the character of which has been already stated.

From the right of Wise to the left of Hoke was about five miles. Besides the artillery, General Beauregard probably had about 14,000 effective force of infantry in these intrenchments early on the 16th. He received no further reinforcements until the morning of the 18th, when Kershaw and Field arrived, and, later in the day, Hill.

The Petersburg intrenchments ran from the Appomattox River east, a mile to the City Point Railroad; then south, three miles to the Norfolk Railroad; then west, four miles to a point a mile west of the Weldon Railroad; then north, two miles to the Appomattox River. The length of the intrenchments from the Norfolk Railroad west to the Jerusalem plank-road was a mile and a half.

On the morning of the 16th General Hancock, who was placed in command of all the troops that were up, made reconnoissances in his front, in the course of which, he says, General Egan's brigade made a spirited attack upon a redoubt on Birney's left (Redan No. 12), and carried it in his, Egan's, usual intrepid manner. General Hancock was now ordered to attack in his front at six P.M., General Meade having arrived upon the ground. This programme was carried out, and a spirited assault was made by the Second Corps, supported by two brigades of the Eighteenth on the right, and two of the Ninth on the left, which resulted in the capture of Redans No. 4 on the right, and Nos. 13 and 14 on the left, together with their connecting lines, and in driving back the enemy along the whole line. The attacking force suffered severely. The heavy fighting ceased at dark, but several vigorous attempts were made by the enemy during the night to retake their ground. The gallant commander of the Irish brigade of the Second Corps, Colonel Patrick Kelly, Eighty-eighth New York, was killed, leading his command, and Colonel Beaver, One Hundred and Forty-eighth Pennsylvania, severely wounded.

At the first dawn of day in the morning of the 17th, the division of General Potter (Ninth Corps) carried, in the most gallant manner, the redans and lines on the ridge where the Shind or Shand house stood, capturing four guns, five colors, 600 prisoners, and 1,500 stands of small arms.

The troops, Griffin's and Curtin's brigades of Potter's division, were formed in two lines in a deep ravine with precipitous slopes, close up to the works they were to attack. They were ordered not to fire a shot, but to depend on the bayonet. The command, *Forward*, was passed along the lines in whispers, and the lines, without firing a shot, at once swept over the enemy's works, taking them completely by surprise, and carrying everything before them. The Confederate troops were asleep, with their arms in their hands.[1]

---

[1] General Griffin, in a paper contributed to the Massachusetts Historical Society, says that General Potter entrusted him with the charge of the assault, assigning Curtin's brigade to his support. He says : " I then spent the entire night moving my troops through the felled timber, getting them in proper position, and preparing for the attack. I placed my brigade on the left of the Second Corps in a ravine immediately in front of the Shand house, which the enemy held, and within one hundred yards of their lines, with Curtin on my left and a little further to the rear on account of the conformation of the ground. We were so near the enemy that all our movements had to be made with the utmost care and caution ; canteens were placed in knapsacks to prevent rattling, and all commands were given in whispers. I formed my brigade in two lines. . . . . Colonel Curtin formed his in the same way. . . . . My orders were not to fire a shot, but to depend wholly on the bayonet in carrying the lines.

" Just as the dawn began to light up the east, I gave the command, ' Forward.' It was passed along the lines in whispers, the men sprang to their feet and both brigades moved forward at once in well-formed lines, sweeping directly over the enemy's works, taking them completely by surprise, and carrying all before us.

" One gunner saw us approaching and fired his piece. That was all we heard from them, and almost the only shot fired on either side. The rebels were asleep

The ground in the ravine from which General Potter made his attack was covered thickly with slashed timber, making it difficult to get up Ledlie's division to follow up Potter's success. Potter, however, pushed forward until he found the enemy in a new intrenched position on the west slope of Harrison's Creek, which extended from Redan No. 3, near the Appomattox to the works at and in the vicinity of the Norfolk Railroad.

In the course of the day General Willcox [1] made an attack on this line, but owing to the musketry fire in front, and artillery fire from the left, without success. General Barlow supported him on the right and pushed forward his line with sharp fighting. Late in the afternoon General Ledlie's division (commanded by Colonel Gould, Fifty-ninth Massachusetts) was directed to attack at the point where Willcox had failed. This attack after some time succeeded, a portion of

---

with their arms in their hands, and many of them sprang up and ran away as we came over. Others surrendered without resistance.

" We swept their line for a mile from where my right rested, gathering in prisoners and abandoned arms and equipments all the way. Four pieces of artillery, with caissons and horses, a stand of colors, 600 prisoners, fifteen hundred stand of arms, and some ammunition fell into our hands."

[1] On the morning of the 17th, General Meade requested me to pass the day with General Burnside, who was to attack on the left of the Second Corps. The day before I had examined the enemy's works as far to our left as the Norfolk Railroad, and got the impression that the Ninth Corps would attack there, and the Fifth Corps in the course of the day on its left, that is, about where the Jerusalem plank road passed through the line of works, and where, according to General Beauregard, there were no troops. Not seeing the Ninth Corps anywhere (they were at that time in some of the numerous deep ravines), I rode to the Norfolk Railroad, and remained there some hours, expecting from time to time that the Ninth Corps would arrive. The enemy at the Norfolk Railroad redan seemed uneasy at the presence there of my small party, and kept up a pretty constant fire of shrapnel upon us, but without hurting any one.

Seeing neither the Ninth nor the Fifth Corps, I was satisfied at length that I had mistaken the place of attack, and rode back to where I knew the Second Corps to be, and found General Burnside at battery or Redan No. 14, which had been captured on the afternoon of the 16th, and in front of which General Willcox was attacking. This position was a mile north of the Norfolk Railroad redan. The line of intrenchments under attack by the Second and Ninth Corps was about two miles in extent.

the intrenchments being carried, but only after many casualties. A hundred prisoners and a stand of colors were captured. The attacking force was under a severe musketry fire in front as well as an artillery fire on the right and left, the opposing batteries keeping up a quick and effective fire throughout. The part of the division that carried the line exhausted its ammunition, and was then driven out of the trenches it had captured, General Beauregard says, by Gracie's brigade, which took many prisoners. General Barlow supported the attack of the Ninth Corps on the right, losing heavily ; [1] General Crawford of the Fifth Corps supported the last attack on the left ; Gibbon and Birney pushed forward during the day, making lodgments close to the enemy's intrenchments on the west side of Harrison's Creek. But at midnight the enemy still held from the Appomattox to Redan No. 3, their intrenchments from that point running south along the high ground west of Harrison's Creek to the Norfolk Railroad.

During the 17th General Beauregard determined to withdraw in the night from the position he was holding, across a ravine five hundred yards in his rear, where his line of battle would be much shortened, and the position would be advantageous. He sent his Chief Engineer, Colonel D. B. Harris of Virginia, to lay out the line and make all the preliminary arrangements with staff officers of the generals of his command. The new line was from five hundred to one thousand yards in rear of the one he was occupying, and intersected

---

[1] It is stated that this capture was made at or before sunset, and the intrenchments held until ten o'clock, but I think it must have been later when the enemy's line was penetrated, as I witnessed the contest from a near point of view, and the attack had not succeeded up to the time of my leaving the Ninth Corps, which was after dark. Nor does it seem probable that it was held so long as stated, for General Burnside was near at hand, and General Warren not far off, and we cannot suppose that either would have failed to throw forward more troops at once when they learnt the intrenchment was carried. The line was probably retaken before either knew it had been captured.

the original line of intrenchments in the vicinity of the Jeru-salem plank road. He withdrew to it after midnight, and the work of intrenchment at once began.

When General Grant learnt on the 16th that General Butler occupied Beauregard's Bermuda Hundred lines, being anxious that they should be held, and a footing on the rail-road secured, he directed General Meade to send General Wright with two of his divisions by boat to General Butler, when they abandoned the crossing-place of the army. Ac-cordingly they embarked at midnight, and on the morning of the 17th General Wright reported with them to General Butler, but Beauregard's lines were then held by Pickett and Field, and General Wright was directed to support Gen-eral Terry in an attack upon them. The attack, however, giving no great promise of success, was not made.

About two o'clock in the afternoon of the 17th, General Lee telegraphed General Beauregard :

" The Fifth Corps, Warren's, crossed the Chickahominy at Long Bridge on the 13th—was driven from Riddel's shop by Hill, leaving many dead and prisoners on our hands. That night it marched to Westover. . . . Have not heard from it since. . . ."

At half past three he telegraphed General W. H. F. Lee, at Malvern Hill, to push after the enemy and endeavor to as-certain what had become of Grant's army, and to inform General Hill.

At half-past four he telegraphed General Hill at Riddell's shop that General Beauregard reported that large numbers of Grant's troops had crossed James River above Fort Pow-hatan the day before, and, if he had nothing contradictory of it to move to Chapin's Bluff.

At five o'clock he telegraphed Mr. Davis at Richmond, that at four o'clock he had assaulted that portion of his Ber-muda Hundred front line held by the enemy, and had driven him from it, and that he held the entire line.

General Osborn, whom I have already quoted, on the contrary, says that at daybreak of the 17th the enemy again assaulted their line (their original advance picket line, now strengthened and held by them in force), and were repulsed, and that at four P.M. the enemy made another fierce attack, *and for a time gained some little advantage, breaking into the line and driving back a part of it.* But this was soon regained.

Beauregard had made urgent calls upon Lee for troops, and Kershaw having arrived at the Bermuda lines, marched at three o'clock in the morning of the 18th for Petersburg, followed by Field, leaving Pickett to hold the lines. Both were in position on Beauregard's right in the morning, Kershaw relieving Johnson's division, Field on his right. General Lee arrived with them. Hill got up in the course of the day, and was posted on the right of Anderson.

Late at night on the 17th General Meade ordered an assault in strong columns, well supported, upon the enemy's works at four o'clock in the following morning, by the Fifth, Ninth, and Second Corps.

Brigadier-General Neill, temporarily commanding the Second Division of the Sixth Corps, had relieved the Eighteenth Corps on the 17th, except Martindale's division, and General Smith returned to General Butler at Bermuda Hundred. Martindale and Neill were held ready to support an attack.

Upon advancing to the assault on the morning of the 18th, it was found that the enemy had abandoned the intrenchments they had so successfully held the day before. The ground in front of the points assaulted was thickly covered with the killed, and the trenches at those points were filled with Confederate dead.

Finding the line abandoned, General Meade at once ordered the army to press forward and attack before reinforcements could arrive, for he had learnt from prisoners that Beauregard's intrenchments were merely such as he had been able to put up after occupying his new position, and they must necessarily be imperfect. He had also learnt from the same source what force Beauregard actually had. This information was communicated to the corps commanders, but before any assault was made Anderson's corps, Field's and Kershaw's divisions, was in position, and before the assaults in the afternoon Hill's troops had begun to arrive.

General Birney was temporarily in command of the Second Corps, General Hancock being disabled by the opening of his wound in the evening of the 17th.

The Second Corps found itself sooner than the other troops close to the enemy's new intrenchments, being at the Hare house (near which were both the enemy's new and abandoned lines), only some three hundred yards distant. Its advance was in great part concealed by woods. The Ninth Corps, on the left of the Second, had to advance nearly a mile, when it found itself in contact with a force of the enemy occupying the Norfolk Railroad cut, and a ravine some four or five hundred yards in advance of and nearly parallel with their main line. The Fifth Corps, on the left of the Ninth, had a still greater distance to advance over, and had similar obstacles in its front interposed between it and the enemy's main line as the Ninth Corps, that is, deep ravines and the Norfolk Railroad cut, which was here very deep and difficult to cross, and was held by the enemy at its northern end. Its direction was such, curving to the north, as to embarrass troops advancing in line of battle. General Meade, finding that serious delays were occurring from the attempt to make a simultaneous attack, without fixing the hour, owing to the different conditions existing on the fronts of the several corps, fixed it himself and ordered all the corps to attack at twelve o'clock, with strong columns of assault. Birney carried out this order, making two assaults about midday, with Gibbon's division, on the right of the Prince George Court

House road, both of which were repulsed with severe loss, Brigadier-General Pierce and Colonel Ramsey, brigade commanders, being wounded.

General Burnside was occupied in endeavoring to drive the enemy out of the railroad cut in his front as a necessary preliminary to getting close enough to the intrenchments to assault. General Warren was similarly engaged. The ground he had to pass over was intricate and difficult to cross, and being chiefly in open ground, was exposed to the enemy's artillery fire for a long distance. General Meade again ordered assaults by all the corps, with their whole force at all hazards, as soon as possible, as he found it useless to appoint an hour to effect co-operation. All the corps assaulted late in the afternoon, and at hours not widely apart, General Birney with all his disposable force—Mott from the Hare house, on the left of the Prince George Court House road, supported by one of Gibbon's brigades, Barlow on Mott's left—but was repulsed with considerable loss.

General Burnside found the task of driving the enemy out of the railroad cut a formidable one, but succeeded, and, assaulting, established his corps within a hundred yards of the enemy's main line. He praises highly the manner in which Potter's and Willcox's divisions, under Major-General Parke's directions, accomplished this.

General Warren's assault was well made, some of Griffin's men being killed within twenty feet of the enemy's works, but it was no more successful than the others. His losses were very severe. Among the desperately wounded was Colonel Chamberlain, of the Twentieth Maine, who led his brigade under a destructive fire. On previous occasions he had been recommended for promotion for gallant conduct and efficient service.

On the right, Martindale advanced and gained some rifle-pits, but did not assault the main line.

The positions gained by the several corps close against the enemy were intrenched, and the two opposing lines in this part of the ground remained substantially the same in position to the close of the war.

Toward evening General Meade had reason to believe that General Beauregard had been reinforced by Lee's army, and that reinforcements were still arriving.

At the close of the day General Grant, expressing himself perfectly satisfied that all had been done that could be done, and that the assaults were called for by all the information that could be obtained, directed that the troops should be put under cover and have some rest, which, indeed, they greatly needed.

The Medical Director states that during this attempt to take Petersburg, from the 15th to the 18th of June, the number of wounded brought to the hospitals from the different corps was: from the Second Corps, 2,212; from the Fifth Corps, 1,145; from the Ninth Corps, 1,197; and, in addition, 1,656, the corps of which he does not note. This makes a total brought to the hospitals of 6,210. Taking the usual proportion for the killed, we have 1,240, and killed and wounded, 7,450. The number of killed and wounded of the Eighteenth Corps is not included. It was probably not less than 700.[1]

This makes the loss in killed and wounded to be 8,150. The Tabular Statement of the " Medical and Surgical History " has under the head of " Missing," 1,814. The total is then 9,964.

The figures of the Tabular Statement are: killed, 1,298; wounded, 7,474; killed and wounded, 8,772; missing, 1,814. Total loss, 10,586. The stragglers are probably included in these numbers.

---

[1] The class the Medical Director designates as stragglers wounded, that is, who, slightly wounded, will not report to the hospitals, but try to straggle away, must have numbered five or six hundred; they are not included in the figures above.

I can find no official statement of the losses of Lee's and Beauregard's troops during these operations, but notwithstanding that they were intrenched, my own observation leads me to believe they were severe.

The incessant movements, day and night, for so long a period, the constant close contact with the enemy during all that time, the almost daily assaults upon intrenchments having entanglements in front, and defended by artillery and musketry in front and flank, exhausted officers and men. The larger part of the officers, who literally led their commands, were killed or wounded, and a large number of those that filled the ranks at the beginning of the campaign were absent. It is unreasonable to suppose that the troops were not, for a time, so exhausted as to need rest, and equally unreasonable to suppose that their opponents were not in a similar condition, though to a less degree, since they had not marched so much at night nor attacked intrenchments.

10*

CHAPTER VIII.

MOVEMENT AGAINST THE WELDON AND SOUTH SIDE
RAILROADS—THE CAVALRY ENGAGEMENTS IN THE
VICINITY OF TREVYLIAN STATION ON THE VIR-
GINIA CENTRAL RAILROAD, AND REAMS'S STATION
ON THE WELDON RAILROAD—THE CASUALTIES IN
THE ARMY OF THE POTOMAC FROM THE COM-
MENCEMENT OF THE CAMPAIGN UNTIL THE 30TH
OF JUNE—THE DEMONSTRATION AGAINST WASH-
INGTON.

IT was now determined to invest Petersburg partially by a
line of intrenchments directed toward the Lynchburg (South
Side) Railroad. These intrenchments were to consist of redoubts connected by lines of infantry parapets, with ditches
and entanglements of slashing or abatis, which the army
might be withdrawn from at any time, leaving a sufficient
force to hold them, and move to intercept the railroads and
attack Lee's army in unexpected quarters south, or even
north, of the James. The work of intrenching went on on
both sides, at first with constant picket and artillery firing.
The Confederate intrenchments were similar to ours except
that their works were not closed in the rear.

General Kautz had returned to General Butler in the night
of the 16th and 17th, and a small cavalry force watched the
left of the army. The two divisions of the Sixth Corps were
returned to the Army of the Potomac on the evening of the
19th.

On the 21st the Ninth Corps extended its right to the

Prince George Court House road at the Hare house, so as to join the troops of the Eighteenth Corps, and relieve the Second and Sixth Corps. The right of the Fifth Corps joined the left of the Ninth; its left, on the evening of the 21st, rested on the Jerusalem plank-road, where, a short time afterward, Fort Sedgwick was built.

The Second Corps, followed by the Sixth, was moved, on the 21st, across the Jerusalem plank-road, with the intention of taking possession of the Weldon Railroad on the next day, and with the expectation of securing the Lynchburg or South Side Railroad. The Second Corps was placed in position on the left of the Fifth, the Sixth Corps at night being in rear of the left of the Second. During the day General Barlow made a reconnoissance toward the Weldon Railroad, and a considerable force of the enemy moved down the road to meet it.

General Birney was instructed by General Meade, on the 21st, that he was to take position on the left of the Fifth Corps, and extend as far as practicable to the left, enveloping and keeping as close as possible to the enemy's line; that it was hoped he would be able to get possession of the Weldon Railroad, though it was probable the enemy would attempt to cover and defend it; that the Sixth Corps would be sent at night to take post on his left, and that it was desired to stretch to the Appomattox.

On the evening of the 21st General Wright was directed by General Meade to take position on the left of Birney, and pressing up against the enemy, drive them into their main works, but not to take the offensive so far as to assault them;[1] that General Birney was forming on Warren's left, which rested on the Jerusalem plank-road, and would extend as far as possible, holding his line defensively; that the ob-

---

[1] The enemy's intrenchments west of the Jerusalem plank-road were the original works, running here east and west.

ject of the transfer of the two corps to the left was to encir-
cle Petersburg so far as to hold the two railroads, the Weldon and the Lynchburg; that he would therefore extend
from Birney's left as far as practicable consistent with its
security as a defensive line.

In order that the enveloping line should be at a suitable
distance from the Confederate works, General Birney, commanding the Second Corps, was further directed, on the 22d,
to swing forward its left, the right of Gibbon's division,
which connected with the Fifth Corps, being the pivot, and
then intrench; and General Wright was directed to move to
the Weldon Railroad by the Williams house road (the distance between the Jerusalem plank-road and the Weldon
Railroad being about three miles), get possession of the railroad and intrench, connecting with Birney. At first these
corps commanders were directed to keep up connection; but
as that led to misapprehensions between their troops and to
delays, they were ordered to move irrespective of each other,
taking the requisite precaution to insure the safety of their
exposed flanks. The two corps were moving chiefly through
densely-wooded thickets, the Second Corps to the edge of
the open ground in front of the enemy's works, the Sixth
Corps nearly at right angles to it, toward the Weldon Railroad near the Globe tavern. The enemy's skirmishers were
very active and embarrassing on the front and flank of the
Sixth Corps, the main line of which did not advance more
than half-way to the railroad. It was late in the afternoon
before General Gibbon had intrenched his part of the new
line, General Mott was still at work upon his, General Barlow was only partially in position, but General Birney had
not taken the requisite precautions to secure his left in
swinging forward.

General A. P. Hill had been sent down the Weldon Railroad to meet Meade's attempt upon it, having Wilcox's and

Mahone's divisions with him, supported by B. R. Johnson's. Leaving Wilcox to make head against Wright, he passed through the opening between Birney and Wright, and the first information Birney had of his presence was a fire upon the flank and rear of Barlow's division, which sent it back in some confusion to the position it had in the morning; and with the loss of many prisoners. Mott's division, partly seeing what had occurred, went back precipitately also to the position from which it had advanced, and by doing so lost much fewer prisoners than Barlow's division, but left Gibbon's division, without any warning, to receive a fire in the rear of its left brigade, which at once followed the example of the troops on its left, and abandoned a battery of four guns on its right to the enemy, who quickly turned it on them. So sudden and unexpected was this attack on Gibbon's left, that the greater part of several regiments were captured with their colors. An immediate attempt was made by General Gibbon to recover his line, but without success. He lost about as many prisoners as the First Division, the total loss of the corps being about 1,700 prisoners, four guns, and several colors. The loss in killed and wounded was not severe. Hill returned to his intrenchments at dusk, leaving some force on the railroad.

The Second Corps was thrown forward that evening, but it was not until early the next morning that it advanced and established itself on the line it had been driven from. The Sixth Corps formed on its left, thrown back facing the Weldon Railroad, and about a mile and a half from it, its picket line close to the road.

In this general position the two armies remained for some weeks. Two strong redoubts were built on the line running south on the Jerusalem plank-road, about half a mile apart, the first, Fort Davis, being half a mile from Fort Sedgwick. They were finished and occupied about the 11th of July.

By this time the musketry and artillery fire, which had been continuous on the lines from the Appomattox to the left of the Fifth Corps, and was especially severe on the Ninth Corps front, where the two lines were very close to each other, had gradually ceased during the day, but was con- tinued during the night, because of the danger of a surprise.[1]

It has been already stated that on the morning of the 7th of June, General Sheridan, with two of his divisions, with certain supplies, train, and a canvas ponton bridge equipage, marched for Charlottesville, from which point he was to be- gin the destruction of the Central Railroad, and to continue it to Hanover Junction, which being accomplished, he was to rejoin the Army of the Potomac. It was expected that he would meet General Hunter at Charlottesville, and that both forces would join the Army of the Potomac when the de- struction of the railroad was completed.

Moving up the north bank of the North Anna, General Sheridan crossed that river on the evening of the 10th at Carpenter's ford and encamped there for the night on the road to Trevylian Station (on the Central Railroad), which was nine or ten miles distant in a southwest direction. On the 9th he had learnt that Breckinridge's infantry division was moving slowly up the railroad to Gordonsville,[2] and that the enemy's cavalry were marching on Gordonsville by the Richmond and Gordonsville road, on the south side of the North Anna.

General Hampton with his division encamped on the night of the 10th in Green Spring Valley, three miles north- west of Trevylian Station ; Fitzhugh Lee near Louisa Court House, about six miles east of Trevylian Station. Hearing

---

[1] The men themselves gave each other notice, upon the approach of night, be- fore they commenced firing.

[2] This was erroneous. Breckinridge, according to Confederate authorities, moved direct from Cold Harbor to Lynchburg, a very important point for the Confederates to hold against Hunter.

during the night where General Sheridan's force was, General Hampton determined to attack it at Clayton's store, which is on the road from Carpenter's ford to Trevylian Station, and about equidistant from both. His division was to move by way of the station, Fitz Lee's by a direct road from Louisa Court House to the store, a march of about six miles. By this movement General Hampton expected also to prevent General Sheridan from reaching Gordonsville by passing his left. At daylight Hampton had reached Trevylian Station and was moving out the road to Clayton's store with two of his brigades, Butler's and Young's, Rosser's advancing in the same direction by a road on his left. Fitz Lee was moving from Louisa Court House to the same point, but separated by several miles from Hampton. Movements of this character are always risky when the opponent is enterprising, and especially so in a wooded country, so favorable to concealed enterprises.

Hampton and Lee met Sheridan's forces before reaching Clayton's store, and before uniting, for General Sheridan, advancing on the morning of the 11th on the road to Trevylian Station, Torbert's division leading, encountered Hampton's division about three miles from Trevylian Station, in dense timber, and, General Sheridan says, behind a line of breastworks. General Custer was now sent by a wood road on his left to Hampton's rear, to attack the horses of his troops that were fighting on foot. Custer passed unnoticed between Hampton and Lee, and got to Trevylian Station unopposed. General Sheridan says that as soon as he learnt this, the two remaining brigades of Torbert's division were dismounted, assailed the enemy's works, and carried them, driving Hampton's division pell-mell, and at a run, back on Custer at Trevylian Station, some of it through Custer's lines, and that Custer commenced fighting in all directions, capturing many of Hampton's men. Gregg in the meantime

attacked Fitz Lee on the Louisa Court House road, drove
him in that direction, and continued the pursuit until night.
Hampton's division made its way in the direction of Gordonsville, and was joined by Fitz Lee during the night, he
making a detour for that purpose. General Sheridan encamped at Trevylian Station.[1]

General Hampton says of this encounter, that whilst he
was driving the enemy in his front, who at first had taken
position behind works, he found that Custer's brigade had got
in his rear, passing between his division and Lee's. "This
forced me," he says, "to withdraw in front, and to take up
a new line. This was soon done, and the brigade which attacked me in rear, Custer's, was severely punished, for I recalled Rosser's brigade, which charged them in front, driving
them back against General Lee, who was moving up to
Trevylian's, and capturing many prisoners. In this sudden
attack on my rear the enemy captured some of my led horses,
a few ambulances and wagons, and three caissons. These
were all recaptured by General Ros er and General Lee, the
latter taking, in addition, four caissons, and the headquarters
wagon of Brigadier-General Custer.[2] My new line being established, I directed General Lee to join me with his command as soon as possible. The enemy tried to dislodge me
from my new position, but failed, and the relative positions
of the opposing forces remained the same during the night.
The next day, at twelve M., General Lee reported to me, and

---

[1] See General Sheridan's report for this account.

[2] Upon meeting General Ewell in Philadelphia in the autumn of 1865, his first
inquiry was concerning the orders of movement issued from the Headquarters of
the Army of the Potomac; and he stated that in Custer's baggage, captured at
Trevylian Station in June, 1864, copies were found of the series of orders from
those headquarters directing the movements of the Army of the Potomac in the
campaign then going on, and he asked several questions concerning them, for he
thought both the orders and the system of furnishing them to the general officers
of the army admirable, adding that they had nothing of that kind in the Army of
Northern Virginia.

his division was placed so as to support mine in case the
enemy attacked." General Hampton's new position was evidently west of Trevylian Station.

It is apparent from these accounts that General Hampton was defeated and driven several miles from the position he had determined to hold against Sheridan's further
advance.

At night General Sheridan learnt from prisoners (he had
captured about 500) that General Hunter was moving on
Lynchburg; that Ewell's corps was on its way there, moving
by the south side of James River;[1] and that General Breckinridge was at Gordonsville or Charlottesville, having passed
up the railroad. He therefore determined to return, and especially as another engagement would have reduced the supply of ammunition to a very small amount.

The conclusion of Sheridan on the night of the 12th was
evidently sound; the movement of Hunter had rendered it
impracticable for him to carry out his orders in the presence
of Hampton. Hampton's being there accomplished the object of General Lee in sending him.

On the morning of the 12th Gregg's division was set to
work destroying the railroad toward Louisa Court House,
and in the afternoon Torbert was sent up the Gordonsville
road to secure a by-road leading over Mallory's ford of the
North Anna to the Catharpin road, as General Sheridan intended to return by way of Spottsylvania Court House and
the White House. Torbert, he says, became heavily engaged
with the enemy, the battle continuing until after dark, and
the result made it impossible to cross at Mallory's ford next
day without a battle, in which case his ammunition would
have been consumed, leaving none to get back with.

During the night of the 12th he moved back, recrossing

---

[1] The information about Ewell's corps was altogether erroneous.

the North Anna at Carpenter's ford, leaving three hospitals with 90 of his own wounded not transportable, and many of the enemy's, carrying with him, in such vehicles as could be collected in the country, about 500 of his own wounded. He also carried with him about 500 prisoners. He reached the White House on the 21st, where he found supplies, and drove off such of Hampton's force as were attacking General Abercrombie.

General Hampton says that "at 3.30 P.M. (of the 12th) a heavy attack was made on my left, where Butler's brigade was posted. Being repulsed, the enemy made a succession of determined assaults, which were all handsomely repulsed. In the meantime General Lee had, by my direction, reinforced Butler's left with Wickham's brigade, while he took Lomax's across to the Gordonsville road so as to strike the enemy on his right flank.[1] This movement was successful, and the enemy, who had been heavily punished in front, when attacked on his flank, fell back in confusion," etc. "I immediately gave orders to follow him up, but it was daylight before these orders could be carried out, the fight not having ended until ten P.M. In this interval the enemy had withdrawn entirely," etc. "We captured, in addition to the wounded in the fight and pursuit, 570 prisoners. My loss, in my own division, was 59 killed, 258 wounded, and 295 missing—total, 612." Among the killed of his division was Lieutenant-Colonel McAllister, Seventh Georgia, "who behaved with great gallantry." Among the wounded was Brigadier-General Rosser, while charging at the head of his brigade, Colonel Aiken, Sixth South Carolina, and Lieutenant-Colonel King, Cobb Legion (Georgia).

The loss of General Lee's division is not given.

General Hampton moved to the White House, keeping on

---

[1] Lee's cavalry dismounted were mistaken by General Torbert and General Sheridan for infantry.

the south side of the North Anna, having, he says, no pontons.[1]

The dépôt at White House was broken up on the 22d, and
a train of nine hundred wagons set out under cover of General Sheridan to cross the James on the ponton bridge at
Bermuda Hundred. It crossed the Chickahominy at Jones's
bridge and moved to Charles City Court House, en route
past Malvern Hill, in advance of which were Hampton and
Fitz Lee. Holding Torbert with the train, Gregg was sent
to St. Mary's Church to cover the exposed flank, and, General Hampton says, intrenched in a strong position. There,
on the 24th, he was attacked by Hampton and Lee in front
and on his right flank, and after a stubborn fight, which
lasted until after dark, was forced to give way, when he
retired in some confusion, pursued by the enemy to within
two and a half miles of Charles City Court House.

The trains were moved back to Douthard's Landing on the
25th, and were ferried over the James, the cavalry following
them. On the 26th, before their crossing was completed,
General Meade directed General Sheridan as soon as he had
crossed to take position on the Jerusalem plank-road on the
left flank of the army, and on the 27th to join the army as
soon as practicable to aid the return of General Wilson. A
force of more than 1,000 cavalry had been seen on the morning of the 27th moving south from Petersburg, near the
Weldon Railroad. It was a part of W. H. F. Lee's division.
Respecting this movement of the trains, General Meade was
of opinion that Sheridan would not get to the Bermuda Hundred ponton bridge in the face of Hampton, unless he was
able to give him a serious defeat.

When it was perceived by the enemy that General Sheridan was crossing the James, General Hampton and General

---

[1] See Appendix I, for some remarks on General Hampton's report.

Fitz Lee were ordered to Drury's Bluff, where they arrived on the evening of the 26th, and, on the following morning, were directed against General Wilson, who was engaged in a raid upon the Petersburg and Lynchburg and Richmond and Danville railroads.

Resting a few days after crossing James River, General Wilson was directed to move at two o'clock in the morning of the 22d by the shortest routes to the intersection of the Petersburg and Lynchburg, and Richmond and Danville railroads at Burkesville, and destroy both those roads to the greatest extent possible, continuing their destruction until driven from it by such attacks of the enemy as he could no longer resist. He was informed that the destruction of those roads to such an extent that they could not be used by the enemy in connection with Richmond during the remainder of the campaign was an important part in the plan of campaign. He was notified that General Sheridan had reached the White House, and that General Hampton was before that place, and that, for that reason, he should march out at the earliest moment.[1] He was also informed that General Hunter was, according to most recent intelligence, near Lynchburg. General Meade in his correspondence with General Grant stated that he trusted General Sheridan would keep General Hampton occupied on the north bank of the James during General Wilson's raid.[2]

---

[1] See Appendix J, for General Wilson's instructions.

[2] In the evening of the 21st I received a despatch from General Wilson, acknowledging the receipt of his orders, and stating in what manner he should carry them out. He inquired: "Before starting I would like to know if our infantry forces cross the Weldon Road?" To this I replied that they did not, but that we should take that road the next day, the 22d, and that we expected to take possession of the Petersburg and Lynchburg Railroad soon after. At this day I hold the same opinion that I held then, that we ought to have taken possession of the Weldon Railroad on the 22d, and have made the attempt upon the Lynchburg Railroad immediately afterward, though the possession of that road, owing to its great importance to the enemy, could only be gained by a heavy battle. Respecting the extent of his raid, he remarked, "If Sheridan will look after Hampton, I appre-

General Wilson set out on the expedition against the rail-roads as ordered, his force consisting of his own division and Kautz's, the whole numbering about 5,500.

Crossing the Weldon Railroad at Reams's Station, which was destroyed, he reached the Lynchburg Railroad about fourteen miles from Petersburg. From this point to the crossing of the Danville Railroad, at Burkesville, thirty miles of the Lynchburg Railroad was destroyed. At the Burkesville Junction everything was destroyed, and the command then turned to and moved along the Danville Railroad, destroying it as they advanced, until they reached Staunton River, by which time about thirty miles of this road also were destroyed.

General W. H. F. Lee with his cavalry division had fol-lowed Wilson closely, and on the Lynchburg Railroad, near Nottoway Court House, interposed between Wilson and Kautz, bringing on a sharp engagement, but did not materi-ally interfere with the destruction of the roads.

At Staunton River the bridge was guarded on the south bank by a large force of militia, intrenched, with artillery. The river was not fordable. Kautz attacked, but could not gain possession of the bridge. At the same time Lee at-tacked Wilson in rear. Finding that he could not push further south (he was now nearly one hundred miles from Petersburg), General Wilson determined to return, and, marching at midnight, moved eastward eighty miles or more, through Christiansburg and Greensborough, crossing the Meherrin River at Saffold's bridge, and arrived at the Double bridges over the Nottoway River at noon of the 28th. This point is about thirty miles south, and eight or ten west

hend no difficulty and hope to be able to do the enemy great damage." Regard-ing this condition, having already informed him that Sheridan and Hampton were at and near White House, I referred as an assurance that they would con-tinue near each other to Hampton's close contact with Sheridan since early in June. See Appendix J, for General Wilson's letter.

of Petersburg, and ten miles west of the Weldon Railroad at Jarratt's Station. The left of the Army of the Potomac was not across the Weldon Railroad, but about two miles east of it. This, however, General Wilson had no means of knowing; on the contrary, he had every reason to believe that we held the road. But if we had taken the Lynchburg Railroad he would necessarily have heard of it from the people of the country, since it would have been necessary to fight a battle for its possession, an event that would have been known far and wide.

At the Double bridges General Wilson learned that there was only a small force of the enemy's cavalry and infantry at Stony Creek Dépôt on the Weldon Railroad, about ten miles northeast of him. The road from Double bridges to Prince George Court House, Wilson's most direct route to the rear of the army, passes two miles west of this dépôt, intersecting there the road from the dépôt to Dinwiddie Court House, and as he could learn of no other force being there than the small one mentioned, General Wilson moved rapidly to that point.

General W. H. F. Lee, who had continued to follow Wilson closely, kept General Lee well informed of Wilson's route. To intercept him on his return General Hampton was sent on the 27th to Stony Creek Dépôt, which he reached at midday on the 28th, finding there General Chambliss's brigade of W. H. F. Lee's division. General Fitz Lee followed General Hampton as far as Reams's Station, where also, at the suggestion of General Hampton, Mahone, with two of his brigades of infantry, and some artillery, was subsequently posted. Reams's Station is about ten miles north of Stony Creek Dépôt, and the same distance south of Petersburg. It was between eight and ten miles from our left by the road we must take.

When General Wilson arrived at the crossing of the Stony

Creek Dépôt and Dinwiddie Court House road, near Sappony Church, he was attacked in force by Hampton, the fight continuing until ten o'clock at night. Finding so strong a force in his front, General Wilson endeavored to evade it by moving westward to the old stage-road to Petersburg (called the Halifax road), Kautz being sent in advance. But it was daylight before he could begin to withdraw his own division. His first line he withdrew, but before he could withdraw his second, Hampton attacked its left flank with Butler's and Rosser's brigades, while his other force attacked its front, driving it to the rear, and separating it for a time from the other part of Wilson's command. Following Wilson closely for two miles, and seeing in what direction he was moving, General Hampton turned back and moved past Stony Creek Dépôt so as to get on the Halifax road and intercept Wilson should he try to cross the Weldon Railroad south of Reams's Station, but Wilson's main force had already passed before Hampton gained the Halifax road, and he encountered only the rear of Wilson's column. Kautz arrived at Reams's Station early in the morning of the 29th, and finding Fitz Lee's cavalry there, he intrenched, expecting assistance from General Meade, to whom Captain Whitaker of General Wilson's staff was sent. This officer dashed through a thin part of the enemy's lines, losing half his escort, and reached General Meade's headquarters on the Jerusalem plank-road, about eight miles from Reams's Station, between ten and eleven o'clock. When Wilson joined Kautz he learnt that the Weldon Railroad was not in our possession, and the enemy's infantry now made their appearance.

Finding himself so nearly surrounded with so heavy a force,[1] he issued all his ammunition, destroyed his wagons

---

[1] According to the Return of the Army of Northern Virginia of July 10, 1864, there were 8,962 officers and enlisted men of cavalry present for duty. The Return of June 30 is imperfect.

and caissons, and at noon began to move back by way of the stage (Halifax) road and Double bridges to the south side of the Nottoway River, intending, after he had crossed that river, to move eastward some twenty miles before turning north again toward Petersburg.   General Fitz Lee, screened by woods, had moved his division, part of it dismounted, past Wilson's left, and when Mahone attacked Wilson's covering force in front, and broke in between Kautz and McIntosh, Lee took McIntosh in flank and reverse, and Wilson's whole rear was thrown into confusion.   Kautz, finding that he could not reach the stage-road and reunite with Wilson, endeavored to get around the enemy's left, which he succeeded in doing without opposition, crossed the railroad between Reams's Station and Rowanty Creek, and reached the lines of the Army of the Potomac after dark.   As he passed through woods, his artillery could not get through with him, and was abandoned in a swamp, the guns spiked. McIntosh, of Wilson's division, succeeded in forming a strong rear guard, though Maynadier's battery was abandoned in woods.

At Stony Creek the enemy made a vigorous push, opening with artillery, and throwing the rear into some confusion, but the troops got over.   A thousand negroes who had followed Wilson were necessarily abandoned.   After crossing Stony Creek the contest was not renewed, and General Wilson succeeded in crossing the Nottoway River between ten and eleven o'clock at night without serious opposition.   He then moved eastward to Jarratt's Station, where he halted until daylight of the 30th.   Continuing his march eastward, he crossed the Nottoway again at Peters's bridge, where he rested five or six hours, resuming his march at half-past six in the evening for Blunt's bridge over the Blackwater.   The bridge was in great part destroyed, and the river not fordable.   Cutting string-pieces from the woods, he repaired the bridge, crossed over and destroyed it, for Hampton and Fitz Lee were following him. Here their pursuit ended, and General Wilson arrived at Light House Point in the afternoon of the 2d of July, having been gone ten and a half days, during which time he had marched over three hundred miles, and destroyed sixty miles of railroad. At no place had he rested more than six hours, and for the last four days at no time longer than four hours. Great credit, he says, was due the officers and men for their endurance, sleepless exertions, and gallantry.

His casualties in both divisions were 240 killed and wounded, and 1,261 missing, making a total of 1,501. Twelve guns were abandoned; his wagons were burnt or captured.

Kautz says all his efficient men came through; 1,000 of Wilson's division came with him, while 500 of his men came in with Wilson. For nine days and nights, he says, his men were in the saddle, or destroying railroads, and were so tired they fell asleep under fire; many were captured asleep on the road.

Captain Whitaker brought General Meade the first intelligence he had received from General Wilson since he had set out on his expedition. A division of the Sixth Corps was at once sent to Wilson's assistance, followed by the whole corps as soon as it could be drawn out of its lines. The corps was at Reams's Station that afternoon, but the enemy had withdrawn before the leading division reached there. General Sheridan, who was moving up from Fort Powhatan, near which he had crossed the James, was also ordered to Reams's Station, but, as already stated, the enemy's infantry withdrew at once to their lines, and their cavalry by circuitous routes on the 1st of July.

Notwithstanding our attempts to destroy the Confederate lines of supply, they still remained sufficient for the wants of the Confederacy. The Virginia Central Railroad, with its connections along the Valley of Virginia and with Lynchburg, remained under their control, and there were large supplies of food in southwestern Virginia. There was railroad communication also from Lynchburg to the crossing of the Danville Railroad at Burkesville, and thence by the Danville Railroad to Richmond. The Weldon Railroad remained in their hands, the injuries to it being soon repaired. The repair of the two roads injured by Wilson was begun at once.

There has been some discussion, perhaps controversy, as to the casualties in the Army of the Potomac from the beginning of the campaign in May until June 30th, or until a later day.

From May 4th to June 19th, including the Eighteenth Corps at Cold Harbor and Petersburg, the total killed were 8,802; wounded, 40,518; missing, 9,544. Total, killed, wounded, and missing, 58,864. Deducting the killed, wounded, and missing of the Eighteenth Corps (2,700), we have for the Army of the Potomac, 56,164 killed, wounded, and missing. To these must be added the casualties of Sheridan on the Trevylian Station expedition, and of Wilson on his raid: that is 840 killed and wounded, and over 1,400 missing. The losses of the infantry corps before Petersburg, from the 20th to the 30th of June, were not less than 1,000 killed and wounded and 2,000 missing; making a total of the Army of the Potomac to that date of 61,400, and of killed and wounded nearly 50,000.

Tne Army of the James lost during this period, not including the smaller actions on the picket line, killed, wounded, and missing, 4,203, exclusive of the losses of the Eighteenth Corps at Cold Harbor and before Petersburg from the 15th to the 30th of June. Including the losses of that corps the number was 6,903.

A large number of sick were sent from the army during this period.

The information that I have been able to collect concerning

the casualties in the Army of Northern Virginia during that period does not admit of any precise or even general statement concerning them. It was evidently their policy not to make public their losses, and the few official data to be got concerning them do not afford the means of making any comparative statement.

The weather had become oppressively hot. No rain fell from the 3d of June to the 19th of July, a period of forty-seven days. There was no surface-water; the springs, the marshes, the ponds, and even streams of some magnitude were dry. The dust was several inches thick upon the roads and bare plains, and the passage of troops or trains over them raised great clouds of fine dust. Any movement of troops occasioned severe suffering among them. But the surface-soil was porous, and at no great depth below it were strata of clay or marly clay, where there was abundance of cool water that did not prove unhealthy ; and the troops, wherever they halted at once sunk wells.

General Breckinridge and General Early arrived at Lynchburg in time to prevent General Hunter from gaining possession of the town. After remaining two days in front of it, General Hunter withdrew on the 19th of June, and retreated by way of the Great Kanawha River, the Ohio River, and the Baltimore and Ohio Railroad to Harper's Ferry. This left the Shenandoah Valley open for several weeks, and General Early moved down it to make his demonstration against Washington. To meet General Early's movement, General Ricketts, with his division of the Sixth Corps, was sent to Baltimore, arriving there on the morning of the 8th of July, and going by rail to the Monocacy near the crossing of the Baltimore and Ohio Railroad, where he joined the Commander of the Department, General Wallace, who had moved from Baltimore to meet General Early. His troops were mostly new and undisciplined.

General Early crossed the Potomac near Shepherdstown, moved through the passes of South Mountain, and on the 9th attacked and defeated General Wallace, who then fell back upon Baltimore.[1] The next day General Early moved toward Washington, the head of his command arriving before it on the Seventh Street road, its north front, by the afternoon of the 11th.

At midnight of the 9th General Wright, with Getty's and Russell's divisions of the Sixth Corps,[2] marched to City Point and embarked for Washington, arriving there at the same time as General Early's force, and, moving to the point menaced by him, defeated, General Early says, "our hopes of getting possession of the works by surprise," etc.

A part of the Nineteenth Corps, Major-General Emory commanding, brought from New Orleans, arrived in Washington at the same time.

Notwithstanding that a column was seen to file into the intrenchments on the afternoon of the 11th,[3] before his advance force, Rodes's division, could be brought up, and skirmishers were thrown out from their intrenchments and their artillery opened upon him, General Early determined, after consultation with his officers that evening, to assault in the morning, although he had ascertained the formidable character of the works by a personal reconnoissance of them; but hearing that night that two corps of infantry had arrived in Washington, he delayed the attack next morning, and examining the works again, found them lined with our troops.   He then reluctantly abandoned all hope of the capture of Washington, and withdrew from it on the night of the 12th, crossing the Potomac near Leesburg, in Lou-

---

[1] In this action General Ricketts, conspicuous for his gallantry, was severely wounded.

[2] General Getty returned to the command of his division on the 28th of June, having been absent, owing to a severe wound received in the Wilderness.

[3] Six hundred dismounted cavalrymen, Army of the Potomac.

doun County.   General Wright followed in pursuit on the 13th.[1]

Although it was the intention of General Grant to bring the Sixth and Nineteenth Corps to the armies operating against Richmond, leaving General Hunter, who had reached Harper's Ferry, to defend Washington, the subsequent movements of General Early prevented this.

---

[1] According to the report of General Barnard on the Defences of Washington, the line of forts with the connecting infantry intrenchments was garrisoned on the north side of the Potomac by 1,834 artillery and 1,819 infantry (the infantry being 100-days men); on the south side by 1,772 artillery and 4,064 infantry (the infantry 100-days men).   There were besides, in Washington and Alexandria, 3,900 effectives, composed of District of Columbia volunteers, veteran reserves, and detachments; and about 4,400 veteran reserves (six regiments of), five field batteries at the artillery camp of instruction, and 800 cavalry under the command of Colonel C. R. Lowell.   The artillery garrisons must necessarily remain in their works, and such of the 100-days infantry garrison in the vicinity of the points attacked were the only parts of that force available for defence there.   The movable infantry force to man the infantry lines at the point of attack, was the District of Columbia Volunteers, Veteran Reserves, and detachments, numbering 8,300.   To these must be added 2,000 quartermaster employés under General Meigs, that reported for duty on the evening of the 10th, and were put in the lines.

The front, exposed to attack by the two roads leading to Washington from the north, the Seventh Street road and the Georgetown road, was six miles in extent from Fort Totten, on the right (Bladensburg road), to Fort Bayard, on the left of the Georgetown road.

General Barnard, in summing up the troops of every kind, states that they constituted "a total of about 20,400 men. Of that number, however, but 9,600, mostly perfectly raw troops, constituted the garrison of the defences. [They were the artillery and 100-days men.] Of the other troops, a considerable portion were unavailable," etc.

The arrival of the Sixth and a part of the Nineteenth Corps was opportune, and they formed the only force that could follow General Early.

CHAPTER IX.

THE OPERATIONS OF THE ARMY OF THE POTOMAC AGAINST THE INTRENCHMENTS OF PETERSBURG TO BE BY REGULAR APPROACHES—MOVEMENT TO THE NORTH BANK OF THE JAMES—THE PETERS-BURG MINE.

UPON the withdrawal of the Sixth Corps from the Army of the Potomac, the left was drawn in to the Jerusalem plank-road, and refused in the manner heretofore stated.

The greater part of July was devoted to strengthening the line of intrenchments from the Appomattox to the Jerusalem plank-road, and constructing redoubts and siege-batteries.

Colonel H. L. Abbot, an Engineer officer, commanding First Connecticut Artillery, a regiment 1,700 strong, had been directed, on the 20th of April, to prepare a siege train, with which he was to report to Brigadier-General Hunt, Chief of Artillery of the Army of the Potomac, when the time arrived for the use of the train. It consisted of forty rifled siege guns ($4\frac{1}{2}$-inch ordnance, or 30-pounder Parrotts), ten X-inch mortars, thirty VIII-inch mortars, twenty Coehorn mortars, with a reserve of six 100-pounder Parrotts.

Colonel Abbot reported to General Butler with his troops and part of the siege train on the 13th of May, but the whole train did not arrive until the 23d of June, when, by order of General Grant, Colonel Abbot reported to General Hunt.

The dépôt for the train was established at Broadway Landing on the Appomattox.[1]

On the 9th of July an order was issued by General Meade directing the operations of the Army of the Potomac against the intrenched position of the enemy defending Petersburg, to be conducted by regular approaches on the front opposed to General Burnside's and General Warren's corps ; and detailed instructions were issued by him for the conduct of those operations.

On the 25th of July General Grant determined to send the Second Corps and two divisions of cavalry secretly to the north bank of the James by the ponton bridges at Deep Bottom (Jones's Neck, Bermuda Hundred), the cavalry to make a dash upon Richmond if the chances seemed favorable for it, but if not, to destroy the two railroads from the vicinity of Richmond as far as the Anna rivers (which was indeed the chief object of the operation). Kautz's division was to join Sheridan at Deep Bottom. The Second Corps, moving up to Chapin's Bluff, was to support the cavalry if it got into Richmond, but at any rate to prevent the enemy's troops from being sent across at that point to interfere with the

---

[1] Noticing the effect upon our troops produced by the single VIII-inch mortar from the Confederate lines of Yorktown, Colonel Abbot had paid great attention to training the gunners in the use of this arm while in the defences of Washington, especially in those details upon which the effect of vertical fire depends. The enemy suffered severely for the first few days when the mortars were opened upon them at Petersburg. Having no mortars with which to reply, and no bomb-proofs for cover, and yet being compelled, by the proximity of the main lines, to keep their own fully manned in order to guard against assault, the effect upon their troops was depressing. As soon as the enemy could obtain mortars, they placed them in position ; and from that time to the evacuation the mortar fire was frequent and severe, though Colonel Abbot's gunners retained their advantage of greater precision of fire. Mortars were introduced chiefly with a view to preparing for an assault and keeping the enemy's artillery quiet while it was being made. This purpose they effectually accomplished. They were also used to keep down picket firing and to compel the silence of certain very annoying batteries, which from the left bank of the Appomattox River enfiladed the right of our line.

cavalry. This movement General Grant thought might cause such a reduction in the strength of the force holding the Petersburg lines as to give fair promise of success in assaulting them, upon springing a mine General Burnside had prepared. This mine was placed under a redan held by Elliott's brigade of Johnson's division. It was opposite the centre of the Ninth Corps, where the opposing lines were only one hundred yards apart.

The success of this movement, as General Hancock says, depended upon the contingency that the enemy's works would be thinly occupied, and the movement be a surprise.

General Hancock and General Sheridan marched in the afternoon of the 26th, and about two o'clock in the morning of the 27th, the Second Corps, followed by the cavalry, began crossing the James. There were two ponton bridges at Deep Bottom (the north end of Jones's Neck is so called), one just above the mouth of Bailey's Creek, the other just below it; the creek is about twelve miles from Richmond; it is four or five miles long, running from north to south, crossing the Central or Darby road (at Fussell's mill), the Long Bridge road, and the New Market or river-road. It was impassable near its mouth, and probably from its character there gave rise to the name of Deep Bottom. General Foster of the Tenth Corps held the two ponton bridges. There was a considerable force of the enemy intrenched opposite the upper bridge, but their line appeared to extend only a short distance beyond. General Hancock determined to cross by the lower bridge, and turn the enemy's left flank, while General Foster threatened them in front. The Second Corps and cavalry were over the river before daybreak, and as soon as it was light, moved forward, the cavalry on the right. The enemy's advanced force on the east side of Bailey's Creek was soon driven out of the way, and a battery of four 20-pounder Parrott guns captured on the New Market road by the skirmish line of Barlow's division. The command, swinging on its left, advanced by the New Market and Long Bridge roads to Bailey's Creek, the cavalry on the right, on the Long Bridge and Central roads. The enemy was found in strong force intrenched on the west bank of Bailey's Creek, from the mouth to Fussell's mill, where their left was refused. Wilcox's and Kershaw's divisions had been sent across the river from Petersburg before our movement began, and held this line. Heth's division joined them on the 27th.

It was not desired by General Grant that the enemy's works should be assaulted, but that their position should be turned by the cavalry on the Central or on the Charles City road, while Foster should make a vigorous demonstration in his front and the Second Corps on theirs. But the enemy having been reinforced, Kershaw advanced against Sheridan's cavalry and drove it back over the ridge upon which it was posted. Dismounting his men, General Sheridan formed them just behind the crest, where the fire of their repeating carbines at close quarters drove the attacking force back in confusion, leaving 250 prisoners and two colors in the hands of the cavalry. W. H. F. Lee's cavalry division now joined the enemy's infantry on the north side of the James, and on the 29th Field's and Fitz Lee's divisions united with them.

On the night of the 28th Mott's division was sent back to relieve Ord's corps in our intrenchments on the right of Burnside, and on the night of the 29th Hancock and Sheridan recrossed the James to take part in the assault on the Petersburg works in front of Burnside. The expedition had accomplished one important result : it had reduced the force holding the Petersburg intrenchments to three infantry divisions, and had likewise drawn two of their three cavalry divisions to the north bank of the James. The casualties of this movement to the north bank of the James amounted to some 300.

In the latter part of June General Potter proposed to General Burnside to mine a redan of the enemy's works in his front, the proposition coming from Lieutenant-Colonel Pleasants, Forty-eighth Pennsylvania, a regiment composed chiefly of miners from Schuylkill County, Pennsylvania, Colonel Pleasants himself being an experienced and skilful mining engineer. This work was authorized by General Burnside, and its continuance was subsequently assented to by General Meade.

The redan to be mined was known as Elliott's salient, the intrenchments there being held by his brigade. The ground on our side was favorable to running the gallery of the mine screened from observation, but the position was not in other respects suitable, Elliott's salient being a re-entrant of the general line of intrenchments, and the salient itself, as well as all the ground between it and Burnside's advanced line of intrenchments, being exposed to a flank fire on the right and left.

Though the work met with many serious difficulties, it was finished ready for charging by the 23d July.[1]

In continuance of the operations against the enemy, it was in question whether an attack should be made on his intrenchments, or a movement to destroy the Weldon Railroad effectually should be undertaken. The final result of an assault seemed doubtful, as, apparently, the enemy had a second line running along the crest about five hundred yards in rear of the first line, and commanding it. A careful examination of the whole front, including that of Bermuda Hundred, led to the conclusion that the chances of carrying

---

[1] The main gallery was 511 feet long, the two lateral galleries 37 and 38 feet. There were eight magazines, each of which was charged with one thousand pounds of powder.

the enemy's intrenchments were better on Burnside's front than on any other, though the existence of a second line in rear of the first made it more than doubtful whether the attempt would be judicious. Thus matters stood on the 24th of July. But on the 25th and 26th very careful examinations were made of this second line from a newly erected signal station, and it was found that the enemy had detached works, batteries probably, along the ridge in front of Burnside, but not a connected line. This fact increased greatly the chances of a successful assault, and it was determined to make it in connection with the springing of Burnside's mine. General Burnside had reason to believe that the enemy had not discovered his mine. His mining work, however, had not escaped detection by them, and General Beauregard at first directed countermining, but abandoned it, and threw up intrenchments at the gorge of the salient against which the mining was apparently directed. Batteries of VIII- and X-inch mortars were also established by him to give a front and cross fire on the points threatened.

The siege and field artillery of our forces had been put in position to keep down both the front and flank fire of the enemy wherever we might attack their intrenchments, and on Burnside's front great care was taken to establish it so as to keep down their fire upon the flanks of our columns of attack against the Elliott salient, and to keep back their reinforcements.

Upon a call from General Meade on the 26th of July, General Burnside on the same day reported a plan of assault with his corps in connection with the explosion of the mine, by which the two brigades of General Ferrero's colored division in close column of attack were to lead. Upon passing through the openings on the right and left of the mine, the regiments in front were to move down the enemy's lines, while the others moved directly to the crest near the cemetery, about five hundred yards beyond.   These two columns were to be followed by the other divisions of the corps as soon as they could be thrown in.

General Burnside's reason for the selection of Ferrero's division to lead was, that his three divisions, commanded by Potter, Willcox, and Ledlie, owing to their closeness to the enemy's line, had been subjected to a musketry and artillery fire, day and night for thirty-six days, with a daily loss of from 30 to 60 killed and wounded (Colonel Loring, Inspector-General, says, more than 30),[1] while Ferrero's division had not been exposed to the fire of the enemy, and had been drilled to manœuvre with a special view to their use in the assault.   As General Ferrero's division had never been in contact with the enemy, this selection was not approved, and the assault fell to the lot of the First Division, commanded by General Ledlie, an officer whose total unfitness for such a duty ought to have been known to General Burnside, though it is not possible that it could have been.   It was not known to General Meade.

General Lee having sent Field's and Kershaw's divisions of Longstreet's corps, and Heth's and Wilcox's of Hill's corps to the north side of the James (together with the cavalry divisions of the two Lees), leaving only Hoke's, Johnson's, and Mahone's divisions in the Petersburg intrenchments, General Meade, with the approval of General Grant, on the 28th of July, fixed upon the morning of the 30th as the time when the mine should be fired and the assault made.   Hancock and Sheridan were to be withdrawn from the north side of the James as soon as it was dark on the night of the 29th, so as to take part in the operation, and General Ord, now commanding the Eighteenth Corps, with a division of his

---

[1] According to Colonel Loring, a loss in killed and wounded of 1,300.   But this is a very loose way of stating losses.   The enemy had also suffered severely from the same cause.

own corps under General Ames, and one of the Tenth under General Turner, was also to take part in it, General Mott, of the Second Corps, relieving, in due time, the Eighteenth Corps, which held the intrenchments on Burnside's right.

The morning of the 30th was fixed upon because it was desired to put more heavy guns and mortars in position for the attack, and the night of the 29th was required to make such preliminary arrangements as the massing of the troops, removing the parapets and abatis for the passage of the assaulting columns, and bringing into position the supporting troops.

The order for the attack was issued on the 29th. It expresses concisely what was to be done by each commander.[1]

General Burnside was to form his troops during the night for assaulting the enemy's works at daylight of the 30th, prepare his parapets and abatis for the passages of the columns, have the pioneers equipped to open passages for artillery, to destroy the enemy's abatis, etc., and the intrenching-tools of the corps (with which all the corps were amply supplied) distributed for effecting lodgments, etc.

General Warren was to reduce the number of his troops holding the intrenchments to the minimum, and concentrate on his right, prepared to support the assault of General Burnside. He was to make the same preparations as to pioneers and intrenching-tools as the Ninth Corps.

General Ord was to put Mott's division in the intrenchments of the Eighteenth Corps, and form his troops in rear of the Ninth Corps, ready to support it in the assault.

The field artillery of each corps was to be held ready to move.

General Hancock was to move at dark from Deep Bottom, and be in position in rear of Mott's division (resuming command of it) at daylight, ready to follow up the assault.

[1] See Appendix K, for a copy of the order.

General Sheridan was to proceed at dark to Lee's mill, and at daylight against the enemy's troops on our left by roads leading to Petersburg from the southward and westward.

Major Duane was to have the ponton trains close at hand prepared to move (to cross the Appomattox), and supplies of sand-bags, gabions, fascines, etc., near the lines, ready for use.   He was to detail engineer officers for each corps.

General Burnside was to spring his mine at half-past three in the morning of the 30th.   His assaulting columns were to move at once rapidly upon the breach, seize the crest in the rear and effect a lodgment there.   He was to be followed by General Ord on the right, and General Warren on the left.   Upon the explosion of the mine the artillery of all kinds in battery was to open upon those points of the enemy's works whose fire covered the ground over which our columns must move.

These orders were carried out thoroughly by all the commanders except General Burnside.   His parapets and abatis were not prepared for the passage of the columns of attack, his pioneers not effectively prepared for work, nor were his intrenching-tools distributed.   In a personal interview with General Burnside and Generals Willcox, Potter, and Ledlie on the 29th, General Meade had endeavored to impress upon them, first, that immediate advantage must be taken of the confusion of the enemy caused by the explosion of the mine, to gain the crest beyond ; that holding the crater would be of no possible use ; second, that if the assault was unsuccessful the troops must be withdrawn at once.

The work mined was on General Johnson's front, at the centre of General Elliott's brigade.   General Wise's brigade was on Elliott's right, General Ransom's on his left, General Gracie's on Ransom's left.   General Hoke's division held from Johnson's left to the Appomattox ; Colquitt's brigade was sent to Johnson's on the 28th, and was placed on Wise's right. General Mahone's held on Johnson's right, his own right being about a mile and a half from the mine, except one brigade on the Weldon Railroad four miles off.

A defect in the fuse delayed the firing of the mine until twenty minutes to five. At once all the heavy guns and mortars, eighty-one in all, and about the same number of field guns, opened, and kept down the fire of the enemy's salients and his batteries at all points except two, which, owing to the character of the ground and woods that concealed them, could not be effectively reached.

A few minutes after the explosion, General Ledlie's division, the Second Brigade leading, filed through Burnside's advanced intrenchments, and moved up to the crater,[1] into which it filed, filling it with a confused mass. General Ledlie did not accompany, much less lead, his division. He remained, according to the testimony before the Court of Inquiry that followed, in a bomb-proof about fifty yards inside our intrenchments, from which he could see nothing that was going on. He could not have given the instructions he received to his brigade commanders. Had the division advanced in column of attack, led by a resolute, intelligent commander, it would have gained the crest in fifteen minutes after the explosion, and before any serious opposition could have been made to it. It was expected by General Meade that the whole of the Ninth Corps would have been formed in columns of attack in the hollow ground in the vicinity of our advanced line of trenches, and would have advanced quickly on the right and left of the leading division, and that in half an hour after the explosion of the mine the corps would have had possession of the crest.

---

[1] The crater was about one hundred and fifty feet long, sixty wide and twenty-five deep. It was about one hundred yards from Burnside's advanced line of intrenchments.

The mine overwhelmed the battery in Elliott's salient, the whole of the Eighteenth and part of the Twenty-third South Carolina Infantry, and for some minutes caused the utmost consternation among the troops there. For some consider-- able time they abandoned the intrenchments for the space of two or three hundred yards on each side of the mine. But the appearance of General Ledlie's division going into the crater aroused them, and they began a scattering musketry fire, which by the time the rear of Ledlie's division got up. to the crater, was somewhat effective. General Elliott, in endeavoring to form a line on the higher ground beyond the crater, was severely wounded, and the command devolved upon Colonel McMaster, who formed a part of the brigade in a ravine in rear of the crater (the salient), the fire from which, with the flanking fire of the rest of the brigade and Ran- som's troops in the intrenchments on our right of the crater, together with Wright's battery, repulsed all the attempts made to advance from the crater. Of these there were several, but only two or three hundred men could be got be- yond the crest of the mine to make them. It was half an hour after the explosion before the enemy's musketry was at all effective, and nearly an hour before their artillery fire from two batteries, in all six guns, was so. Then Wright's battery of four field guns opened. It was some six hundred yards on our right of the mine, concealed in woods, and well covered by traverses, so that we could not silence it.[1] It swept the ground between our intrenchments and the crater, the crater itself, and the ground on our right of it, firing over the heads of Ransom's troops, who were formed in a covered way running along a ravine. A two-gun battery in

---

[1] Major Coit, who commanded four of the batteries in this part of the Confed- erate intrenchments, says this battery was literally battered, and the ground around it and in its rear was honeycombed by the explosion of mortar shells. The battery was well traversed.

a ravine on our left of the mine, equally difficult to reach with our fire, also became effective, and as the contest continued, batteries were put in position on the crest so often mentioned, though their fire was in a great degree kept down, as was that of their mortars.

General Potter's division went forward by the flank [1] (filed out) soon after General Ledlie's commenced advancing. The leading brigade, General Griffin's, moved toward the right when it reached the vicinity of the mine, and taking possession of the partially abandoned intrenchments, began an attack upon the enemy, whose works at that point were intricate, the ground being cut up with covered-ways and rifle-pits. After a long, sharp contest the intrenchments were taken, and Elliott's troops driven back upon Ransom's, holding in the ravine. [2]

General Willcox's division followed General Ledlie's, his leading brigade going into the crater, his second brigade moving to the left of it, and getting possession of the enemy's intrenchments there, but not without fighting. His instructions, he says, were to bear to the left and take up a position on the Jerusalem plank-road, and that he endeavored to form his division so that its right flank would rest on that road, and protect the left flank of Ledlie's division, but that he was unable to do so; and when, some time after, he was ordered to advance to Cemetery Hill, the enemy had concentrated such a fire that he could not go forward.

An hour after the mine exploded General Meade, receiving a despatch from Colonel Loring, staff officer to General Burnside, stating that Ledlie's division was in the crater, but

---

[1] General Potter says his division was to have been formed left in front, to move forward by the flank, so that when his troops had passed the line of the enemy's intrenchments they would face to the right, to cover the right of Ledlie.

[2] When General Potter first got up there, he says, the intrenchments were partially abandoned by the enemy for the space of two hundred or three hundred yards on each side of the mine.

could not be got forward, at once ordered Burnside to push
with all his troops to the crest, and directed General Ord to
move his troops forward at once; at six o'clock he directed
General Ord to push for the crest independently of Burnside's troops, and make a lodgment there.   Just before this
direction was given, General Burnside having reported that
no enemy was seen in their line of intrenchments, General
Warren was informed of it, and ordered to go forward with
his troops, independently of the Ninth Corps, and try to
carry the works if there was apparently any chance for it.
But he reported that so far as they could see none of the
enemy had left their front, meaning the part of the enemy's
line within his view.   And on Hancock's front the enemy's
intrenchments were well manned, and opened a heavy and
close fire whenever they perceived any indication of an attack.

At six o'clock, prisoners taken having stated that they had
no line in their rear, that they were falling back when our
troops advanced, and that none of the troops had returned
from the north side of the James, General Meade, informing
General Burnside of this, ordered him to push forward his
men, black and white, at all hazards, and rush for the crest.
Ferrero was ordered repeatedly by Burnside to go forward
with his division, but instead of having it massed close to
the advanced line ready to move, it lay crowded in the covered-ways leading down to that line, and it was eight o'clock
before it filed out of them.   As most of the other troops of
the Ninth Corps had done, it passed out of the intrenchments by twos and threes and fours.   It went forward with
alacrity, but a large part of it crowded through the crater of
the mine, notwithstanding the efforts of the commanders of
the two brigades to keep them out of it.   This threw them
into confusion, but a part of them were led off to the right,
and got off into the intrenchments there, when they had

some fighting, capturing 200 prisoners and a color. Its division commander remained in the bomb-proof with General Ledlie.

There was now a crowded mass in and in rear of the crater, and for some distance on its right in and about the somewhat confused intrenchments taken from the enemy. The day was one of intense heat, the thermometer several degrees above 90°, and the sun beating down in the deep hole of the crater caused great suffering.

General Ord's troops were very much delayed in passing through the Ninth Corps intrenchments, owing to the parapets and abatis not having been prepared for it, and the crowds still in them and in the covered-ways.

General Turner says that at half-past six the last of Potter's troops had just passed out, and that seeing the confused mass of troops in and about the crater, and the colored troops lying down and trying to cover themselves in a very short line on the right of the mine, he moved his leading brigade to the right of the colored troops, and took possession of about one hundred yards of the enemy's works. His Second Brigade passed out still further to the right and attacked, but without success. His First Brigade was in the act of charging down the enemy's line to the right, he says, and his Second Brigade about to advance, when looking to the left, he saw the troops in large numbers rushing back, and immediately the whole of his First Brigade, and then his Second, fell back to our intrenchments.

At about six o'clock General Lee was informed of the springing of the mine, and at once ordered two brigades of Mahone's division to be brought up from the right. In a short time he was at the Gee house, a commanding position five hundred yards in rear of the crater, where he met General Beauregard. Hill had gone to the right to bring up the troops, having first sent batteries to the crest.

Mahone arrived with Weisiger's and Wright's brigades between eight and nine o'clock, and seeing what a large body
of our troops were in their intrenchments, sent for Sanders's
brigade of his division. Weisiger's brigade had just formed
a little before nine o'clock in the ravine a short distance in
rear of the mined salient, where, it has been stated, Elliott's
men had aided so effectively in repelling every effort of our
troops in the crater to advance.[1] Wright's brigade was not
yet in position when Colonel Thomas, commanding the
Second Brigade of colored troops, having with Colonel Sig-
fried, commanding the First Brigade, received an order from
General Ferrero to take the crest, attempted to carry out the
order by charging with his brigade, but only succeeded in
getting two of his regiments and part of a third[2] over the
enemy's intrenchments they had possession of, and advancing a short distance, when Weisiger's brigade, with some of
Elliott's, advanced against them, charged and drove them
back in confusion, the whole division rising from the ground
and running in wild disorder back to our intrenchments,
carrying with them many of Potter's troops, both of Turner's
brigades, and most of the men lying around and in rear of
the crater. Some of the colored division took refuge in the
crater, or must have remained there from the beginning, for
many were captured there, and according to General Burnside's report of casualties 801 were missing. Some of Potter's division also were driven into the crater. This attack
left the enemy in possession of nearly all their intrenchments
on our right of the mine.

Satisfied that the time for success had passed, and that
any further attempt would only result in useless sacrifice of
life, General Meade, with the concurrence of General Grant,

---

[1] This ravine extended some distance to our right of the mine.

[2] Colonel Charles S. Russell, commanding one of the regiments, says only 150
or 200 men went forward from the intrenchments.

directed the suspension of further offensive movements, and the withdrawal of the troops to our lines when it could be done with security, leaving it discretionary with General Burnside and General Ord to withdraw them during the day or at night. Our batteries were held ready to keep down the fire of the enemy's that they controlled, should they attempt to open upon the troops in withdrawing. For my own part, I had no expectation of success after reading Colonel Loring's despatch from the mine, written an hour after the explosion, for, if in that time they had not gained the crest in force, the opportunity we had counted on in the surprise and confusion of the enemy upon the springing of the mine must have been lost.

At half-past six a despatch was received from the officer at the signal station on the Jerusalem plank-road, reporting that a column of the enemy's infantry, at least a strong brigade, was marching toward our right, and that they came from the vicinity of the Lead Works (Weldon Railroad), where all the camps had been broken up, and the troops moved toward our right. General Warren was notified of this and instructed to make an attack in that direction if practicable. (The point indicated was at least four miles from his right, where the greater part of his corps was concentrated.)[1]

To this General Warren replied that all his troops were on the right except Crawford's, to whom he had sent directions to do what he could, and asked if he should send Ayres there; but General Meade preferred that Crawford should be heard

---

[1] General Wilson was directed to make a lodgment on the Weldon Railroad and move up along it to the enemy's unoccupied intrenchments, the other cavalry divisions to support him. But the march prescribed for the cavalry was too long to carry out this programme before the operation of the mine was concluded. General Sheridan was then directed to make a reconnoissance instead of an attack, to feel the enemy's right flank, and to be governed in anything further by his own judgment.

from before giving further orders. The report of Crawford, received about eight o'clock, was not favorable to the attempt, owing to the distance of the point of attack. Ayres was directed to attack on Burnside's left and to take the 2-gun battery of the enemy on our left of the mine, which had a most destructive fire in that quarter, and was not only very much concealed, owing to its position in a ravine, but was hidden by a group of trees from our 14-gun battery, where six 4½-inch guns had been put in position, one of its objects being the silencing of this 2-gun battery. General Burnside had been requested and ordered to have these trees cut down, but they remained standing. Ayres was about to go forward when, as already stated, all our troops on the right of the mine fell back in confusion to our intrenchments, and General Meade directed all offensive operations to cease. This was at a quarter of ten. At half-past ten Mahone made an attack on the crater and on Willcox's troops in the enemy's intrenchments on our left of the crater. This was repulsed by the musketry of the troops attacked, and by our artillery, and Mahone's men were forced to seek cover in one of their trenches near by. Between one and two o'clock another, a third and last attack, was made with Johnson's and Mahone's troops, Sanders's brigade having arrived in the meantime.

The order to withdraw from the crater to our own lines was sent by General Burnside at half-past twelve o'clock to the brigade commanders there, leaving them to consult and decide upon the time and manner of withdrawal. This they did, returning the order endorsed with a request that our artillery and infantry should open when they fell back, but before the despatch reached General Burnside the enemy advanced to the last attack, and two of the brigade commanders in the crater, seeing them close at hand, hastily gave the order to retire, when the larger part of the troops fell back to our lines, losing many men by the infantry and artillery fire of the enemy, though the distance to our intrenchments was but little more than one hundred yards. A large number of officers and men were captured in the crater, among them the two brigade commanders of Ledlie's division, Brigadier-General W. F. Bartlett, whom General Burnside mentions as a most brave and efficient officer, who was severely wounded in the Wilderness, and Colonel E. G. Marshall.

General Meade reported his casualties at 4,400 killed, wounded, and missing, all except about 100 being the loss of the Ninth Corps. He also stated that 246 prisoners and two colors had been captured. General Burnside's report does not state what his loss was at the mine, but gives the whole number of his casualties from June 12 to July 30; his missing during that time was 1,396. As his colored division was in no other engagement than the mine during that time, its casualties there are given and are stated to have been 176 killed, 688 wounded, and 801 missing.

The Tabular Statement of the Medical Department puts down the loss at 419 killed, 1,679 wounded and 1,910 missing; total, 4,008. The number of the killed and missing are, I believe, too great: the total was probably 3,500.[1] Its Tabular Statement of the Confederate loss is evidently erroneous, 400 killed, 600 wounded, 200 missing.

Colonel McMaster states that the loss of Elliott's brigade was 677, and that that was more than half the Confederate loss that day. Weisiger's brigade lost heavily also, the commander being among the wounded.

The great mass of the Ninth Corps were so huddled together that they could do no fighting, but those that were disengaged from the mass did good fighting. The proportion of killed and wounded among the officers of the colored troops was unusually large.

---

[1] General Mahone states that the number of prisoners taken in the crater was 1,101.

At the request of General Meade the President ordered a Court of Inquiry to examine into and report upon the facts and circumstances attending this affair, and also to report their opinion, and what officers, if any, were answerable for the want of success of the assault. The statements of most of the officers commanding troops before this Court were not very clear and precise as to their positions, and those of the enemy where the troops were in contact, and the accounts of the details of the contest, are confused.

The opinion of this Court will be found in Appendix K.

The Committee on the Conduct of the War also inquired into the facts in the following winter.

The principal facts being known, it was apparent that the assault failed from mismanagement and misbehavior on the part of several of the chief actors, unless, indeed, which I do not believe, the troops were in such condition that the best management, the best handling, and the best leading would have been lost upon them. This in brief was the opinion of the Court. General Grant, when before the Committee on the Conduct of the War, said that General Meade made his orders most perfectly ; even at the time of giving his testimony, when all the facts were known, he did not think he could improve upon the order, and that if the troops had been properly commanded, and led in accordance with that order, we would have captured Petersburg, but that the opportunity was lost in consequence of the division commanders not going in with their men, but allowing them to go into the enemy's intrenchments and spread themselves there, without going on further, thus giving the enemy time to recover from his surprise, collect his troops, and organize against them.

He said further that General Burnside did not prepare his parapets and abatis as he was ordered to do, and that the preparation ordered was essential to success, and could have been made without its discovery by the enemy; that had he been a corps commander entrusted with the duty General Burnside was charged with, he would have been upon the ground and seen that the preparations were made as ordered; and that had he been a division commander, he would have gone in with his division; and he added that there were a great many officers there (with the army) who would have done the same thing.

General Ledlie left the army a short time after the mine affair, and resigned.

According to the Return of the Army of the Potomac on the 20th of July, its effective force of infantry (enlisted men present for duty equipped) was 37,984; its effective force of cavalry, 10,280.

The effective force of infantry of the Army of the James on the 31st of July was 24,009; of its cavalry, 1,880.

The effective force of infantry of the Army of Northern Virginia on the 10th of July was 39,295; of cavalry, 8,436.

The Sixth Corps of the Army of the Potomac and the Second Corps of the Army of Northern Virginia were detached and are not included in the Returns. Johnson's and Hoke's divisions are included in the strength of the Army of Northern Virginia.[1]

The engineers now went on with perfecting our redoubts

---

[1] General Gibbon, commanding the Second Division, Second Corps, in concluding his report of the service of his division from May 3d to July 31st, states that when the division left its camp on May 3d, it consisted of three brigades with an aggregate number, 6,799 (officers and enlisted men); that between the dates mentioned it had been reinforced to the number of 4,263, making a total of 11,062, and had been divided into four brigades; that it lost 77 officers and 971 enlisted men killed, 202 officers and 3,825 enlisted men wounded, being a total of 5,075; that the brigades had had seventeen different commanders, of whom three had been killed and six wounded. Of the 279 officers killed and wounded, 40 were regimental commanders. That many of the bravest and most efficient officers and men were among those who fell. He continues: "The effect upon the troops of the loss of such leaders as Tyler, Webb, Carroll, Baxter, Conner, McKeon, Ramsey, Blaisdell, Coons, Haskell, Porter, Murphy, McMahon, Macy, Curry, Pierce,

and return-works, so that our lines could be held by a small part of our troops, leaving the larger part free for movement.

A second line of redoubts without connecting lines, in rear of the first line, was contemplated, but was not thrown up.

Abbot, Davis, Curtis. and a host of others can be truly estimated only by one who has witnessed their conduct in the different battles."

The names he mentions are those of general officers and regimental commanders, nearly all of whom I knew personally ; they were soldiers in every meaning of the word, gallant, skilful, full of zeal and energy.

CHAPTER X.

MOVEMENT TO THE NORTH BANK OF THE JAMES TO THREATEN RICHMOND—CAPTURE OF THE WELDON RAILROAD AT THE GLOBE TAVERN—THE BATTLE OF REAMS'S STATION.

EARLY in August General Sheridan was assigned to the command of all the troops operating against General Early, who was then in the vicinity of Winchester; General Hunter on the Monocacy at the railroad crossing.

General Lee sent Kershaw's division and Fitz Lee's cavalry division to reinforce General Early; and General Torbert's and General Wilson's cavalry divisions were sent to General Sheridan.

Between this time and the month of March, 1865, several movements of portions of the Army of the Potomac and of the Army of the James were made to the right and to the left, which resulted in the extension of our lines of intrenchments in both directions, and caused a corresponding extension of the Confederate intrenchments on our left, and their occupation in stronger force of their intrenchments on the north bank of the James. By this process their lines finally became so thinly manned when the last movement to our left was made in March, 1865, as to be vulnerable at one or two points, where some of the obstructions in their front had been in a great measure destroyed by the necessities of the winter.

These flank movements had not only that general object

of Confederate extension in view, but other special objects also, which were important at the time, and which were to a greater or less extent accomplished.

During the period mentioned, the plan of leaving garrisons in the enclosed works and moving in force against the Confederate lines of supply from the south, and to turn Lee's right flank, was never carried out. A partial attempt of this character was made in the latter part of October, by way of the Boydton plank-road, but it failed, and chiefly because it was of a partial character, and not a decided, vigorous attempt with all the force that could have been taken from the lines to turn Lee's right.

Information received from various sources leading General Grant to believe that General Lee had detached three divisions of infantry and one of cavalry from Petersburg to reinforce General Early, he sent General Hancock with his corps and Gregg's cavalry, together with the Tenth Corps, or part of it, under General Birney, to threaten Richmond from the north side of the James, in order to prevent further detachments from being made by Lee, and, if possible, to draw back those sent. General Hancock's instructions were the same as those sent him on the 25th of July for his former movement, except as to the manner of crossing the James. Great care was taken to conceal the movement, and to give the impression that the troops were destined for Washington. The Second Corps was marched to City Point, and embarked on steamers which left City Point for the lower ponton bridge at Deep Bottom at ten o'clock at night of the 13th August. The cavalry and artillery went by land. It was expected that the troops would have disembarked, and the movements have begun by daylight, but the steamers were not adapted to the transportation of troops, and, owing to the shoal water, could not run near enough to the shore, and the tide was ebbing. This caused delay, and it was

nine o'clock in the morning of the 14th before the corps had
disembarked.

The plan of operations was for Mott to move on the river-
road (New Market), and drive the enemy into his intrenched
line behind Bailey's Creek, and beyond it, if practicable.
General Barlow—General Gibbon being absent—with the
First and Second Divisions, to move to Mott's right and assault the enemy's lines near the Jennings house (in the vicinity of Fussell's mill), Gregg to cover the right flank.   If
Barlow carried the lines, he was to move to the left, uncover
Mott's front, and both were then to advance along the river
road.   As soon as the infantry uncovered the Charles City
and Central (Darby) roads, Gregg was to move on the former, make a dash on Richmond, if the chance offered, and if
not, to destroy the railroads entering it.   General Birney
was to attack the enemy's right near the ponton bridge
above the mouth of Bailey's Creek, and if successful, was to
move up the Kingsland, Varina, and Mill roads, all of which
are near the river bank.

If this plan could have been carried out, the enemy's intrenchments would have been turned, and we should have
had possession of Chapin's Bluff, the works of which, with
those of Drury's Bluff, were the chief fortifications guarding
the river approach to Richmond.   But General Field's division had remained at the Deep Bottom or Bailey's Creek intrenchments, and General Wilcox's at Chapin's Bluff, and in
fact, only Kershaw's division of infantry had been sent to
Early.   Wilcox at once joined Field, and Mahone's division,
with Hampton's and W. H. F. Lee's cavalry divisions, were
sent across the river to reinforce them, Dearing's brigade
being the only cavalry force left with Beauregard.

Mott found the enemy in their strong position on Bailey's
Creek at the river road crossing.   It was intended, General
Hancock says, that General Barlow should attack near Fus-

sell's mill with the greater portion of two divisions, when by
mere weight of numbers he would have broken through the
enemy's line, which at that point was thinly held ; but that
he extended from Mott's right to the vicinity of Fussell's (a
distance, according to the maps, of nearly a mile and a half),
through thick woods, and about four o'clock assaulted with
only one brigade (of Gibbon's division), and made several
unsuccessful attempts upon the enemy's line ; that General
Barlow's personal example to the troops was all that could
be expected or desired from his well-known gallantry and
devotion to duty, but was of no avail. He adds that General Barlow's report reflects but little credit on the troops,
and attributes their failure to respond to the leading of their
commander, to the large number of new men among them,
and the small number of experienced officers left to command them.[1] To meet General Barlow's threatening movement, the enemy weakened their right, opposite Birney,
to such an extent that he was able to seize a part of their
line with trifling loss, capturing four guns, but could get
no further.   Gregg advanced well up the Charles City
road.

During the night the greater part of Birney's command
with Colonel Craig's brigade of Mott's division was massed
on the right, in the vicinity of Fussell's, and dispositions
were made for him to attack in the morning. Gibbon's
division, Smythe commanding, was massed on Birney's left,
Barlow's near the fork of the Darby and Long bridge roads,
and Mott's on the river-road.   Birney was to find the enemy's
left the next morning, and turn it, or, failing in that, to at
tack.   Gregg was to cover the movement on the right.   But
General Birney took so wide a circuit to his right between
the Darby and Charles City roads that it was near night be-

---

[1] See the remarks of General Gibbon, at the close of the previous chapter, upon
the loss of officers and enlisted men in the division.

fore he reported that he had found the enemy's line, but could not attack before morning.

Birney was ordered to attack on the 16th, and Gregg, with Miles's brigade of Barlow's division, to move up the Charles City road to divert the enemy's force from Birney.

General Gregg advanced at an early hour to the vicinity of White's tavern (seven miles from Richmond), driving the enemy's advanced force of cavalry before him, their commander, General Chambliss, being killed. At ten o'clock General Terry, with his division of Birney's corps, and Craig's brigade of Mott's division, together with a brigade of colored troops commanded by Brigadier-General Birney, advanced against the enemy's works above Fussell's mill, and after a severe contest carried them, capturing three colors and between 200 and 300 prisoners from Wilcox's and Mahone's divisions. Colonel Craig, who had just returned to the army from an absence on account of wounds received during the campaign, was killed. The enemy soon retook their line, Birney retaining only the advanced line of pits, the picket line. The wooded character of the country prevented personal examination by General Hancock, and it was some hours before he was fully informed of the state of affairs.

Early in the afternoon the enemy's cavalry, now in large force and supported by infantry, advanced upon Gregg and Miles and forced them back to and across Deep Creek. Miles, with his brigade and Brooke's, formed on Birney's right. It was now fully ascertained that the information upon which General Hancock had been sent to the north side of the James was erroneous, but he was retained there during the 17th, 18th, 19th, and 20th, until dark, keeping up a threatening attitude with constant skirmishing, though directed not to assault the enemy's works. On the night of the 20th his command was withdrawn to their former posi-

tions before Petersburg and at Bermuda Hundred.   General
Kautz held the left of the army during General Gregg's absence.

There was a sharp encounter on the afternoon of the 18th,
when the enemy left their works above Fussell's mill and
attacked Birney ; they were repulsed, General Miles on the
right aiding by an attack on their left flank.

The casualties of the command, according to the statement
furnished me from the Adjutant-General's Office by Mr. J. W.
Kirkley, taken by him from the nominal lists of casualties,
were 321 killed, 1,840 wounded, 625 missing ; total, 2,786.[1]
I have not found a statement of the Confederate casualties.
Among the severely wounded of the Second Corps, on the
15th, was Colonel Macy, Twentieth Massachusetts, who was
particularly mentioned by General Barlow for good conduct.
He had only returned to his command on the morning of the
15th, having been absent, owing to a wound received during
the campaign.[2]

While General Hancock was keeping the enemy occupied
on the north bank of the James, General Warren was withdrawn from the lines, the Ninth Corps extending its left to
occupy the place of the Fifth, and sent at four o'clock on the
morning of the 18th, by a route well away from the enemy's
lines, to seize and hold the Weldon Railroad at the Globe
tavern, about four miles south of the outskirts of Petersburg.
As he would need reinforcements, Mott's division was sent
back on the night of the 18th to relieve a part of the Ninth
Corps (now commanded by General Parke) in the intrenchments, so that it might be sent to reinforce the Fifth Corps.

On the night of the 14th and 15th, the Fifth Corps was re-

---

[1] The casualties, according to the Tabular Statement found in Badeau's volumes,
are 1,498 killed and wounded, 515 missing ; total, 2,013.

[2] The effective force of infantry of the Army of the Potomac at this time was
33,684 ; of the Army of the James, 18,449.

lieved by the Ninth in its intrenchments, and held ready to move. On the 16th, General Meade, satisfied, from the report of General Hancock, the observation of signal officers, and other sources of information, that Lee had but three infantry divisions in the Petersburg intrenchments, directed General Warren to move by daylight of the 17th to the Weldon Railroad near the intersection of the Vaughan road (about two miles from Petersburg), and if the enemy held their intrenchments weakly in that vicinity to endeavor to carry them and occupy the crest in the rear of their line opposite the line held by the Ninth and Eighteenth Corps. Kautz was to move on his left flank. But General Grant, not being altogether satisfied as to the disposition of the enemy, preferred to wait for further developments, and the order was suspended.   On the next day General Grant authorized sending the Fifth Corps and some cavalry to destroy as much of the Weldon Railroad as practicable, but not to assault fortifications ; the movement to be rather a reconnoissance in force, during which General Warren might take advantage of any weakness of the enemy he discovered.   In certain contingencies he was to remain on the road.   General Grant's despatch concluded : " I want, if possible, to make such demonstrations as will force Lee to withdraw a portion of his troops from the Valley, so that Sheridan can strike a blow against the balance."

Accordingly General Warren was instructed, on the 17th, to move the next morning at four o'clock, and make a lodgment upon the Weldon Railroad, near the Gurley house (two miles south of the intersection of the Vaughan road), or as near the enemy's lines as practicable, and destroy the road as far south as possible.   In addition to the destruction of the road, he was to consider the movement a reconnoissance in force, and take advantage of any weakness the enemy might betray.   A brigade of cavalry under Colonel Spear

was attached to his command. In the course of General
Warren's operations on the 18th, it was determined to with-
draw General Mott's division from Hancock in the night, to
take the place of a part of the Ninth Corps, and that General
Ord should extend his left, so that the two would enable
Willcox's, White's, and finally Potter's divisions to be sent
to the left on the 19th to co-operate with General Warren.
These three divisions of the Ninth Corps had altogether
about 6,000 men, but all these were not available. General
Warren moved as directed, taking possession of the Weldon
Railroad at the Globe tavern (some three miles west of our
left), finding only Dearing's cavalry brigade to oppose him.
Griffin's division was formed along the road looking west,
and began its destruction. The day was oppressively hot
and close, as were those that followed, and a heavy rain fell
throughout the day. Ayres's division moved up the railroad
a mile or more from Griffin and to within half a mile of the
Vaughan road intersection, having Hayes's brigade on the
right of the railroad, Dushane's Maryland brigade on his left
moving by a flank. Crawford moved up on Ayres's right,
his right in dense woods with close underbrush. A large
field of Indian corn in front of Crawford's left and Ayres's
right hid everything from their view. Cutler's division remained in rear in support.

General Dearing had reported to General Beauregard the
appearance of some force on the railroad, and General Heth,
with Davis's and Walker's brigades, was sent to his support.
Moving out by the Vaughan road, about two o'clock General
Heth made a sudden attack on Ayres's left, caught the
Maryland brigade unawares, and drove it back. Ayres, to
prevent his line of battle being taken in flank, drew it back,
but then advancing, drove the enemy from the ground.
Crawford's left, Lyle's brigade, was partly engaged. Warren's loss was 544 killed and wounded, 392 missing—total,

936. General Warren says the enemy's loss must have exceeded ours ; he left his dead and wounded on the ground.

On the morning of the 19th, General Bragg of Cutler's division was sent with his brigade to the right of Crawford, to support him and establish connection by a skirmish line with the pickets of the Ninth Corps. There was great difficulty in doing this, the whole face of the country being covered with dense woods and underbrush, the wood-roads or cart-tracks through which were unknown to any of our troops. The line was probably imperfectly formed, but at best would constitute a very imperfect guard against an active enemy, acquainted in detail with the woods, which, at the distance of twenty paces, effectually screened everything from sight.

Upon learning from General Beauregard that the Fifth Corps or a part of it was on the Weldon Railroad, General Lee sent Mahone's and Lee's divisions back to Petersburg. In the course of the day Willcox's division, then White's, and later in the afternoon, Potter's, were sent to General Warren.

General A. P. Hill, with Davis's and Walker's brigades under General Heth, and Weisiger's, Colquitt's, and Clingman's under General Mahone, with Lee's cavalry and Pegram's batteries, moved to the Vaughan road intersection. Heth was to attack Ayres, while Mahone, familiar with the woods, was to move concealed by it, some distance beyond Crawford's right, break through Bragg's skirmish line, and take Bragg and Crawford in rear. About half-past four in the afternoon General Mahone with his command formed in columns of fours, broke through Bragg's skirmish line, faced to the right, and swept rapidly down toward General Warren's right flank, taking all Crawford's skirmish line and part of his line of battle in rear. His skirmish line fell back in the greatest confusion, and, in doing so, masked the fire of his line of battle, and forced it to fall back, together with a part of the right of General Ayres's division. Heth at the same time opened on Ayres's centre and left; General Warren, reforming the parts of Ayres's and Crawford's divisions that were broken, brought them forward again and regained the ground temporarily lost, taking some prisoners and two flags. General Willcox was ordered up to attack; and White's division was formed facing to the right, and engaging Colquitt's brigade, drove it back and captured some prisoners. Mahone's command fell back rapidly in great confusion to their intrenchments, carrying with them the parts of Warren's command disorganized by the attack on their rear in the woods, and a large portion of the pickets.

Heth made repeated attempts to drive Ayres back, but failed. General Beauregard, telegraphing General Lee, said Colquitt and Clingman in advancing through thick undergrowth lost their organization and were ordered to their camps to rally them. Mahone's brigade was also ordered into the lines. Heth's two brigades remained.

General Warren's casualties were 382 killed and wounded, 2,518 missing, of which 1,805 were from Crawford's division. General Hayes, of Ayres's division, was among the captured. The enemy's loss, General Warren says, must have been heavy in killed and wounded. General Clingman was among the latter.

The necessity of remaining stationary, even a single day, in a dense wood like that in which the greater part of General Warren's troops were posted, subjects a command to having some part of it taken suddenly in flank or rear, broken, thrown into confusion, and many of them captured.[1]

---

[1] General Warren was directed toward night on the 18th, if his contingent objects could not be accomplished that night, to intrench as close up to the enemy's works as he could get; he was informed that he would be reinforced by the Ninth Corps the next day; on the 19th he was instructed to maintain his hold on the railroad, at all hazards, and, if practicable, extend to connect with the Ninth Corps; he was also to push the enemy back nearer their own lines. These were

Satisfied that the enemy would renew their efforts to drive him from the railroad, General Warren on the 20th selected a position on it a mile or two in rear of his line of battle on the 19th, chiefly in open ground, and favorable for the use of artillery, and intrenched so as to have a considerable infantry reserve.

On the 21st General Lee, finding our forces had been withdrawn from the north side of the James, directed Field to send two of his brigades to Petersburg, and General Hampton to bring over his cavalry division (now commanded by General Butler). Wilcox's division, in whole or in part, had already been moved to Petersburg.

On the morning of the 21st, General A. P. Hill, with his own corps, part of Hoke's division with Lee's cavalry, attacked Warren, opening with thirty guns on his front and right flank, and at ten o'clock assaulting them, but was everywhere repulsed. Later Mahone attempted an assault on the left flank, but the artillery broke his infantry before it came under musketry fire. In the assault, General Warren says, General Hagood's brigade being nearly surrounded close in on our works, every one thought they had surrendered, and ceased firing, but when our troops advanced to bring them in their officers commenced firing. In the mixed condition of his men and the enemy s, his line could not fire, and many of the enemy escaped. However he captured 517 officers and men and six flags, the larger part from Hagood's brigade.

The enemy's loss in killed and wounded must have been severe, as General Warren says 211 of their dead were buried by his troops. General Sanders of Mahone's division was among their killed. Warren's own loss was 301 killed,

---

too many conditions to impose upon him on ground of the character he was operating in. Informed of the general object he was to accomplish, everything else as far as possible should have been left to his judgment.

wounded, and missing.   Colonel Dushane, commanding the
Maryland brigade, a gallant officer, was killed, General Cutler wounded.

General Warren says the heat of the first day was excessive,
and many fell out of the ranks, who were counted among the
missing.   An oppressive, warm rain fell all the time, making
the side roads and fields almost impassable for artillery.

The cavalry under General Spear were active in watching
the left flank and rear ; Steadman's brigade took part in the
repulse of the enemy on the 21st.

No further attempts upon General Warren's position were
made.   The intrenchments were now extended by the Ninth
Corps from the Jerusalem plank-road to unite with General
Warren's on the Weldon Railroad.

The extension of our left to the Weldon Railroad at the
Globe tavern would not prevent the enemy from using that
road as a line of supply up to a point within a day's hauling
by wagon to Petersburg.   By destroying the road as far
down as Rowanty Creek, about thirteen miles beyond Warren's left, they would be obliged to haul by wagon from
Stony Creek Dépôt to Dinwiddie Court House, and thence
by the Boydton plank-road to Petersburg, a distance of thirty
miles at least.   It was determined, therefore, to destroy the
railroad as far as Rowanty Creek, and on the 22d, General
Hancock with his First and Second Divisions and Gregg's
cavalry was charged with this work,[1] and set about it at once,
Gregg looking out for the enemy on the roads leading to the
railroad from the left and to Hancock's rear.[2]   By the night

---

[1] His Third Division, Mott's, held the intrenchments at and in the vicinity of
the Jerusalem plank-road.

[2] General Hancock says of his return march from Deep Bottom, that it was one
of the most fatiguing and difficult performed by the troops during the campaign,
owing to the wretched condition of the roads.   The men arrived in camp greatly
exhausted early in the morning of the 21st.   After a very brief rest they were ordered to the Strong house, and then, in the afternoon, to the Gurley house, in rear
of General Warren's position.

of the 24th they had accomplished the work as far as Malone's cross-road, about three miles south of Reams's Station, and had still about five miles of the road to destroy. The two divisions were held at Reams's Station during the night.

But the Weldon Railroad was deemed to be too important as a line of supply to the Confederate forces to admit of this destruction without an attempt to prevent it, and General A. P. Hill [1] was assigned to this task, having with him the larger part of his own corps, together with Anderson's brigade of Longstreet's corps, and General Hampton with his two cavalry divisions.

About dark of the 24th signal officers reported that there were large bodies of the enemy's infantry, estimated at 8,000 or 10,000, passing south from their intrenchments by the Halifax and Vaughan roads. Both General Hancock and General Warren were advised of this, and that these troops were most probably directed against General Hancock. In the morning of the 25th, General Hancock ascertained that the enemy's cavalry was in force on his left, supported by infantry.

The intrenchments at Reams's Station were slight, and had been hastily thrown up by troops sent to Wilson's relief in June. They ran along the railroad about twelve hundred yards, having a return about eight hundred or one thousand yards long at each end, the returns being nearly at right angles with the railroad. This direction of the returns subjected the troops in them to a reverse artillery fire. The Second Division, commanded by General Gibbon, occupied the left half of these intrenchments; the First Division, commanded by General Miles, occupied the right half.

---

[1] Hill's infantry was McGowan's, Lane's, and Scales's brigades of Wilcox's division, Anderson's brigade of Field's division, and Cock's and McRae's brigades of Heth's division, and two brigades of Mahone's division. General Wilcox was first on the ground, and made the preliminary attacks with his own brigades and Anderson's brigade.

About two P.M. General Wilcox made two spirited attacks on Miles's front, both of which were quickly repulsed. About this time General Hancock received a despatch from General Meade informing him that Mott was directed (about half-past one o'clock) to send him all his available force (about 1,800 men) down the plank-road, taking a battery with it ; and as the railroad could not be further destroyed at present, he might be governed by his own judgment as to withdrawing his command to his former position, or remaining where he was. To this General Hancock replied that, although there was no necessity for his remaining there longer, since the presence of the enemy prevented further destruction of the railroad, and although it was more important that he should join Warren than remain there, yet he was then too closely engaged with the enemy to withdraw, but that he would do so at night. At two, or half-past two, General Meade ordered General Willcox's division to move down the plank-road to General Hancock's support. General Meade notified General Hancock of this, saying all he apprehended was that the enemy might be able to interpose between him and Warren, and some more of Warren's forces were held ready for contingencies. It was this apprehension, no doubt, that induced him to send General Willcox by the plank-road instead of by the railroad. But by the plank-road his march was twelve miles long (about the same length as that of Mott's troops), whereas had he gone by the railroad, which continued open until five o'clock, he would have had not more than five miles to march, would have got to Hancock by half-past four or five, and managing his movement skilfully, might have taken a part of the enemy's force in flank or rear.

Meanwhile Hill was preparing his forces for attack, which he began at five o'clock with a heavy artillery-fire that did little actual damage (that is, caused few casualties), but had the effect of shaking a portion of the command exposed to its reverse fire. The shelling continued about fifteen minutes, when General Heth and General Wilcox, with Cook's and Lane's, McRae's and Scales's brigades, Anderson's and part of McGowan's brigades supporting, assaulted a part of General Miles's front, and, just at the time when a few minutes' longer resistance would have repulsed the enemy (who were thrown into a good deal of disorder by the severity of the fire they received, and the obstacles in the way of their advance), a part of the line, composed of troops recently raised, gave way in confusion. A small reserve brigade of the Second Division was ordered forward to fill the gap, but could neither be made to go forward nor to fire. McKnight's battery was turned on the opening with good effect, but the enemy, running along under cover of the rifle-pits, captured the battery. Murphy's brigade of the Second Division on the left of the break was driven back, and two more batteries fell into the hands of the enemy, after having been served with marked gallantry, and after losing a large proportion of officers, men, and horses. General Hancock ordered Gibbon's division to retake the position and the guns, but his troops responded feebly to the order, and fell back on receiving a slight fire ; being now exposed to attack in reverse and on the flank they were obliged to occupy the reverse side of their breastworks. The moment was a critical one, and General Hancock says, would have ended still more disastrously but for the steadiness of a part of the First Division, and the fine conduct of its commander, General Miles,[1] who succeeded in rallying a small force of the Sixty-first New York, and forming a line at right angles with the breastworks, swept off the enemy, and retook McKnight's guns and a considerable portion of his own line. An at-

---

[1] The historian must, in justice, add,—and the bearing of General Hancock himself.

tempt was made to get some of Gibbon's troops to assist in this operation, but their commanders reported that they could not be got to advance.   Hampton with his dismounted cavalry now made an attack on the left, driving General Gibbon's division from its breastworks, the division offering very little resistance.   Pressing on with loud cheers, Hampton's cavalry was met by a heavy flank fire from Gregg's dismounted cavalry, which checked their advance.   Then they turned upon Gregg, who was forced to fall back and form on the left of the new line which General Gibbon had established a short distance in rear of the intrenchments.

General Miles's troops, with Werner's New Jersey artillery, held the road running to the Jerusalem plank-road until dark, checking every attempt of the enemy to advance beyond the portion of the intrenchments they had captured. General Miles and General Gregg offered to retake their breastworks, but General Gibbon stated that his division could not retake theirs.   As it was essential either to withdraw or to retake the lost works in order to protect the only communication open to the rear, and as no reinforcements had arrived by dark, the troops were then ordered to withdraw.   Neither General Mott's detachment nor General Willcox's division reached the field.   The enemy made no attempt to follow up their advantage, but returned to the Petersburg intrenchments, leaving Hampton's cavalry at the Station.

General Hancock says that if his troops had behaved as well as they had done before, he would have been able to defeat the enemy ; or had a force been sent down the railroad to attack the enemy in flank, or had a small reserve been on the field at about six o'clock, it would have accomplished the same end.   He attributed the bad conduct of some of his troops to their great fatigue and to their heavy losses during the campaign, especially in officers.   Besides, there were several regiments largely made up of recruits and substitutes; one, General Hancock mentions particularly, being entirely new, and some of its officers unable to speak English.

His casualties were 610 officers and enlisted men killed and wounded, the proportion of officers being unusually large; his missing, 1,762, making a total of 2,372. Nine guns were lost.

General A. P. Hill reported his loss to be 720, chiefly, if not almost entirely, killed and wounded. His captures, he stated, were 12 stands of colors, 9 guns, 10 caissons, 2,150 prisoners, 3,100 stands of small arms.

The extent of the injurious effect of the large number of raw recruits recently received had not been anticipated, or reinforcements would have been sent to General Hancock early in the morning.[1]

The work of intrenching the newly-added front and rear went on vigorously during September.

---

[1] The larger part of the troops furnished by the States under the several calls made this year, and until the close of the war, were supplied by the re-enlistment of the veteran regiments whose terms of service expired. But there were many vacancies in those regiments, and in those whose terms had not expired, and those vacancies were filled and new regiments formed by volunteer, drafted, and substitute raw recruits. Owing to the absence on account of wounds and sickness of large numbers of those who had entered the service in the early part of the war, these raw recruits in some cases formed a large majority of those present for duty in old regiments of high reputation, and sometimes completely changed their character temporarily, and not only the character of regiments, but even of brigades and divisions. The large bounties paid volunteers and substitutes, amounting, in some places, to a thousand dollars or more, had a very injurious effect upon the army, for it brought to its ranks many men who were actuated by very different motives from those that had influenced the men who had voluntarily filled the ranks before, and the veterans that now re-enlisted.

All recruits were sent to the army without instruction or discipline. A good many enlisted, intending to escape from the service, and deserted to the enemy. Some of these attempted to enter our lines at the West, in the guise of Confederate deserters, but were detected, brought back to the Army of the Potomac, tried and executed.

CHAPTER XI.

THE two brigades of Field's division, Anderson's and Bratton's, sent to Petersburg in the latter part of August, still
remained there in the latter part of September, and the only
troops in the Confederate intrenchments on the north side of
the James besides the heavy artillery, the two brigades of
the local defence, and Garey's cavalry brigade, were Field's
three brigades, commanded by Benning, Law, and Gregg,
and Colonel Fulton's brigade of Johnson's division.

On the 28th of September General Ord, commanding the
Eighteenth, and General Birney, commanding the Tenth
Corps, were directed to cross the James in the night and ad-
vance upon Richmond, the former by the Varina road, near
the river, the latter by the New Market and Darby roads,
Kautz with his cavalry on the Darby road.   General Ord was
to engage the enemy in his works at and near the river at
Chapin's Bluff, and prevent reinforcements being sent from
the south side against Birney's column.   He was to cross the
James by a ponton bridge to be established during the early

part of the night at Aiken's, two miles below Dutch Gap, where the Varina road abutted on the river. General Birney was to cross at Deep Bottom by the upper ponton bridge; General Kautz was to follow him.

General Ord selected for the purpose 2,000 men from each of his First and Second divisions, one commanded by Brigadier-General Stannard, the other by Brigadier-General Heckman. His Third Division (colored), commanded by Brigadier-General Paine, reported to Major-General Birney, whose column, composed of his First and Second divisions, under Generals Terry and Ames and General William Birney's brigade of colored troops, was, with Paine's addition, about 10,000 strong. General Ord from the Bermuda front, and General Birney from the Petersburg front, each left sufficient force in the intrenchments to maintain them.

Both columns were over the river and moving on the routes designated by daylight, driving before them the enemy's skirmishers and advance troops. Every precaution had been taken to keep the knowledge of the movement from the enemy and make the attack a surprise.

By half-past seven General Ord had reached the open ground around Fort Harrison on Chapin's farm, the strongest work on the main line of intrenchments, about a mile and a quarter from the works on the river at Chapin's Bluff, with which it was connected by more than one line of intrenchments. While one line of advanced intrenchments held by the Confederate pickets or skirmishers ran from Fort Harrison in a northeast direction, the main line, soon after leaving the fort ran north about three-fourths of a mile to Fort Gilmer, which was also connected with the works on the river at Chapin's Bluff by two intrenched lines. The main advanced line of Richmond intrenchments continued north from Fort Gilmer about three-fourths of a mile, then ran northeast to the Chickahominy at New Bridge. The pos-

session of Fort Harrison did not give possession of the defences at Chapin's Bluff, but the possession of Fort Gilmer
would give it.

Ord having arrived upon the ground, the artillery of the fort
and adjacent works opened upon him. The disposition for
attack was quickly made by him. Stannard's division, General Burnham's brigade leading, was to push forward on the
left of the Varina road, in column of divisions, over the open
ground in front of the works, preceded by skirmishers. The
distance it had to traverse was about fourteen hundred yards.
General Heckman was to move his division, as soon as it
came up, along the edge of the wood that skirted the Varina
road on the right, until opposite Fort Harrison, and then to
attack it on the front toward the wood—the east front. This
would envelop the work on the south and east. Reinforcements were now seen entering Fort Harrison from the
enemy's left. Stannard's division advanced in quick time,
and when they reached the foot of the hill which the work
crowned, Burnham's brigade ran up it under a severe fire of
artillery and musketry, and after a very sharp encounter captured the work with sixteen guns and a number of prisoners,
including the Lieutenant-Colonel in command of it. General Burnham was killed in the assault. Colonel Stevens,
the officer who succeeded to the command of the brigade,
was severely wounded, and his successor also. The division
lost 594 killed and wounded during the day.

The enemy was next driven from the intrenchments on the
right and left of the Fort, including two lunettes six hundred
yards apart, which were captured with their artillery, six guns.
General Ord now endeavored to sweep down the captured
intrenchments to the remaining redan, which was on the river
bank, so as to secure the enemy's ponton bridge, but this
redan was covered by the Confederate gunboats, and by a
battery in the rear, and the attempt was unsuccessful. In

making it General Ord was so severely wounded in the leg
as to completely disable him, and the command devolved
upon General Heckman. He, General Ord says, in advancing
went too far into the woods ; his brigades became scattered,
and were not available at the right time.   While the fighting
for the possession of the intrenchments adjoining Fort Harrison was going on, General Ord says he saw through the
smoke what he thought was General Heckman's division entering Fort Gilmer, but they soon proved to be reinforcements of the enemy, and that work and the adjacent lines
were now defended by Gregg's and Benning's brigades of
Field's division, and Fulton's brigade of Johnson's division.
Soon after he had succeeded to the command of the corps,
General Heckman attacked Fort Gilmer with his division but
was repulsed with heavy loss.   In the afternoon General
Field arrived at the fort with Law's brigade to aid in its defence.

In the meantime Major-General Birney, driving the advance troops of the enemy before him, advanced upon the
New Market road, and with sharp encounters captured the
skirmish or picket line of intrenchments of the enemy,
which has been mentioned as running from Fort Harrison
in a northeast direction, and crossing the New Market and
Darby roads.   The main line was from one-half to three-
quarters of a mile in rear of this.   Communication was established between the two columns, the Varina and New
Market roads being about a mile apart here.

General Grant, who had arrived at Fort Harrison, now informed Major-General Birney of Ord's success, and that the
Eighteenth Corps was ready to advance in conjunction with
his (Birney's) and directed him to push forward.   Kautz
had advanced along the Darby road, abreast of Birney, and
Terry's division was sent to his support.

About three o'clock in the afternoon Major-General Birney with Ames's division, and Brigadier-General Birney's colored brigade, made a determined, but unsuccessful attack upon Fort Gilmer, the adjacent works, and the main line of intrenchments as far as the New Market road. The troops advanced half a mile or more under the fire of the enemy's artillery, the greater part of Ames's division crossing three ravines filled with fallen trees, but upon emerging from the third ravine, which was close upon the works, the fire of canister and musketry broke the line and forced it to fall back, part of it in some confusion. The leading troops of Birney's colored brigade went forward to the attack on Fort Gilmer with great gallantry, jumped into the ditch of the fort, and endeavored to climb up on each other's shoulders to the parapet, but nearly all that reached the ditch were killed.

The assaults of to-day were made with great gallantry.

As the left and rear of our forces on the north bank of the James were open to the enemy, Birney's command was drawn into the New Market road, and slight intrenchments (afterward strengthened) were extended around them, and a line was run from Fort Harrison to the river, just above Dutch Gap. General Weitzel was placed in command of the Eighteenth Corps.

General Ewell was in command of the Confederate troops on the north side, where he was joined by General Lee during the day. Bratton's and Anderson's brigades were brought from the Confederate extreme right by railroad, getting into position on the north side in the evening. Colonel Montague, with four regiments of Pickett's troops was also brought to the north side, and during the night of the 29th, Hoke, with Kirkland's, Clingman's, and Colquitt's brigades, and Scales's brigade of Wilcox's division were brought over. Ten brigades in all were concentrated at and near Fort Gilmer, to assault Fort Harrison and its dependent works on the following day.   During the night and the next morning large parties were at work to make Fort Harrison an enclosed work.

At two o'clock in the afternoon of the 30th General Anderson, commanding Longstreet's corps, assaulted with Law, Anderson, Bratton, Clingman, and Colquitt.   General Stannard, who held the fort, says of the attack, that twelve guns opened on his centre and left, the enemy's infantry advancing on his right; that he reserved his musketry fire until their lines emerged from the thick underbrush in front, and that he repulsed them with musketry alone.   Quickly reforming, they attacked a second, and a third time, but were repulsed each time, and with heavy loss, leaving a large number of killed and wounded on the ground.

I can find no report from General Heckman or from General Weitzel, who now commanded the Eighteenth Corps, of the part taken by General Heckman's division in repulsing this assault.   It undoubtedly took part in it, as did Birney's colored brigade, the loss of which in the engagements of the 29th and 30th amounted to 434.   General Stannard lost his arm in the second assault.   He had four staff officers wounded in the two days, and mentions many of the officers of his command who were conspicuous for their gallantry.

The losses of the enemy in this assault must have been severe.   General Bratton says he had 377 killed and wounded out of his brigade of 1,165 enlisted men and 129 officers.   The Tabular Statement of the "Medical and Surgical History of the War" puts the Confederate loss at 2,000.

According to the Tabular Statement prepared in the Adjutant-General's Office, which I have heretofore referred to, our casualties in the two days were 394 killed, 1,554 wounded, and 324 missing—total, 2,272.

In co-operation with the movement against the Richmond

defences on the north side of the James, just described,
General Meade, under instructions from General Grant,
made such semi-concealed changes of position of part of
his troops on the 28th as to give the enemy the impression, when they should discover the absence of much of
the Tenth and Eighteenth Corps, on the morning of the
29th, that we were concentrating on our left, and, in that
way, would lead General Lee to delay reinforcing the real
point of attack north of the James. In addition, the Army
of the Potomac was got under arms at four o'clock in the
morning of the 29th, General Warren and General Parke,
each with two divisions of his corps ready to move. All the
corps commanders made dispositions to withdraw from the
intrenchments, leaving garrisons in the redoubts and enclosed batteries, and arranged for the further contingency
of withdrawing entirely from the intrenchments.[1] These
dispositions undoubtedly had the effect of delaying the
transfer of Confederate troops to meet the attack of Ord and
Birney. But there was another object that General Grant
had in view, which was, should the enemy draw off such a
force from the defences of Petersburg as, in General Meade's
opinion, would justify his moving against the South Side
Railroad or Petersburg, he was to do so. If he got possession of the road he was to maintain it at all hazards, reinforcing from the troops left in the intrenchments.

It was not deemed advisable by General Grant that General Meade should move on the 29th, the reduction of the

---

[1] Gregg was sent to the crossing of Hatcher's Run, by the Vaughn road, and
up that road and the Squirrel Level road to the vicinity of the Peebles and Pegram farms. At the former point the enemy had a redoubt at the termination of
the intrenchments they had constructed and were still going on with. This intrenchment was nearly parallel with the Weldon Railroad, and joined the Petersburg intrenchments. Peebles's farm was two miles west of our intrenchments on
the Weldon Railroad. The enemy was found in position at all these points, and
General Gregg was attacked by General Hampton upon his return march.

enemy's force around Petersburg not seeming to justify it that day, nor until eight o'clock in the morning of the 30th. The object then in view was to secure the junction of two roads coming from the southwest, the Squirrel Level, and the Poplar Spring Church roads. This junction was at the Peebles farm, where a redoubt terminated, the Confederate intrenchment covering the roads. From that point an advance was to be made in a northwest direction toward the Boydton plank-road and South Side Railroad, if the conditions would justify it.

General Warren, with Griffin's and Ayres's divisions, was directed against the junction of the roads ; General Parke, with Willcox's and Potter's divisions, was to follow him, form on his left, and both were then to advance toward the Boydton road. General Gregg was to move on the Vaughan and other roads on our left.

Griffin's troops advanced against the Peebles intrenchments, passing over six hundred yards of open ground, and carried them, the infantry parapets being held by infantry and Dearing's dismounted cavalry, and flanked by artillery in the redoubt. Colonel Welch, commanding the Sixteenth Michigan, was killed on the parapet of the work. The loss otherwise was small. A gun and some prisoners were taken.

General Ayres carried the redoubt on the right of Griffin. These two captures gave us the whole of the line of intrenchment. General Parke advanced Potter's division to support Griffin on his left, and as soon as Willcox got up, moved forward with his two divisions through the Pegram farm in a northwest direction toward the Boydton road, Willcox on Potter's left in support, as General Parke expected Griffin's division to support his right.

The force holding the Petersburg intrenchments was Hill's corps and Johnson's division, with Hampton's two cavalry divisions and Dearing's brigade, all under the command of

General Hill, General Beauregard having been sent south to take charge of affairs in that direction. The main line of Petersburg intrenchments had been extended in a southwest direction to, or nearly to, Hatcher's Run, covering the Boyd-ton plank road and the South Side Railroad.

To meet the advance of Meade, General Hill threw out Heth's and Wilcox's divisions as far as the Jones house, on the road leading to the Pegram farm. Potter, passing through a wood, found himself within eight hundred yards of the enemy's main line of intrenchments, and quite near Heth's and Wilcox's troops, which he advanced to attack. He was met by an advance on their part, attacked vigor-ously, his right outflanked, and his division driven back in some confusion, as well as one of Willcox's brigades. But a new line was at once established by General Parke with Willcox's troops, which, with Griffin's line on the right, put a stop to the enemy's advance. General Parke lost 485 killed and wounded, and heavily in prisoners. Hampton, on the Confederate right, shared in the captures.

Mott's division arrived on Parke's left in the afternoon of the 1st of October, and on the next day General Parke ad-vanced, with artillery and musketry firing, and established a line of intrenchments about a mile from the enemy's. This was connected with the Weldon Railroad works, and was extended to the rear on the left, having its proper number of redoubts and batteries.

The casualties in this operation were, according to the Table of the Adjutant-General's Office, 661 killed and wounded, 1,348 missing ; total, 2,009.[1]

---

[1] General Parke, in his report of this affair, remarks : " The large amount of raw material in the ranks has diminished greatly the efficiency of the corps. All the new material, good as well as bad, requires instruction and disciplining. The drafted and substitute recruits are entirely different from those formerly ob-tained.

The Table of the Medical Department is evidently erroneous. The Confederate loss I have never seen stated except
in that Table, which puts it down at 800 wounded. Apparently this is as erroneous as the numbers it gives for our
loss.

Kautz, with 1,700 men and two batteries, looking out from
the right of the force on the north side of the James, held
the Darby road at the old Confederate line of intrenchments,
which had been captured on the 29th of September. There
was a swamp on his right, which ran around his rear, crossing the Darby road. To drive him from this threatening
position, Field and Hoke, with the larger part of their divisions, were brought over to the Darby road on the night of
the 6th of October, and at sunrise of the 7th Field advanced upon him, with Anderson's and Bratton's brigades,
while Gary's cavalry, supported by Lane, moved by the
Charles City road around his right. He could not stand up
against the attack of the two infantry brigades in his front,
and in falling back on the narrow road, through the swamp
in his rear, found Gary's cavalry, or part of it, there, and
thus lost eight of his guns. Kautz succeeded in crossing
over to the New Market road and getting under cover of the
Tenth Corps, which was moving out to his assistance, but
losing, besides the guns, 72 killed and wounded, and 202
missing.

Field, following Kautz passed over to the New Market
road, through the dense swamps of one of the chief affluents
of the White Oak Swamp, and attacked the right of the
Tenth Corps, which had moved out to Kautz's assistance,
but was repulsed, and fell back to his intrenchments. In
this attack, General Gregg, commanding the Texan brigade,
a gallant commander of a gallant brigade, was killed, and
General Bratton was wounded.

On the 13th of October, General Butler made a reconnoissance in force of the enemy's intrenchments on the Darby road, and found them to be of a formidable character, with slashing in front of the greater part. Colonel Pond's brigade of Ames's division, Tenth Corps, assaulted them at a point where there was no slashing, but was repulsed.

On the 24th of October General Grant wrote General Meade :

" Make your preparations to march out at an early hour on the 27th to gain possession of the South Side Railroad, and to hold it, and fortify back to your present left. In commencing your advance, move in three columns, exactly as proposed by yourself in our conversation of last evening, and with the same force you proposed to take. Parke, who starts out nearest to the enemy, should be instructed that, if he finds the enemy intrenched, and their works well manned, he is not to attack, but confront him and be prepared to advance promptly when he finds that by the movement of the other two columns to the right and rear of them they begin to give way," etc.

According to the information we had, the Petersburg intrenchments had been extended to Hatcher's Run at a point two miles above the Vaughan road crossing of that stream and about a mile above Armstrong's mill, but were in a very incomplete condition. They did not cross or extend up the run. At Burgess's mill, where the Boydton plank-road crossed Hatcher's Run, there were emplacements for artillery and some infantry parapets, but no line of intrenchments, nor were there any further up the run.

The Confederate Petersburg lines from the Appomattox to Battery 31 (west of the Jerusalem plank-road) were held by Johnson's division. General Hill held the remainder of the line, Heth on the right, Wilcox on the left, Mahone in reserve. Hampton's two divisions of cavalry (Lee's and Butler's) with Dearing's brigade were on the right flank.

The general plan of the contemplated movement was to leave sufficient force in the redoubts to hold them, and with from 30,000 to 35,000 effective force of infantry, a due proportion of artillery, and Gregg's division of cavalry, about 3,000 strong, to move to our left.   Hancock, with Gregg on his left, to cross Hatcher's Run by the Vaughan road, move to the Boydton plank-road past Dabney's mill, thence by the White Oak road to its intersection with the Claiborne road, recross Hatcher's Run, near there (two miles above Burgess's mill), and then march to the South Side Railroad, striking it at a point about three miles east of Sutherland Station.   General Parke, with the Ninth Corps, was first to endeavor to surprise the incomplete intrenchments near Hatcher's Run at daylight (it was thought they were thinly held), but failing in that, to remain confronting them while the Second and Fifth Corps moved to turn their right.

General Warren, with the Fifth Corps, was to move to the vicinity of Armstrong's mill, support General Parke, and if his attack was successful, to follow it up, moving on the left of the Ninth Corps.   If General Parke did not break the enemy's line, General Warren was to cross Hatcher's Run, and endeavor to turn the enemy's right by recrossing the run above the Boydton plank-road bridge (Burgess's mill bridge), keeping on the right of Hancock, and, being over the stream, to open the Burgess's mill bridge.[1]

On the 25th General Hancock withdrew Mott's and Gibbon's divisions from the intrenchments and massed them in a concealed position in rear of the lines (General Egan commanding Gibbon's division in the absence of that officer).   Miles's division held the Petersburg line from the Appomattox River to Battery 24, half way between the Jerusalem plank-road and the Weldon Railroad.   General

---

[1] The troops were to take four days' rations.   The supply and quartermaster's trains were to be sent to City Point.   Pack animals were to be used instead of light wagons.   The ammunition and other wagons that were to be taken with the troops were not to accompany them on the morning of the 27th.

Hancock took with him an effective infantry force of about 10,000.

On the 26th Mott and Egan were moved along the rear line of intrenchments to the vicinity of the Weldon Railroad. General Parke assigned 1,500 men to hold his intrenchments ; General Warren 2,500 under the command of General Baxter, to hold his.   Each had about 11,000 effective infantry.[1]

The columns were to move at half-past three o'clock in the morning of the 27th.   It was a dark, rainy morning, and the movement in the wooded ground was necessarily delayed, so that the enemy were not taken by surprise.   General Parke and General Warren, driving in their pickets, found their intrenchments to consist of breastworks, with abatis and slashing, and held with such force as not to justify an attempt to carry them.   Griffin was in front of the extreme right of the enemy's intrenchments, his skirmishers extending to Hatcher's Run.   This was about nine o'clock.

Being on the ground and satisfied that an assault here should not be made, and having learnt by a despatch from General Hancock that he had crossed Hatcher's Run, and consequently that the Dabney mill road was clear for General Warren's troops to follow, and considering it important that a portion, at least, of his command should cross, and communicate with Hancock as soon as possible, I directed him at nine o'clock to cross some of them at once at Armstrong's mill, and communicate with General Hancock.   I then rode to meet General Meade and General Grant, who were coming out, and inform them of the condition of affairs, and of the directions I had given General Warren.

After some consultation when General Grant and General Meade got upon the ground, General Warren was directed

---

[1] General Warren says that 3,913 of his men had never fired a musket, and that 1,649 of them were ignorant of the manual.

to send a division across Hatcher's Run, place its right flank on the stream, move up it supporting Hancock (the Dabney mill road was but a mile distant from the run), and upon arriving opposite the right of the enemy's intrenchments, which Griffin was fronting, to attack it in flank, and endeavor to drive the enemy from the line, and open the way for the rest of the Fifth Corps and for the Ninth Corps. Crawford's division was assigned to this duty as it was nearest at hand. Griffin, with Ayres supporting, was left on the north side of the run, Ayres sending his Maryland brigade to join Crawford. General Parke's corps set about intrenching in their front and back to our works.

It was a quarter of twelve o'clock when the head of Crawford's division crossed the run, General Warren accompanying it. His line was formed with the right of Bragg's brigade on the run, Hoffman's brigade covering the left, and the Maryland brigade in reserve. At half-past twelve Crawford began to advance, but the dense low growth of wood, and the crookedness of the stream caused serious delay. A large tributary was mistaken for the main stream and caused still further embarrassment, the trees in and along it having been slashed by the enemy, making it very difficult to cross. As a guide for the movement General Griffin was ordered at one o'clock to set his skirmish line at work, and be ready to take advantage of any effect Crawford's operations might have. After getting over the tributary stream, General Crawford began skirmishing. At four o'clock he was at the right flank of the enemy's works that Griffin was fronting, and the firing became sharp. It had taken all that time to move a mile and a half up the stream. The crossing of the run was naturally difficult; the enemy had dammed it, and had slashed timber in it and on its banks, and were very active in opposing Crawford's progress. It was difficult to communicate with him. The forest was dense and of great extent, and the troops were getting separated and lost, and to enable him to get his division in order General Warren directed General Crawford to halt it and reform, but, at the same time, to press forward with his skirmishers. Between General Crawford and the open ground of the Boydton plank-road there was a thicket forest of more than a mile, and there was no road or path leading to it known to any one, or that had been come across. The Dabney's mill road was a mile distant on Crawford's left.

The head of General Hancock's infantry column was at the Vaughan road crossing of Hatcher's Run by daylight. The ford had been obstructed by fallen trees. Smyth's brigade of Egan's division crossed the stream waist-deep, and carried the rifle-pits on the opposite bank in a gallant manner. Egan, followed by Mott, moved past Dabney's mill (the road being only a narrow track used for carting lumber), and entered the Boydton road about a mile south of Burgess's mill. Gregg, in the meantime, crossed Hatcher's Run below the infantry, moved along the Vaughan, and then the Quaker road, encountering part of Hampton's troops, and united with the infantry on the Boydton road soon after they entered it.

When Hancock emerged from the thicket forest into the open ground of the plank-road he was met by the enemy's artillery fire from Burgess's tavern and from the White Oak road on his left. But Beck's artillery soon silenced that of the enemy at the tavern. Egan was sent along the Boydton road toward the Burgess's mill bridge to drive the enemy across the run, and Mott's division was set in motion for the White Oak road, Egan to follow him as soon as he was relieved by the cavalry. At this time, about one o'clock, General Hancock received instructions from General Meade to halt at the plank-road, and in compliance with this instruction General Mott formed De Trobriand's brigade looking toward the Claiborne road bridge, while General Egan with Smyth's brigade drove the enemy's troops opposing them here (some of Hampton's dismounted cavalry) over the run. A despatch to General Hancock now notified him that Crawford's division was feeling its way up along the south bank of the run, and cautioned him against the vacant space between his right and the Fifth Corps which he was requested to assist in closing by extending his right. General Meade and General Grant now came upon the ground.

General Egan, by Hancock's order, deployed his division across the plank-road at the intersection of the White Oak road, having two of his brigades on the right of it, one on the left, and sent two regiments to his right as far as they could reach to connect with Crawford, whom Major Bingham, of Hancock's staff, reported to be three-quarters of a mile on the right. In the meantime the enemy placed nine guns in position on the north bank in front of Egan, and five on the White Oak road, from which an annoying fire was opened, but replied to effectively by four guns of Beck's Battery, Fifth Artillery.

Upon the return of Major Bingham from General Crawford, General Grant and General Meade left the field, directing General Hancock to hold his position until morning, and then fall back by the route he had come. The South Side Railroad was still six miles distant from the leading corps. It was essential to the success of the operation that the objective points should have been reached during the first day. That had not been done. In view of the character of the country our starting-points were too distant from our points of destination ; we were ignorant of the topography of the country to be passed over. It was evident that we must extend our intrenchments more to the left before advancing to the South Side Railroad, so as to give us more and better roads to move the infantry columns on. In our present movement we had had but a narrow cart track on which to pass two corps from the Vaughan to the Boydton road, a distance of three or four miles. Had the Fifth Corps followed Hancock closely over to the Boydton road by the Dabney saw-mill road, as originally intended, the result might have been more favorable. We could have carried the high ground on the north bank of Hatcher's Run at Burgess's mill easily and thus have turned Lee's right, and most probably have secured a footing on the South Side Railroad. But the attempted movement up Hatcher's Run failed of any favorable result. It kept two-thirds of our force at the right of Lee's intrenchments substantially doing nothing, when the two-thirds should have been at the movable end of the column. Only Wilcox's division was retained in the Confederate intrenchments by the presence of the Ninth and Fifth Corps in front of them.

As the character of our movement developed itself the enemy concentrated Hampton's cavalry and Heth's and Mahone's divisions about the Boydton crossing of Hatcher's Run ; Hampton was so placed as to attack Hancock's left flank and rear, while Heth, whose most distant troops had been but four miles from the bridge, opposed his advance toward Petersburg on the Boydton road, and Mahone was sent to cross Hatcher's Run about a mile below Burgess's mill, and following a narrow wood-road, make a sudden attack from the edge of the thick wood upon Hancock's right flank.[1] At the time the attack was made reinforcements of infantry were seen moving down the Boydton plank-road to Heth's support.

General Hancock, knowing the views of General Meade and General Grant, determined to gain possession of the

---

[1] According to the Return of October 20, 1864, the effective force of Hill's three infantry divisions was 13,638 ; of Hampton's cavalry, 5,453.

high ground north of Hatcher's Run in the vicinity of Burgess's mill, with Egan's division, supported by McAllister's
brigade of Mott's division.   De Trobriand's brigade was on
the left of the plank-road, near the intersection of the Dabney's mill road, and looking toward the upper bridge, Kerwin's brigade of dismounted cavalry on his left.   Pierce's
brigade of Mott's division was supporting Metcalf's section
of Beck's battery on the east side of the Boydton road,
posted on a ridge half way between Egan and De Trobriand ;
these two guns and Pierce's brigade looked north toward the
run.   Constant firing, General Hancock says, had been heard
on his right, which was attributed to Crawford's advance.
Becoming uneasy at this firing, General Hancock sent two
regiments of Pierce's brigade well into the wood to ascertain
what was there, and despatched Lieutenant Stacey of his
staff to inform General Crawford that he was about to assault the bridge.   In fact at that time his artillery near the
bridge had opened, and the advance of the storming party
had pushed across it, secured the bridge, and captured a
gun.   But at that moment, about four o'clock, a volley of
musketry immediately on his right, followed by a continuous
fire, left no doubt that the enemy was advancing on his right.
Pierce's small force in the woods was soon overrun, and the
enemy, Mahone's division, broke out of the woods just where
Metcalf's section was placed.   Changing front, Metcalf fired
a few rounds ; Pierce's brigade endeavored to change front,
but was driven back in confusion to the plank-road where it
rallied ; the section of artillery (two guns) fell into the
hands of the enemy.

At the first sound of this attack General Hancock sent
Major Mitchell of his staff to General Egan with orders for

---

[1] General Warren says that he must have been with General Crawford when
this attack was made on Hancock, but that the wood was so dense that no sound
of the musketry reached him.

him to desist from the assault of the bridge, face to the rear, and attack the enemy with his whole command. When Major Mitchell reached General Egan, he found him, " with the instinct of the true soldier," General Hancock says, already in motion to attack the force in his rear. Mahone pushed rapidly across the ridge on which Metcalf's section and Pierce's brigade had been posted, rested his right across the Boydton road, faced south and began firing upon De Trobriand and Kerwin. They had been quickly formed across the Boydton road just in front of the Dabney's mill road, and with Roder's and Beck's batteries opened on Mahone. General Egan swept down upon his flank with Smyth's, Willet's, and McAllister's brigades, De Trobriand and Kerwin advancing against him at the same time. Mahone was swept from the field, and driven into the woods in complete confusion, losing two colors and several hundred prisoners. Metcalf's two captured guns were retaken. Almost simultaneously with Mahone's attack Hampton commenced pressing Hancock's left and rear, and Mott's skirmishers in the direction of the Claiborne bridge, and Gregg's cavalry were sharply engaged. The enemy in front had scarcely been driven from the ground when the firing in the rear became so brisk that General Hancock was obliged to send Gregg all his cavalry. The attack on Gregg, General Hancock says, was made by five brigades of Hampton's cavalry, and was pressed vigorously until after dark, but that Gregg held his own.

Upon learning what had occurred, General Meade directed General Warren to send a division to Hancock's support, but it was dark by the time it (Ayres's division) reached the Armstrong mill crossing. As reserve ammunition could not be got forward to Hancock by daylight the next morning, together with the troops with which it was deemed desirable to reinforce him, it was concluded that he should withdraw that night, which was done, the infantry marching by the Dabney's mill road, the cavalry by the Quaker and Vaughan roads. Having an insufficient number of ambulances, 250 wounded were left in charge of surgeons at the Rainey house, and on the field. It rained heavily all night.

On the 28th, the troops were withdrawn to their former positions.[1]

Hancock's loss, according to his report, was 123 killed, 734 wounded ; total, killed and wounded, 857. His missing were 625. General Hancock mentions in high terms the conduct of General Egan, General Mott, General Gregg, and several other officers.[2]

General Warren's loss was 211 killed and wounded, and 48 missing.[3]

I have not been able to find any Confederate report or account of this day's operations on our left, except two tele-. graphic despatches of General Lee from Chapin's Bluff, which are on the files of the War Department. (See foot note [4] for

[1] In the course of the afternoon of the 27th, some of the enemy got on the Dabney's mill road, and captured some ambulances, but were themselves subsequently captured with the ambulances. Staff officers on that road and in the forest suddenly found themselves prisoners within the enemy's lines, but most, if not all, escaped. Parties of the enemy became so bewildered in the woods that 200 of them strayed into Crawford's lines and were captured.

[2] By some neglect seventy men of the First Minnesota under Captain Farwell were left on the field, and remained there until nine o'clock on the morning of the 28th, when they withdrew safely, though followed by the enemy's cavalry.

[3] One of Warren's staff, with a few men, went to the Boydton plank-road at eight o'clock on the morning of the 28th, finding only cavalry pickets there.

[4] " *October 27th.*—General Hill reports that the enemy crossed Rowanty Creek below Burgess's mill, and forced back the cavalry. In the afternoon General Heth attacked, and at first drove them, but found them in too strong force. Afterward the enemy attacked and was repulsed. They still hold the plank-road at Burgess's mill. Heth took colors and some prisoners."

" *October 28th.*—General Hill reports that the attack of General Heth upon the enemy on the Boydton plank-road, mentioned in my despatch last evening, was made by three brigades under General Mahone in front, and by General Hampton in rear. Mahone captured 400 prisoners, three stands of colors, and six pieces of artillery. The latter could not be brought off, the enemy having possession of the bridge. In the attack subsequently made by the enemy, General Ma-these despatches.)   The Confederate losses must have at least equalled ours.

In support of the movement to the left, General Butler, having been directed to make a demonstration on the north side of the James, sent part of the Eighteenth Corps, under General Weitzel, to make a demonstration on the Williamsburg road north of the White Oak swamp, and part of the Tenth Corps, under General Terry, to demonstrate on the Charles City and Darby roads.   Under cover of General Terry's demonstration, General Weitzel was to push through the White Oak swamp at Hobson's crossing, and move up the Williamsburg road to the Confederate line of intrenchments.

The plan was carried out successfully, General Weitzel arriving at the road near the Seven Pines battlefield at one o'clock in the afternoon.   Moving up the road toward Richmond, at the end of a mile and a half he found himself in front of the Confederate intrenchments, which, upon examination, he found to be thinly held by a small body of dismounted cavalry with three guns, and determined to attack, believing he could easily carry them.   At the same time he sent Colonel Holman, commanding the First Brigade, Third Division, colored troops, across the York River Railroad to find the enemy's left and turn it.

In the meantime the enemy were not idle.   On the 19th of October General Longstreet returned to his corps and took command on the north side of the James and on the Bermuda Hundred front.   North of the James he had the

---

hone broke three lines of battle, and during the night the enemy retreated, leaving his wounded and more than 250 dead on the field.   Later.—The total number of prisoners, according to General Hill's report, is 700."

According to the Table of the Adjutant-General's Office, our casualties were 143 killed, 653 wounded, and 488 missing.   The errors of this table, as heretofore explained, are in the numbers of the wounded.   Its numbers of killed and missing are, undoubtedly correct.

troops known as the Local Defences, under General Ewell, Hoke's division, Field's division, and Gary's cavalry brigade. These troops, in the order mentioned, held from the river to the White Oak swamp. Pickett's division still held the Bermuda Hundred front.

Longstreet perceived on the morning of the 27th that General Butler was moving against his left, and anticipated that the heavy skirmishing from the New Market to the Charles City road was designed, because of its long continuance, not to precede an assault, but to cover an attempt to turn his left flank by pushing a column through the White Oak swamp, taking possession of the unoccupied works on the Williamsburg and Nine Mile or New Bridge roads, and moving down them. He accordingly directed Field and Hoke to move to the left along the works, leaving only skirmishers in them, and sent General Gary to the Nine Mile road to hold the works there. Moving rapidly, the left of Field had just crossed the Williamsburg road, when Weitzel's skirmishers, preceding his line of battle, were advancing to attack.

General Weitzel had for his attacking force, Colonel Cullen's brigade of his First Division, which was formed in line of battle on the right of the Williamsburg road, supported by the First and Third brigades, General Marston commanding the division. On the left of the road the attacking force was Colonel H. S. Fairchild's brigade of the Second Division in line of battle, the division commanded by General Heckman. This force, preceded by skirmishers, advanced to the attack over open ground, at half past three o'clock, but instead of the fire of a thin line, were met with a heavy musketry fire, together with that of some guns. They got close to the works, but were repulsed with considerable loss in killed, wounded, and missing, each brigade losing three colors.

Colonel Holman crossed the railroad and upon the New Bridge road came upon a salient held by some of Gary's men, dismounted, the last occupied part of the intrenchments. This a part of the brigade charged upon and captured, taking two guns, but Gary then came upon the field, and charging along the line of works, took Holman's men in flank, recaptured the guns, and forced Holman to fall back. As they fell back, Colonel Holman received General Weitzel's order to return to his command.

Colonel Kiddoo was severely wounded in this affair while leading his regiment.

Shortly after dark General Weitzel began to withdraw to the Charles City road, the rain, darkness, mud, and narrow road making it very fatiguing for the troops, who were marching all night.

At four o'clock in the afternoon, General Terry was ordered to press his demonstration, and, if the chance occurred, to carry the enemy's intrenchments. This was attempted, but the whole attack was repulsed.

The loss in the two commands is not given in the reports. By the Table of the Adjutant General's Office it was 516 killed and wounded, and 587 missing.

Being covered by intrenchments, the casualties of General Longstreet's command must have been much less. On the Williamsburg road he reports his loss (Field's division and Gary's brigade) to have been 64 killed, wounded, and missing.

It may be in place here, at the close of active operations in 1864, to mention that on the 7th of November, Surgeon McParlin, Medical Director of the Army of the Potomac, reported to General Meade, "that the number of wounded of the Army of the Potomac from May 3 to October 31, 1864, may be considered as amounting to 57,495. This was exclusive of the Eighteenth Corps while it served with the

Army of the Potomac, and does not include the Ninth Corps at the Wilderness and Spottsylvania Court House. According to a memorandum of General Warren, the killed and wounded of the Fifth Corps during the period stated by Surgeon McParlin exceeded 11,000.

In the latter part of November, the season for active operations having ceased, General Hancock was called to Washington by the Secretary of War to organize the new First Army Corps, which, it was expected, would be ready to take the field in the spring, when the roads and country would admit of the resumption of active operations.

He had served in the Army of the Potomac with the greatest distinction from its earliest operations at Williamsburg down to the time of his leaving it, being conspicuous in all its battles and operations.

CHAPTER XII.

THE WINTER OF 1864-65—MOVEMENT TO BREAK UP THE WAGON-TRAIN ROUTE OF SUPPLY FROM HICKSFORD, ON THE WELDON RAILROAD, TO PETERSBURG, AND EXTENSION OF OUR INTRENCHMENTS TO HATCHER'S RUN—THE CAPTURE AND RECAPTURE OF FORT STEDMAN — PREPARATIONS TO MOVE AGAINST LEE'S RIGHT FLANK AND THE DANVILLE AND SOUTH SIDE RAILROADS.

THE defeat of General Early at Cedar Creek on the 19th of October by General Sheridan substantially closed the campaign in the Valley of Virginia.

The Sixth Corps was returned to the Army of the Potomac, arriving before Petersburg by divisions between the 4th and 16th of December, and Brig.-General T. M. Harris's division of the Army of West Virginia was also detached from General Sheridan's command, and was sent to the Army of the James.

About the same time General Early's corps, now commanded by General Gordon, rejoined the Army of Northern Virginia. Kershaw's division had returned to it in the latter part of November. The Army of Northern Virginia now had an effective force of infantry amounting to 50,000.[1]

---

[1] Return of December 20, 1864:

	Officers.	Enlisted men.
Longstreet's, First Corps (including Hoke's division).	1,503	20,010
Gordon's, Second Corps	505	8,179
Hill's, Third Corps	1,097	15,274
Anderson (Johnson's division only)	504	6,692
Total	3,609	50,155

Wise's brigade is not included in the above numbers. Wise's brigade in the Return of December 20th, and that of November 30th, and in Returns preceding it, is

In December the Twenty-fourth Corps was organized from the white troops of the Army of the James, and the Twenty-fifth Corps from the colored troops of that army, to which Ferrero's division of the Ninth Corps was added. General Ord was in command of the Twenty-fourth Corps ; General Weitzel of the Twenty-fifth. The Tenth and Eighteenth Corps were discontinued.

In January General Terry was detached from the Army of the James, having with him General Ames's division and Colonel J. C. Abbott's brigade of the Twenty-fourth Corps, and General Chas. J. Paine's division of the Twenty-fifth Corps, in all a force of 8,000 infantry, to take part with the Navy in the attack on Fort Fisher at the northern entrance to the Cape Fear River. When that was accomplished, he was to unite with the Twenty-third Corps under Major-General Schofield. This corps was to be brought from the West, and after taking Wilmington on the Cape Fear River, was to join General Sherman when he should advance northward from Savannah.

In the same month General Hoke with his division (whose effective strength was 5,517) was sent to aid in the defence of Fort Fisher and Wilmington.

During the winter General Butler's cavalry division (formerly Hampton's) was allowed to return to South Carolina to obtain fresh horses, and fill up the ranks. General Hampton at the same time was placed on duty in the South.

---

not included in Johnson's division, but is reported separately as the First Military District. November 10th, the effective force of Johnson was 6,494, the effective force of Wise 2,271. November 30th, Johnson 6,504 ; Wise, 2,345. December 20th, Johnson, 6,692 ; Wise, 520. It is not stated where the other three-fourths of Wise's brigade were on December 20th. Evidently they are not included in Johnson's division.

Wise's brigade was present at the closing operations around Petersburg, but does not appear in the Return of the Army of Northern Virginia of February 20th, 1865, the last Return of that army to be found among the Confederate archives in the possession of the War Department.

During December General Warren, having Mott's division of the Second Corps and Gregg's cavalry added to his own corps, destroyed the Weldon Railroad, as far as Hicksford on the Meherrin River, about forty miles from Petersburg. General A. P. Hill was sent to interrupt him, but not in time. The work was completed and the troops returned to their camps without his encountering them.

During the winter the Army of Northern Virginia was posted in its intrenchments in the following manner : General Hill, on the Confederate right, held from Hatcher's Run to Fort Gregg ; Generals Gordon and Anderson held from his left to the Appomattox, and General Longstreet from the Appomattox to the Confederate left at White Oak Swamp.

In the course of the winter the imperfect intrenchments at and in the vicinity of Hatcher's Run were very much strengthened, and new and strong intrenchments were thrown up on the south side of Hatcher's Run at the Crow house, a mile and a half above Armstrong's mill, and at Burgess's mill, where the Boydton plank-road crosses the run, and along the south side of the run covering the White Oak road as far as its intersection by the Claiborne road, then northward covering that road also as far as Hatcher's Run, upon which the works terminated. Heavy slashing covered the front of these new works. They were not occupied in strength but watched.[1]

---

[1] In the spring of 1865, when these works were completed, the Confederate intrenchments were thirty-seven miles in length from the White Oak Swamp on their left to the Claiborne road crossing of Hatcher's Run on their right. This length is not measured along the irregularities of the general line of intrenchments, m ch less along those of the parapet line. Eight miles of these intrenchments were north of James River, five were on the Bermuda Hundred front, and sixteen on the Petersburg line. The space along James River between Chapin's Bluff and Bermuda Hundred, which was held by heavy artillery was four miles in length. The space along the Appomattox River from the Bermuda Hundred intrenchments to the left of their Petersburg intrenchments, which space was held by batteries of artillery, was also four miles in length.

The winter of 1864-65 was one of unusual severity, making the picket duty in front of the intrenchments very severe. It was especially so to the Confederate troops with their threadbare, insufficient clothing, and meagre food, chiefly corn bread made of the coarsest meal. Meat they had but little of, and their Subsistence Department was actually importing it from abroad. Of coffee or tea and sugar, they had none except in the hospitals.

It is stated that in a secret session of the Confederate Congress the condition of the Confederacy as to subsistence was declared to be:

That there was not meat enough in the Southern Confederacy for the armies it had in the field.

That there was not in Virginia either meat or bread enough for the armies within her limits.

That the supply of bread for those armies to be obtained from other places depended absolutely upon keeping open the railroad connections of the South.

That the meat must be obtained from abroad through a seaport.

That the transportation was not now adequate, from whatever cause, to meet the necessary demands of the service.

That the supply of fresh meat to General Lee's army was precarious, and if the army fell back from Richmond and Petersburg, that there was every probability that it would cease altogether.

The condition of the deserters who constantly came into our lines during the winter appeared to prove that there was no exaggeration in this statement.

Some time in February the Confederate commissariat was got into better condition, and Lee's army was better rationed from that time until the fall of Richmond and Petersburg, and reserve dépôts were maintained at Richmond, Lynchburg, Danville, and Greensboro', containing three and a half millions rations of meat and two and a half millions rations of bread. But the rolling stock of the railroads was so worn that it could no longer bring the necessary number of rations to Lee's army in addition to the other requirements made upon it. Wagon trains were resorted to wherever practicable.

It was reported that supplies were brought to Petersburg by wagon trains from Hicksford on the Weldon Railroad, the route of the trains being up the Meherrin River to the Boydton plank road, and thence on that road through Dinwiddie Court House to Petersburg. To intercept those trains, and break up this route of supply, General Gregg was directed to march at three o'clock in the morning of the fifth of February, by way of Reams's Station to Dinwiddie Court House, move up and down the Boydton plank road, and endeavor to intercept the trains said to be on it, and do such other injury as he was able to the enemy in that direction. General Warren was directed to cross Hatcher's Run below the Vaughan road, and take position on that road, half way between Hatcher's Run and Dinwiddie Court House, and support General Gregg. General Humphreys, commanding the Second Corps since the retirement of General Hancock from it, was directed to take his two reserve divisions to the crossing of the Vaughan road over Hatcher's Run, and to Armstrong's mill, hold those two points, keep up communication with General Warren (four miles distant) and support him; and also keep up communication with our intrenchments, between three and four miles off.[1]

At the Vaughan road crossing the run was found to be dammed and obstructed by fallen trees and held by a few infantry who were merely on the lookout, and were soon dispersed, and Mott's division put in position on the south side of the run. General Smyth's division was established on the north side of the run at Armstrong's mill. They both intrenched sufficiently. Communication was opened with

---

[1] The Second Corps held the left of these intrenchments. The First Division, General Miles, remained in them.

General Warren. Opposite Smyth's centre the enemy's new intrenchments were in full view, about one thousand yards distant. Opposite his left they were hidden by woods. His right rested on a small, wooded swamp. On the right of this swamp was the open ground of the Thompson house, in front of which was a wood extending to the enemy's intrenchments. A road led from those intrenchments through this wood to the open ground at Thompson's. Further to the right was another swamp. To sit down in this way all day close to the enemy's intrenchments was to invite an attempt on one's flanks, and I anticipated that one would be made on Smyth's right, expecting the enemy to come along the wood road into the open ground at Thompson's. I therefore brought over McAllister's brigade of Mott's division and put it along the edge of the wood, though it did not cover half the space that should have been occupied. Subsequently, with General Meade's authority, I sent to General Miles for a brigade, which arrived in due time. McAllister intrenched the whole line.

A little after five o'clock the enemy's artillery opened upon Smyth, and his infantry, moving along the edge of the wood in front of Smyth's right, made a determined attack. At the same time a column of infantry emerged from the woods into the open ground of the Thompson house by the road already mentioned, evidently expecting to find it unoccupied, and that they would take Smyth in flank and rear. But McAllister had been in his intrenchments on the right of this road, and had just drawn his brigade out and formed part of it perpendicular to them. He promptly opened a heavy and unexpected fire upon the enemy's column, which fell back at once through the woods to their intrenchments. Smyth had by this time repulsed the attack on his front, but the enemy's artillery kept up a fire upon both Smyth and McAllister for some time after.

General Lee, advised of our appearance on his right flank, and being with good reason sensitive to any movement upon it, had concentrated parts of Hill's and Gordon's corps to meet it. It was this force that made the attack just described. General Lee says of it : "In the afternoon, parts of Hill's and Gordon's troops demonstrated against the enemy on the left of Hatcher's Run, near Armstrong's mill. Finding him intrenched they were withdrawn after dark."

Upon ascertaining what force of the enemy was here, General Meade ordered Hartranft's division of the Ninth Corps and Wheaton's of the Sixth to join me, and when they arrived in the night they were placed on my right.

General Gregg upon reaching the Boydton road captured some wagons and prisoners, but found that the road was but little used, and returned in the evening to Malone's bridge on Rowanty Creek. From this place he was ordered up to the Vaughan road crossing, where he arrived early in the morning of the 6th with General Warren, who had also been ordered to the same point.

A reconnoissance on the morning of the 6th showed that the enemy was not outside his intrenchments north of the run. Warren, with Gregg, was in position on the south bank. Wheaton's division and De Trobriand's brigade were held ready to support him, Mott's division having been brought to the north bank of the run.

About 1 o'clock in the afternoon General Warren made a reconnoissance with Crawford's division along the Vaughan and Dabney's mill roads, Ayres following on his left, Gregg being sent down the Vaughan road to Gravelly Run to watch the left. Griffin remained in reserve and with part of his division supported Gregg, who was heavily attacked by a part of Pegram's division of Gordon's corps, which, however, with the support Griffin gave him he pressed back. Crawford also encountered a part of Pegram's division, which he forced back to Dabney's mill, where Evans's division of Gordon's corps came to his support, and Crawford in turn had his left flank forced back. Two brigades of Ayres were now brought up to Crawford's support, and one brigade of Griffin's division, and at the same time Mahone's division arrived and formed between Evans and Pegram. The enemy's whole line then advanced to the attack, and spite of the exertions of the leading officers and the good conduct of many of the men, Warren's line gave way and fell back rapidly, but with little loss. General Wheaton's leading brigade came upon the scene of action at this time and got into line ; others reformed with it, and the enemy was checked.

A large part of one of General Warren's divisions was composed of new troops.

General Warren made a reconnoissance on the 7th, meeting the enemy, but not in force.

He states that the enemy in his encounters with them met with losses nearly equal to his own. General Pegram was killed when his division was forced back to Dabney's mill.

General Warren's total loss, including the cavalry, was 1,165 killed and wounded and 154 missing.

The loss of the Second Corps was 138 killed and wounded, among them, Colonel Murphy, Sixty-ninth New York, commanding Second Brigade, Second Division, mortally wounded. Wheaton's division lost 17 killed and wounded.

Our intrenchments were now extended to Hatcher's Run at the Vaughan road crossing, and the Second Corps held the left of the army, the Sixth Corps taking the intrenchments at Fort Fisher and the Signal Tower. The Fifth Corps was massed in rear of the left.

During the whole period of our partial investment of Petersburg and Richmond, there were frequent affairs on the picket lines, especially in front of the Petersburg intrenchments, where the affair sometimes became of a serious character, drawing into it brigades, sometimes a division. Some of these encounters occurred at points where the lines were so close as to cause apprehension of a successful night attack, and hence the effort to force back the pickets. These attacks gave occasion for the exhibition of dexterity and daring on both sides, but did not result in any appreciable modification of the lines. The loss they entailed in killed and wounded was by no means trifling.

On the 27th of February General Sheridan, with two divisions of cavalry, moved from Winchester up the valley of the Shenandoah to Staunton, thence to Charlottesville, destroying the railroad between those towns, and from Charlottesville toward Gordonsville, and also to within a short distance of Lynchburg. The James River Canal was also destroyed from New Market to near Goochland Court House, completely obliterating it as a line of supply. On the 27th of March he formed a junction with the Armies of the Potomac and the James.

There had been indications for some time past that General Lee would abandon his Petersburg and Richmond intrenchments for the purpose of uniting with General Johnston, then in front of Sherman, and General Grant was apprehensive this might be done before he was prepared for an effective pursuit. Accordingly on the 24th of March he issued the order for the movement to the left on the 29th by the armies operating against Richmond, with a view to destroy the Danville and the South Side (Lynchburg) railroads, turn Lee's right, and force him to abandon his intrenchments. Indeed as early as the 14th of March instructions had been issued to the Army of the Potomac for its guidance, in anticipation of a general movement.

Early in March, it was determined in a conference between Mr. Jefferson Davis and General Lee, that as soon as the roads would admit of movement, the Richmond and Peters-

burg lines should be abandoned, and the Army of Northern
Virginia move to Danville, unite with General Johnston and
attack General Sherman. Preparations were made accordingly. General Lee proposed in the meantime to make a
sortie in order to gain some of the works on the right of the
line held by the Army of the Potomac near the Appomattox
River, and the ridge in their rear, with the expectation that
this would oblige General Grant to concentrate there by
drawing in his left, and thus postpone the threatened necessity for abandoning Richmond and Petersburg until the
weather was favorable for falling back to Danville. This
being assented to, General Gordon was selected for the service, and his corps was brought to the intrenchments nearest
Petersburg, with its left on the Appomattox. The point of
attack was Fort Stedman, where the opposing lines were only
one hundred and fifty yards apart; the pickets fifty yards
apart. General Gordon was sanguine that this redoubt could
be taken by a night assault, and that through the breach
thus made a sufficient force could be thrown to disorganize
and destroy Grant's left wing before he could recover and
concentrate his forces from the right.

General Gordon says General Lee placed at his disposal, in
addition to his own corps, a portion of A. P. Hill's and a portion of Longstreet's, and a detachment of cavalry, in all
about one-half of the Army.

The attack was well arranged; picked men preceded the
storming party to cut away the fraise and abatis in front of
the intrenchments; the storming party was followed by three
columns, which were to push through the gap made by the
capture of Fort Stedman and seize three forts on the high
ground that commanded Fort Stedman, and the lines on the
right and left of it. These forts were supposed to be open
at the gorge. But, in point of fact, there were no such forts.
The redoubts that had a commanding fire upon Fort Sted-

man and the lines and open batteries on its right and left, were on the main line.   In front of them was the line of intrenchments erected by our troops on the 18th of June, which probably led to the misapprehension of General Gordon.

A division of infantry, moving by its left flank, was to follow the three detachments, and when halted and fronted was to move down our intrenchments to our left, being joined by the other troops as their fronts were cleared. Next were the cavalry, who were to cut our telegraphic lines and destroy the ponton bridges over the Appomattox.   Next all the remaining force was to unite in the attack.

The Ninth Corps was on our right, holding from the Appomattox to Fort Howard, a line about seven miles in length, General Willcox on the right, General Potter on the left, General Hartranft in reserve, his right at the Dunn house, his left near Fort Howard.   Taking advantage, General Parke says, of the order allowing deserters to bring their arms with them, the enemy at half-past four in the morning of the 25th quietly gained possession of several picket posts, the storming party instantly followed, and with a rush overpowered the trench guard, broke the main line between Batteries 9 and 10, turned to the right and left, gained Battery 10, overpowered the garrison of Fort Stedman after a spirited resistance, capturing the greater part of it, and then turned its artillery, four 12-pounders, and the guns of Battery 10 against Willcox's troops ; but not until they had been used effectively by the garrison.   Batteries 11 and 12, open works, were also captured.   It was so dark, General Parke says, that friends could not be distinguished from foes, and artillery could not therefore at first be used, but Brigadier-General McLaughlin, whose brigade occupied this part of the line, opened a mortar fire on Battery 11, and recaptured it with the bayonet, but entering Fort Stedman in ignorance of its capture, was himself taken prisoner.

As soon as General Parke learnt what had occurred he ordered General Willcox to recapture the works, General Hartranft to concentrate and support him, and General Tidball to post his artillery on the high ground in rear of the main line, and open at once, together with the artillery in the forts on the right and left of Fort Stedman. General Hartranft promptly concentrated his division, and while doing so, with one of his regiments and some of Willcox's troops, attacked the enemy's skirmishers, who were moving in the direction of City Point and were already at our military railroad and telegraph line, and drove them back to their own troops in our works.[1] The enemy now moved from Fort Stedman and assaulted the forts on the right and left of it, but were repulsed. By half-past seven General Parke had regained Batteries 11 and 12, had drawn a cordon of troops around Fort Stedman and Battery 10, had forced the enemy back into them, and had concentrated a fire upon them from all the artillery in the works and on the high ground in rear that bore upon them. General Hartranft was assigned to the recapture of Fort Stedman and Battery 10. At a quarter of eight o'clock he advanced to the attack and carried the fort with comparatively small loss. The cross-fire of artillery and infantry on the space between the lines prevented the enemy who were in our works from escaping, and reinforcements from coming to them. Many were killed and wounded trying to get back to their own lines ; 1,949 prisoners, including 71 officers and nine stands of colors, fell into General Parke's hands. His loss was 494 killed and wounded and 523 missing ; a total of 1,017.

General Gordon says that guides were sent with the commanders of the detachments that were to seize the forts in rear of Stedman, but that the guides were lost or had de-

---

[1] Those whom General Parke calls skirmishers were probably the three detachments of Gordon's troops sent to capture the rear forts.

serted, and that the commanders could not find the forts'
which, as I have already explained, were in fact on the main
line. Nearly all of the troops composing these detachments
were killed or captured.

General Gordon says that " a large body of the troops
sent by General Lee from General Longstreet's corps were
delayed by the breaking down of trains, or by some other
cause, and did not arrive at the appointed hour, which
caused so great a delay that we did not get in the fort and
upon the enemy's flank at as early an hour as was expected,
and daylight found us with the plan only half executed."

General Meade had passed the night of the 24th at City
Point, the telegraph to which place was cut by the enemy.
At half-past five General Parke telegraphed General Webb,
Chief of Staff, what had occurred, and at a quarter-past six
learnt in reply that General Meade was at City Point, and
that he, General Parke, was in command (being the senior
in rank). He then directed General Wright to send him a
division, which got to the ground just as our works were retaken, and General Warren, who had the Fifth Corps under
arms ready to move toward General Parke's right, to move
up with his corps. By the time the works were retaken telegraphic communication with General Meade at City Point
was opened.

At a quarter before six I received a telegram from General
Hunt, Chief of Artillery, informing me that the enemy had
broken through our right, captured Fort Stedman and were
moving toward City Point. I at once got the Second Corps
under arms ready to move, ordered the division commanders
to make strong reconnoissances and ascertain the condition
of the enemy in my front, and to attack their intrenched
picket line with a view to assaulting their main works, if the
force holding them had been materially weakened. This
was duly communicated to General Parke and General

Meade, and approved by them. The intrenched picket line of the enemy was captured, and our line was advanced beyond it under the close fire of the artillery and musketry of their main works, which proved to be held by a force sufficient to maintain them against assault. In fact, General Hill's force here had not been reduced, probably in expectation of a counter-attack. Under cover of the artillery and musketry fire of their works the enemy moved out repeatedly with strong force at several points to recapture their picket intrenchments, but were always driven back.

The loss of the Second Corps was 513 killed and wounded and 177 missing; total, 690.

The enemy's number of killed and wounded was probably about the same as that of the Second Corps ; 358 officers and enlisted men were captured from them.

General Wright also attacked and captured the enemy's intrenched picket line, losing about 400 in the encounters, and capturing 547 prisoners.

It was this capture of the intrenched picket line of the enemy that made it practicable for General Wright to carry the enemy's main line of intrenchments by assault on the morning of the 2d of April.

The total loss of the enemy in the operations of the 25th of March must have been nearly 4,000 ; ours, about 2,000.

CHAPTER XIII.

MOVEMENT TO TURN LEE'S RIGHT—ACTIONS OF WHITE OAK RIDGE AND DINWIDDIE COURT HOUSE—THE BATTLE OF FIVE FORKS—LEE'S INTRENCHMENTS WEST OF PETERSBURG CARRIED—HE ABANDONS THE RICHMOND AND PETERSBURG LINES, AND RETREATS TOWARD DANVILLE.

HAVING established his army at Goldsboro', North Carolina, about 145 miles south of Petersburg, General Sherman visited General Grant at City Point on the 27th of March, and stated, as he had done before by letter, that he would be ready to move by the 10th of April, if it should be necessary to bring his army in co-operation with the forces in front of Richmond and Petersburg. He proposed, in the event of such a movement, to threaten Raleigh, and then, turning suddenly to the right, reach the Roanoke River near Weldon (60 miles south of Petersburg), from which point he could move to the Richmond and Danville Railroad at its junction with the Petersburg and Lynchburg Railroad, Burke's junction, which would cut off Lee's retreat to Danville and to Lynchburg, or could join the armies operating against Richmond, as might be deemed best. This plan, General Grant says, he was directed to carry out, if, in the meantime, he received no further directions. The movement ordered for the 29th of March was explained to him.

Apprehensive that General Lee might any night abandon his intrenchments, and being satisfied that he would do so as soon as he heard that General Sherman had crossed the

Roanoke, General Grant determined not to delay the movement ordered for the 29th, but to take the initiative.

On the night of the 27th, General Ord, commanding the Army of the James, taking with him General Gibbon, with Turner's and Foster's divisions of the Twenty-fourth Corps, Brigadier-General Birney's division (colored) of the Twenty-fifth Corps, and General Mackenzie's cavalry (formerly Kautz's) made a secret march of 36 miles to the left of the Army of the Potomac, taking post in rear of the Second Corps on the evening of the 28th. He managed this movement so well that the enemy remained in ignorance of it until the 2d of April.

General Devens's division of Gibbon's corps remained in the intrenchments on the north side of the James; General Weitzel's two divisions of the Twenty-fifth Corps in the Bermuda Hundred intrenchments, he having command there and on the north side of the James.

Upon the resumption of active operations in the spring of 1865, the effective force of the two contending armies, according to the latest returns of each, was as follows:

The effective force of infantry of the Army of the Potomac was 69,000; of field artillery, 6,000, with 243 guns.

The effective force of infantry of the Army of the James was 32,000; of field artillery, 3,000, with 126 guns; and of cavalry, 1,700. General Ord took with him, on the 27th of March, about one-half the infantry and all the cavalry of his army.

The present for duty of the enlisted men of cavalry under General Sheridan was 13,000.

Total of all arms of the three independent commands 124,700.

The effective force of Lee's infantry was not less than 46,000; of his field artillery, not less than 5,000; and of his cavalry, 6,000; making a total of not less than 57,000.[1]

---

[1] See Appendix L.

On the 28th of March General Grant instructed General Sheridan to move at an early hour on the morning of the 29th, cross Hatcher's Run below where it would be crossed by the Fifth Corps (at Monk's Neck bridge), pass near to or through Dinwiddie Court House, and reach the right and rear of the enemy as soon as practicable. He was informed that the Second and Fifth Corps would be in position on the Vaughan road, south of Hatcher's Run, extending to, or near to Dinwiddie Court House. It was not the intention, he said, to attack the enemy in his intrenched position, but to force him out, if possible, with a view to attacking him. Should the enemy remain within his main intrenched line, then General Sheridan might " cut loose and push for the Danville Road." If practicable, he was to cross the South Side Railroad between Petersburg and Burkesville, destroy it as much as practicable without interfering with the complete destruction of the Danville Railroad, which he was to strike as near the Appomattox as possible. That being done, the South Side Railroad west of Burkesville was to be similarly destroyed.

Having accomplished the destruction of these two roads, he might return to the two armies, or join General Sherman. These instructions were preliminary, and might be changed on the following day.

General Humphreys was directed to cross Hatcher's Run by the Vaughan road on the morning of the 29th, as soon as General Ord's troops occupied the intrenchments held by the Second Corps, and take position with his right near Hatcher's Run, and his left in communication or connection with the Fifth Corps, and advance toward the enemy's position.

General Warren was directed to cross Hatcher's Run at Monk's Neck bridge early on the morning of the 29th, but not to proceed beyond the junction of the Vaughan and

Quaker roads until the Second Corps was in position, when he would advance toward the enemy by the Boydton road, his right connecting with the Second Corps; but at mid-day on the 29th he was directed to move up the Quaker road.

General Wright was directed to hold himself ready to with-draw the Sixth Corps from the intrenchments it was hold-ing; General Parks to remain in the intrenchments manned by the Ninth Corps, and be prepared to take up the return-works from his left at Fort Sedgwick, when the Sixth Corps should be withdrawn.

In accordance with these instructions, General Sheridan marched to Dinwiddie Court House on the 29th, by way of Reams's Station and Malone's crossing of Rowanty Creek, encountering only small pickets of the enemy's cavalry; but learning that a strong force of the enemy's cavalry was on the south side of Stony Creek, near the railroad depot, Custer's division was directed to remain near Malone's crossing to protect the trains. This Confederate cavalry force consisted of W. H. F. Lee's and Rosser's divisions.

General Warren, moving as directed, after advancing Grif-fin's division to within two miles of Dinwiddie Court House, withdrew it to the Quaker road, under his modified instruc-tions, and in the afternoon moved up that road, Griffin in advance. About a mile from its junction with the Boydton plank-road, in the vicinity of the steam sawmill, his leading brigade, General Chamberlain's, came in contact with Wise's and Wallace's brigades of Anderson's command, when a sharp engagement took place, in which the enemy was forced to fall back into their intrenchments on the White Oak road, after suffering severely, losing some 200 prisoners, besides the wounded left on the field. A portion of Bartlett's bri-gade took part in the action toward its close. The loss in Griffin's division was 367 killed and wounded, Brigadier-

General Sickle among the latter. The loss of the enemy was evidently greater.

General Humphreys, taking position as directed, moved forward, meeting with little opposition until darkness put a stop to further progress.

As soon as the movement of our troops was perceived by the enemy on the morning of the 29th, General Lee sent General Anderson, with Bushrod Johnson's division and Wise's brigade, to the extreme right of his intrenchments along the White Oak road. A part of this force, as we have seen, encountered Griffin's division in the afternoon of that day. Pickett's division, which had been relieved from the charge of the Bermuda Hundred intrenchments by Mahone's division early in March, was likewise transferred to the extreme right of the intrenchments, reaching there at daylight on the 30th.

General Fitz Lee's division was on the extreme left of the Confederate army, when, on March 28th, General Lee, learning that Sheridan's cavalry was held on the left of the Army of the Potomac, and surmising that it was to move against the South Side Railroad and his right rear, directed General Fitz Lee to move at once to Five Forks, assume the command of all the cavalry, and with the infantry supports he would send, attack General Sheridan in that vicinity. General Fitz Lee arrived at Sutherland Station with his division on the night of the 29th.

General Hill extended to his right in the course of the night of the 29th, and early in the morning of the 30th, Mc-Gowan's and McRae's brigades, moving into the intrenchments on the White Oak road on Johnson's left, Scales's and Cooke's brigades into the intrenchments in front of Burgess's mill and along the south side of Hatcher's Run, probably including the Crow house intrenchments, while Lane's, Davis's, McComb's, and Thomas's brigades held those maintained by Hill north of Hatcher's Run. General Heth commanded the brigades south of the run, General Wilcox those north of it.[1]

_ In the course of the 29th, General Grant instructed General Sheridan not to move against the enemy's railroads for the present, but to endeavor, on the following morning, to push around the enemy and get on his right rear.

The rain fell heavily all the night of the 29th, and all the next day, rendering the roads impassable for artillery and wagons until corduroyed. The country was flat, covered generally with dense forest and tangled undergrowth, with numerous small, swampy streams, that, owing to the flatness of the country, did not drain the downfall quickly. The soil was a mixture of clay and sand, partaking in some places of the nature of quicksand.

On the 30th General Humphreys continued his advance, driving the enemy inside his intrenchments along Hatcher's Run from the Crow house to the Boydton road, pressing close up against them, but not assaulting.

General Warren moved up the Quaker and Boydton roads as far as the Dabney Mill road, and occupied a line covering the Boydton road as far as Gravelly Run. A reconnoissance was made by General Ayres's division northwestward to the vicinity of the point where the White Oak road intrenchments turned north to cover the Claiborne road, and a picket line was established in that vicinity, supported by a part of his division, the other part remaining on Griffin's left in advance of the Boydton road.

General Sheridan directed General Merritt to gain possession of Five Forks with Devin's division, supported by Davies's brigade of Crook's division, while General Crook guarded the Boydton road crossing of Stony Creek. Gen-

---

[1] For the space of a mile above the Crow house intrenchments the run was dammed so as to be impassable, and required only a picket line to watch it.

eral Merritt advanced to the forks of the road, near J. Boisseau's, from which point reconnoissances were sent on the
left hand or Five Forks road, and on the right hand road
leading past Dr. Boisseau's to the White Oak road. On
both these roads the enemy's cavalry was encountered and
heavy skirmishing ensued. Devin halted for the night at
the forks near J. Boisseau's.

Early on the morning of the 30th, General Fitz Lee
marched to Five Forks by the most direct road, and advancing toward Dinwiddie Court House, encountered Sheridan's
cavalry, when sharp skirmishing ensued, in which Lee lost a
general officer wounded. At dark General W. H. F. Lee
and General Rosser joined him. At sunset General Pickett
arrived at Five Forks, by way of the White Oak road, with
Corse's, Terry's, and Steuart's brigades of his own division,
and Ransom's and Wallace's brigades of Johnson's division.
General Sheridan was soon made aware of Pickett's arrival
there, and reported it to General Grant.

According to the Return of February 20th, the cavalry divisions of the two Lees numbered 5,760 enlisted men, including Roberts's brigade, which, under the orders of General
Anderson, picketed the White Oak road from the right of
the Confederate intrenchments to Five Forks. The infantry
under Pickett, by the same return, numbered about 3,600 enlisted men of his own division and 3,000 of Johnson's, making a total of 6,600. Hunton's brigade, of Pickett's division,
and Fulton's and Moody's brigades, of Johnson's division, together with Wise's brigade, remained in the intrenchments
along the White Oak road.

Upon arriving at Five Forks, General Pickett assumed
command of the operation to be undertaken the following
morning against General Sheridan. In connection with
Pickett's attack, General Lee intended to get on the left flank
of the Fifth Corps, with part of Hill's and Anderson's troops,

and roll it up, the troops that remained in the intrenchments to join successively this flank attacking force as it arrived in front of the intrenchments held by them.   In this way he hoped to defeat the attempt upon the South Side Railroad and his right rear.

General Lee's line was now so extended on his right that it was apparent that some part of it must be very thinly held, and Generals Ord, Wright, and Parke were directed on the 30th to ascertain the feasibility of carrying the intrenchments in their fronts by assault.   Both Generals Wright and Parke reported that it was practicable to carry them in that way.

It was now General Grant's intention to reinforce General Sheridan with an infantry corps to enable him to turn Lee's right, and while he was accomplishing this to assault the Petersburg lines with the other infantry corps ; but the condition of the roads prevented immediate movement.

Late in the afternoon General Warren, in reporting the result of General Ayres's reconnoissance, suggested that a division of the Second Corps should take Griffin's place during the night, and that the Fifth Corps should occupy the White Oak road early the next morning, an important object, since it would cut Lee's direct communication with Pickett at Five Forks.   This was so far approved that General Humphreys was directed to relieve General Griffin's division during the night (which was done with Miles's division before daylight of the 31st), and General Warren was directed to place Crawford's and Griffin's divisions within supporting distance of Ayres.   General Ayres was directed by General Warren to reinforce his advance by daylight of the 31st with his whole division, General Crawford to hold his command ready to follow General Ayres, and General Griffin to take up the position Ayres had held at Mrs. Butler's, as soon as his division was relieved by troops of the Second Corps.   The position taken by General Ayres was in the open ground on the south side of the White Oak road, near W. Dabney's, and about 600 yards from that road.

At 7 A.M. of the 31st General Crawford was ordered to move out to the Holliday house, about 500 yards in rear of Ayres, and support him. General Griffin was about 1,000 yards in rear of Crawford on the south or east side of a branch of Gravelly Run, which had become very much swollen during the night, and was on that account difficult to cross.

At 8 o'clock General Ayres was informed of Pickett's presence at Five Forks, about four miles from his left, and was cautioned to be prepared for an attack against his left flank as well as on his front. General Ayres formed his division, with General Winthrop's brigade looking north fronting the White Oak road, General Denison's Maryland brigade along a ravine on Winthrop's left looking west, his third brigade somewhat to Winthrop's right, and a brigade which Crawford sent him in rear of his centre.

At half-past eight o'clock corps commanders were notified that there would be no movement of troops that day, owing to the almost impassable condition of the roads and country, caused by the continuous heavy rain that had fallen. But at 9.40 A.M. General Warren telegraphed General Meade that the enemy's pickets covered the White Oak road, and that he had sent word to General Ayres to drive them off or ascertain with what force the enemy held the road. General Meade replied to this, that if his reconnoissance should show that he could get possession of and hold the White Oak road, he was to do so, notwithstanding the order to suspend operations during the day.

General Lee, in furtherance of his plan of attacking the left flank of the Fifth Corps on the morning of the 31st, directed General McGowan to take his own brigade and Gracie's (commanded by Colonel Sanford) and move out of the intrenchments by the White Oak road, get across the flank of the Fifth Corps, and attack. General Hunton's brigade was drawn up on the edge of the wood along the north side of the White Oak road, fronting the open ground of W. Dabney. General Wise's brigade was formed on his left, but at precisely what hour does not appear. General Lee was on the ground, directing the movement in person.

General McGowan had not quite got into the position he intended to take, and General Hunton had just formed his brigade, when, at eleven o'clock, General Winthrop's brigade moved forward, supported on the right by the Third Brigade, commanded by General James Gwyn. When within 50 yards of the White Oak road the enemy's line of battle moved forward out of the wood across the road into the open field to meet them, and the firing began. Seeing that he had a much superior force to encounter, General Winthrop faced his brigade about, General Ayres says, and marched back across the field in good order. It was now General Ayres's intention to form his line of battle along the edge of the wood on the south side of the field, but the supports could not be held, due, in part, he says, to the enemy's attack on his left flank at the same time that the front attack was made. Again he endeavored to form his troops along a ravine, but in this he also failed, and they fell back to the ground they had occupied the day before, behind a branch of Gravelly Run, where Griffin was in position, and to the intrenchments along the Boydton road, along the left of Miles's division. Brigadier-General Denison was among the wounded. Crawford's division fell back in confusion, Colonel Kellogg attempting with his brigade to make a stand, but uselessly.

General Hunton, in his testimony before the Warren Court of Inquiry, says of this affair that he had scarcely formed line of battle when a large force of infantry marched out upon them; that he had no orders to attack or charge, but that a lieutenant in his brigade, promoted for gallantry, rushed out from his company, waved his sword, and said, "Follow me, boys," and from that the three brigades, McGowan's, Gracie's, and his own, made the charge. General McGowan says of it, that he had not completed his movement to the right across the left flank of Ayres when the firing in front began, and he at once ordered the charge to be made; that it was successful; and although the enemy attempted to rally two or three times, yet they were driven from the ground and across a branch of Gravelly Run, on the other side of which was a strong force with artillery. General Hunton mentions the successive attempts to reform made by Warren's troops when they were falling back. His brigade, he says, did not advance to the run, but about two-thirds of the way to it from the White Oak Road, that is, not much beyond the Holliday fields.

The sudden burst of heavy musketry firing, coming from the position of Warren's advance troops, followed soon by a large and increasing number of stragglers coming to the rear, satisfied General Humphreys that Warren's advance needed support, and he at once ordered General Miles to go forward quickly with two of his brigades and attack the enemy's left flank. This was done in a prompt and spirited manner. The other two brigades of his division followed soon after. Mott was ordered to attack in his front, and Hays the Crow house intrenchments. These directions were in conformity to those subsequently received from General Meade.

Wise's brigade had advanced on the left of Hunton's, and being struck in front and flank by Miles, fell back rapidly into the intrenchments with severe loss of killed, wounded, and prisoners. The prisoners taken numbered more than 300, some of whom belonged to Hunton's brigade. The flag of an Alabama regiment was also captured.

Wise being driven from the ground, Hunton was forced to fall back also, and General Warren having by that time got some part of Griffin's division across the run, with which he threatened McGowan's right flank, the whole force fell back to the position occupied by Ayres in the morning near the W. Dabney house.

The enemy's intrenchments covering the White Oak road were on the crest of a long slope, with wide slashings in front, and abatis along the ditch, with artillery at short intervals. The works were unused and in good order.

General Mott attempted to carry the redoubts and intrenchments covering the Boydton road crossing of Hatcher's Run, but without success. General Hays attempted to carry the Crow house redoubt, but although he kept down the fire of their artillery, the heavy slashing in front of the works was absolutely impassable to even a small body of troops.[1]

By half-past two o'clock General Warren had formed his corps on the north side of the branch of Gravelly Run ready to move forward to the White Oak road where the morning's engagement had begun, Griffin in the centre (Chamberlain's brigade leading), Ayres's division on Griffin's left, Crawford's on his right, both in echelon. General Chamberlain, driving in some skirmishers as he went forward, came in front of Hunton's brigade, in slight breastworks, from which he received a sharp fire. General Gregory came to his support, moving into the wood on his right. Chamberlain then charged the breastworks in his front, General Hunton says,

---

[1] General Wilcox says of these attempts of Mott and Hays, and of the pressing of General Ord's troops close up against the intrenchments north of Hatcher's Run, that during most of the day, while the fighting was severe further to the right there was a very heavy skirmish going on about Burgess's mill, and on Cooke's brigade below the mill and on Lane's brigade. It was so heavy and threatening about the mill (Mott's attack) that General Heth sent to him for a brigade, but that the firing was increasing so on his own front (Hays's and Ord's troops) that he could not send any assistance to Heth.

in the most gallant manner, carried them, capturing some prisoners and a battle-flag, while Gregory turned their left. Hunton was driven into the White Oak road intrenchments, and McGowan, seeing Hunton's line give way, fell back at once with his two brigades into their main works.

The killed and wounded in General Warren's corps to-day were 173 in the First Division. 325 in the Second, and 431 in the Third, and 7 in the artillery and escort. Total, 936. The missing were 470, making an aggregate of 1,406.

The casualties in General Humphreys's corps were 374 killed and wounded, officers and enlisted men.

General Ord pushed up close to the enemy's works, losing sharply in doing so, and capturing many prisoners.

In the morning of the 31st General Fitz Lee moved with his cavalry toward Dinwiddie Court House on the direct road to it from Five Forks, encountering Devin's division, which was moving toward Five Forks. Pickett's infantry had not yet moved. Leaving Munford (Fitz Lee's division) in contact with Devin, near the fork of the Gravelly Run Church road, Pickett moved with his infantry, Fitz Lee with W. H. F. Lee's and Rosser's cavalry divisions leading, by way of Little Five Forks, west of Chamberlain's Creek or bed, intending to cross that stream at Fitzgerald's and Danse's and attack General Sheridan's left flank, while Munford attacked his front.

General Crook was holding Fitzgerald's crossing with General Smith's brigade, Danse's crossing, a mile above, with Davies's brigade, keeping Gregg in reserve. Fitzgerald's crossing was two and one-half miles from Dinwiddie Court House, measured by the road, and in a direct line a mile and three-quarters from it in a northwest direction. As soon as General W. H. F. Lee arrived upon the ground he attempted to force the passage of Chamberlain's bed at Fitzgerald's crossing, and succeeded in getting over, but was driven back with heavy loss. No better success was met with at Danse's crossing at first, but about one o'clock the infantry, Corse's brigade leading, succeeded in carrying it after sharp fighting, in which it met with severe loss. Gregg attacking held them here for a time. Munford meanwhile had forced Devin back, and Pickett's infantry driving Davies upon Devin's left, passed between Devin and Crook. Being thus isolated, and unable to withdraw to Dinwiddie Court House by the direct road, Devin and Davies were ordered to retire, fighting, toward the Boydton road, and by that road to reach the Court House. Gibbs (of Devin's division) withdrew his brigade toward the Court House and joined Crook's command. W. H. F. Lee had now forced the crossing of Chamberlain's Run, and moving up the road through the Adams farms, united with and formed the right of Pickett's troops—Munford his left. Crook's two brigades, Smith's and Gregg's, had been forced to fall back.

Pickett having exposed his rear in following Devin and Davies toward the Boydton road, General Sheridan ordered Gibbs and Gregg to attack him, and directed Custer to bring up two of his brigades, Pennington's and Capehart's, to join in the attack. This attack freed Devin and Davies from further molestation, and forced Pickett to face about and meet Sheridan's line of battle in front of the Court House. A spirited, obstinate contest ensued, which lasted until night, Smith's brigade, General Sheridan says, bearing the brunt of the cavalry attack.

Devin and Davies reached the Court House by way of the Boydton road, but not in time to take part in the closing action.

The ground over which the greater part of the fighting took place during the day was very heavy ; a large part of it was densely wooded.

The two contending lines of battle lay very close to each

other that night, Pickett's infantry across the road from Din-widdie Court House to Five Forks, with cavalry on each flank, whose pickets extended on his left to the vicinity of the Boydton road near G. U. Brooks's, and on his right to Fitzgerald's crossing of Chamberlain's Run. Custer held Sheridan's front, supported by Devin.

About five o'clock in the afternoon General Warren, then at W. Dabney's on the White Oak road, heard the sound of General Sheridan's engagement coming from a southwest direction. It seemed to him to have receded and to be still receding. He at once sent General Bartlett with his brigade of Griffin's division across the country to General Sheridan's support, with directions to attack the enemy in flank. He sent his topographer, Major Cope, with him. A little later he received directions from General Meade to push a brigade down the White Oak road so as to open it for General Sheri-dan, and to support the brigade if necessary. At half-past six he was directed to send the force which had been ordered to move out the White Oak road down the Boydton plank-road as promptly as possible, as a staff-officer of General Merritt had reported to General Meade that the enemy had penetrated between General Sheridan's main command and Warren's position.

But as General Bartlett was at that time too distant to be recalled for the prompt execution of this order, General Warren directed General Pearson, who was then on the Boyd-ton road with three regiments, to move at once toward Din-widdie Court House. But the bridge at the Boydton road crossing of Gravelly Run had been destroyed by the enemy on the 29th, and the stream, swollen by the rains, had be-come unfordable for infantry, and General Pearson was com-pelled to stop there. At eight o'clock General Warren was advised by General Meade that General Sheridan had been forced back to Dinwiddie Court House by a strong force of

cavalry supported by infantry, and as this left the rear of the
Fifth and Second Corps open on the Boydton road, it would
require great vigilance on their part; that the brigade sent
down the Boydton road should not go farther than Gravelly
Run.   But about half-past nine General Warren received orders to withdraw his command from the White Oak road to
the Boydton road, and send Griffin's division at once to General Sheridan by the Boydton road.

General Humphreys was directed to throw back the left
of the Second Corps.

General Warren at once sent a staff officer, and afterward
Captain Benyaurd, of the Engineers, to examine and repair,
or rebuild the bridge, which, it was found, required the
building of a span forty feet in length, and prepared to withdraw to the plank-road, and send Griffin to General Sheridan,
advising General Meade of the position and condition of his
several divisions.   Somewhat later General Warren was notified that the division to be sent to General Sheridan must
start at once.   In replying to this, General Warren stated
that the bridge was broken, and that it would take he did
not know how long to repair or rebuild it; that he would
make every effort to render it passable by the time General
Griffin reached it.

At 8.40 General Warren telegraphed General Meade,[1] suggesting that he should move with his corps, and attack the
enemy near Dinwiddie Court House on one side, while General Sheridan attacked on the other, *provided the enemy did
not threaten us south of Gravelly Run, east of the plank-road.*

---

[1] General Meade's headquarters were at the Vaughan road crossing of Hatcher's
Run, about five miles from General Warren's, which were on the Boydton road.
General Grant's headquarters were near Dabney's mill, about two miles from
General Meade's.   It is evident, from the great length of time that was required
to communicate between these headquarters, that the telegraph was working
badly.   General Grant's headquarters were about eight miles from Dinwiddie
Court House.

At 9.45 General Meade submitted this proposition (which, under the circumstances, was the best thing on all accounts to do) to General Grant, and at the same time stated that Bartlett's brigade was at or near Gravelly Run, on the road running north from Dinwiddie Court House, past J. Boisseau's, to the White Oak road ; that Warren could move at once that way and take the force threatening Sheridan in rear, or he could send one division to support Sheridan near Dinwiddie Court House, and move on the enemy's rear with the two other divisions of the Fifth Corps.   To this General Grant replied, " Let Warren move in the way you propose, and urge him not to stop for anything.   Let Griffin go on as he was first directed."

At 10.50 General Warren received General Meade's reply to his suggestion of 8.40, which, conforming to General Grant's despatch just quoted, directed General Warren to send Griffin promptly, as ordered, by the Boydton road, and to move the rest of his corps by the road Bartlett was on, and strike the enemy in rear.   He was informed that General Sheridan reported his own position to be north of Dinwiddie Court House, near Dr. Smith's, and that the enemy held the cross-roads at that point.   He was directed to be very prompt in this movement, and get the forks of the Brooks cross-road, so as to open communication by it with the Boydton road, and cautioned not to encumber himself with anything that would impede his progress or prevent his moving in any direction.

General Meade informed General Sheridan of the orders given General Warren, and what had been done to get troops to him, and by what routes part of them would unite with him, and part co-operate with him.   General Grant also informed him of the orders given for the same object, and that he had also sent Mackenzie's cavalry to him.

Upon receiving the above order at 10.50, General Warren

replied that he would send Ayres instead of Griffin to General Sheridan by the Boydton road, as in withdrawing his troops to that road in accordance with previous orders, Ayres's division was necessarily the first to reach it ; and that he would move with Griffin's and Crawford's divisions against the enemy, as the last despatch from General Meade directed.   At the same time he gave the preliminary orders for the movement of these two divisions.

His despatches do not clearly explain why he did not move with these two divisions as quickly as the troops could be got in motion, though it is to be inferred from the subsequent despatches that it was because he apprehended that Ayres might not get to General Sheridan in time to prevent him from being forced back to the Vaughan road, and that in that case the best route for the whole corps would be by the Boydton road.   The tenor of General Meade's instructions to him before and after 11 P.M., was, that the first and most important object for him to accomplish was to get a division to General Sheridan by the Boydton, or any other road not closed by the enemy, at the earliest possible moment, and in time to go into action at daylight.

It was not until one o'clock in the morning of the 1st of April that General Warren had a reply from General Meade, concerning the destruction of the bridge over Gravelly Run, which neither General Meade nor General Grant had been aware of, and in which it was suggested that the troops for General Sheridan should go by the Quaker road ; and stating that time was of the utmost importance ; that General Sheridan could not maintain himself at Dinwiddie Court House without reinforcements ; that he, General Warren, must use every exertion to get troops to him as soor as possible.   If necessary to insure that, he could send troops by both roads, and give up the rear attack.   If General Sheridan was

not reinforced and was compelled to fall back, he would retire by the Vaughan road.   But the distance from the position of General Warren's troops to Dinwiddie Court House,
by the Quaker road, was from 9 to 10 miles, and by that
route they could scarcely reach General Sheridan before
eight o'clock in the morning—too late an hour to accomplish
the object of their going.   Of this General Meade was advised, but General Warren added that if he failed to send
reinforcements by the Vaughan road, he would send them
by the Quaker road.

In case General Sheridan should be obliged to retire by
the Vaughan road, the best route, in General Warren's opinion, by which the rear of the enemy could be attacked would
be by the Boydton road.   As it appeared to General Warren
that this despatch left it discretionary with him as to how
he could best reinforce General Sheridan, he determined to
abide by the movement already in progress.

At two o'clock in the morning the bridge over Gravelly
Run was practicable for the passage of infantry, and General
Ayres was crossing it, in his advance toward Dinwiddie
Court House.   Of this General Warren at once advised Gen-
eral Meade.

An hour before daybreak, when about two miles from the
Court House, General Ayres was met by an officer of General
Sheridan's staff, who led him back about a mile to the
Brooks road, and along it to the road leading north from the
Court House to the White Oak road, where, by direction of
General Sheridan, the division was massed to await further
orders.   General Ayres says that about the dawn of day,
soon after entering the Brooks Road, one of Munford's ve-
dettes was seen moving off.

At half-past four o'clock General Warren learnt that Ayres
had communicated with General Sheridan, and he was about
joining Generals Griffin and Crawford to move across the

country against Pickett's rear, when he received General Sheridan's despatch sent at 3 A.M.[1]

But General Warren should have moved with Griffin and Crawford as soon as practicable after receiving Meade's order at 10.50 P.M., though it will be observed that subsequent to that hour General Meade subordinated all General Warren's efforts to ensuring the presence of one of his divisions with General Sheridan by daylight.[2]

---

[1] This despatch said: "I am holding in front of Dinwiddie Court House, on the road leading to Five Forks, for three-quarters of a mile, with General Custer's division. The enemy are in his immediate front, lying so as to cover the road just this side of the Adams House, which leads out across Chamberlain's Bed or Run. I understand you have a division at J. Boiseau's [Dr. Boisseau's was meant]; if so you are in rear of the enemy's line, and almost on his flank. I will hold on here. Possibly they may attack Custer at daylight; if so, have this division attack instantly and in full force. Attack at daylight anyway, and I will make an effort to get the road this side of Adams' house, and if I do, you can capture the whole of them. Any force moving down the road I am holding, or on the White Oak road, will be in the enemy's rear, and in all probability get any force that may escape you by a flank attack. Do not fear my leaving here. If the enemy remain I shall fight at daylight."

[2] The Court of Inquiry which was appointed by the President, at the request of General Warren, to investigate this and other matters, say of this:

"Notwithstanding that dispositions suitable for the contingency of Sheridan's falling back from Dinwiddie might well have occupied and perplexed General Warren's mind during the night, the court is of the opinion that he should have moved the two divisions by the Crump road in obedience to the orders and expectations of his commander, upon whom alone rested the responsibility of the consequences.

"It appears from the despatches and General Warren's testimony, that neither Generals Meade, Sheridan, nor Warren expressed an intention of having this column attack before daylight.

"The court is further of the opinion that General Warren should have started with two divisions, as directed by General Meade's despatch (CIV., heretofore quoted), as early after its receipt at 10.50 P.M., as he could be assured of the prospect of Ayres's departure down the Boydton plank-road, and should have advanced on the Crump road as far as directed in that despatch, or as far as might be practicable or necessary to fulfil General Meade's intentions; whereas the evidence shows that he did not start until between five and six o'clock on the morning of the 1st of April, and did not reach J. Boisseau's with the head of the column till about seven o'clock in the morning.

"The despatches show that Generals Meade and Warren anticipated a withdrawal during the night of the enemy's forces fronting General Sheridan, which was rendered highly probable from the known position in their rear of a portion

General Bartlett had moved with his brigade from the vicinity of W. Dabney's on the White Oak road, at five o'clock in the afternoon of the 31st, by a wood-road toward the sound of firing near Dinwiddie Court House. This brought him to Dr. Boisseau's, on the most direct road from the White Oak road to the Court House, where his skirmishers met those of the enemy, and drove them across Gravelly Run on that road and at Crump's. A picket line was then established by Bartlett along the run. It was dark before this was accomplished.

The presence of General Bartlett's brigade along the main branch of Gravelly Run, at the crossing of these roads, became known to General Pickett about ten o'clock at night. Its subsequent withdrawal, near midnight, was not known to the enemy. General Fitz Lee says that General Pickett believing it to be the advance of the Fifth Corps, determined to withdraw to Five Forks during the night. Accordingly the ambulance and ammunition trains and the artillery began to move back about midnight, followed by the infantry, which took the most direct road to Five Forks, the last brigade, Corse's, getting off just before, or about, daylight. Munford's division followed on the route of the infantry about daylight. W. H. F. Lee's and Rosser's divisions at the same time crossed Chamberlain's Bed, and returned to Five Forks by way of Little Five Forks.[1] Having reported

---

of the Fifth Corps (Bartlett's brigade) at G. Boisseau's, [Dr. Boisseau's is meant. —A. A. H.] and the event justified the anticipation."—*Proceedings, Findings, and Opinions of Court of Inquiry in Case of Gen. G. K. Warren*, pp. 1558–9.

[1] General Fitz Lee says, in his testimony before the Warren Court of Inquiry, that in consultation with General Pickett, when they learnt, about ten o'clock at night, that our infantry was moving against them, it was decided to withdraw, and that nearly all the artillery, ammunition, and ambulance trains which preceded the troops got off by midnight.

He further says that W. H. F. Lee's and Rosser's divisions were ordered by him to withdraw at four o'clock in the morning, and that Munford's division withdrew at daylight, following the infantry.

General W. H. F. Lee states in his testimony that he began his withdrawal a little before day; that his impression was that the infantry withdrew about mid-

this action by telegraph to General Lee, General Pickett was directed to maintain the position of Five Forks, in order to cover the South Side Railroad and the wagon-roads south of the Appomattox, which Lee intended to use in abandoning Petersburg and Richmond, and moving toward Danville or Lynchburg.   He at once intrenched as much as practicable.

At 5 A.M. General Griffin moved from the White Oak road across the country to Crump's, and thence to the forks of the road at J. Boisseau's, where, about seven o'clock in the morning, he met General Devin with his cavalry division, and reported to General Sheridan.   General Crawford followed him. General Warren was directed by General Sheridan to remain at J. Boisseau's, refresh his men, and be ready to move to the front when required ; and General Mackenzie, who had reported with his cavalry, was directed to rest at Dinwiddie Court House until further orders.

At daylight General Merritt, with the First and Third Cavalry Divisions moved forward toward Five Forks, pressing the rear of the enemy ; Custer's division, dismounted, on the left (the country being impracticable for mounted men),

---

night or after midnight; that the news came to him about midnight that the infantry would retire.

The despatch of his Adjutant-General to General Beale was shown to him, dated 2 A.M., April 1, 1865, saying, " General Lee wishes you to withdraw your command to this side of the creek when General Pickett's infantry has withdrawn, at 4 A.M.   You will bivouac on this side."

This despatch shows that it was expected that the infantry would have been out of the way by four o'clock, which conforms to General Corse's statement that his brigade, the rear of the infantry, withdrew or started to retire about daylight, perhaps a little before; it was very early dawn, just about the dawn of day.

Colonel Walter Harrison, Adjutant and Inspector-General of Pickett's division, says Pickett's command started back toward Five Forks about two o'clock in the morning of April 1st.

Colonel Mayo, commanding Terry's brigade, says he began to withdraw at 2 A.M., as had been agreed upon by the brigade commander to whom General Pickett left the arrangements for the withdrawal.

General Pickett states in his report that, ascertaining that General Sheridan was being reinforced with infantry, he was " induced to fall back, at daylight in the morning, to the Five Forks."

Devin on the right.   Custer's left moved along Chamberlain's Run.   General Crook was held in support.

General Pickett had, in the meanwhile, intrenched his infantry along the White Oak road, extending about a mile west of Five Forks, and about three-quarters of a mile east of it, with a short return about one hundred yards long at his left.   General W. H. F. Lee's cavalry division was on his right, along the west line of the Gilliam field, then followed in succession Corse's brigade (whose line lay along the north edge of the Gilliam field), Terry's, Steuart's, Ransom's, and Wallace's brigades, with Pegram's battalion of artillery on the line, three guns on Corse's right, and three at the Five Forks, with McGregor's battery of four guns on the left.   Munford's cavalry division, dismounted, was posted on the left so as to cover the ground between Wallace's left and Hatcher's Run. It connected with Roberts's brigade, which picketed toward the right of their main line of intrenchments, covering the Claiborne road.   General Rosser guarded the trains on the north side of Hatcher's Run, near the Ford road.

General Merritt pressed close up to Pickett's intrenchments.

General Sheridan's plan of attack was to make a feint of turning the enemy's right flank with Merritt's cavalry, while he assaulted their left flank with the Fifth Corps, Merritt's cavalry to attack the intrenchments in his front as soon as he heard the firing of the Fifth Corps attack.

If this attack proved to be successful Pickett's troops would be cut off from the rest of Lee's forces and driven westward.

At one o'clock General Sheridan directed General Warren to bring up the Fifth Corps and form it on the right of Devin, between 600 and 800 yards south of the White Oak road.   The ground where the Fifth Corps formed had been previously examined by Captain Gillespie, an Engineer officer on General Sheridan's staff, and is known in this operation as the ground about Gravelly Run Church. General Warren's statement as to the information and instructions he received from General Sheridan, besides the general plan of the battle, was "that the enemy was in line of battle along the White Oak road, their left resting about where the road that I was to turn off on crossed the White Oak road;[1] and that he wanted me to form my line so that I should strike with the right centre on the angle of the works and let the left engage the front, and place one division behind the right to support the attack on the angle where we thought the fight would be the heaviest; and to so place the men oblique to the road as to bring this heaviest force of mine on the angle of the works—give it a direction whose obliquity to the road would correspond with that supposed position of the enemy and his works. We talked that over until I understood it, I think; and he was convinced that I understood him."

See General Warren's diagram and instructions herewith (taken from Record of Court of Inquiry):

April 1, 3 P.M.

The following is the movement now about to be executed:

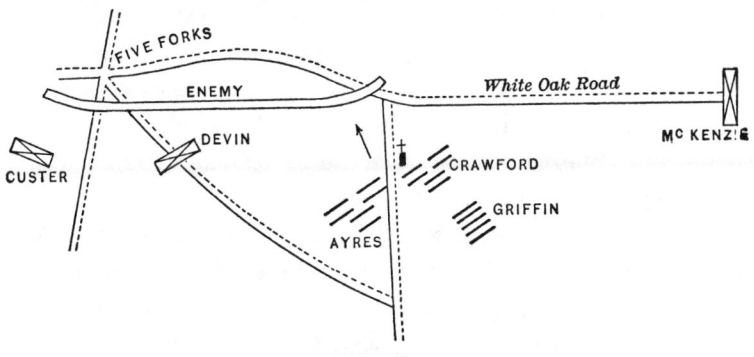

---

[1] The road General Warren turned off *from* was the Dinwiddie Court House and Five Forks road. The road he got on by turning off was the Gravelly Run Church road.

The line will move forward as formed till it reaches the White Oak road, when it will swing round to the left, perpendicular to the White Oak road. General Merritt's and General Custer's cavalry will charge the enemy's line as soon as the infantry get engaged. The cavalry is on the left of the infantry, except Mackenzie's, which is moving up the White Oak road from the right.

The divisions came upon the ground in the order of Crawford, Griffin, and Ayres. General Crawford's division was placed on the right of the Gravelly Run Church road, so that his centre would strike the angle and be the first to encounter the works; General Griffin's division was placed behind Crawford's. These were the largest divisions. General Ayres's division, the smallest, was placed on the left of the road, as General Warren supposed, from the position of the enemy as stated to him, that General Crawford's centre would fall right on the angle of their line, and that if he was not able to carry it, General Griffin would be there to sustain him and to take advantage of any success. General Ayres was to engage the enemy's front and prevent reinforcements being sent to the angle.

A copy of the diagram with the instructions on it was given to each division commander, and the plan was explained to them verbally besides. The line was to move forward until it reached the White Oak road, when it was to swing round to the left, perpendicular to the White Oak road.

General Sheridan states that he gave General Warren instructions about engaging the enemy after he had ordered him to bring up his corps; that he gave him orders for the formation of his troops and method of attack while his troops were coming up and forming; that he talked several times with General Warren as to what was to be done; that the order of General Warren (referring to the diagram and directions on it) conformed substantially to the orders he gave him; that "there was a good deal of conversation explanatory of that, but that embodies about it generally."

General Mackenzie had been sent from Dinwiddie Court House to get possession of the White Oak road at a point about three miles east of Five Forks, which he accomplished, having a sharp skirmish with some of the enemy's cavalry there, and moved down to the right of the Fifth Corps. He was directed to move in conjunction with that corps on its right, and come in on the flank and rear of the enemy and hold the Ford road crossing of Gravelly Run to intercept the enemy's retreat.

As soon as Ayres's division was formed (which was about four o'clock) the order was given to the Fifth Corps to attack. Advancing and receiving only a skirmish fire in its front on crossing the White Oak road, his right crossing the road sooner than his left, General Warren thought it probable that the enemy's line of battle was in the edge of the wood, about 300 yards north of the road, and continued to advance in the direction in which his line had started, until very soon after crossing that road General Ayres received a musketry and artillery fire on his left, which evidently came from the enemy's intrenchment at the return, showing that their intrenchment did not extend to the near vicinity of the Gravelly Run Church road. The return was, in fact, according to the map before the Warren Court of Inquiry, seven or eight hundred yards west of that road.[1] General Ayres understanding the

---

[1] In his testimony before the Warren Court of Inquiry, Colonel Gillespie stated that he had made no reconnoissance of the enemy's works before the attack; that the cavalry had moved directly up the road and gradually pressed the enemy behind his works; that he did not know that there was a return, nor did he know its direction from the position where the Fifth Corps was formed; that he was instructed by General Sheridan to select ground which would hold General Warren's corps close under the right flank of Devin's command and beyond the observation of the enemy, as he wanted to put General Warren in as a turning column.

Apparently no attempt was made to ascertain with precision the position of the enemy's left, lest the attempt might put them on their guard and betray the plan of attack.

meaning of this fire immediately changed front and faced
the return, bringing up Winthrop's brigade (which was in
reserve) in double-quick on the left of the new line, and then
advanced against the return under a heavy fire, his right
overlapping it, and finally carried the works, the key to the
position, capturing a large number of prisoners and many
battle-flags.

When the fire on General Ayres's left opened, General
Warren, perceiving that the fight at the angle of the return
would fall on Ayres and not on Crawford, as planned, at once
directed General Winthrop to form on Ayres's left so as to
connect with Devin, sent orders to General Griffin to come
in as quickly as he could to support Ayres on the right, and
to General Crawford to change direction to the left, at right
angles to the line he was following. A large part of Crawford's and Griffin's divisions had already entered the woods
north of the open space along the White Oak road.

General Sheridan, who accompanied General Ayres's division throughout the greater part of the battle, immediately
upon its receiving the flank fire, sent orders to General
Griffin and General Crawford to come in on Ayres's right.

After sending the orders mentioned, General Warren directed Colonel Kellogg to form his brigade (Crawford's left)
at right angles to its former direction, and to hold it there
for the division to form on ; then he directed Coulter's brigade (following in reserve) to form on Kellogg. Not finding
General Crawford, for the wood was dense, General Warren
sent renewed orders to him to change direction to the left,
and keep closed on Kellogg in advancing against the rear of
the enemy. Returning to Kellogg's position, General Warren found it vacant, for a staff officer of General Sheridan
had endeavored to take it against the rear of the enemy.
Every staff officer of General Warren had now been sent to
bring Griffin and Crawford against the rear of Pickett's in-

trenchments. Many of General Sheridan's had been sent for the same purpose. The country was thickly wooded, and troops moving rapidly through it could not be readily overtaken, but the direction of both Griffin's and Crawford's divisions had soon been changed to the left, for both entered the open ground of the Sydnor farm at its northern end about 800 yards from the enemy's intrenchments near the return. There General Warren found General Griffin with his division, moving southwest against the rear of the enemy's intrenchments, and directed him to attack a body of the enemy's infantry, composed of Ransom's brigade and some of Wallace's, that had formed a new line, with slight intrenchment connected with and at right angles to their main line of intrenchment, in order to oppose the further progress of the Fifth Corps, for General Ayres had by this time carried the return. Griffin at once set about doing what General Warren directed, but found the resistance stubborn; the enemy's fire was quick, sharp, decisive, and lasted about half an hour,[1] though Griffin was finally successful. General Gwyn's brigade of Ayres's division, and Coulter's of Crawford's, joined him in the latter part of the encounter.

While this was going on, General Warren rode to General Ayres, and found that he had carried the return and was reforming his troops at right angles to the enemy's intrenchments.

He now endeavored to find General Crawford, who had entered the Sydnor field before General Griffin, and had passed through it, driving General Munford's division of

---

[1] A singular circumstance connected with this battle is the fact that General Pickett was all this time, and until near the close of the action, on the north side of Hatcher's Run, where he had heard no sound of the engagement, nor had he received any information concerning it. There was no Confederate commander on the field; otherwise Terry's (Mayo's) brigade would probably have been brought into action with Ransom's and Wallace's brigades when General Ransom formed his new line, or earlier still, when Ayres was moving to attack the return.

dismounted cavalry westward before him. Following in Crawford's track from the Sydnor field, marked by his killed and wounded, General Warren found him in the Young-Boisseau farm (through which the Ford road runs) with his division in good order, facing west. Kellogg's brigade had now joined its division. Changing the direction of the division to the south, General Warren led it along the Ford road toward the rear of the enemy's intrenchments, meeting at the edge of the wood, on the south side of the farm, a sharp fire from the enemy, who had formed a line across the Ford road.

General Pickett finding his left had been captured, and that the Fifth Corps was moving westward along the line of his intrenchments, and coming in on his rear, had drawn Terry's brigade (Colonel Mayo commanding) out of the intrenchments between Corse and Steuart, and had brought them to this point to make head, if he could, against the rear attack. Some of Ransom's force, just dislodged by Griffin from the southwest corner of the Sydnor field, joined Mayo. McGregor's battery of four guns, that had been at the return with Ransom's and Wallace's brigades, was also here; but the resistance was brief, and the four guns were captured. Part of Bartlett's brigade joined Crawford in this field, but neither Griffin nor Ayres had yet reached this point. Colonel Mayo, finding that he could not withstand Crawford's attack, fell back with a part of his brigade toward Corse, moving along the Fork road to the Five Forks battery, and along the intrenchments to Corse, when he was ordered by General Pickett to get across the country to the South Side Railroad, which he succeeded in doing, though in great disorder. The guns at the Five Forks battery were still in position, and part of Steuart's brigade still held on when Mayo passed there.

General Devin's division, as previously stated, was formed

in front of the enemy's intrenchments, with its left on the road from Dinwiddie Court House to Five Forks, and when the Fifth Corps moved to attack, it dismounted and advanced against the intrenchments, keeping up a constant fire upon them, and receiving in reply the fire of the infantry and of the three guns at the Five Forks battery.

Custer's division, on our left of the Five Forks battery, had but one brigade, Pennington's, dismounted, which in open order kept up a constant fire upon the intrenchments held by Corse's and Terry's brigades. With his two other brigades General Custer made a charge upon General W. H. F. Lee's right. One of Lee's brigades was with Corse, dismounted. With the other General Lee advanced to meet Custer's charge, when a brilliant encounter took place. Lee, however, maintained his position on the right.

When General Pickett saw that Mayo could not maintain himself upon the Ford road, he directed General Corse to form a line running along the west side of the Gilliam field at right angles to the main intrenchments, and extending into the woods north of it, so that the escape of the other infantry, the greater part of which was now pouring through the woods in complete disorder, could be in some measure covered. This was quickly effected, and a line of partial intrenchment prepared.

Soon after Colonel Mayo passed the Five Forks battery, falling back upon Corse from the Young-Boisseau field, Colonel Fitzhugh's brigade of Devin's division charged the intrenchments and carried them, capturing the three guns, two battle-flags, and over a thousand of the enemy.

General Warren, with Crawford's division, pursuing the troops falling back toward Corse, came upon the Gilliam field, along the east side of which, in the edge of the woods, Crawford's troops were formed, the right being north of the White Oak road in woods. There was some little hesitation

in Crawford's line about advancing against the enemy's intrenchments on the west side of the field, from which a
sharp fire was kept up, until Warren, riding forward with the
Corps flag in his hands, led his troops across the field.   Custer, south of him, advanced at the same time, having sent him
word by a staff-officer that he would do so.   The fire close up
was severe, but in a few minutes the intrenchment was carried
and a large part of the force captured.   It was now in the
dusk of evening.   General Warren says he continued the pursuit west for half a mile, when no enemy being in sight, the
command was halted.   Some little skirmishing was still going on in the woods north of the road, apparently with the
enemy's rear guard.   General Custer passed General Warren
at this time on his left hand.

When General Pickett ordered General Corse to form his
new line, he directed General W. H. F. Lee to withdraw from
the field toward the South Side Railroad covering his dismounted brigade, which he effected along the W. Dabney
Road, pressed close by Custer.   The routed infantry moved
in confusion through the woods.

The pursuit by Griffin and Ayres was continued along the
White Oak road until after dark, by which time the cavalry
was out of sight and hearing of the infantry.

When upon the Young-Boisseau farm, General Warren sent
Colonel Spear to hold the Ford road crossing of Hatcher's
Run, where he became sharply engaged with Rosser's cav-
alry on the north side.

General Mackenzie, moving on Crawford's right, was pushed
by his infantry to the right against Hatcher's Run, which h
crossed at one point, but the heavy firing being in a south
or southwest direction from him he recrossed, and moving
west came upon the Ford road north of the Young-Boisseau
farm, which he had been directed to hold, and where his
command remained.

When the battle began General Pickett and General Fitz Lee were on the north side of Hatcher's Run. Owing to the density of the woods no sound of firing reached them, and when General Pickett was notified of the engagement going on he had barely time to ride rapidly down the Ford road to Five Forks, under the fire of General Crawford's troops that were then close on the road approaching it. As soon as he got to his troops he ordered up Mayo's brigade, as heretofore mentioned. Munford, after being driven across the Ford road, mounted his division and rode to the Confederate right, where he was ordered by General Pickett to withdaw at once to the north side of Hatcher's Run and join General Fitz Lee, who had been notified of the battle too late to cross to the south side of the run, Crawford's troops having possession of the Ford road.

General Sheridan's success was complete. Pickett had been routed with a loss, according to the reports of the Fifth Corps and Cavalry, of not less than 4,500 prisoners, 13 colors, and 6 guns.[1] His killed and wounded did not probably exceed those of General Sheridan. The casualties of his cavalry were not large.

General Warren states that the Fifth Corps in this battle captured 3,244 men with their arms, 11 regimental colors, and 1 four-gun battery. The larger part of the prisoners were captured by Ayres's and Griffin's divisions. The corps

---

[1] According to the statement furnished the Warren Court of Inquiry from the Adjutant-General's Office, showing the number of Confederate prisoners captured at Five Forks, and as appeared from the records of military prisons on file in the Adjutant-General's Office, the number was :

Five Forks, April 1, 1865	2,063
Dinwiddie Court House, April 1, 1865	223
Hatcher's Run, April 1, 1865	116
Five Forks, April 2, 1865	164
Dinwiddie Court House, April 2, 1865	33
Total	2,599

"lost in killed, wounded, and missing 634, of which 300 were in General Crawford's division, 205 in General Ayres's division, and 125 in General Griffin's division." Among the killed was General Fred. Winthrop, commanding the First Brigade of Ayres's division, who "was mortally wounded at the head of his command while making a successful assault."

The number of casualties in the cavalry was not large. I do not find it stated for this battle separate from the whole number in the campaign. The proportion of cavalry officers killed and wounded was large.

Two divisions of the Fifth Corps were posted for the night across the White Oak road near Gravelly Run Church, and one on the Ford road. The cavalry were at and near Five Forks, except Mackenzie's division, which remained at the Ford road crossing of Hatcher's Run.

General W. H. F. Lee's and General Munford's divisions after crossing Hatcher's Run united with General Fitz Lee at the Ford road crossing of that stream, and their cavalry was then withdrawn to the South Side Railroad, where the Ford road crosses it. There they were joined during the night, first by Hunton's brigade of Pickett's division, then, later, by General Johnson with Wise's, Gracie's, and Fulton's brigades, all under the command of General R. H. Anderson. They marched by routes north of Hatcher's Run.

These troops were sent by General R. E. Lee to cover the collection of Pickett's disorganized command, and with it to take up a position at Sutherland Station, to close, if possible, that avenue of approach to Petersburg. With intrenchments, and some assistance from Longstreet, this might have been possible, but it was not possible for Lee to send sufficient troops to overmatch the force with General Sheridan, and at the same time maintain the Petersburg and Richmond lines. He had lost possession of the South Side

Railroad, but the Danville Railroad and its connections with the Lynchburg (or South Side) Railroad still remained, with the rolling stock of both roads, and it was rolling stock they most needed. So long as his intrenchments remained intact he might still defer his movement to Danville until the wagon-roads were passable.

These troops sent to cover the reassembling of Pickett's scattered forces were drawn from General Lee's right at the Claiborne road crossing of Hatcher's Run, where they had been concentrated on the 30th of March. Their withdrawal left in their intrenchments from the Claiborne road to Burgess's mill on the south side of Hatcher's Run, McGowan's, McRae's, Scales's, and Cook's brigades of Hill's corps.

Pickett's infantry, after wading across Hatcher's Run, got into the W. Dabney road, and assembled in some shape near the South Side Railroad, when General Pickett moved them in the direction of Exeter mills at the mouth of Whipponock Creek, as he intended to cross the Appomattox there and rejoin the army, but early next morning he received orders to unite with General R. H. Anderson at Sutherland Station.

It has always seemed to me to have been a grave mistake to require General Pickett to fight at Five Forks. There he was isolated. Had he moved at once with his infantry to Sutherland Station, when he fell back from Dinwiddie Court House, leaving his cavalry to maintain the crossings of Hatcher's Run as long as practicable, he could have been reinforced from Lee's right with the infantry sent to him in the night of the 1st of April, and with some of Longstreet's force, and slight intrenchments extending on his right to the Appomattox, and on his left to the Claiborne road crossing of Hatcher's Run, he would have fought under conditions much more favorable to him.

General Warren states that after the last of the enemy had

been captured at Five Forks, he received at 7 p.m. an order from Major-General Sheridan relieving him from duty, and directing him to report for orders to Lieutenant-General Grant. This action of General Sheridan was taken under an authority sent him by General Grant some time in the morning of the 1st of April, " to relieve General Warren if, in his judgment, it was for the best interests of the service for him to do so." [1]

In his report of this battle, dated May 16, 1865, General Sheridan states that in bringing up and forming his corps at Gravelly Run Church, " General Warren did not exert himself to get up his corps as rapidly as he might have done, and his manner gave me the impression that he wished the sun to go down before dispositions for the attack

---

[1] The circumstances under which this authority was sent are narrated by Capt. E. R. Warner, 3d U. S. Artillery, at the time of the battle on the staff of General Hunt, Chief of Artillery. He was sent by General Hunt on some artillery duty to the old headquarters camp of the Fifth Corps, on the morning of the 1st of April, where General Warren had, early in the morning, left several of his staff officers sleeping, among them Colonel Locke, Adjutant-General. Captain Warner was directed by General Rawlins to ascertain where the Fifth Corps was. Captain Warner saw Colonel Locke, and some other Fifth Corps staff officers, about nine o'clock, and in reply to his inquiry Colonel Locke told him that a portion of the Fifth Corps, when he last heard from them, had halted to bridge a stream (General Warren had insisted upon his staff getting some sleep during the night, and this statement of Colonel Locke merely means that he went to sleep before the bridge was built, and slept until after General Warren and the staff officers, who had been up during the latter part of the night, had left the camp).

Upon returning to Headquarters about ten o'clock, Captain Warner stated to General Rawlins that the Fifth Corps, or a portion of it, when last heard from, was delayed building a bridge, and that they were then still delayed.

At times, during the campaign beginning in May, there had been misunderstandings between General Meade and General Warren, the latter sometimes modifying the plan of operations prescribed by the orders of the day for the Fifth Corps, so as to make them accord with his own judgment, as the day went on, modifications which General Meade sometimes did not approve, and hence something like controversy grew up occasionally in the despatches that passed between them. It appears to be probable that General Grant apprehended that something of this kind might occur between General Sheridan and General Warren, and considering the time to be a critical one, sent the message mentioned to General Sheridan.

could be completed." Further he states: " During this attack [that of the Fifth Corps and the Cavalry upon Pickett's intrenched position] I again became dissatisfied with General Warren. During the engagement portions of his lines gave way when not exposed to a heavy fire, and simply for want of confidence on the part of the troops, which General Warren did not exert himself to inspire. I therefore relieved him from the command of the Fifth Corps, authority for the action having been sent to me, before the battle, unsolicited."

These are very grave accusations or imputations, and of such serious character that no officer could rest under them. Any officer against whom they were made would be entitled, whatever his rank might be, to an investigation of them before a proper court.

A Court of Inquiry was finally appointed by the President, after General Warren had repeatedly requested it. Before that court, which entered into an extended and minute investigation of the circumstances attending the battle of Five Forks, many Confederate as well as United States officers engaged in the battle appeared. General Sheridan explained further to that court that, though his troops were victorious at Five Forks, they were isolated from the Army of the Potomac, and that the extreme left of that army had been thrown back to the Boydton road, while the enemy held strongly at the intersection of the White Oak and Claiborne roads, and directly in his rear, and distant from Five Forks only three and a half miles, and might march down the White Oak road that night or early the next morning, and take his command in rear ; that General Warren having disappointed him in the movement of his corps, and in its management in the battle, he deemed it to be for the best interests of the service to relieve him, and did so. (In point of fact, however, the White Oak road, close to the enemy's intrenchments at the intersection of the Claiborne road, was, by direction of Generals Grant and Meade, held strongly by the Second Corps at the time of the close of the battle of Five Forks. Still, General Sheridan's force would have been exposed to attack if General Lee had had a sufficient number of troops to admit of it without abandoning his intrenchments, which he had not.)

Respecting the giving way of portions of General Warren s troops, it appears from the testimony that the skirmish line of Ayres's division, when it entered the woods north of the open ground on the north side of the White Oak road, fell back, lay down, and began to fire in the air, and that they were made to go forward by General Sheridan and General Ayres and their staff; and it further appears that when General Ayres changed front, General Gwyn's brigade on his right, or part of it, fell into some disorder and confusion, which made General Sheridan doubt if he would be successful, and that this confusion was remedied by General Sheridan and General Ayres and their staff. But General Ayres in his testimony does not appear to have considered this disorder as serious. General Warren was at that time endeavoring to rectify the position and direction of movement of Griffin's and Crawford's divisions. In such cases of disorder or confusion, or want of steadiness and ardor, commanders of very high rank usually act in accordance with their temperaments, whatever their command may be.

The report and opinion of the court upon the first quoted imputation or accusation are as follows:

THIRD IMPUTATION.

The third imputation is found in an extract from General Sheridan's report of May 16, 1865 (see Record, pp. 21 and 48), as follows:

" . . . General Warren did not exert himself to get up his corps as rapidly as he might have done, and his manner gave me the impression that he wished the sun to go down before dispositions for the attack could be completed."

On the afternoon of April 1st the Fifth Corps was massed as follows: Crawford's and Griffin's divisions at the forks of the Crump road and the main road from Dinwiddie Court House to Five Forks, and Ayres's division on the Brooke's road, about one-fourth of a mile east from the forks of that road and the road to Five Forks.

The distance from the position of Griffin and Crawford to the place of formation of the Fifth Corps, near Gravelly Run Church, was about two and a half miles, and the length of the corps, when spread out in column of route, would be about two and three-eighths miles. The last file of the column required as much time to reach the place of formation as it would have taken to march about five miles.

General Warren received his orders near Gravelly Run Church to move up his corps at 1 P.M., and it took some time to communicate those orders to the divisions and for the movement to begin.

The route to the place of formation was along a narrow road, very muddy and slippery, somewhat encumbered with wagons and led horses of the Cavalry Corps, and the men were fatigued. The testimony of the brigade and division commanders is to the effect that the corps in line of march was well closed up, and that no unnecessary delay was incurred.

The corps reached its destination, and was formed ready to advance against the enemy at 4 P.M.

It is in evidence that General Warren remained near Gravelly Run Church, directing the formation, explaining the mode of attack to the division and brigade commanders, with sketches prepared for the purpose.

General Warren also repeatedly sent out staff officers to the division commanders in order to expedite the march.

OPINION.

The Court is of the opinion that there was no unnecessary delay in this march of the Fifth Corps, and that General Warren took the usual methods of a corps commander to prevent delay.

The question regarding General Warren's manner appears to be too intangible and the evidence on it too contradictory for the Court to decide, separate from the context, that he appeared to wish "the sun to go down before dispositions for the attack could be completed;" but his actions, as shown by the evidence, do not appear to have corre-sponded with such wish, if ever he entertained it.[1]

Respecting the second quoted imputation, the report and opinion of the Court are :

FOURTH IMPUTATION.

The fourth imputation is found in an extract from General Sheridan's report of May 16, 1865 (see Record, pp. 22 and 48), as follows :

.   .   .   .

"During this attack I again became dissatisfied with General Warren. During the engagement portions of his line gave way when not exposed to a heavy fire, and simply from want of confidence on the part of the troops, which General Warren did not exert himself to inspire."

.   .   .   .

When the Fifth Corps moved up to the attack, General Sheridan said to General Ayres, "I will ride with you." General Warren was on the left of Crawford's division, between Crawford and Ayres.

When General Ayres's command struck the White Oak road it received a fire in flank from the enemy's "return" nearly at right angles to the road. He changed front immediately at right angles and faced the "return," his right receiving a fire from Munford's Confederate division of dismounted cavalry distributed along the edge of the woods to the north of the White Oak road. There was some confusion, which was immediately checked by the exertions of General Sheridan, General Ayres, and other officers.

The evidence shows that General Warren was observant of Ayres, because he sent orders to Winthrop's reserve brigade to form on the left of Ayres's new line.

---

[1] Respecting the impression that General Warren's manner made upon General Sheridan, it is to be said that General Sheridan knew but little of him. General Chamberlain, after the war Governor of Maine, who served in the Fifth Corps during all the time General Warren commanded it, says, in his evidence before the Court, that he noticed no apathy or indifference of manner in General Warren at the battle of Five Forks ; that he was not apathetic that morning, but energetic. He said further, that those who did not know General Warren's temperament might think him to be negative when he was deeply intent. Instead of showing excitement he generally showed an intense concentration, and those who did not know him might take his deep concentrated thought and purpose for apathy. A stranger looking at him and not seeing indications of excitement and resolution on his face, might judge him to be apathetic, when in fact that conclusion might be far from the truth.

This necessary change of front of Ayres increased the interval between him and Crawford on his right; the latter was marching without change of direction until, as he expressed it, he would clear the right of Ayres, when he was also to change front to the left.

At this moment Warren, who saw that Crawford, with Griffin following, was disappearing in the woods to the north of the White Oak road, sent a staff-officer to Griffin to come as quickly as he could to sustain Ayres; went himself to the left brigade of Crawford and caused a line to be marked out, facing to the west, directing the brigade commander to form on it; then went into the woods and gave orders to the right brigade of Crawford to form on the same line. When he returned to the open ground the brigade he had directed to change front had disappeared, as appears by the evidence, in consequence of orders given by an officer of General Sheridan's staff. General Warren sent repeated orders by staff-officers to both Griffin and Crawford to change direction, and went himself to both; and finally by these means corrected, as far as was possible under the circumstances, the divergence of these two divisions.

It appears from evidence that these two divisions were operating in the woods and over a difficult country, and received a fire in their front from the dismounted cavalry of Munford posted in the woods to the north of the White Oak road, which led to the belief, for some time, that the enemy had a line of battle in front; and this may furnish one reason why it was so difficult at first to change their direction to the proper one.

OPINION.

General Warren's attention appears to have been drawn, almost immediately after Ayres received the flank fire from the "return" and his consequent change of front, to the probability of Crawford with Griffin diverging too much from and being separated from Ayres, and by continuous exertions of himself and staff substantially remedied matters; and the Court thinks that this was for him the essential point to be attended to, which also exacted his whole efforts to accomplish.[1]

These are the reports and opinions of a court composed of officers of high character and great experience, formed under the sanctity of an oath to examine and inquire into the mat‹

---

[1] Warren Court of Inquiry, Part II., pp. 1559-1561.

ter according to the evidence, without partiality, favor, affec-
tion, prejudice, or hope of reward.

At half-past five in the afternoon of the 1st of April, General Grant having learnt that General Sheridan was about to
assault at Five Forks (at the time the staff officer carrying
the information left General Sheridan's command), directed
that the left of the Second Corps should be thrown forward,
so as to hold the White Oak road and prevent the enemy
from sending any force against General Sheridan by that
road. This was done at once, and the road was held strongly
by Miles's division. By nine o'clock General Grant had received intelligence of the defeat and rout of Pickett at Five
Forks, and apprehending that General Lee might hastily
abandon his lines and fall upon General Sheridan, ordered
that General Humphreys should at once feel for a vulnerable
point in the enemy's intrenchments, and, if one was found,
to assault immediately, and if successful to push on at once
after the enemy. If he could not carry their lines by midnight, then he must send General Miles's division to General
Sheridan. The artillery of the corps was opened, and both
Miles and Mott attacked at once, drove in the enemy's pickets and got up close to the slashings of the intrenchments,
but could not carry them. The enemy was vigilant and active, and opened heavily with his artillery. As the lines
were not vulnerable, General Miles was sent down the White
Oak road to General Sheridan shortly after midnight, communication with his cavalry along the road having been previously opened. The left of Mott was then thrown back, but
he kept up constant attacks throughout the night, both he
and General Hays feeling the enemy closely and holding
their divisions ready to take advantage of any weakening on
his part and assault. A general bombardment of the Confederate lines was carried on throughout the night.

General Ord, General Wright, and General Parke had,

during the three days of their quiet, been carefully examining the enemy's works and ground in their front, and planning and arranging for the assault which they were now ordered to make at four o'clock in the morning of the 2d of April. Upon carrying the works they were to move toward Petersburg. The Second Corps was to be thrown forward in the same direction. General Sheridan was to start at daylight and sweep up the White Oak road and all north of it to Petersburg.

The Confederate intrenchments in front of General Ord's and General Wright's commands were held by four brigades of Hill's corps, under the command of General Wilcox, Davis's, McComb's, Lane's, and Thomas's, numbering, according to the return of February 20th, about 4,000 enlisted men. The intrenchments in front of General Parke's command were held by General Gordon's corps, numbering, according to the same return, about 7,600 enlisted men.

The account that General Wright gives of his assault on the morning of the 2d of April, by which the enemy's intrenchments were carried and General Lee forced to abandon his lines, is so clear and so instructive that I shall use his own language in the narrative as far as I can. He says :

As early as the evening of the 30th of March he was instructed to be prepared to assault the enemy's works in his front. On the evening of the 1st of April he was directed to make the attack at 4 A.M. next day. The works to be attacked were those extending from the Jones house to a point opposite the left of the Sixth Corps.

The point chosen for assault was selected after the most careful consideration, based upon personal examination and the reports of a large number of officers who had scanned the works for a long time. It was in front of Forts Fisher and Welch. The ground to be passed over was perfectly cleared of trees, and offered few natural obstacles except the

marshes with which the front of the enemy's line was intersected.   The point was near the left of the corps line ; on its
right was an inundation which was impracticable, while still
further to the right, before reaching the Ninth Corps, were
the strong original defensive works, in the vicinity of the
Lead Works ; after-observation showed that the selection was
the best that could have been made.   The parapets had high
relief and deep ditches, preceded (it was found) by two lines
of abatis, well constructed, with a fraise between them.
Every few hundred yards were batteries well supplied with
artillery.   But for the capture of the enemy's intrenched
picket line on the 25th of March, the attack of the 2d of
April could not have succeeded.   The position then gained
was indispensable to the operations on the main lines, by affording a place for assembling the assaulting columns within
striking distance of the enemy's main intrenchments.

The troops were drawn out of the intrenchments, leaving
the smallest garrison possible in the forts and very few men
in the connecting lines.   The three divisions were formed for
the assault just in rear of the picket line ; the First Division
on the right ; the Second in the centre ; the Third on the
left ; the centre division being in advance of the others.   All
were formed by brigade with regiment-front.   Every precaution was taken to ensure success.   There were pioneers
in front, and artillerymen provided with implements so that
captured guns might be turned on the enemy were with the
columns.

Careful instructions were given to guide the movement of
the troops when they captured the works.   There was not
light enough to see until 4.40 A.M.; then the men could see to
step, though nothing could be distinguished at the distance
of a few yards.   Then the signal, the firing of a gun at Fort
Fisher, was given.   The columns moved promptly at the signal, broke over the enemy's picket line, meeting little resist-

ance, and poured in masses over the main défenses, under a musketry fire from the parapets and a heavy artillery fire from the batteries. Abatis were cut away, and through the openings thus made, *and through those made by the enemy for his convenience of access to the front*, the works were gained. A brief but sharp conflict occurred, which soon resulted in giving us possession of the whole front of attack.[1] In the ardor of the attack some troops from each division crossed the Boydton road and reached the South Side Railroad.[2] Reforming the lines, the troops moved down the works to Hatcher's Run, capturing all the artillery and a very large number of prisoners. A brigade of the Sixth Corps was left to hold the captured works and gain more to the right, which it did, but it was temporarily unable to hold a part of those gained against an attempt to recover them made by General Wilcox, until reinforced by Foster's division and two brigades of Turner's division of General Gibbon's corps. About 7 A.M. Harris's brigade of Turner's division carried the enemy's line near Hatcher's Run, and met the Sixth Corps there sweeping everything before it.

On reaching Hatcher's Run the Sixth Corps faced about and moved toward Petersburg. At the request of General Gibbon, commanding the Twenty-fourth Corps, he was allowed to pass the Sixth, which followed on his right and left, and halted in front of the enemy's lines, closing on the Appomattox near the Whitworth house.

General Wright's troops were so exhausted, having been eighteen hours under arms, that it was considered unadvisable to attack until the next morning.

---

[1] General Wright told me that this was the weakest part of all the line he saw, and the only point where it could have been carried. His loss in killed and wounded was 1,100, all of which occurred in the space of fifteen minutes.—A. A. H.

[2] It is probable that General A. P. Hill was killed by one of these parties. He was shot west of the Boydton Road early in the action of the day. He had served with distinction in the Army of Northern Virginia from the beginning of the war.

General Parke kept up the fire of all his artillery until I
A.M. of the 2d of April, reopening it at four o'clock, when
General Willcox made a demonstration against the enemy's
works opposite Fort Stedman.

For the assault General Parke concentrated Hartranft's
division on the right of Fort Sedgwick, and massed Potter's
on its left. The columns of assault (columns of regiments)
were formed between his intrenchments and his picket line
at 3 A.M., storming pioneer parties, carrying axes, being
placed in front. At half-past four o'clock the assaulting
columns went forward; the pioneers cut away abatis and
chevaux-de-frise, and under a heavy musketry, gun, and
mortar fire the enemy's works were captured, with 12 guns,
some colors, and 800 prisoners. Turning to the right, Miller's salient was captured; turning to the left, the intrenchment was found to be heavily traversed, and the fighting
went on from traverse to traverse.

But a rear line of works remained in possession of the
enemy, which General Parke endeavored to carry, but unsuc-
cessfully. His loss in officers was severe. Among the
wounded was General Potter.

The position gained by General Parke extended 400 yards
on each side of the Jerusalem plank-road, and included
several forts and redans. Frequent attempts were made by
General Gordon during the day to retake the works, but
without success. The firing continued all day and into the
night.

During the night of the 1st and 2d of April, General
Humphreys was directed not to attack the Crow house redoubts in consequence of the absence of one of his divisions,
but about 6 A.M., being informed by General Meade that both
Generals Parke and Wright had carried and held positions
of the enemy's lines, General Humphreys directed General
Hays to assault the redoubts, preparations for which had

been made in the night. The attack was successful, the works, their artillery, and the greater part of the garrison being captured. About half-past seven General Mott captured the intrenched picket line at the Burgess's mill works under severe artillery and musketry fire, and about half-past eight the enemy were moving rapidly out of their intrenchments by their right flank, attacked sharply by Mott.

At nine o'clock, receiving intelligence from General Miles that he was on his return, being, when he sent word, on the White Oak road about two miles west of the enemy's intrenchments at the Claiborne road junction, General Humphreys directed General Miles, General Mott, and General Hays to pursue the enemy by the Claiborne road toward Sutherland Station. He expected by this movement to close in on the rear of all the enemy's force, which General Wright, by penetrating their works, had cut off from Petersburg, while General Sheridan would probably strike their flank and front. This force consisted of McGowan's, McRae's, Scales's, and Cook's brigades of Hill's corps under General Heth, and Anderson's command, consisting of Johnson's and Pickett's divisions and Fitz Lee's cavalry. General Meade was at once advised of this, as it was not in accordance with his orders, and as he did not approve of this movement the orders to the division commanders were changed. Mott and Hays were ordered to move on the Boydton road toward Petersburg and connect on the right with General Wright, and Miles to move toward Petersburg by the first road met after crossing Hatcher's Run.

Overtaking Miles's division near Sutherland Station on the South Side Railroad, General Humphreys found that it had just come up with the brigades under General Heth, which were forced to halt and give battle. General Heth selected a position for them on the summit of a smooth open ridge, at the foot of which, some six or eight hundred yards in front of the crest, was a small stream. The ground then rose again to the same height, the slope being covered with oak and pine wood. The Confederate position was intrenched hastily as well as time admitted. Finding that General Miles was satisfied that he could defeat the force before him, General Humphreys left him to accomplish it and rejoined his two other divisions, that in the meantime were moving toward Petersburg, in front of which they were formed on the left of Wright.

As soon as General Miles examined the position of General Cook, who now commanded the force opposed to him (General Heth having been called to Petersburg to take command of Hill's corps), he attacked impetuously with the brigades of Nugent and Madill, and was repulsed, Madill being severely wounded.

About half-past twelve General Miles attacked the Confederate left with Madill's brigade, General McDougall commanding, but notwithstanding the gallant manner in which the attack was made, aided by the artillery of the division, it was repulsed, General McDougall being among the wounded.

About three o'clock General Miles, having enveloped the enemy's right with a strong skirmish line, attacked his left with Ramsey's brigade with complete success, sweeping down inside the breastworks, capturing 600 prisoners, one battle-flag, and two guns. The enemy retreated in confusion toward the Appomattox, some crossing to the north side at Exeter mills; but the body of them moved up the river in disorder toward Amelia Court House, where they arrived at noon of the 4th.

About half-past two General Meade, having learned that General Miles needed support, directed General Humphreys to take one of his divisions toward Sutherland Station for that purpose. Arriving there by the Coxe road, General 'Humphreys found that General Miles's last attack had been completely successful. Probably the whole force would have been captured in the morning had the Second Corps continued its march toward Sutherland Station.

The main line of the Confederate intrenchments closing upon the Appomattox west of Petersburg ran along the east bank of Old Town or Indian Town Creek. In front of this line on the opposite side of the creek, about 1,000 yards distant, were some advanced works, the most important of which were Forts Gregg and Whitworth, the former enclosed at the rear with a ditch eight or ten feet deep, of about the same width, and the parapet of corresponding height and thickness. Fort Whitworth was of similar dimensions, but open at the gorge.

Field's division of Longstreet's corps, two brigades of Gordon's, and some of Wilcox's troops were placed in the main line of works. General Wilcox says, the 200 infantry in Fort Gregg was composed of detachments from Thomas's and Lane's brigades of Hill's corps, and Harris's of Gordon's corps. There were two guns in Gregg, three in Whitworth; General Harris's brigade formed the garrison of the latter work.

As soon as General Ord's and General Wright's commands arrived before these works, Foster's division of Gibbon's Corps was ordered to charge them, and moved forward steadily under artillery and musketry fire, to find Fort Gregg surrounded by a deep, wide ditch partially filled with water, and flanked by fire on the right and left. Turner's First and Second brigades were now pushed up as supports, while his Third Brigade, General Harris's, assailed Fort Whitworth. The enemy, General Gibbon says, made a desperate resistance, and it was not until Fort Gregg was nearly surrounded, and his men had succeeded in climbing upon the parapet under a murderous fire, that the place was finally taken by the last of several determined dashes with the bayonet. General Harris and a portion of the First Division, he says, carried Fort Whitworth at the same time. General Wilcox says the troops were ordered to retire from this work to prevent further sacrifice.

General Gibbon says, of the assault upon Fort Gregg, that it was one of the most desperate of the war, that fifty-five of the enemy were found dead inside the fort, whilst his own loss during the day, most of which occurred around these two works, was 10 officers and 112 enlisted men killed, and 27 officers and 565 enlisted men wounded, making a total loss of 714. Two guns (in Fort Gregg), several colors, and about 300 officers and men were captured.

When the Confederate lines were carried, General Anderson was directed to move up along the Appomattox River toward Amelia Court House, on the road to which he was joined by such force as General Pickett had, and by the troops of Hill's corps under General Cook. His rear was covered by General Fitz Lee.

General Sheridan's cavalry, General Merrit leading, moved northward, crossing the South Side Railroad midway between Ford's and Sutherland's depots, near Ford's Meeting House, pushing the enemy's cavalry, who resisted their advance up to the crossing of Namozine Creek, where, General Merritt says, a spirited fight took place with the enemy's infantry.

General Sheridan moved the Fifth Corps up the White Oak road two miles toward the Claiborne road, when it returned to Five Forks and moved across Hatcher's Run on the Ford road, and across the South Side Railroad to the Coxe road, driving out of the way some dismounted cavalry, then moved eastward along the Coxe road toward Sutherland Station, but turned off on the Namozine road, and halted for the night near Williamson's, at the intersection of the Namozine by the River road. General Crawford's division was sent forward to General Merritt at the crossing of Namozine Creek.

When the Confederate intrenchments were carried by the Sixth Corps on the morning of the 2d, General Lee at once notified Mr. Jefferson Davis that he would be compelled to abandon his lines during the following night, and that he would endeavor to reach Danville. Mr. Davis at once took measures to withdraw the personnel and the archives of the Confederate Government from Richmond by the Danville Railroad.[1]

At three o'clock in the afternoon, General Lee gave the final orders for the retreat, which commenced at eight o'clock, at night, the artillery preceding the infantry, the wagon trains keeping as much as possible upon roads where there were to be no troops. The trains and troops crossed to the north side of the Appomattox by the ponton, Pocahontas and railroad bridges. The point of assemblage was Amelia Court House. General Longstreet, with Field's division, and Heth's and Wilcox's divisions of Hill's corps, led the column, moving on the River road, intending to recross the river at Bevil's bridge, but that being out of order, used the ponton bridge laid at Goode's bridge.

General Gordon, taking the Hickory road, recrossed the Appomattox at Goode's bridge, following Longstreet, and Mahone's division, passing through Chesterfield Court House, also crossed at Goode's bridge, following Gordon. General Ewell's command, composed of General Kershaw's and General Custis Lee's divisions, crossed the James River at and below Richmond, and taking the Genito road, followed by Gary's cavalry, crossed the Appomattox by the Danville Railroad bridge. The larger part of General Anderson's command, composed of Pickett's and Bushrod Johnson's divisions, moved up along the south bank of the

---

[1] Had General Lee abandoned his lines on the night of the 1st of April to attack General Sheridan, there would have been only six or seven hours of night for this withdrawal, too short a time to effect it. They now had twenty hours.

Appomattox, General Fitz Lee, with his cavalry, bringing up the rear.

Orders were given by General Grant for the assault of the Petersburg and Richmond lines early on the morning of the 3d, but at three o'clock in the morning it was discovered that General Lee had abandoned all his intrenchments. Petersburg was taken possession of by General Willcox with his division, his troops and those at City Point being placed under the command of General Warren.

The formal surrender of Richmond was made to General Weitzel at the City Hall, at 8.15 A.M.[1]

---

[1] The United States flag was raised on the Capitol at Richmond by Lieutenant Johnston L. de Peyster, and Captain Loomis L. Langdon, U. S. Artillery, Chief of Artillery, both of General Weitzel's staff. The former, the son of Major-General J. Watts de Peyster, a youth of eighteen, had carried the flag upon the pommel of his saddle, with this object in view, for several days, expecting to assault.

CHAPTER XIV.

LEE'S ARMY ASSEMBLED AT AMELIA COURT HOUSE—
NIGHT MARCH PAST MEADE'S AND SHERIDAN'S LEFT
FLANK—ATTACKED WHILE RETREATING—BATTLES
OF SAILOR'S CREEK—RETREAT CONTINUED DURING
THE NIGHT — HALTS NEAR FARMVILLE — CORRE-
SPONDENCE BETWEEN GRANT AND LEE—SURREN-
DER OF LEE AT APPOMATTOX — SURRENDER OF
ALL OTHER CONFEDERATE ARMIES—ARMY OF THE
POTOMAC DISBANDED.

IT was well understood that General Lee would move either
to Danville or to Lynchburg, and General Grant's directions
for the march of the armies were such as to intercept his retreat, whichever route he might take. General Sheridan,
with his cavalry and the Fifth Corps were to move in a westerly direction, south of and near to the Appomattox River,
so as to feel Lee's army constantly, and at the same time to
strike the Danville Railroad between its crossing of the Appomattox and its crossing of the Lynchburg Railroad at Burke's
Junction. General Meade, with the Second and Sixth Corps,
was to follow General Sheridan, moving westward in the general direction of Amelia Old Court House, with similar general objects in view. General Ord, with the Twenty-fourth
Corps and Birney's colored troops, followed by the Ninth
Corps, was to move along the South Side Railroad to Burke's
Junction.

The pursuit of Lee was taken up early on the 3d, the leading brigade of Custer's division, commanded by Colonel
Welles, overtaking near Namozine Church the rear of Fitz
Lee's cavalry, Barringer's brigade, which suffered severely
in the contest, the commander and many others being captured.   At Deep Creek General Fitz Lee placed his command in a strong defensive position, Wise's and Hunton's
brigades forming part of the rear guard.   A sharp engagement took place about dark, Merritt's troops attacking.   The
cavalry halted here for the night, the Fifth, Second, and
Sixth Corps well closed up.

General Sheridan having ascertained that General Lee was
probably concentrating at Amelia Court House, ordered General Crook, on the 4th, to strike the Danville Railroad between Burke's Junction and Jetersville, and then move toward the latter place, and General Griffin to march direct to
Jetersville.   Both commands reached there late in the afternoon, when General Sheridan learnt that General Lee's army
was at Amelia Court House, about eight miles northeast from
Jetersville.   General Mackenzie's division at the same time
had got to within a few miles of the Court House, on the
south approach to it.   The Fifth Corps intrenched so as to
hold the position until Meade's troops could be got up.   General Sheridan at once sent the information he had obtained
to General Meade and General Grant.

The Second and Sixth Corps had followed the Fifth Corps
closely until about eleven o'clock in the morning of the 4th,
when Merritt's cavalry, coming in from the right, and having
precedence necessarily delayed the progress of the infantry,
so that it was night by the time it reached Deep Creek.

General Meade, upon receiving the information sent him
by General Sheridan, directed the Second Corps to march
for Jetersville at one o'clock in the morning of the 5th
and the Sixth Corps to follow ; but a short distance beyond

Deep Creek, General Merritt's cavalry, which had been to the vicinity of Bevil's bridge, on the Appomattox, again came into the road from the right on its way to Jetersville, so that it was half-past two in the afternoon of the 5th, when the Second Corps began to arrive at Jetersville, followed by the Sixth Corps. Both went into position, the Second Corps on the left, the Sixth on the right of the Fifth Corps.[1]

But, in fact, Lee's army was not concentrated at Amelia Court House by the night of the 4th. Longstreet's command was there on the afternoon of the 4th; Gordon's, if not there, was not more than four or five miles distant. Mahone's division was near Goode's bridge, ten or twelve miles off. Ewell's command did not arrive at the Court House before midday of the 5th.[2] Anderson's command, the rear brought up by Fitz Lee's cavalry, arrived on the morning of the 5th. General Mahone's division was now assigned to General Longstreet's command. General Ewell retained the troops that had marched with him, the Navy battalion commanded by Commodore Tucker being attached to General Custis Lee's division. General Anderson retained Pickett's and Bushrod Johnson's divisions, and General Gordon his own corps.

Rations were obtained here by a part of Lee's army, but some of his troops were already suffering for the want of food, want of sleep, and from excessive fatigue. The roads were very heavy owing to the copious rains, and in fact were nearly impassable for wagon trains.

On the 5th General Lee sent forward his spare artillery (under General Lindsey Walker) and his trains by roads on

[1] Large working parties from the Second and Sixth Corps were at work on the roads during the 3d, 4th, and 5th, for they were nearly impassable for wagon trains.

[2] Custis Lee's division had its subsistence and baggage wagons destroyed by Mackenzie.

the right flank of those his troops would take in moving
toward Danville, or Lynchburg, and in the afternoon advanced toward Jetersville, with a view to attacking if no
heavy force of infantry had reinforced Sheridan's command;
but his cavalry, General W. H. F. Lee's division, advising
him that Sheridan had been heavily reinforced, he turned
his column northward toward a bridge across Flat Creek,
some five miles from the position now held by Sheridan and
Meade in force.   Flat Creek, a tributary of the Appomattox,
is eighty or one hundred feet wide, and so deep (in its shal-
lowest places coming up to the armpits of infantry) that
bridges are essential to its passage by an army.   Just after
sunset the head of Lee's column, Longstreet's corps, had
crossed the creek, and had arrived at Amelia Sulphur
Springs, which is on the creek near the bridge over that
stream on the road from the springs to Jetersville.   General
Lee still hoped, by a well-conducted night march westward,
to get so far in advance that he might certainly reach Lynchburg by passing through Deatonsville, Rice's Station, and
Farmville, and possibly might reach Danville.

On the morning of the 5th General Sheridan sent General
Davies's brigade of Crook's division to make a reconnoissance
to Paine's Cross-Roads (Paineville), about five miles north
of Amelia Springs, to ascertain if the enemy were making
any movement toward that flank to escape.   At Paineville
Davies found a wagon train moving westward, escorted by
Gary's cavalry brigade; it attacked, drove off the escort
(taking some prisoners), burned the wagons, and captured
five pieces of artillery, probably part of those in General
Walker's charge.   It is said that the papers of General
Robert E. Lee's Headquarters, containing many valuable
reports, copies of but few of which are now to be found,
were destroyed by the burning of these wagons.   General
Fitz Lee says that his own Headquarters' wagons were

among those destroyed. General Fitz Lee, with Munford's and Rosser's divisions, was sent against Davies, whom he followed closely, attacking him at Amelia Springs about sunset, just before he recrossed Flat Creek, by which time he was supported by General Crook, with Gregg's and Smith's brigades.

The march of the army of Northern Virginia was continued throughout the night, the head of Longstreet's column arriving at Rice's Station, on the Lynchburg Railroad, about sunrise of the 6th, where it was joined by General Lee in the course of the morning. There Longstreet was to wait the coming up of the rest of Lee's army. Anderson followed Longstreet, Ewell, Anderson. Ewell was at Amelia Springs about eight o'clock in the morning. Gordon formed the rear guard. At daylight of the 6th, Fitz Lee with his cavalry, which had halted for the night at Amelia Springs, marched toward Rice's Station, where he joined Longstreet.

The trains, which were long, kept on the roads on the right flank of the troops and were to cross Sailor's Creek at Perkinson's mill, near its mouth in the Appomattox. The troops were to cross it two or three miles higher up, on the road to Rice's Station. The bridges over Flat Creek, by which Lee's troops and trains crossed, as well as that at Amelia Springs, were destroyed.

At eight o'clock on the night of the 5th, General Meade, in his despatch to General Grant, who had not yet arrived at Jetersville, informed him that as the Sixth Corps could not get up until about six o'clock, he was unable to attack that night, but that he would attack Lee at six o'clock on the morning of the 6th with the Second, Fifth, and Sixth Corps, in conjunction with General Sheridan. In accordance with that despatch, he directed those corps to advance the next morning at that hour on the enemy at Amelia Court House, and attack him, the Fifth Corps to move along the railroad, the Second Corps on its left, the Sixth Corps on its right.

General Ord, with Gibbon's Twenty-fourth Corps troops, arrived at Burke's Junction late at night on the 5th, having marched fifty-two miles since the morning of the 3d. Birney's colored troops were left at Blacks and Whites Station. On the evening of the 5th, General Ord learned from General Sheridan that he was at Jetersville with his cavalry and the Fifth Corps, and that Lee's army was at Amelia Court House. Before arriving at Burke's Junction, General Ord received directions from General Grant to destroy High Bridge and the other bridges in Lee's front, in order to interrupt his movement toward Danville or Lynchburg. Before daylight of the 6th, General Ord sent two small regiments of infantry, together only 500 strong, and his Headquarters cavalry, 80 in number, under Colonel Washburn, of the Fifth Massachusetts, General Theodore Read of his staff conducting the party, to burn High Bridge and the bridges at Farmville, if not too well guarded.

On the morning of the 6th General Meade began to advance toward Amelia Court House, but at half-past eight, when the troops were about four miles out, General Humphreys discovered a strong column of the enemy's infantry on the north bank of Flat Creek, moving westward (a part of the column had already entered the woods in their front), and directing General Mott to send a brigade across the creek, to attack and develop the force, halted the rest of his command, communicated the information to General Meade, and began preparations to cross the creek. General Miles meanwhile brought some guns to the bank of the creek and opened upon the column. This, even if not effective (which it was), would give notice that the enemy had been come up with. Apparently it was the rear of Lee's army.

A short time before this took place, Meade's signal officers had discovered trains several miles distant in a northwest direction near Deatonsville, with cavalry escorting them, moving west. General Griffin, at Hill's Shop, received undoubted information that Lee had left Amelia Court House and had moved west. At half-past nine General Meade's signal officers discovered an infantry column three or four miles distant in a straight line, in a northwest direction, and another six or seven miles distant, both moving quickly. All this information left no doubt that General Lee had been passing our left during the night, and General Meade at once faced his army about, and directed the Second Corps to move on Deatonsville, the Fifth Corps through Paineville on the right of the Second, and the Sixth Corps to move through Jetersville and take position on the left of the Second.

The Second Corps at once began crossing Flat Creek, some of the troops wading across with the water up to their armpits, while bridges were built in an incredibly short space of time for the passage of the rest of the infantry and of the artillery and ambulances.

A sharp running fight commenced at once with Gordon's corps, which was continued over a distance of fourteen miles, during which several partially intrenched positions were carried. The country was broken, consisting of woods with dense undergrowth and swamps, alternating with open fields, through and over which the lines of battle followed closely on the skirmish line, with a rapidity and good order that is believed to be unexampled. Artillery moved with our skirmish line.

General Anderson halted some time in the morning at a point about three miles west of Deatonsville, at J. Hott's house, where the road from Deatonsville forks, one branch turning abruptly to the right and running down Sailor's Creek at about a mile's distance from it ; the other branch of the fork is the road to Rice's Station, and does not change its direction.   The ground at this fork is high, declining in an even slope of clear ground to Sailor's Creek, about a mile off.

Early on the morning of the 6th, General Sheridan directed General Crook to move to Deatonsville, and General Merritt to follow him.   Moving on the Pride's Church road, General Crook ascertained that the enemy were passing through Deatonsville, their trains on the Jamestown road.   These he endeavored, about midday, to cut off at the forks of the road near Hott's, but found them strongly guarded by Anderson, who repelled the attempt.   The head of Ewell's troops was about a mile in rear of Anderson at this time, coming up, and after its arrival took part in repulsing a second attempt of Crook, aided by Merritt, upon the trains at this point. Pickett had crossed Sailor's Creek, and when the head of Gordon's corps began to arrive at the forks of the road, Anderson crossed the creek with Johnson's division, and, with Pickett, formed across the road to Rice's Station on high ground, where they made some temporary breastworks. Ewell followed Anderson across the creek, halting upon it.

General Merritt and General Crook moved parallel with the enemy's line of march, on its left flank, impeding the movement of the column wherever practicable, and crossing Sailor's Creek.   General Custer, when south of the creek, succeeded in striking the column at a weak point, destroying a large number of wagons and capturing Huger's part of three batteries (12 guns).   Stagg's brigade of Devin's division remained near the forks of the road and subsequently united with the Sixth Corps in its attack on Ewell.   Gordon, after the passage of the main trains of Lee's army, took the right-hand fork, covering them, the Second Corps close upon him.

Upon arriving at the forks near Hott's at about half-past four o'clock, General Humphreys perceived Ewell's troops, or part of them, apparently forming line of battle along the north side of Sailor's Creek. They appeared to be about two brigades strong. Knowing that General Sheridan's cavalry were close upon the enemy on the Rice's Station road, though not aware that Anderson's command was across that road on the crest beyond Ewell, and seeing the whole of the Sixth Corps near at hand (a brigade of Seymour's division was temporarily mixed with the Second Corps near Hott's), General Humphreys continued his pursuit of Gordon's corps, which had turned down the creek on the right-hand fork of the road. The running contest with Gordon's corps continued for three miles further, the road for many miles being strewn with tents, camp equipage, baggage, battery-forges, limbers, and wagons. Its last attempted stand was near Perkinson's mills on Sailor's Creek, where just before dark a short, sharp contest gave us 13 flags, 3 guns, several hundred prisoners, and a large part of the main trains of Lee's army, which were huddled together in a confused mass at the crossing of the creek. Gordon attempted to form on the high ground on the opposite side of the creek, but fell back quickly from it as our troops crossed. Night put a stop to the pursuit until daylight of the 7th, for the country and roads were unknown to us. General Gordon reached High Bridge that night.

The captures of the corps were 13 flags, 4 guns, and 1,700 prisoners. The enemy's killed and wounded probably exceeded our own, and their total loss could not have been less than 2,000. The destruction of the wagon trains must have caused much additional suffering in Lee's army.

Our own killed and wounded were 311 of the First and Second divisions, General Mott being among the wounded.

When at the Amelia Springs in the morning General Humphreys was informed that there was a column of the enemy moving along the Paineville road, and therefore directed General Barlow, who commanded the Second Division (having just reported for duty in the morning), to move on the extreme right of the corps; but the information having been altogether erroneous, that division did not become engaged.

The Fifth Corps, forming the right of the army, moved on the Paineville road to Ligontown Ferry, a distance of thirty-two miles, but encountered none of the enemy.

General Crook moving to the left found General Anderson strongly posted on high ground with temporary breastworks running across the Rice's Station road, and sent Gregg, dismounted, to take possession of and form across the road. General Smith, his brigade dismounted, formed on Gregg's right; Davies, mounted, was formed in front of Anderson's works. General Merritt formed Devin and Custer on the right of Crook.

As soon as Seymour's and Wheaton's divisions of the Sixth Corps arrived, General Wright formed them for attack on the north side of Sailor's Creek, on the open slope descending from Hott's to the creek, Seymour's division on the right of the road, his left resting on it, Wheaton's division on Seymour's left. Wright's artillery at short distance opened with a destructive fire without receiving any response from Ewell, showing that he had no artillery with him, which in fact neither he nor Anderson had.

General Ewell had formed his troops in a good position some little distance from the creek on a crest, in front of which was a thicket of young pines, beyond or in front of which was the creek. Facing north to meet the Sixth Corps, General Kershaw was on the right of the road, General Custis Lee on the left. The Navy battalion was in rear of his right as a reserve.

When General Ewell learnt from General Anderson that the cavalry held the road in his front, he proposed that they should strike through the woods to their right and reach a road further west that led to Farmville, or unite and attack the cavalry in Anderson's front; but before they could arrange for either attempt the Sixth Corps was forming close to them. Seymour's and Wheaton's divisions now charged Ewell's position and carried it handsomely, except, General Wright says, at a point on the right of the road, where the Navy battalion made a countercharge upon that part of his line. These troops, he says, were surrounded by Seymour's and Wheaton's divisions on their flanks, the artillery, supported by Getty's division, in their front, and the cavalry in their rear; he had ceased firing supposing them to be prisoners, but at once opened again the artillery and infantry fire upon them, when they surrendered. General Stagg with his brigade of cavalry, directed by General Sheridan, struck Ewell's right flank.

As soon as General Wright's artillery was in position, General Sheridan ordered General Crook and General Merritt to attack, when a general assault was made by them, Crook's two dismounted brigades on the left turning and going over Anderson's works, while Davies, General Crook says, "made one of the finest charges of the war, riding over and capturing the works and their defenders. The enemy on the right who were thus cut off from retreat surrendered, and were taken by different parties."

General Ewell says that he held on until Anderson was broken, and until the Sixth Corps line came round his left and indeed was already in his rear, his right also completely enveloped, when he surrendered. The whole of Ewell's command was either killed, wounded, or captured, except 250 of Kershaw's division.

According to the most reliable information I have been able to obtain, General Ewell had about 3,600 men on the ground, General Anderson about 6,300, making a total force of about 10,000. General Ewell lost about 3,400, General Anderson about 2,600, making the total loss of both com-

mands about 6,000 in killed, wounded, and prisoners. Among
the prisoners were Generals Ewell, Kershaw, Custis Lee, and
Dubose, of Ewell's command, and Generals Hunton and
Corse, of Pickett's division.[1]

The total loss to Lee's army to-day in its actions with the
Cavalry and Sixth Corps and with the Second Corps was not
less than 8,000.

I have no means of stating the number of the killed and
wounded in the Cavalry. The loss of the Sixth Corps in
killed and wounded was 442.

General Devin advanced with his cavalry as far as one of
the main branches of Sailor's Creek, where he halted for the
night. Mahone's division was on the opposite bank, having
been sent back by General Longstreet from Rice's Station to
cover the escape of the fugitives.

---

[1] General Ewell states that his command numbered only about 3,000, having
lost half its numbers since leaving Richmond by the fatigue of four days' and
nights' almost constant marching, the last two days with nothing to eat.

General Kershaw states that he had 2,000 men on the ground. General Custis
Lee's troops being unaccustomed to marching or the hardships of the field, undoubtedly suffered much more than General Kershaw's.

It appears probable, according to a paper of Captain McHenry Howard, of General Custis Lee's staff, published in the Southern Historical Society Transactions,
1874-75, that he had about 1,600 men on the ground ; 250 of Kershaw's escaped
capture and formed a battalion. The loss of Ewell according to these figures was
about 3,400. General Bushrod Johnson, whose division numbered about 3,800,
says that his loss was small ; that Wise's and Wallace's brigades remained to him,
250 of Moody's, but only 80 of Ransom's. He probably lost some 1,100. Of Pickett's division, that numbered about 2,500, about 1,000 escaped capture, making the
loss of Anderson's command 2,600 ; the loss of both commands, Ewell's and Anderson's, 6,000.

The disorder in which those brigades of Johnson's and Pickett's divisions that
were engaged at Five Forks got away from the field on the night of the 1st of
April, and the disorder with which the four brigades of Hill's troops retreated
from Miles at Sunderland Station on the 2d, as well as the disorder of those brigades along the lines carried by General Wright, doubtless scattered them to such
an extent that many being without rations did not rejoin their commands.

In the movement to Amelia Court House, and from that point to Sailor's Creek,
Farmville, and Appomattox Court House, having but scanty supplies and being
exhausted by want of sleep and food and overcome with fatigue, many men fell
out or wandered in search of food.

General Getty advanced two miles beyond the battlefield, the two other divisions of the Sixth Corps closing up on him.

General Ord, having been notified by General Sheridan, on the 6th, that General Lee was apparently moving toward Burke's Junction, at first prepared to meet him there, but subsequently, with a view to intercept him, moved along the Lynchburg Railroad with Gibbon's two divisions (orders to that effect also having been sent him by General Grant), and after marching eight or ten miles came upon Longstreet, intrenched at Rice's Station; it was night, however, before his troops got into position. General Ord endeavored to warn General Read of the movement of Lee's army, but unsuccessfully, and that officer passing through Farmville was within two miles of High Bridge when he was encountered about midday by General Rosser with his own and Munford's division of cavalry. Read's force, General Ord says, consisted of 80 cavalry and 500 infantry. A most gallant fight ensued, in which General Read, Colonel Washburn, and all the cavalry officers were killed. After heavy loss the rest of the force surrendered. General Dearing, Colonel Boston, and Major Thompson of Rosser's command were among the killed.

It has been seen that General Longstreet remained halted at Rice's Station all day waiting for Anderson, Ewell, and Gordon to unite with him. They were covering the trains, but notwithstanding their efforts the greater part of them were destroyed. Ewell's whole force was lost, together with nearly half of Anderson's and a large part of Gordon's, all in a useless effort to save the trains.

When Mr. Davis and General Lee determined to abandon the Richmond intrenchments as soon as the roads ceased to be impassable, had preparations then been made for abandoning all surplus artillery and discarding all camp equipage, baggage, etc., except that which could be carried without encumbrance on pack-animals, retaining heavy wagons only for ammunition and hospital supplies (with ambulances) and establishing temporary depots of supplies at railroad stations, Lee thus lightly equipped might have united with Johnston at Danville, or at least have reached the mountains near Lynchburg. But that would only have protracted the war for a brief period.

As soon as night set in General Longstreet, with Field, Heth, and Wilcox, marched for Farmville, crossed to the north bank of the Appomattox there, and on the morning of the 7th began to move out on the road passing through Appomattox Court House to Lynchburg. He retained some force on the river to delay our crossing. General Fitz Lee, with all his cavalry, followed Longstreet, crossing the river by a ford above the bridges, leaving some force in the vicinity of Farmville.

At Farmville rations were distributed to Lee's army, 80,000 having been placed there to await its arrival. Many of the officers and men had had little else than parched or raw Indian corn on the 5th and 6th.

General Gordon, to whose command General Bushrod Johnson's division had been attached, crossed to the north bank of the Appomattox at High Bridge, where there is a wagon-road bridge as well as a railroad bridge. General Mahone's division followed Gordon's troops early in the morning of the 7th.

Early on the same morning General Ord, finding that General Longstreet had moved in the night toward Farmville, followed to that town. Birney's colored division had now joined him.

General Sheridan sent Merritt's cavalry toward Prince Edward Court House to intercept any movement of the enemy toward Danville, and Crook's to Farmville.

General Meade directed Griffin to move to Prince Edward

Court House, General Humphreys and General Wright to continue the direct pursuit as long as it promised success. General Wright moved to Farmville, following General Ord. By the time the head of Crook's cavalry reached Farmville the enemy had crossed there and burnt the bridges. The cavalry ford was too deep for infantry.

The Second Corps resumed the pursuit at half-past five in the morning of the 7th, keeping near to the river and taking routes which appeared to have been marched on by the largest bodies of infantry, and came upon High Bridge just as the enemy had blown up the redoubt that formed the bridge-head and had set fire to the railroad bridge [1] and were trying to burn the wagon-road bridge. But General Barlow, whose division was in advance, promptly sent his leading men in double-quick to secure the wagon-road bridge, a matter of importance since the river was not fordable for infantry.

There were but few of the enemy at the bridge, and those Barlow's men drove off. Seeing their mistake, the enemy sent back a cloud of skirmishers to drive off the few men of the Second Corps that had as yet come up, but they being reinforced secured the bridge, and the Second Corps began crossing the river at once. Mahone's division was drawn up on the high ground of the north bank, apparently to oppose the passage, his position being strengthened by two redoubts, but moved off in a northwest direction, Gordon's corps moving up the river along the railroad bed in the direction of Farmville.

---

[1] The railroad bridge is called High Bridge because built upon piers about 60 feet high across the narrow river and the wide marshy low ground on the north bank.

This railroad bridge was saved, with the loss of four spans at the north end, chiefly by the exertions of Colonel Livermore, of General Humphreys's staff, whose party put out the fire while the enemy's skirmishers were fighting under their feet. It was an open deck bridge.

Believing that General Lee was moving toward Lynch-burg by the old stage-road north of the Appomattox River, General Humphreys moved with Miles and De Trobriand (the latter now commanding the Third Division) on a road running northwest, which intersects the stage-road about four miles north of Farmville, but lest he might be mistaken in the route Lee intended to pursue, he sent General Barlow to follow General Gordon along the railroad bed toward Farmville.   Artillery could not accompany him.

General Barlow found Farmville still in possession of a strong force of the enemy, who had set the bridges on fire and were covering a wagon-train on the north bank that was moving toward Lynchburg.

The bridges were burnt and our troops concentrated about Farmville during the day, were, with the exception of Crook's cavalry, prevented from crossing, as the river was not fordable for infantry, and barely for cavalry.

General Barlow overtaking part of Gordon's corps, at once attacked and cut off a large number of wagons, which were burnt.   In this attack, Brigadier-General Smyth, command-ing the Third Brigade, a gallant and highly meritorious offi-cer, was mortally wounded.   His fall led to the loss of some part of the skirmish line.

General Humphreys, with Miles and De Trobriand, arrived near the Lynchburg stage-road about one o'clock, when he suddenly came in contact with the enemy, who opened on him with Poague's sixteen guns ; dispositions were at once made for attack, and a heavy skirmish line was pressed close up against the enemy to develop his position.   It was soon found, from the prisoners taken, that Lee's whole army was present in a strong position covering the stage and plank roads to Lynchburg, which had been intrenched sufficiently for cover, and had artillery in place.   It was on the crest of a long slope of open ground.   Fitz Lee's cavalry was covering their rear toward Farmville, supported by Heth's infantry. A heavy skirmish line was pressed against the enemy, and an attack threatened with the two divisions, both of which were now up, and an unsuccessful attempt was made to take them in flank. Barlow was now sent for,[1] and General Meade informed that Lee's whole remaining force, probably about 18,000 infantry, had been come up with, and suggesting that a corps should attack Lee from the direction of Farmville at the same time that the Second Corps attacked from the opposite direction. Upon this General Meade sent directions for General Gibbon, with the Twenty-fourth Corps, and General Wright, with the Sixth Corps, both of which were then at or near Farmville, to cross the river there and attack jointly with the Second Corps But neither General Meade nor General Humphreys was aware that the river at Farmville was impassable, and that there was no ponton bridge available, and that it would be night before the Sixth Corps, which had arrived at Farmville by two o'clock, could get across after building a foot bridge and a ponton bridge.

While General Humpheys, fully expecting that an attack from the direction of Farmville would be made, was waiting the arrival of Barlow, the enemy was observed, at half-past four, to shorten his right flank, and some firing being heard in the direction of Farmville, which was supposed to be the Sixth Corps advancing, General Humphreys contracted his left, and extended his right to envelop the enemy's left flank. While this was being done General Miles thought he saw an opportunity for attack, and at once made it with a part of his First Brigade, which was, however, repulsed with considerable loss. The ground was rough and the position and the intrenchments strong. The attack fell on Mahone's division,

---

[1] The information received from Headquarters in the morning was that Lee was probably moving toward Danville, and for that reason Barlow had been sent toward Farmville.

which was on the Confederate left. supported by Anderson's brigade of Field's division.   Poague's artillery was on Mahone's right, then Gordon's corps, with Longstreet's troops on its right.   The firing in the direction of Farmville, which was light and ceased very soon, came from an encounter with Crook's cavalry division, which had crossed the river with great difficulty, by wading, at Farmville.   Moving forward by the Plank-road, General Gregg's brigade, which was leading, was attacked by General Fitz Lee, General Munford in front, General Rosser in flank, General Heth supporting. General Gregg was captured with other prisoners, and his brigade driven back.   General Crook was now recalled to Farmville, and directed to move to Prospect Station on the Lynchburg Railroad, 10 or 12 miles from Farmville, which station he reached about midnight.

General Barlow rejoined his corps about sunset, but it was dark before he could be put in position.[1]

The loss of the Second Corps to-day was five hundred and seventy-one officers and men killed, wounded, and missing. Nothing could have been finer than the spirit and promptness of the officers and men.[2]   Without it the wagon-road bridge at High Bridge could not have been secured, and no infantry could have crossed and detained Lee from midday to night at Farmville heights.

Among the enemy's loss was Brigadier-General Lewis of

---

[1] The following quotation from "McGowan's South Carolina Brigade," upon what took place where two divisions of the Second Corps overtook Lee's force on the 7th, may serve as an example of what is meant by pressing up against an enemy without serious fighting.

"The enemy seemed ubiquitous. We were instructed to be prepared to fight on either flank. On our right flank firing was pretty steadily kept up; in our front a regular battle was going on. Mahone's division was engaged, and a portion of Field's. . . . The firing increased in rapidity and extent until three sides were at once set upon by the enemy. . . . I never was so bewildered as on this occasion. . . ."

[2] All commanding officers were at the head of their commands, literally leading them, as they should in a pursuit.

Walker's division, Gordon's Corps, who was severely wounded, and fell into our hands with other wounded officers.

It was anticipated that General Lee would move off in the night, which he did, General Fitz Lee, who brought up the rear, leaving the ground about midnight.

By the detention until night at this place, General Lee lost invaluable time, which he could not regain by night-marching, lost the supplies awaiting him at Appomattox Station, and gave time to Sheridan with his cavalry, and Ord with the Fifth and Twenty-fourth Corps, to post themselves across his path at Appomattox Court House. If no infantry had crossed the Appomattox on the 7th he could have reached New Store that night, Appomattox Station on the afternoon of the 8th, obtained the rations there, and moved that evening toward Lynchburg. A march the next day, the 9th, would have brought him to Lynchburg. Ord's two infantry corps did not reach Appomattox Court House until ten o'clock in the morning of the 9th of April.

About half-past eight o'clock in the evening, when still in contact with Lee as described, General Seth Williams, Adjutant-General, brought General Humphreys General Grant's first letter to General Lee, asking the surrender of his army, which letter General Humphreys was requested to have delivered to General Lee. He sent it at once through his picket-line, at the same time authorizing a truce for an hour at that point to enable the enemy to gather up their wounded, that were lying between the lines, an authority which they had informally asked for. The opposing troops were only a few hundred yards apart. General Lee's answer was brought back within an hour, and General Williams set out at once to return to General Grant at Farmville, by the circuitous route of High Bridge.

The letter of General Grant and the reply of General Lee are marked Nos. 1 and 2 in Appendix M.

The pursuit was resumed by the Second Corps, followed by the Sixth Corps, at half-past five on the morning of the 8th, on the road to Lynchburg. In the morning, while on the march, General Williams brought to General Humphreys General Grant's second letter to General Lee, which was sent to him through Fitz Lee's cavalry rear guard close in General Humphreys's front. General Lee's answer to this second letter of General Grant was received by General Humphreys at dusk, when he had halted for two or three hours to rest his troops some two miles beyond New Store, after a march of twenty miles.   See Letters Nos. 2 and 3 in Appendix M.

General Humphreys at once sent the reply of General Lee by his Adjutant-General, Colonel Whittier, to General Grant, who received it about midnight, he and General Meade having halted for the night at Curdsville, about ten miles back.

After some two or three hours' rest, in view of despatches received from Headquarters, though somewhat against General Humphreys' judgment, he resumed the march with the object of coming up with the main force of the enemy, but finding the men dropping out of the ranks from exhaustion, owing to want of food, and to fatigue, halted the head of his column at midnight, after a march of twenty-six miles, Longstreet's troops about three miles in front.   The supply-train with two days' rations was just in rear, and got up in the morning of the 9th.

On the morning of the 9th, General Humphreys received from General Grant his third letter to General Lee, written that morning at Curdsville [see No. 5, Appendix M], which letter General Humphreys sent forward by Colonel Whittier, who, after riding a few miles, met, first, one of Lee's couriers, and immediately afterward, Colonel Marshall of General Lee's staff.   The latter conducted him to General Lee, to whom General Grant's letter was delivered.

General Lee dictated his answer to General Grant Colonel,

Marshall writing it.   (While doing so artillery firing in the direction of Appomattox Court House was heard, and a Confederate officer rode up with some apparently important communication to General Lee.)   The letter was signed by Lee, and delivered to Colonel Whittier by Colonel Marshall, with verbal messages to General Grant from General Lee expressive of regret at not having met him.   This letter was written about nine o'clock in the morning.

Mr. Jefferson Davis, in his "Rise and Fall of the Confederate Government," mentions as a matter of some interest the following incident in connection with the surrender-correspondence :

"On the next morning [the morning of the 9th of April], before daylight, Lee sent Colonel Venable, one of his staff, to Gordon, commanding the advance, to learn his opinion as to the chances of a successful attack, to which Gordon replied, 'My old corps is reduced to a frazzle, and unless I am supported by Longstreet heavily, I do not think we can do anything more.'   When Colonel Venable returned with this answer to General Lee, he said, 'Then there is nothing left me but to go and see General Grant.' " [1]

This interview General Lee sought after a consultation with his principal and most highly esteemed officers—a consultation necessarily of a very painful kind, but, controlled by motives of an exalted character, General Lee submitted with dignity to a necessity that was inevitable.

Passing through General Longstreet's lines, General Lee was met by Colonel Whittier, received General Grant's letter and replied to it as already described.   See No. 6, of Appendix M.

This letter was sent to General Grant by the hands of Col-

---

[1] Colonel Venable stated substantially the same thing at the Lee Memorial meeting in Richmond, on the 3d of November, 1870.

onel Whittier, who delivered it to General Meade at about ten o'clock.

It was forwarded by him to General Grant, who, near New Store, had left the route followed by the Second and Sixth Corps, and had taken a cross-road to get into the road south of the Appomattox River, which also led to the Court House and along or near the routes of Sheridan and Ord.

Lieutenant Pease carried this letter, as well as one from General Meade, to General Grant, and after a ride of twelve or fourteen miles from the vicinity of New Store, delivered it to him at 11.50 A.M., at which time General Grant was about eight miles from Appomattox Court House. General Grant's letter to General Lee, acknowledging the receipt of his letter of the morning of the 9th, was undoubtedly sent to General Lee through General Sheridan's and General Ord's lines. For the letter see No. 7, Appendix M.

Had General Grant remained on the route of the Second and Sixth Corps, the surrender would have taken place before mid-day. About half-past ten the troops of the Second Corps, closely followed by the Sixth Corps, began to over-take General Longstreet's, when General Humphreys received two earnest verbal requests from General Lee by a staff officer (Colonel Marshall or Colonel Taylor) with a flag of truce, not to press forward upon him, but to halt, as negotiations were going on for a surrender. General Humphreys did not feel himself authorized to comply with these requests, since he had not received such information and authority from General Meade or General Grant as would sanction it, and so replied to General Lee, and continued to press forward.

In fact, with the letters from General Grant for General Lee, General Humphreys had been notified that this correspondence was in no way to interfere with his operations; and although this message did not accompany the last letter received from General Grant, the previous messages were evidently designed to govern General Humphreys' actions. General Humphreys notified General Meade of these messages from General Lee and of his replies.

When the request by General Lee's staff officer was made the last time (the Second Corps was then close on General Longstreet) he was very urgent—so urgent that General Humphreys had to send him word twice that the request could not be complied with, and that he must withdraw from the ground at once. He was in full sight on the road, not a hundred yards distant from the head of the Second Corps.

About half a mile beyond this, at eleven o'clock, the Second Corps had come up with Longstreet's command, intrenched in the vicinity of Appomattox Court House. It was at once formed for attack, the Sixth Corps formed on the right, which, at the moment when it was about to begin, was suspended by the arrival of General Meade, who sent a written communication to General Lee granting a truce on his (Meade's) line for an hour, in view of the negotiations for a surrender. General Meade had read General Lee's letter of nine o'clock before sending it on to General Grant. General Meade's despatch to General Grant at ten o'clock that morning stated that he (Meade) had just written to General Lee. The communication just mentioned granting a truce is the letter Meade referred to. It was sent through the lines by General Humphreys, and delivered to a Confederate officer by Colonel Whittier, and was received by General Lee between eleven and twelve o'clock.

Lee halted for the night of the 8th at and in the vicinity of Appomattox Court House.

General Merritt marching early in the morning of the 7th toward Prince Edward Court House, on the flank of the infantry, halted for the night beyond it on Spring Creek, and resuming the march early the next morning toward Appomattox Station, reached that vicinity during the early part of the night, Custer, in advance, capturing Walker's train of artillery and wagons, and three trains of cars with subsistence sent back from Farmville by Lee. Merritt then moved up to the vicinity of the Court House and formed across the road the enemy were moving on.

General Crook, General Mackenzie following him, reached Appomattox Station on the evening of the 8th, having burned subsistence trains at Pamphlin's Station on the way. From the station he sent Smith's brigade to the vicinity of Appomattox Court House to hold the road from that place to Lynchburg.

General Griffin halted for the night of the 7th at Prince Edward Court House, and resuming the march early on the 8th, joined the Twenty-fourth Corps at Prospect Station, coming then under the command of General Ord.

Continuing the march for twenty-nine miles toward Appomattox Court House, General Ord halted for three hours' rest between midnight and the morning of the 9th. Resuming the march, he says he arrived near the Court House about ten o'clock in the morning of the 9th, when he deployed his two corps across Lee's route just as his advance was pushing out of it.

General Fitz Lee says that on the evening of the 8th his cavalry, which had formed the rear guard, was moved to the front; that the corps commanders were called to Headquarters, where General Lee explained the situation fully, and submitted the correspondence he had had with General Grant to them. It was decided that Fitz Lee, supported by Gordon, should attack Sheridan's cavalry at daylight, and in case nothing but cavalry was found, they were to open a way for the remaining troops; but in case the cavalry was supported by heavy bodies of infantry, the Commanding General must be at once notified.

At daybreak on the 9th Gordon's command was formed in line of battle half a mile west of the Court House on the Lynchburg road. The cavalry was posted on his right, W. H. F. Lee's division next to the infantry, Rosser's in the centre, Munford's on the right, making, General Fitz Lee says, a mounted force of about 2,400 men. "Our attack," he continues, "was made about sunrise, and the enemy's cavalry quickly driven out of the way, with a loss of two guns and a number of prisoners. The arrival at this time of two corps of their infantry necessitated the retiring of our lines." [1]

General Crook says : "At about 9 A.M. the enemy made a strong attack on my front and flanks with a large force of infantry, while their cavalry attacked my rear. Mackenzie and Smith were forced to retire by overwhelming numbers until relieved by the infantry, when we reorganized and were getting ready to go to the front when an order for the cessation of hostilities reached me."

General Merritt says the enemy advanced against Crook in heavy force. The cavalry was forced back. Custer was brought up and the cavalry retired slowly, but of necessity. Soon the Twenty-fourth Corps took up Crook's line on the left of Devin, and the Fifth Corps deployed in rear of him. As soon as the columns of the enemy discovered we had infantry in position, they retired precipitately toward the Valley. The cavalry was thrown out rapidly to the right, taking possession of the high ground on the enemy's left, and opened artillery.

General Ord states that he was barely in time on the morning of the 9th, "for in spite of General Sheridan's attempts the cavalry was falling back in confusion before Lee's infantry ; but," he says, "we soon deployed and went in, Gibbon on the left, at double-quick, with Foster's and Turner's

---

[1] General Fitz Lee, seeing that immediate surrender was inevitable, withdrew at once toward Lynchburg, that road, he says, being clear, where and in the vicinity of which he and his command surrendered shortly after.

divisions, in beautiful style, and the colored troops also at the double-quick under these commanders, with the Fifth Corps under Griffin, when a white flag met" him "at the Fifth Corps front with a request for a cessation of arms until General Lee could meet General Grant and confer on the terms." General Ord continues: "As I knew that a surrender had been called for and terms asked for and made known, I knew this second request meant acceptance, and the bugles were sounded to halt."

General Sheridan says: "A white flag was presented to General Custer, who had the advance, and who sent the information to me at once that the enemy desired to surrender.

"Riding over to the left at Appomattox Court House,[1] I met Major-General Gordon, of the rebel service, and Major-General Wilcox. General Gordon requested a suspension of hostilities pending negotiations for a surrender then being held between Lieutenant-General Grant and General Lee. I notified him that I desired to prevent the unnecessary effusion of blood, but as there was nothing definitely settled in the correspondence, and as an attack had been made on my lines with a view to escape under the impression that our force was only cavalry, I must have some assurance of an intended surrender. This General Gordon gave by saying that there was no doubt of the surrender of General Lee's army. I then separated from him, with an agreement to meet those officers again in half an hour at Appomattox Court House. At the specified time, in company with General Ord, who commanded the infantry, I again met this officer, and also Lieutenant-General Longstreet, and received from them the same assurance, and hostilities ceased until the arrival of Lieutenant-General Grant."[2]

---

[1] Appomattox Court House was between the picket lines of the opposing forces.

[2] The author of "With General Sheridan in Lee's Last Campaign, by a Staff Officer," states that General Longstreet bore a despatch from General Lee to

General Grant arrived at Appomattox Court House about one o'clock, when the meeting between himself and General Lee took place. After a brief conference the two letters of General Grant and General Lee [Nos. 8 and 9, Appendix M], respectively presenting and accepting the terms of surrender, having been written in each other's presence, were exchanged.

At about four o'clock the surrender of the Army of Northern Virginia was announced to the Army of the Potomac.

The surrender of General Johnston's army took place on the 25th of April, and that of the other Confederate forces soon followed.

According to the Records of the War Department, the number of officers and enlisted men of the Army of Northern Virginia paroled on the 9th of April, 1865, was:

	Officers.	Enlisted men.	Aggregate.
General Lee and Staff.	15	......	15
Longstreet's Corps	1,521	13,312	14,833
Gordon's Corps	695	6,505	7,200
Ewell's Corps	19	268	287
Total Infantry	2,250	20,085	22,335
Cavalry Corps	132	1,654	1,786
Artillery Corps	192	2,394	2,586
Total Infantry, Cavalry, and Artillery.	2,574	24,133	26,707
Detachments [1]	288	1,361	1,649
Grand Total	2,862	25,494	28,356

General Grant, and gives a copy of the despatch. It is a copy or duplicate of the despatch written by General Lee at nine o'clock in the morning, and delivered to General Humphreys' staff officer, Colonel Whittier, and placed in General Grant's hands by Lieutenant Pease, of General Meade's staff, at 11.55 A.M., when General Grant was still eight miles from Appomattox Court House, and at about the hour when General Longstreet delivered the duplicate to General Sheridan and General Ord.

[1] Detachments consisted of some of the Navy Battalion, the Provost Guard, Headquarters Cavalry escort, some odds and ends of troops, and civilian employés.

It has been stated that of the troops surrendered, only 8,000 had arms.

If, indeed, that is correct, then the greater part of those men who had no arms must have thrown them away when they found that they must surrender. This was not difficult to do unobserved by their officers. The country was thickly wooded and open to them on the west and northwest. A walk of half an hour would bring them to ground that neither their officers nor ours would pass over during their brief stay in the vicinity of the Court House.

Our casualties in these closing operations from the 29th of March to the 9th of April were 8,268 officers and enlisted men killed and wounded, and 1,676 missing, making a total loss of 9,944. They were distributed as shown below.[1]

The Army of the Potomac marched to Washington, was reviewed by the President and his Cabinet, and was disbanded by the 30th of June following.

It has not seemed to me necessary to attempt a eulogy upon the Army of the Potomac or the Army of Northern Virginia.

[1] Cavalry,	1,151	officers	and	enlisted	men	killed	and	wounded,	339	missing.
2d Corps,	1,394	"	"	"	"	"	"	"	630	"
5th "	1,919	"	"	"	"	"	"	"	546	"
6th "	1,542	"	"	"	"	"	"	"	...	"
9th "	1,548	"	"	"	"	"	"	"	161	"
24th "	714	"	"	"	"	"	"	"	...	"
Total,	8,268	"	"	"	"	"	"	"	1,676	"
Missing,	1,676									
Total,	9,944	"	"	"	"	"	"	"	and	"

APPENDIX A.

ORGANIZATION OF THE ARMY OF THE POTOMAC, COMMANDED BY MAJOR-GENERAL GEORGE G. MEADE, ON MAY 4, 1864.

[Compiled from the records of the Adjutant-General's Office.]

GENERAL HEADQUARTERS.

Provost Guard.

Brigadier-General MARSENA R. PATRICK.

1st Massachusetts Cavalry, Companies C and D.
80th New York Infantry (20th Militia).

3d Pennsylvania Cavalry.
68th Pennsylvania Infantry.
114th Pennsylvania Infantry.

Volunteer Engineer Brigade.

Brigadier-General HENRY W. BENHAM.
15th New York Engineers.   50th New York Engineers.

Battalion United States Engineers.

Captain GEORGE H. MENDELL.

Guards and Orderlies.

Captain DANIEL P. MANN.
Independent Company Oneida (N. Y.) Cavalry.

ARTILLERY.
BRIGADIER-GENERAL HENRY J. HUNT.

ARTILLERY RESERVE.
COLONEL HENRY S. BURTON.

First Brigade.

Colonel J. HOWARD KITCHING.
6th New York Heavy Artillery.   15th New York Heavy Artillery.

Second Brigade.

Major JOHN A. TOMPKINS.
Maine Light Artillery, 5th Battery.
New York Light Artillery, 5th Battery.
New York Light Artillery, 12th Battery.
New York Light Artillery, 15th Battery.
New Jersey Light Artillery, Battery A.
New Jersey Light Artillery, Battery B.

First Brigade Horse Artillery.[1]

Captain JOHN M. ROBERTSON.
New York Light Artillery, 6th Battery.
2d U. S. Artillery, Batteries B and L.
2d U. S. Artillery, Battery D.
2d U. S. Artillery, Batter. M.
4th U. S. Artillery, Battery A.
4th U. S. Artillery, Batteries C and E.

---

[1] Detached with Cavalry Corps.

Second Brigade Horse Artillery.

Captain DUNBAR R. RANSOM.

1st U. S. Artillery, Batteries E and G.
1st U. S. Artillery, Batteries H and I.
1st U. S. Artillery, Battery K.
2d U. S. Artillery, Battery A.
2d U. S. Artillery, Battery G.
3d U. S. Art., Batteries C, F, and K.

Third Brigade.

Major ROBERT H. FITZHUGH.

Massachusetts Light Art'y, 9th Battery.
1st New York Light Art'y, Battery B.
1st New York Light Art'y. Battery C.
New York Light Art'y, 11th Battery.
1st Ohio Light Artillery, Battery H.
5th U. S. Artillery, Battery E.

SECOND ARMY CORPS.

MAJOR-GENERAL W. S. HANCOCK.

Escort.

Captain JOHN H. HAZELTON.
1st Vermont Cavalry, Company M.

FIRST DIVISION.

BRIGADIER-GENERAL FRANCIS C. BARLOW.

First Brigade.

Colonel NELSON A. MILES.
26th Michigan.
61st New York.
81st Pennsylvania.
140th Pennsylvania.
183d Pennsylvania.

Second Brigade.

Colonel THOMAS A. SMYTH.
28th Massachusetts.
63d New York.
69th New York.
88th New York.
116th Pennsylvania.

Third Brigade.

Colonel PAUL FRANK.
39th New York.
52d New York.
57th New York.
111th New York.
125th New York.
126th New York.

Fourth Brigade.

Colonel JOHN R. BROOKE.
2d Delaware.
64th New York.
66th New York.
53d Pennsylvania.
145th Pennsylvania.
148th Pennsylvania.

SECOND DIVISION.

BRIGADIER-GENERAL JOHN GIBBON.

First Brigade.

Brig.-Gen. ALEX. S. WEBB.
19th Maine.
1st Co. Andrew (Mass.) S. S.
15th Massachusetts.
19th Massachusetts.
20th Massachusetts.
7th Michigan.
42d New York.
59th New York.
82d New York.

Second Brigade.

Brig.-Gen. JOSHUA T. OWEN.
152d New York.
69th Pennsylvania.
71st Pennsylvania.
72d Pennsylvania.
106th Pennsylvania.

Third Brigade.

Col. SAMUEL S. CARROLL.
14th Connecticut.
10th New York.
108th New York.
12th New Jersey.
1st Delaware.
7th West Virginia.
4th Ohio.
8th Ohio.
14th Indiana.

Not Brigaded.
2d Company Minnesota Sharpshooters.

THIRD DIVISION.
MAJOR GENERAL DAVID B. BIRNEY.

First Brigade.

Brig.-Gen. J. H. H. WARD.
3d Maine.
40th New York.
86th New York.
124th New York.
99th Pennsylvania.
110th Pennsylvania
141st Pennsylvania.
20th Indiana.
2d U. S. Sharpshooters.

Second Brigade.

Brig.-Gen. ALEXANDER HAYS.
4th Maine.
17th Maine.
93d New York.
57th Pennsylvania.
63d Pennsylvania.
105th Pennsylvania.
3d Michigan.
5th Michigan.
1st U. S. Sharpshooters.

FOURTH DIVISION.
BRIGADIER-GENERAL GERSHOM MOTT.

First Brigade.

Colonel **ROBERT McALLISTER.**
1st Massachusetts.
16th Massachusetts.
5th New Jersey.
6th New Jersey.
7th New Jersey.
8th New Jersey.
11th New Jersey.
26th Pennsylvania.
115th Pennsylvania.

Second Brigade.

Colonel **WILLIAM R. BREWSTER.**
11th Massachusetts.
70th New York.
71st New York.
72d New York.
73d New York.
74th New York.
120th New York.
84th Pennsylvania.

Artillery Brigade.

Colonel **JOHN C. TIDBALL.**
Maine Light Artillery, 6th Battery.
New Hampshire Light Artillery, 1st Battery.
Massachusetts Light Artillery, 10th Battery.
1st Rhode Island Light Artillery, Battery A.
1st Rhode Island Light Artillery, Battery B.
1st Rhode Island Light Artillery, Battery G.
4th New York Heavy Artillery, 3d Battalion.
1st Pennsylvania Light Artillery, Battery F.
4th U. S. Artillery, Battery K.
5th U. S. Artillery, Batteries C and I.

FIFTH ARMY CORPS.
MAJOR-GENERAL G. K. WARREN.

Provost Guard.

Major HENRY W. RYDER.
12th New York Battalion.

FIRST DIVISION.
BRIGADIER-GENERAL CHARLES GRIFFIN.
First Brigade.

Brigadier-General ROMEYN B. AYRES.
140th New York.   146th New York.   91st Pennsylvania.
155th Pennsylvania.
2d United States, Companies B, C, F, H, I, and K.
11th United States, Companies B, C, D, E, F, and G, 1st Battalion.
12th United States, Companies A, B, C, D, and G, 1st Battalion.
12th United States, Companies A, C, D, F, and H, 2d Battalion.
14th United States, 1st Battalion.
17th United States, Companies A, C, D, G. and H, 1st Battalion.
17th United States, Companies A, B, and C, 2d Battalion.

Second Brigade.

Colonel JACOB B. SWEITZER.
9th Massachusetts.
22d Massachusetts.
32d Massachusetts.
62d Pennsylvania.
4th Michigan.

Third Brigade.

Brig. Gen. JOSEPH J. BARTLETT.
20th Maine.
18th Massachusetts.
44th New York.
83d Pennsylvania.
118th Pennsylvania.
1st Michigan.
16th Michigan.

SECOND DIVISION.

BRIGADIER-GENERAL JOHN C. ROBINSON.

First Brigade.

Col. SAM'L H. LEONARD.
16th Maine.
13th Massachusetts.
39th Massachusetts.
104th New York.

Second Brigade.

Bg.-Gen. HENRY BAXTER.
12th Massachusetts.
83d New York.
97th New York.
11th Pennsylvania.
88th Pennsylvania.
90th Pennsylvania.

Third Brigade.

Col. ANDREW W. DENISON.
1st Maryland.
4th Maryland.
7th Maryland.
8th Maryland.

THIRD DIVISION.

BRIGADIER-GENERAL SAMUEL W. CRAWFORD.

First Brigade.

Colonel WILLIAM McCANDLESS.
1st Pennsylvania Reserves.
2d Pennsylvania Reserves.
6th Pennsylvania Reserves.
7th Pennsylvania Reserves.
11th Pennsylvania Reserves.
13th Pennsylvania Reserves (1st Rifles).

Third Brigade.

Colonel JOSEPH W. FISHER.
5th Pennsylvania Reserves.
8th Pennsylvania Reserves.
9th Pennsylvania Reserves.
10th Pennsylvania Reserves.
12th Pennsylvania Reserves.

FOURTH DIVISION.

BRIGADIER-GENERAL JAMES S. WADSWORTH.

First Brigade.

Bg.-Gen. LYSANDER CUTLER.
1st N. Y. Battalion Sharpshooters.
7th Indiana.
19th Indiana.
24th Michigan.
2d Wisconsin.
6th Wisconsin.
7th Wisconsin.

Second Brigade.

Bg.-Gen. JAS. C. RICE.
76th New York.
84th New York.
95th New York.
147th New York.
56th Pennsylvania.

Third Brigade.

Colonel ROY STONE.
121st Pennsylvania.
142d Pennsylvania.
143d Pennsylvania.
149th Pennsylvania.
150th Pennsylvania.

Artillery Brigade.

Colonel CHARLES S. WAINWRIGHT.
Massachusetts Light Artillery, Battery C.
Massachusetts Light Artillery, Battery E.
1st New York Light Artillery, Battery D.
1st New York Light Artillery, Batteries E and L.
1st New York Light Artillery, Battery H.
4th New York Heavy Artillery, 2d Battalion.
4th New York Heavy Artillery, Company E.
1st Pennsylvania Light Artillery, Battery B.
4th United States Artillery, Battery B.
5th United States Artillery, Battery D.

SIXTH ARMY CORPS.

Major-General JOHN SEDGWICK.

Escort.

Captain CHARLES E. FELLOWS.
8th Pennsylvania Cavalry, Company A.

FIRST DIVISION.

Brigadier-General HORATIO G. WRIGHT.

First Brigade.

Colonel HENRY W. BROWN.
1st New Jersey.
2d New Jersey.
3d New Jersey.
4th New Jersey.
10th New Jersey.
15th New Jersey.

Second Brigade.

Colonel EMORY UPTON.
5th Maine.
121st New York.
95th Pennsylvania.
96th Pennsylvania.

Third Brigade.

Brig.-Gen. DAVID A. RUSSELL.
6th Maine.
49th Pennsylvania.
119th Pennsylvania.
5th Wisconsin.

Fourth Brigade.

Brig.-Gen. ALEXANDER SHALER.
65th New York.
67th New York.
122d New York.
23d Pennsylvania.
82d Pennsylvania.

SECOND DIVISION.

Brigadier General GEORGE W. GETTY.

First Brigade.

Brig.-Gen. FRANK WHEATON.
62d New York.
93d Pennsylvania.
98th Pennsylvania.
102d Pennsylvania.
139th Pennsylvania.

Second Brigade.

Colonel LEWIS A. GRANT.
2d Vermont.
3d Vermont.
4th Vermont.
5th Vermont.
6th Vermont.

Third Brigade.

Brig.-Gen. THOMAS H. NEILL.
7th Maine.
43d New York.
49th New York.
77th New York.
61st Pennsylvania.

Fourth Brigade.

Brig.-Gen. HENRY L. EUSTIS.
7th Massachusetts.
10th Massachusetts.
37th Massachusetts.
2d Rhode Island.

THIRD DIVISION.

Brigadier-General JAMES B. RICKETTS.

First Brigade.

Brig.-Gen. WILLIAM H. MORRIS.
10th Vermont.
106th New York.
151st New York.
14th New Jersey.
87th Pennsylvania.

Second Brigade.

Colonel BENJAMIN F. SMITH.[1]
67th Pennsylvania.
138th Pennsylvania.
6th Maryland.
110th Ohio.
122d Ohio.
126th Ohio.

---

[1] Relieved May 5th by Brigadier-General Truman Seymour.

Artillery Brigade.

Colonel CHARLES H. TOMPKINS.

Maine Light Artillery, 4th Battery (D).
Massachusetts Light Artillery, 1st Battery (A).
1st Rhode Island Light Artillery, Battery C.
1st Rhode Island Light Artillery, Battery E.
1st Rhode Island Light Artillery, Battery G.
New York Light Artillery, 1st Battery.
New York Light Artillery, 3d Battery.
4th New York Heavy Artillery, 1st Battalion.
5th United States Artillery, Battery M.

CAVALRY CORPS.

MAJOR-GENERAL PHILIP H. SHERIDAN.

Escort.

Captain IRA W. CLAFLIN.

6th United States.

FIRST DIVISION.

BRIGADIER-GENERAL A. T. A. TORBERT.

First Brigade.	*Second Brigade.*	*Reserve Brigade.*
Bg.-Gen. GEO. A. CUSTER.	Col. THOS. C. DEVIN.	Bg.-Gen. WESLEY MERRITT.
1st Michigan.	4th New York.	1st New York (Dragoons.)
5th Michigan.	6th New York.	6th Pennsylvania.
6th Michigan.	9th New York.	1st United States.
7th Michigan.	17th Pennsylvania.	2d United States.
		5th United States.

SECOND DIVISION.

BRIGADIER-GENERAL DAVID McM. GREGG.

First Brigade.	*Second Brigade.*
Brig.-Gen. HENRY E. DAVIES, Jr.	Colonel J. IRVIN GREGG.
1st Massachusetts.	1st Maine.
1st New Jersey.	10th New York.
1st Pennsylvania.	2d Pennsylvania.
6th Ohio.	4th Pennsylvania.
	8th Pennsylvania.
	13th Pennsylvania.
	16th Pennsylvania.

THIRD DIVISION.

BRIGADIER-GENERAL JAMES H. WILSON.

First Brigade.	*Second Brigade.*
Colonel TIMOTHY M. BRYAN, Jr.	Colonel GEORGE H. CHAPMAN.
1st Connecticut.	1st Vermont.
2d New York.	8th New York.
5th New York.	3d Indiana.
18th Pennsylvania.	8th Illinois.

ORGANIZATION. OF THE NINTH ARMY CORPS, COMMANDED BY MAJOR-GENERAL AMBROSE E. BURNSIDE, ON MAY 4, 1864.[1]

Provost Guard.
Captain MILTON COGSWELL.
8th United States Infantry.

FIRST DIVISION.

BRIGADIER-GENERAL THOMAS G. STEVENSON.

First Brigade.
Colonel SUMNER CARRUTH.
35th Massachusetts.
56th Massachusetts.
57th Massachusetts.
59th Massachusetts.
4th United States.
10th United States.

Second Brigade.
Colonel DANIEL LEASURE.
21st Massachusetts.
100th Pennsylvania.
3d Maryland.

Artillery.
Maine Light Artillery, 2d Battery (B).
Massachusetts Light Artillery, 14th Battery.

SECOND DIVISION.

BRIGADIER-GENERAL ROBERT B. POTTER.

First Brigade.
Colonel ZENAS R. BLISS.
36th Massachusetts.
58th Massachusetts.
7th Rhode Island.
51st New York.
45th Pennsylvania.
48th Pennsylvania.

Second Brigade.
Colonel SIMON G. GRIFFIN.
31st Maine.
32d Maine.
6th New Hampshire.
9th New Hampshire.
11th New Hampshire.
17th Vermont.

Artillery.
Massachusetts Light Artillery, 11th Battery.
New York Light Artillery, 19th Battery.

THIRD DIVISION.

BRIGADIER-GENERAL ORLANDO B. WILLCOX.

First Brigade.
Colonel JOHN F. HARTRANFT.
109th New York.
51st Pennsylvania.
2d Michigan.
8th Michigan.
17th Michigan.
27th Michigan.

Second Brigade.
Colonel BENJAMIN C. CHRIST.
79th New York.
50th Pennsylvania.
60th Ohio.
1st Michigan Sharpshooters.
20th Michigan.

Artillery.
Maine Light Artillery, 7th Battery.
New York Light Artillery, 34th Battery.

---

[1] This corps was under the direct orders of Lieutenant-General U. S. Grant until May 24, 1864, when assigned to the Army of the Potomac.

FOURTH DIVISION.

BRIGADIER-GENERAL EDWARD FERRERO.

First Brigade.	*Second Brigade.*
Colonel JOSHUA K. SIGFRIED.	Colonel HENRY G. THOMAS.
27th United States Colored Troops.	30th Connecticut (colored).
30th United States Colored Troops.	19th United States Colored Troops.
39th United States Colored Troops.	23d United States Colored Troops.
43d United States Colored Troops.	

Artillery.

Vermont Light Artillery, 3d Battery.   Pennsylvania Light Art'y, Battery D.

Cavalry.

3d New Jersey.   13th Pennsylvania.   2d Ohio.

Reserve Artillery.	*Provisional Brigade.*
1st R. I. Light Artillery, Battery D.	Colonel ELISHA G. MARSHALL.
1st R. I. Light Artillery, Battery H.	24th New York Cavalry (dismounted).
N. Y. Light Artillery, 27th Battery.	14th New York Heavy Artillery.
2d United States Artillery, Battery E.	2d Pennsylvania Prov. Heavy Artillery.
3d United States Artillery, Battery G.	
3d U. S. Art., Batteries L and M.	

APPENDIX B.

Extract from Consolidated Morning Report of the Army of the Potomac, April 30, 1864.

	PRESENT FOR DUTY, EQUIPPED.				
			Artillery.		
	Officers.	Enlisted men.	Officers.	Enlisted men.	Guns.
Provost Guard	70	1,048			
Engineers...............	50	2,226			
Reserve Artillery—Infantry Guard.	59	2,391	64	2,052	92
Infantry—Second Corps	1.276	25,405	50	1,602	54
Infantry—Fifth Corps............	1,227	22.898	45	1,525	48
Infantry—Sixth Corps............	1,003	21,581	43	1,536	48
Total of Infantry.............	3,506	69,884	138	4,663	150
Cavalry Corps...................	585	11,839	24	839	32

The grand aggregate of the above officers and enlisted men, 99,438. Excluding engineers it is 97.162, which is 111 less than given by General Drum, the difference between us being my omission of 61 guards and orderlies with General Ingalls and 50 cavalry with the Sixth Corps. There were:

	Officers.	Enlisted men.
On extra or daily duty.................	946	18,149
In arrest or confinement.......................	80	851
Sick..	199	4,377

All teamsters, ambulance and spring-wagon drivers, hospital attendants, men in the Quartermaster and Subsistence Departments, that is the whole personnel of the Staff Departments and trains, was composed of officers and enlisted men detailed for "extra or daily duty" from the regiments forming the army. They were not available for any other duty.

The artillery consisted of 49 batteries, having 274 field guns (120 12-pounder Napoleons, 148 10-pounder and 3-inch rifles, and 6 20-pounder Parrotts). There were also 8 24-pounder coehorns.

Two hundred and seventy rounds of ammunition were carried for each gun.

There were 657 artillery carriages, including caissons, battery-wagons, and forges, the horses for which numbered 6,239; besides, there were 609 wagons (ordinary army wagons) and 3,721 animals for transport of ammunition.

In the Annual Report of the Hon. Edwin M. Stanton, Secretary of War, dated November 22, 1865, he states, on page 5, in a tabular statement of the numerical strength of the several Military Departments and Armies, that "*The aggregate available force present for duty, May 1, 1864*," of the Army of the Potomac, the Ninth Corps not included, was 120,384.

Upon an examination of the original tabular statement on the files of the Adjutant-General's Office, prepared for Mr. Stanton, the figures of which are exactly those presented by him in the Annual Report specified, I found that those figures included not only the officers and enlisted men of every branch of the service "*present for duty*," but all those on "*extra or daily duty*," as well as all those "*in arrest or confinement.*"

There is no column of "*Aggregate available force present for duty*" in any return or morning report. The column "*present for duty equipped*" is intended to give the number of enlisted men that form the fighting force of the army, together with those that may be made available for it, such as the Provost Guard, but does not include those on extra or daily duty, who form no part whatever of that force, and are not available for it.

The foot-note shows that on April 30, 1864, there were about 19,000 officers and enlisted men on extra or daily duty, and about 900 in arrest or confinement.

The tabular statement used by Mr. Stanton was prepared from the Return of the Army of the Potomac for April, 1864, between which and the consolidated morning report of April 30, 1864, there is some discrepancy. The morning report gives a better presentation of the condition of the army for that day than the monthly report.

Upon ascertaining how Mr. Stanton's tabular statement was prepared, I addressed a letter to General Drum, Adjutant-General of the Army, asking him for an official statement as to the classes of officers and enlisted men, and the number of each that go to the making up the numbers given in the Report of the Secretary of War. My letter and General Drum's reply are herewith.

WASHINGTON, December 1, 1881.

BRIGADIER-GENERAL RICHARD C. DRUM,
  Adjutant-General U. S. Army, Washington :

GENERAL—In the Annual Report of the Hon. Edwin M. Stanton, Secretary of War, dated November 22, 1865, he states on page 5 that "The aggregate available force present for duty May 1, 1864, was distributed as follows." Here follows a tabular statement of the numerical strength of the several military departments and armies, the second on the list being,

"Army of the Potomac............................ 120,384 "

It is chiefly to the numbers given for the "available force present for duty" with the Army of the Potomac that I desire to ask the attention of the Honorable the Secretary of War.

Upon an examination of the original tabular statement on the files of the Adjutant-General's Office, prepared for Mr. Stanton, the figures of which are exactly those presented by him in the Annual Report, I find that those figures include not only the officers and enlisted men of every branch of the service present for duty, but all those on extra or daily duty, as well as all those in arrest and confinement.

In this manner it appears that the number, on 1st of May, 1864, of officers and enlisted men of the Army of the Potomac in the line of battle or available for it, that is present for duty, according to the Tabular Statement, is about twenty thousand greater than the actual number ; for the officers and enlisted men on extra or daily duty are not in the line of battle nor are they available for it. They form the personnel of the trains. Neither are those in arrest or confinement in or available for the line of battle, though some of them may be temporarily released for it on the eve of a battle. In the present case they numbered 931.

The same kind of error will, I believe, be found to exist in all the numbers of the Table.

I understand that the Tabular Statement was prepared from the returns of the armies and military departments for the month of April, and not from the Morning Reports of the 30th of April, usually called the Tri-monthly Reports, because made every ten days. These Morning Reports give a better presentation of the condition of the army than the Monthly Return. In the present case there is evidently a large error in the Monthly Return for April of the Army of the Potomac in the number of officers and enlisted men present for duty, and in those on extra or daily duty, especially in the Second Corps.

On page 14 of the same Annual Report of the Secretary of War there is a tabular statement of " The aggregate available force present for duty on the 1st of March," 1865, which contains an error of the same kind as that just pointed out in the numbers given for the Army of the Potomac, by which its actual numerical strength of present for duty is increased by 16,000. The same kind of error undoubtedly exists in the numbers given for the other armies and for the military departments.

The object of this communication is to suggest whether the Tabular Statements of the Secretary of War's Report of November, 1865, cannot be officially examined and a statement made as to the classes of officers and enlisted men, and the number of each that go to making up the numbers given in the Report.

Very respectfully, your obedient servant,

A. A. HUMPHREYS,
Brig.-Gen., etc., etc., Retired, Maj.-Gen. Vols.

HEADQUARTERS OF THE ARMY,
ADJUTANT-GENERAL'S OFFICE,
WASHINGTON, December 23, 1881.

GENERAL A. A. HUMPHREYS, U. S. A., Washington, D. C.:

GENERAL—In reply to your communication of December 1, 1881, relative to the strength of the Army of the Potomac on the 1st of May, 1864, and the 1st of March, 1865, as shown in the report of the Hon. Secretary of War, dated November 22, 1865, I have the honor to furnish the following information:

The strength of the Army of the Potomac on the 1st of May, 1864, as given by the Hon. Secretary of War in his report of November 22, 1865, was obtained from a tabular statement prepared in this office. In his report Mr. Stanton designates the strength therein stated at 120,384. as "the aggregate available force present for duty," while the tabular statement made in the Adjutant-General's Office styles it the " present available for duty."

In reporting the available or effective strength of the army, or any portion thereof, it is the common practice to give either the " present for duty " or the " present for duty equipped," preferably the latter when obtainable, which shows the force available for conflict. But this custom seems not to have been observed in the preparation of the statement upon which the Secretary of War based his report. In calculating the number " available for duty " as given therein, the following classes of officers and men were included :

Present for duty	103,789
" on extra duty	15,629
" in arrest, suspension, or confinement	870
" in blank column (artillery reserve)	92

In computing the "available for duty" only the *sick*, numbering 4,222, were excluded from the aggregate " present " (124,602), leaving 120,380, or four less than given by Mr. Stanton. An examination of the records leads to the assumption that this slight difference is a typographical error in the Secretary's printed report.

The above figures were compiled from the regular monthly return of the Army of the Potomac for April, 1864, but which was not made out until July 18, 1864.

Turning to the consolidated morning report, or tri-monthly return (as it is more generally known), for April 30, 1864, the following figures are obtained, viz.:

Total present for duty	102,869
On special, extra, or daily duty	19,095
Sick	4,576
In arrest or confinement	931
Aggregate present	127,471
Of the total present for duty there were equipped	97,273

The latter is understood to represent the "effective force," or number of officers and men "available for line of battle," and was usually ascertained by deducting from the "present for duty" all non-combatants, and those who from lack of arms or other causes could not be placed in line of battle.

By comparing the numbers reported on the monthly return and those borne on the tri-monthly, both purporting to be for the same date (April 30), it is found that a discrepancy of 920 exists in the "present for duty" alone, the monthly return showing that many more than the tri-monthly. There are some other differences between the two returns, but this office has no means at command by which to furnish any certain and satisfactory explanation of the matter. It is believed, however, that in this particular case the tri-monthly return for April 30, 1864, and which bears date of May 2, 1864, only two days after the date it represents, contains the most reliable data.

In reference to Mr. Stanton's report of the strength of the Army of the Potomac on the 1st of March, 1865, it may be stated that his figures were obtained from the tri-monthly return for February 28, 1865, which furnishes the following:

Total present for duty	87,268
On special, extra, or daily duty	15,422
Sick	5,361
In arrest or confinement	583
Aggregate present	108,634

Deducting from this the sick (5,361), gives the 103,273 reported by the Hon. Secretary of War as the "aggregate available force present for duty."

This method of calculating the "available for duty" appears to have been applied to all the commands of the Army mentioned on pages 5 and 14 of the Report of the Secretary of War, dated November 22, 1865.

Very respectfully, your obedient servant,
R. C. DRUM,
Adjutant-General.

APPENDIX C.

Organization of the Army of Northern Virginia, Commanded by General Robert E. Lee, January 31, 1864.

SECOND ARMY CORPS.
Lieutenant-General R. S. EWELL Commanding.

EARLY'S DIVISION.
Major-General JUBAL A. EARLY.

Hays's Brigade.	*Pegram's Brigade.*
Brig.-Gen. H. T. HAYS.	Brig.-Gen. JOHN PEGRAM.
5th Louisiana, Col. Henry Forno.	13th Virginia, Col. J. B. Terrill.
6th Louisiana, Col. Wm. Monaghan.	31st Virginia, Col. J. S. Hoffman.
7th Louisiana, Col. D. B. Penn.	49th Virginia, Col. J. C. Gibson.
8th Louisiana, Lt.-Col. A. DeBlanc.	52d Virginia, Col. James H. Skinner.
9th Louisiana, Col. W. R. Peck.	58th Virginia, Col. F. H. Board.

Gordon's Brigade.

Brig.-Gen. JOHN B. GORDON.
13th Georgia, Col. James M. Smith.
36th Georgia, Col. J. D. Matthews.
31st [26th] Georgia, Col. E. N. Atkinson.
38th [31st] Georgia, Col. C. A. Evans.
60th Georgia, Col. W. H. Stiles.
61st Georgia, Col. J. H. Lamar.

Hoke's Brigade.

Brig.-Gen. R. F. HOKE.
6th N. Carolina, Col. R. F. Webb.
21st N. Carolina, Lt.-Col. W. S. Rankin.
54th N. Carolina, Col. K. M. Murchison.
57th N. Carolina, Col. A. C. Godwin.
1st N. C. Battalion, Capt. J. A. Cooper.

JOHNSON'S DIVISION.
MAJOR-GENERAL EDWARD JOHNSON.

Stonewall Brigade.

Brig.-Gen. J. A. WALKER.
2d Virginia, Col. J. Q. A. Nadenbousch.
4th Virginia, Col. William Terry.
5th Virginia, Col. J. H. S. Funk.
27th Virginia, Lt.-Col. [C. L.] Haynes.
33d Virginia, Col. F. W. M. Holliday.

Jones's Brigade.

Brig.-Gen. J. M. JONES.
21st Virginia, Col. W. A. Witcher.
25th Virginia, Col. J. C. Higginbotham.
42d Virginia, Colonel R. W. Withers.
44th Virginia, Col. Norvell Cobb.
48th Virginia, Col. R. H. Dungan.
50th Virginia, Col. A. S. Vanderventer.

Steuart's Brigade.

Brig.-Gen. GEORGE H. STEUART.
10th Virginia, Col. E. T. H. Warren.
23d Virginia, Col. A. G. Taljaferro.
37th Virginia, Col. T. V. Williams.
1st N. Carolina, Col. J. A. McDowell.
3d N. Carolina, Col. S. D. Thruston.

Stafford's Brigade.

Brig.-Gen. L. A. STAFFORD.
1st Louisiana, Col. W. R. Shivers.
2d Louisiana, Col. J. M. Williams.
10th Louisiana, Col. E. Waggaman.
14th Louisiana, Col. Z. York.
15th Louisiana, Col. E. Pendleton.

RODES'S DIVISION.
MAJOR-GENERAL ROBERT E. RODES.

Daniel's Brigade.

Brig.-Gen. JUNIUS DANIEL.
32d N. Carolina, Col. E. C. Brabble.
43d N. Carolina, Col. Thos. S. Kenan.
45th N. Carolina, Col. Sam'l H. Boyd.
53d N. Carolina, Col. Wm. A. Owens.
2d N. C. Batt., Maj. John M. Hancock.

Doles's Brigade.

Brig.-Gen. GEORGE DOLES.
4th Georgia, Col. Philip Cook.
12th Georgia, Col. Edward Willis.
21st Georgia, Col. John T. Mercer.
44th Georgia, Col. William H. Peebles.

Ramseur's Brigade.

Brig. Gen. S. D. RAMSEUR.
2d N. Carolina, Col. W. R. Cox.
4th N. Carolina, Col. Bryan Grimes.
14th N. Carolina, Col. R. T. Bennett.
30th N. Carolina, Col. F. M. Parker.

Battle's Brigade.

Brig.-Gen. C. A. BATTLE.
3d Alabama, Col. C. Forsyth.
5th Alabama, Col. J. M. Hall.
6th Alabama, Col. J. N. Lightfoot.
12th Alabama, Col. S. B. Pickens.
26th Alabama, Col. E. A. O'Neal.

Johnston's Brigade.

Brigadier-General R. D. JOHNSTON.
5th N. C., Col. Thomas M. Garrett.   20th N. C., [Lieut.] Col. Thomas F. Toon
12th N. C., Col. H. E. Coleman.   23d N. C., Major C. C. Blacknall.

THIRD ARMY CORPS.

LIEUTENANT-GENERAL A. P. HILL COMMANDING.
ANDERSON'S DIVISION.
MAJOR-GENERAL R. H. ANDERSON.

Wilcox's (late) Brigade.

8th Alabama, Col. Y. L. Royston.
9th Alabama, Col. J. H. King.
10th Alabama, Col. W. H. Forney.
11th Alabama, Col. J. C. C. Sanders.
14th Alabama, Col. L. Pinckard.

Mahone's Brigade.

Brig.-Gen. WILLIAM MAHONE.
6th Virginia, Col. George T. Rogers.
12th Virginia, Col. D. A. Weisiger.
16th Virginia, Col. Joseph [H.] Ham.
41st Virginia, Col. W. A. Parham.
61st Virginia, Col. V. D. Groner.

Posey's (late) Brigade.

12th Mississippi, Col. W. H. Taylor.
16th Mississippi, Col. S. E. Baker.
19th Mississippi, Col. N. H. Harris.
48th Mississippi, Col. J. M. Jayne.

Wright's Brigade.

Brig.-Gen. A. R. WRIGHT.
3d Georgia, Col. E. J. Walker.
22d Georgia, Col. [George H. Jones].
48th Georgia, Col. William Gibson.
2d Georgia Battalion, Maj. C. J. Moffitt.

Perry's Brigade.

Brigadier-General E. A. PERRY.

2d Florida, Col. L. G. Pyles.   5th Florida, Col. T. B. Lamar.
8th Florida, Col. David Lang.

HETH'S DIVISION.

MAJOR-GENERAL HENRY HETH.

Davis's Brigade.

Brig.-Gen. J. R. DAVIS.
2d Mississippi, Col. J. M. Stone.
11th Mississippi, Col. F. M. Green.
42d Mississippi, Col. H. Moseley.
55th N. Carolina, Col. J. K. Connally.

Kirkland's Brigade.

Brig.-Gen. W. W. KIRKLAND.
11th N. Carolina, Col. C. Leventhorpe.
26th N. Carolina, Col. J. R. Lane.
44th N. Carolina, Col. T. C. Singeltary.
47th N. Carolina, Col. G. H. Faribault.
52d N. Carolina, Col. J. K. Marshall.

Cooke's Brigade.

Brigadier-General J. R. COOKE.
15th North Carolina, Colonel William McRae.
27th North Carolina, Colonel John A. Gilmer [Jr.].
46th North Carolina, Colonel E. D. Hall.
48th North Carolina, Colonel [S. H. Walkup].

WILCOX'S DIVISION.

MAJOR-GENERAL C. M. WILCOX.

Lane's Brigade.

Brig.-Gen. J. H. LANE.
7th N. Carolina, Col. E. G. Haywood.
18th N. Carolina, Col. J. D. Barry.
28th N. Carolina, Col. S. D. Lowe.
33d N. Carolina, Col. C. M. Avery.
37th N. Carolina, Col. W. M. Barbour.

McGowan's Brigade.

Brig. Gen. S. McGOWAN.
1st S. Carolina, Maj. C. W. McCreary.
12th S. Carolina, Col. J. L. Miller.
13th S. Carolina, Col. B. T. Brockman.
14th S. Carolina, Col. Jos. N. Brown.
Orr's (1st) S. C. Rifles, Col. F. E. Harrison

Scales's Brigade.

Brigadier-General A. M. SCALES.

13th N. Carolina, Col. J. H. Hyman.
16th N. Carolina, Lt.-Col. W. A. Stowe.
22d N. Carolina, Col. T. S. Galloway.

34th N. Carolina, Col. W. L. J. Lowrance.
38th N. Carolina, Col. W. J. Hoke.

CAVALRY CORPS.

MAJOR-GENERAL J. E. B. STUART COMMANDING.

HAMPTON'S DIVISION.

MAJOR-GENERAL WADE HAMPTON COMMANDING.

Gordon's Brigade.

Brig.-Gen. JAMES B. GORDON.
1st N. Carolina Cav., Col. W. H. Cheek.
2d N. C. Cav., Col. [Wm. G.] Robinson.
4th N. C. Cav., Col. D. D. Ferebee.
5th N. Carolina Cav., Col. [Lt.-Col. S. B. Evans].

Young's Brigade.

Brig.-Gen. P. M. B. YOUNG.
1st S. Carolina Cav., Col. J. L. Black.
2d S. Carolina Cav., Col. T. J. Lipscomb.
Cobb's Georgia Legion (Cav.), Col. G. J. Wright.
Phillips' Georgia Legion (Cav.), Lt.-Col. W. W. Rich.
Jeff. Davis Legion (Cav.), Lt.-Col. J. F Waring.

Rosser's Brigade.

Brigadier-General T. L. ROSSER.

7th Virginia Cav., Col. R. H. Dulany.   12th Virginia Cav., Col. A. W. Harman.
11th Virginia Cav., Col. O. R. Funsten.   35th Bat'n, Va. Cav., Lt.-Col. E.V.White

LEE'S DIVISION.

MAJOR-GENERAL FITZHUGH LEE.

W. H. F. Lee's Brigade.   *Lomax's Brigade.*

Brig.-Gen. J. R. CHAMBLISS Com'd'g.   Brig.-Gen. L. L. LOMAX.
9th Virginia Cav., Col. R. L. T. Beale. 5th Virginia Cav., Lt.-Col. H. Clay Pate.
10th Va. Cav., Col. J. Lucius Davis.   6th Virginia Cav., Col. Julien Harrison.
13th Va. Cav., Col. [J. C. Phillips].   15th Va. Cav., Lt.-Col. John Critcher.

Wickham's Brigade.

Brigadier-General W. C. WICKHAM.

1st Virginia Cav., Col. R. W. Carter.   3d Virginia Cav., Col. T. H. Owen.
2d Virginia Cav., Col. T. T. Munford.   4th Virginia Cav., Lt.-Col. W. H. Payne.

VALLEY DISTRICT.

MAJOR-GENERAL J. A. EARLY COMMANDING.

UNATTACHED COMMANDS.

Imboden's Brigade.   *Thomas's Brigade.*

Brig.-Gen. J. D. IMBODEN.   Brig. Gen. E. L. THOMAS.
62d Va. Inf. (mt'd), Col. Geo. H. Smith. 14th Georgia, Col. R. W. Folsom.
18th Va. Cavalry, Col. G. W. Imboden.   35th Georgia, Col. B. H. Holt.
41st Va. Cav. Batt., Lieut.-Col. Robert 45th Georgia, Col. T. J. Simmons.
White.   •   49th Georgia, Col. S. T. Player.
Gilmor's Md. Cav. Batt., Major H. W.
Gilmor.
McClanahan's Battery, Capt. —— Mc-
Clanahan.

Walker's Brigade.   *Archer's Brigade.*

Brig.-Gen. H. H. WALKER.   Brig.-Gen. J. J. ARCHER.
40th Virginia, Col. J. M. Brockenbrough. 1st Tennessee, Col. P. Turney.
47th Virginia, Col. R. M. Mayo.   7th Tennessee, [Col. John A. Fite].
55th Virginia, Col. [Wm. S.] Christian. 14th Tennessee, [Col. Wm. McComb].
22d Virginia Batt., Lt.-Col. E. P. Tayloe. 13th Alabama, —— ——.

Provost Guard.   *Scouts, Guides, and Couriers.*

1st Virginia Batt., Major D. B. Bridg- 39th Virginia Cav. Batt., Major J. H.
ford.   Richardson.

MARYLAND LINE.

COLONEL BRADLEY T. JOHNSON COMMANDING.

1st Md. Cav., Lieut.-Col. Ridgely Brown. 2d Md. Art., Capt. H. Griffin.
2d Md. Inf., Lieut.-Col. Jas. R. Herbert. Cooper's Va. Bat., Capt. [R. L.] Cooper.

ARTILLERY CORPS.

BRIG.-GENERAL W. N. PENDLETON, CHIEF OF ARTILLERY.

ARTILLERY WITH SECOND CORPS.

BRIGADIER-GENERAL A. L. LONG, CHIEF OF ARTILLERY.

Braxton's Battalion.   *Jones's Battalion.*

Major C. M. BRAXTON, of Virginia.   Lieut.-Col. H. P. JONES, of Va.
Lee Battery (Va.), Capt. C. W. Statham. Maj. J. B. BROCKENBROUGH, of Va.
1st Maryland Art., Capt. W. F. Dement. Charlottesville Art. (Va.), Capt. J. McD.
Chesapeake Art. (Md.), Lieut. W. S.   Carrington.
Chew.   Staunton Art. (Va.), Capt. A.W.Garber.
Alleghany Art. (Va.), Capt. J. C. Car- Courtney Art. (Va.), Capt. W. A. Tan-
penter.   ner.

Carter's Battalion.

Lieut.-Colonel T. H. CARTER, of Virginia.
Morris Art. (Va.), Capt. R. C. Page.
Orange Art. (Va.), Capt. C. M. Fry.
King William Art. (Va.), Capt. W. P. Carter.
Jeff. Davis Art.(Ala.), Capt.W. J. Reese.

Nelson's Battalion.

Lieut.-Col. W. NELSON and Major T. J. PAGE, of Virginia.
Amherst Art. (Va.), Capt. T. J. Kirkpatrick.
Milledge Art. (Ga.), Capt. John Milledge.
Fluvanna Art. (Va.), Capt. John L. Massie.

First Regiment Virginia Artillery.

Colonel J. T. BROWN, of Virginia, and Major R. A. HARDAWAY, of Alabama.
Powhatan Artillery, Captain Willis J. Dance.
2d Richmond Howitzers, Captain David Watson.
3d Richmond Howitzers, Capt. B. H. Smith, Jr.
Rockbridge Artillery. Captain Archie Graham.
Salem Flying Artillery, Captain Charles B. Griffin.

ARTILLERY WITH THIRD CORPS.
COLONEL R. L. WALKER, CHIEF OF ARTILLERY.

Cutts's Battalion.

Lieut.-Col. A. S. CUTTS and Major JOHN LANE, of Georgia.
Ross's Battery (Ga.), Capt. H. M. Ross.
Patterson's Battery (Ga.), Capt. G. M. Patterson.
Irvine Artillery (Ga.), Capt. J. T. Wingfield.

Garnett's Battalion.

Lieut.-Col. J. J. GARNETT and Major C. RICHARDSON, of Virginia.
Lewis Artillery (Va.), Capt. N. Penick.
Donaldsonville Artillery (La.), Capt. V. Maurin.
Norfolk Light Artillery (Va.), Capt. C. R. Grandy.
Huger Art. (Va.), Capt. J. D. Moore.

McIntosh's Battalion.

Major D. G. McINTOSH, of S. Carolina.
Johnson's Artillery (Va.), Captain M. Johnson.
Hardaway Art. (Ala.), Capt.W. B. Hurt.
Danville Art. (Va.), Capt. R. S. Rice.
2d Rockbridge Artillery (Va.), Capt. L. Donald.

Pegram's Battalion.

Major W. J. PEGRAM, of Virginia.
Pedee Art. (S. C.), Capt. E. D. Brunson.
Fredericksburg Art. (Va.), Capt. E. A. Marye.
Purcell Battery (Va.), Capt. J. McGraw.
Letcher Art. (Va.), Capt. T. A. Brander.
Crenshaw Battery (Va.), Capt. T. Ellett.

Poague's Battalion.

Major W. T. POAGUE. of Missouri.
Madison Art. (Miss.), Capt. Geo. Ward.
Albemarle Art. (Va.), Capt. J.W.Wyatt.
Brooke Battery (Va.), Capt. A.W. Utterback.
Graham's Bat. (Ala.), Capt. J. Graham.

Haskell's Battalion.

Major J. C. HASKELL, of South Carolina.
Palmetto Bat. (S.C.),Capt. H.R.Garden.
Branch Art.(N. C.), Capt. J. R.Potts.
Rowan Artillery (N. C.), Capt. John A. Ramsay.
Nelson Art. (Va.), Capt. J. N. Lamkin.

ARTILLERY WITH CAVALRY CORPS.
Beckham's Battalion.

Major R. F. BECKHAM.
Chew's Battery (Virginia), Captain R. P. Chew.
Moorman's Battery (Virginia), Captain M. N. Moorman.
Hart's Battery (South Carolina). Captain James F. Hart.
Breathed's Battery (Maryland), Captain J. Breathed.
McGregor's Battery (Virginia), Captain W. M. McGregor.

RESERVE ARTILLERY.
Cabell's Battalion.

Colonel H. C. CABELL, of Virginia, and Major S. P. HAMILTON, of Georgia.
Company A, 1st Artillery (North Carolina), Captain B. C. Manly.
1st Richmond Howitzers (Virginia), Captain E. S. McCarthy.
Troup Artillery (Georgia), Captain H. H. Carlton.
Savannah Artillery (Georgia), Lieut. M. Calloway.

Organization of the Army of Northern Virginia, Commanded by General Robert E. Lee, August, 1864.

FIRST ARMY CORPS.
Lieutenant-General R. H. ANDERSON Commanding.

PICKETT'S DIVISION.
Major-General GEORGE E. PICKETT.

Barton's Brigade.
Brig.-Gen. SETH M. BARTON.
9th Virginia, Col. J. J. Phillips.
14th Virginia, Col. William White.
38th Virginia, Col. George K. Griggs.
53d Virginia, Col. W. R. Aylett.
57th Virginia, Col. C. R. Fontaine.

Corse's Brigade.
Brig.-Gen. M. D. CORSE.
15th Virginia, Col. T. P. August.
17th Virginia, Col. Arthur Herbert.
29th Virginia, Col. James Giles.
30th Virginia, Col. A. T. Harrison.
32d Virginia, Col. E. B. Montague.

Hunton's Brigade.
Brig.-Gen. EPPA HUNTON.
8th Virginia, Col. N. Berkeley.
18th Virginia, Col. H. A. Carrington.
19th Virginia, Col. Henry Gantt.
28th Virginia, Col. William Watts.
56th Virginia, Col. P. P. Slaughter.

Terry's Brigade.
Brig.-Gen. WILLIAM R. TERRY.
1st Virginia, Col. F. G. Skinner.
3d Virginia, Col. Joseph Mayo, Jr.
7th Virginia, Col. C. C. Flowerree.
11th Virginia, Col. M. S. Langhorne.
24th Virginia, Lt.-Col. R. L. Maury.

FIELD'S DIVISION.
Major-General C. W. FIELD.

Anderson's Brigade.
Brig.-Gen. G. T. ANDERSON.
7th Georgia, Col. G. H. Carmical.
8th Georgia, Col. J. R. Towers.
9th Georgia, Lt.-Col. E. F. Hoge.
11th Georgia, Col. F. H. Little.
59th Georgia, Col. Jack Brown.

Law's Brigade.
Brig.-Gen. E. M. LAW.
4th Alabama, Col. P. D. Bowles.
15th Alabama, Col. A. A. Lowther.
44th Alabama, Col. W. F. Perry.
47th Alabama, Col. M. J. Bulger.
48th Alabama, Lt.-Col. W. M. Hardwick.

Bratton's Brigade.
Brigadier-General JOHN BRATTON.
1st South Carolina, Col. J. R. Hagood.
2d South Carolina [Rifles], Col. R. E. Bowen.
5th South Carolina, Col. A. Coward.
6th South Carolina, Col. J. M. Steedman.
Palmetto Sharpshooters, Col. Jos. Walker.

KERSHAW'S DIVISION.
Major-General J. B. KERSHAW.

Wofford's Brigade.
Brig.-Gen. W. T. WOFFORD.
16th Georgia, Major James S. Gholston.
18th Georgia, Col. Joseph Armstrong.
24th Georgia, Col. C. C. Sanders.
3d Georgia Battalion (Sharpshooters), Lt.-Col. N. L. Hutchins.
Phillips' Legion. Lt.-Col. Jos. Hamilton.
Cobb's Legion, Lt.-Col. L. J. Glenn.

Humphreys's Brigade.
Brig.-Gen. B. G. HUMPHREYS.
13th Mississippi, Lt.-Col. A. G. O'Brien.
17th Mississippi, Capt. J. C. Cochran.
18th Mississippi, Col. T. M. Griffin.
21st Mississippi, Col. D. N. Moody.

Bryan's Brigade.

Brig.-Gen. GOODE BRYAN.
10th Georgia, Col. W. C. Holt.
50th Georgia, Col. P. McGlashan.
51st Georgia, Col. E. Ball.
53d Georgia, Col. James P. Sims.

Kershaw's [Old] Brigade.

2d South Carolina, Col. J. D. Kennedy.
3d So :th Carolina, Col. W. D. Rutherford.
7th South Carolina, Capt. E. J. Goggans.
8th South Carolina, Col. J. W. Henagan.
15th South Carolina, Col. J. B Davis.
20th South Carolina, Col. S. M. Boykin.
3d S. C. Batt., Lt.-[Col.] W. G. Rice.

SECOND ARMY CORPS.
MAJOR-GENERAL JUBAL A. EARLY COMMANDING.

GORDON'S DIVISION.
MAJOR-GENERAL JOHN B. GORDON.

Hays's Brigade.

Brig.-Gen. H. T. HAYS.
5th Louisiana, Col. Henry Forno.
6th Louisiana, Col. William Monaghan.
7th Louisiana, Col. D. B. Penn.
8th Louisiana, Col. A. DeBlanc.
9th Louisiana, Col. William R. Peck.

Pegram's Brigade.

Brig.-Gen. JOHN PEGRAM.
13th Virginia, Col. J. B. Terrill.
31st Virginia, Col. J. S. Hoffman.
49th Virginia, Col. J. C. Gibson.
52d Virginia, Col. James H. Skinner.
58th Virginia, Col. F. H. Board.

Gordon's Brigade.

Brig. Gen. J. B. GORDON.
13th Georgia, Lt.-Col. J. H. Baker.
26th Georgia, Col. E. N. Atkinson.
31st Georgia, Col. C. A. Evans.
38th Georgia, Col. J. D. Ma'thews.
60th Georgia, Col. W. H. Stiles.
61st Georgia, Col. J. H. Lamar.

Hoke's Brigade.

Brig.-Gen. R. F. HOKE.
6th North Carolina, Col. R. F. Webb.
21st North Carolina, Lt.-Col.W.S. Rankin.
54th North Carolina, Col. K. M. Murchison.
57th North Carolina, Col. A. C. Godwin.
1st N. C. Batt., Major [R. W.] Wharton.

JOHNSON'S DIVISION.
MAJOR-GENERAL EDWARD JOHNSON.

Stonewall Brigade.

Brig.-Gen. J. A. WALKER.
2d Virginia, Col. J. Q. A. Nadenbousch.
4th Virginia, Col, William Terry.
5th Virginia, Col. J. H. S. Funk.
27th Virginia, Lt.-Col. Charles [L.]
Haynes.
33d Virginia, Col. F. W. M. Holliday.

Jones's Brigade.

Brig.-Gen. J. M. JONES.
21st Virginia, Col. W. A. Witcher.
25th Virginia, Col. J. C. Higginbotham.
42d Virginia, Col. R. W. Withers.
44th Virginia, Colonel Norvell Cobb.
48th Virginia, Col. R. H. Dungan.
50th Virginia, Col. A. S. Vanderventer.

Steuart's Brigade.

Brig.-Gen. GEORGE H. STEUART.
10th Virginia, Col. E. T. H. Warren.
23d Virginia, Col. A. G. Taliaferro.
37th Virginia, Col. T. V. Williams.
1st North Carolina, Col. H. A. Brown.
3d North Carolina, Col. S. D. Thruston.

Stafford's Brigade.

Brig.-Gen. L. A. STAFFORD.
1st Louisiana, Col. W. R. Shivers.
2d Louisiana, Col. J. M. Williams.
10th Louisiana, Col. E. Waggaman.
14th Louisiana, Col. Z. York.
15th Louisiana, Col. E. Pendleton.

RODES'S DIVISION.
MAJOR-GENERAL R. E. RODES.

Daniel's Brigade.

Brig.-Gen. J. DANIEL.
32d North Carolina, Col. E. C. Brabble.
43d North Carolina, Col. Thos. S. Kenan.
45th North Carolina, Col. Samuel H. Boyd.
53d North Carolina, Col. Wm. A. Owens.
2d N. C. Batt., Major John M. Hancock.

Doles's Brigade.

Brig.-Gen. GEORGE DOLES.
4th Georgia, Col. Philip Cook.
12th Georgia, Col. Edward Willis.
21st Georgia, Col. John T. Mercer.
44th Georgia, Col. W. H. Peebles.

Ramseur's Brigade.

Brig.-Gen. S. D. RAMSEUR.
2d North Carolina, Col. W. R. Cox.
4th North Carolina, Col. Bryan Grimes.
14th North Carolina, Col. R. T. Bennett.
30th North Carolina, Col. F. M. Parker.

Battle's Brigade.

Brig.-Gen. C. A. BATTLE.
3d Alabama, Col. Charles Forsyth.
5th Alabama, Col. J. M. Hall.
6th Alabama, Col. J. N. Lightfoot.
12th Alabama, Col. S. B. Pickens.
61st Alabama, Maj. [Lt.-Col.] L. H. Hill

Johnston's Brigade.

Brigadier-General R. D. JOHNSTON.
5th North Carolina, Colonel T. M. Garrett.
12th North Carolina, Colonel H. E. Coleman.
20th North Carolina, Colonel T. F. Toon.
23d North Carolina, Maj. C. C. Blackwell.

THIRD ARMY CORPS.

LIEUTENANT-GENERAL A. P. HILL COMMANDING.

MAHONE'S DIVISION.

MAJOR GENERAL WILLIAM MAHONE.

Sanders's Brigade.

Brig.-Gen. J. C. C. SANDERS.
8th Alabama, Col. Y. L. Royston.
9th Alabama, Col. J. H. King.
10th Alabama, Col. W. H. Forney.
11th Alabama, Lt.-Col. G. E. Tayloe.
14th Alabama, Col. L. Pinckard.

Mahone's Brigade.

6th Virginia, Col. G. T. Rogers.
12th Virginia, Col. D. A. Weisiger.
16th Virginia, Col. Joseph H. Ham.
41st Virginia, Col. W. A. Parham.
61st Virginia, Col. V. D. Groner.

Harris's Brigade.

Brig.-Gen. N. H. HARRIS.
12th Mississippi, Col. M. B. Harris.
16th Mississippi, Col. E. C. Council.
19th Mississippi, Col. R. W. Phipps.
48th Mississippi, Col. J. M. Jayne.

Wright's Brigade.

Brig.-Gen. A. R. WRIGHT.
2d Georgia Battalion, Major C. J. Mofflitt.
10th Ga. Batt., Capt. J. D. Frederick.
3d Georgia, Col. E. J. Walker.
22d Georgia, Col. G. H. Jones.
48th Georgia, Col. William Gibson.
64th Georgia, Major W. H. Weems.

Finegan's Brigade.

Brigadier-General JOSEPH FINEGAN.
2d Florida, Major W. [R.] Moore.
5th Florida, Col. T. B. Lamar.
8th Florida, Col. D. Lang.
9th Florida, Col. J. M. Martin.
10th Florida, Col. C. [F.] Hopkins.
11th Florida, Col. T. W. Brevard.

WILCOX'S DIVISION.

MAJOR-GENERAL C. M. WILCOX.

Thomas's Brigade.

Brig.-Gen. E. L. THOMAS.
14th Georgia, Lieut.-Col. R. P. Lester.
35th Georgia, Col. B. H. Holt.
45th Georgia, Col. T. J. Simmons.
49th Georgia, Col. John T. Jordan.

Lane's Brigade.

Brig.-Gen. JAMES H. LANE.
7th North Carolina, Col. E. G. Haywood,
18th North Carolina, Col. J. D. Barry.
28th North Carolina, Major S. N. Stowe.
33d North Carolina, Col. R. V. Cowan.
37th North Carolina, Col. W. M. Barbour.

McGowan's Brigade.

Brig.-Gen. SAMUEL McGOWAN.
1st S. Carolina, Col. C. W. McCreary.
12th S. Carolina, Lt.-Col. E. F. Bookter.
13th S. Carolina, Col. Isaac F. Hunt.
14th S. Carolina, Col. J. N. Brown.
Orr's Rifles, Col. McD. Miller.

Scales's Brigade.

Brig.-Gen. ALFRED M. SCALES.
13th N. Carolina, Col. J. H. Hyman.
16th N. Carolina, Col. W. A. Stowe.
22d N. C., Col. T. S. Galloway [Jr.].
34th N. C., Col. W. L. J. Lowrance.
38th N. Carolina, Col. John Ashford.

HETH'S DIVISION.

MAJOR-GENERAL H. HETH.

Davis's Brigade.

Brig.-Gen. J. R. DAVIS.
2d Mississippi, Col. J. M. Stone.
11th Mississippi, Lt.-Col. W. B. Lowry.
26th Mississippi, Lt.-Col. A. E. Reynolds.
42d Mississippi, Lt.-Col. A. M. Nelson.
1st Confederate Battalion, —— ——.

McRae's Brigade.

Brig.-Gen. D. McRAE.
11th N. Carolina, Col. W. J. Martin.
26th N. Carolina, Col. J. R. Lane.
44th N. Carolina, Col. T. C. Singeltary.
47th N. Carolina. Col. G. H. Faribault.
52d N. Carolina, Col. M. A. Parks.

Cooke's Brigade.

Brig.-Gen. JOHN R. COOKE.
15th N. C., Lt.-Col. W. H. Yarborough.
27th N. Carolina, Col. J. A. Gilmer, Jr.
46th N. Carolina, Col. W. L. Saunders.
48th N. Carolina, Col. S. H. Walkup.

Archer's Brigade.

Brig.-Gen. J. J. ARCHER.
1st Tennessee, Lieut.-Col. N. A. George.
7th Tennessee, Col. J. A. Fite.
14th Tennessee, Col. W. McComb.
13th Alabama, Lt.-Col. James Aiken.[1]

Walker's Brigade.

Brigadier-General H. H. WALKER.
22d Virginia Battalion, Lieut.-Colonel E. P. Tayloe.
40th Virginia, Lieut.-Colonel A. S. Cunningham.
47th Virginia, Colonel R. M. Mayo.
55th Virginia, Colonel W. S. Christian.
2d Maryland Battalion, Lieut.-Colonel James R. Herbert.

CAVALRY CORPS.

LIEUTENANT-GENERAL WADE HAMPTON COMMANDING.

LEE'S DIVISION.

MAJOR-GENERAL FITZHUGH LEE.

Wickham's Brigade.

Brig.-Gen. W. C. WICKHAM.
1st Virginia, Col. R. W. Carter.
2d Virginia, Col. T. T. Munford.
3d Virginia, Col. T. H. Owen.
4th Virginia, Col. W. H. Payne.

Lomax's Brigade.

Brig.-Gen. L. L. LOMAX.
5th Virginia, Col. H. Clay Pate.
6th Virginia, Col. Julien Harrison.
15th Virginia, Col. C. R. Collins.

BUTLER'S DIVISION.

MAJOR-GENERAL M. C. BUTLER.

Dunovant's Brigade.

Brig.-Gen. JOHN DUNOVANT.
3d S. Carolina [Col. C. J. Colcock].
4th S. Carolina [Col. B. H. Rutledge].
5th S. Carolina, Col. [H. K.] Aiken.

Young's Brigade.

Brig.-Gen. P. M. B. YOUNG.
Cobb's Ga. Legion. Col. G. J. Wright.
Phillips' Legion, Lt.-Col. W. W. Rich.
Jeff. Davis Legion, Lt.-Col. J. F. Waring.
Miller's Legion, —— ——.
Love's Legion, —— ——.
7th Georgia, Col. [R. H.] Anderson.

Rosser's Brigade.

Brigadier-General THOMAS L. ROSSER.
7th Virginia, Col. R. H. Dulany.
11th Virginia, Col. O. R. Funsten.
12th Virginia, Col. A. W. Harman.
35th Virginia Batt., Lt.-Col. E. V. White.

---

[1] James Aiken was Colonel in October, 1864, according to signature.

LEE'S DIVISION.

MAJOR-GENERAL W. H. F. LEE.

Barringer's Brigade.

Brig.-Gen. RUFUS BARRINGER.
1st N. Carolina, Col. W. H. Cheek.
2d North Carolina, Col. C. M. Andrews [1]
[Col. W. P. Roberts].
4th N. Carolina, Lt.-Col. D. D. Ferebee.
5th N. Carolina, Lt.-Col. S. B. Evans.

Chambliss's Brigade.

Brig.-Gen. J. R. CHAMBLISS, Jr.
9th Virginia, Col. R. L. T. Beale.
10th Virg·nia, Col. J. Lucius Davis.
13th Virginia, Col. J. C. Phillips.

ARTILLERY RESERVE.

BRIGADIER-GENERAL W. N. PENDLETON COMMANDING.

Cabell's Battalion.

Colonel H. C. CABELL.
Manly's Battery, Capt. B. C. Manly.
1st Company Richmond Howitzers, Capt.
R. M. Anderson.
Carlton's Battery, Capt. H. H. Carlton.
Calloway's Bat., 1st Lieut. M. Calloway.

Huger's Battalion.

Major F. HUGER.
Smith's Battery, Capt. [John D.] Smith.
Moody Battery, Lieut. [G.] Poindexter.
Woolfolk Bat'y, Lieut. [Jas.] Woolfolk.
Parker's Battery, Capt. [W. W.] Parker.
Taylor's Battery, Capt. [O. B.] Taylor.
Fickling's Bat.. Capt. [W. W.] Fickling.
Martin's Battery, Capt. —— Martin.

Haskell's Battalion.

Major J. C. HASKELL.
Branch's Battery. Captain —— Flanner.
Nelson's Battery, Lt. [W. B.] Stanfield.
Garden's Battery, Capt. [H. R.] Garden.
Rowan Battery, Lieut. —— Myers.

Gibbs's Battalion.

—— GIBBS.
Davidson's Bat., Lt. [J. H.] Chamber-
layne.
Dickenson's Bat'y, Capt. [C.] Dickenson.
Otey's Battery, Capt. [D. N.] Walker.

LONG'S DIVISION.

BRIGADIER-GENERAL A. L. LONG.

Braxton's Battalion.

Major CARTER M. BRAXTON.
Lee Battery, Lieut. W. W. Hardwick.
1st Md. Artillery, Capt. W. F. Dement.
Stafford Artillery, Capt. W. T. Cooper.
Alleghany Art., Capt. J. C. Carpenter.

Cutshaw's Battalion.

Major [W. E.] CUTSHAW.
Charlottesville Artillery, Capt. J. McD.
Carrington.
Staunton Artillery, Capt. A. W. Garber.
Courtney Artillery, Capt. W. A. Tanner.

Carter's Battalion.

Lieut. Col. THOMAS H. CARTER.
Morris Artillery, Capt. S. H. Pendleton.
Orange Artillery, Capt. C. W. Fry.
King William Art., Capt. Wm. P. Carter.
Jeff. Davis Artillery, Capt. W. J. Reese.

Nelson's Battalion.

Lieut.-Col. [WILLIAM] NELSON.
Amherst Artillery, Capt. T. J. Kirk-
patrick.
Milledge Artille y, Capt. John Milledge.
Fluvanna Artillery, Capt. J. L. Massie.

Brown's Battalion.

Colonel J. T BROWN.
Powhatan Artillery, Captain W. J. Dance.
2d Richmond Howitzers, Captain L. F Jones.
3d Richmond Howitzers. Captain B. H. Smith, Jr.
Rockbridge Artillery, Captain A. Graham.
Salem Flying Artillery, Captain C. B. Griffin.

[1] On the original of this; was killed June 23, 1864.

WALKER'S DIVISION.
Colonel R. L. WALKER.

Cutts's Battalion.

Lieut. Col. A. S. CUTTS.
Ross's Battery, Capt. H. M. Ross.
Patterson's Bat'y, Capt. G. M. Patterson.
Irwin Artillery, Capt. J. T. Wingfield.

McIntosh's Battalion.

Lieut.-Col. D. G. McINTOSH.
Johnson's Battery, Capt. [V. J. Clutter].
Hurdaway Artillery, Capt. W. B. Hurt.
Danville Artillery, Capt. R. S. Rice.
2d Rockbridge Art., Capt. L. Donald.

Richardson's Battalion.

Lieut.-Col. C. RICHARDSÓN.
Lewis Artillery, Capt. N. Penick.
Donaldsonville Art., Capt. V. Maurin.
Norfolk Light Art., Capt. C. R. Grandy.
Huger Artillery, Capt. J. D. Moore.

Pegram's Battalion.

Lieut.-Colonel W. J. PEGRAM.
Peedee Artillery [Capt. E. B. Brunson].
Fredericksburg Art., Capt. E. A. Marye.
Letcher Artillery, Capt. T. A. Brander.
Purcell Battery [Capt. Geo. M. Cayce].
Crenshaw's Battery, Capt. T. Ellett.

Poague's Battalion.

Lieutenant-Colonel W. T. POAGUE.
Madison Artillery [Captain T. J. Richards].
Albemarle Artillery, Captain J. W. Wyatt.
Brooke Artillery, Captain A. W. Utterback.
Charlotte Artillery, Captain —— Williams.

APPENDIX D.

HEADQUARTERS, ARMY OF THE POTOMAC,
May 2, 1864.

ORDERS.

1. The army will move on Wednesday, the 4th May, 1864.

2. On the day previous, Tuesday, the 3d May, Major-General Sheridan, commanding Cavalry Corps, will move Gregg's cavalry division to the vicinity of Richardsville. It will be accompanied by one-half of the canvas ponton train, the engineer troops with which will repair the road to Ely's ford as far as practicable without exposing their work to the observation of the enemy.

Guards will be placed in all the occupied houses on or in the vicinity of the route of the cavalry, and in advance toward the Rapidan, so as to prevent any communication with the enemy by the inhabitants. The same precaution will be taken at the same time in front of the First and Third Cavalry Divisions, and wherever it may be considered necessary.

At 2 o'clock A.M., on the 4th May, Gregg's division will move to Ely's ford, cross the Rapidan as soon as the canvas ponton bridge is laid, if the river is not fordable, and as soon as the infantry of the Second Corps is up will move to the vicinity of Piney Branch Church, or in that section, throwing reconnoissances well out on the Pamunkey road toward Spottsylvania Court House, Hamilton's crossing, and Fredericksburg.

The roads past Piney Branch Church, Tod's tavern, etc., will be kept clear for the passage of the infantry the following day.

The cavalry division will remain in this position to cover the passage of the army trains, and will move with them and cover their left flank.

At midnight on the 3d May the Third Cavalry Division, with one-half the canvas ponton bridge train, which will join it after dark, will move to Germanna ford, taking the plank-road and cross the Rapidan as soon as the bridge is laid, if the river is not fordable, and hold the crossing until the infantry of the Fifth Corps is up; it will then move to Parker's store on the Orange Court House plank-road or that vicinity, sending out strong reconnoissances on the Orange plank and pike roads, and the Catharpin and Pamunkey roads, until they feel the enemy, and at least as far as Robertson's tavern, the Hope Church, and Ormond's or Robinson's.

All intelligence concerning the enemy will be communicated with promptitude to headquarters, and to the corps and division commanders of the nearest infantry troops.

3. Major General Warren, commanding Fifth Corps, will send two divisions at midnight of the 3d instant by way of Stevensburg and the plank-road to the crossing of Germanna ford. So much bridge train as may be necessary to bridge the Rapidan at Germanna ford, with such artillery as may be required, will accompany these divisions, which will be followed by the remainder of the corps at such hour that the column will cross the Rapidan without delay. Such disposition of the troops and artillery as may be found necessary to cover the bridge will be made by the corps commander, who, after crossing, will move to the vicinity of the Old Wilderness tavern on the Orange Court House pike. The corps will move the following day past the head of Cartharpin Run, crossing the Orange Court House plank-road at Parker's store.

4. Major-General Sedgwick, commanding Sixth Corps, will move at 4 A.M. on the 4th inst, by way of Stevensburg and the Germanna plank-road to Germanna ford, following the Fifth Corps, and after crossing the Rapidan will bivouac on the heights beyond. The canvas ponton train will be taken up as soon as the troops of the Sixth Corps have crossed, and will follow immediately in rear of the troops of that corps.

So much of the bridge train of the Sixth Corps as may be necessary to bridge the Rapidan at Culpeper Mine ford will proceed to Richardsville in rear of the reserve artillery, and as soon as it is ascertained that the reserve artillery are crossing, it will move to Culpeper Mine ford, where the bridge will be established.

The engineers of this bridge train will at once open a road from Culpeper Mine ford direct to Richardsville.

5. Major-General Hancock, commanding Second Corps, will send two divisions, with so much of the bridge train as may be necessary to bridge the Rapidan at Ely's ford, and such artillery as may be required, at midnight of the 3d instant, to Ely's ford. The remainder of the corps will follow at such hour that the column will cross the Rapidan without delay.

The canvas ponton train at this ford will be taken up as soon as the troops of this corps have passed, and will move with it at the head of the trains that accompany the troops. The wooden ponton bridge will remain.

The Second Corps will enter the Stevensburg and Richardsville road at Madden's, in order that the route from Stevensburg to the plank-road may be free for the Fifth and Sixth Corps. After crossing the Rapidan the Second Corps will move to the vicinity of Chandler's or Chancellorville.

6. It is expected that the advance divisions of the Fifth and Second Corps, with the wooden ponton trains, will be at the designated points of crossing not later than 6 A.M. of the 4th instant.

7. The reserve artillery will move at 3 A.M. of the 4th instant and follow the Second Corps, passing Mountain Run at Ross's mills or Hamilton's crossing at Ely's ford, take the road to Chancellorville, and halt for the night at Hunting Creek.

8. Great care will be taken by the corps commanders that the roads are promptly repaired by the pioneers wherever needed, not only for the temporary wants of the division or corps to which the pioneers belong, but for the passage of the troops and trains that follow on the same route.

9. During the movement on the 4th and following days, the commanders of the Fifth and Sixth Corps will occupy the roads on the right flank to cover the passage of their corps, and will keep their flankers well out in that direction.

The commanders of the Second Corps and reserve artillery will in a similar manner look out for the left flank.

Wherever practicable, double columns will be used to shorten the columns. Corps commanders will keep in communication and connection with each other, and co-operate wherever necessary. Their picket lines will be connected. They will keep the Commanding General constantly advised of their progress and of everything important that occurs, and will send staff officers to acquaint him with the location of their headquarters. During the movement of the 4th instant headquarters will be on the route of the Fifth and Sixth Corps. It will be established at night between those corps and the Germanna plank-road.

10. The infantry troops will take with them fifty rounds of ammunition upon the person, three (3) days' full rations in the haversacks, three (3) days' bread and small rations in the knapsacks, and three days' beef on the hoof.

Each corps will take with it one-half of its intrenching tools, one hospital wagon, and one medium wagon for each brigade ; one-half of the ambulance trains and the light spring-wagons, and pack animals allowed at the various headquarters.

No other trains or means of transportation than those just specified will accompany the corps, except such wagons as may be necessary for the forage for immediate use for five (5) days. The artillery will have with them the ammunition of the caissons only.

11. The subsistence and other trains loaded with the amount of rations, forage, infantry and artillery ammunition, etc., heretofore ordered, the surplus wooden pontons of the different corps, etc., will be assembled under the direction of the Chief Quartermaster of the army in the vicinity of Richardsville, with a view to crossing the Rapidan by bridges at Ely's ford and Culpeper Mine ford.

12. A detail of 1,000 or 1,200 men will be made from each corps as guard for its subsistence and other trains; this detail will be composed of entire regiments as far as practicable. No other guards whatever for regimental, brigade, division, or corps wagons will be allowed. Each detail will be under the command of an officer selected for that purpose, and the whole will be commanded by the senior officer of the three.

This guard will be so disposed as to protect the trains on the march and in park. The trains are likewise protected by cavalry on the flank and rear.

13. Major-General Sheridan, commanding the Cavalry Corps, will direct the First Cavalry Division to call in its pickets and patrols on the right on the morning of the 4th instant and hold itself ready to move and cover the trains of the army; it will picket and watch the fords of the Rapidan from Rapidan Station to Germanna ford. On the morning of the 5th the First Cavalry Division will cross the Rapidan at Germanna ford and cover the right flank of the trains while crossing the Rapidan and during their movement in rear of the army.

The signal stations on Cedar, Poney, and Stoney Mountains will be maintained as long as practicable.

14. The wooden ponton train at Germanna and Ely's fords will remain for the passage of General Burnside's Army. That at Culpeper Mine ford will be taken up under the direction of the Chief Engineer as soon as the trains have crossed, and will move with the train of its corps.

By command of MAJOR-GENERAL MEADE,

S. WILLIAMS,
Asst. Adjutant-General.

APPENDIX E.

HEADQUARTERS, ARMY OF THE POTOMAC,
May 4, 1864, 6 P.M.

ORDERS.

The following movements are ordered for the 5th May, 1864 :

1. Major-General Sheridan, commanding Cavalry Corps, will move with Gregg's and Torbert's divisions against the enemy's cavalry in the direction of Hamilton's crossing. General Wilson, with the Third Cavalry Division, will move at 5 A.M. to Craig's Meeting House, on the Catharpin road. He will keep out parties on the Orange Court House pike and plank-road, the Catharpin road, Pamunkey road (road to Orange Spring), and in the direction of Twyman s store and Andrew's tavern, or Good Hope Church.

2. Major-General Hancock, commanding Second Corps, will move at 5 A.M. to Shady Grove Church, and extend his right toward the Fifth Corps at Parker's store.

3. Major General Warren, commanding Fifth Corps, will move at 5 A.M. to Parker's store, on the Orange Court House plank-road, and extend his right toward the Sixth Corps, at the Old Wilderness tavern.

4. Major-General Sedgwick, commanding Sixth Corps, will move to Old Wilderness tavern on the Orange Court House pike as soon as the road is clear. He will leave a division to cover the bridge at Germanna ford until informed from these headquarters of the arrival of General Burnside's troops there.

5. The Reserve Artillery will move to Corbin's bridge as soon as the road is clear.

6. The trains will be parked in the vicinity of Todd's tavern.

7. Headquarters will be on the Orange Court House plank-road, near the Fifth Corps.

8. After reaching the points designated, the army will be held ready to move forward.

9. The commanders of the Fifth and Sixth Corps will keep out detachments on the roads on their right flank. The commander of the Second Corps will do the same on the roads in his front.

Their flankers and pickets will be thrown well out, and their troops be held ready to meet the enemy at any moment.

By command of MAJOR-GENERAL MEADE.

S. WILLIAMS,
Assistant Adjutant-General.

APPENDIX F.

ACCORDING to a tabular statement of killed, wounded, and missing in the Army of the Potomac and the Army of the James from May 5, 1864, to April 9, 1865, prepared in the Office of the Adjutant-General of the Army from the regimental records (the muster-rolls) for General Badeau, found on page 713, Vol. III., of his "Military Life of General Grant," the casualties of the Army of the Potomac in the battle of the Wilderness were 2,261 killed, 8,785 wounded, 2,902 missing. The number of killed and missing in a battle can be correctly obtained from the regimental records, but the number of wounded not necessarily so, especially for the battle of the Wilderness, and probably for that of Spottsylvania Court House and other battles. The first muster-roll made out after the battle of the Wilderness was for the 30th of June; the muster-rolls are made at the end of every two months. By the 30th of June many of the wounded, even the severely wounded, had returned to duty with the army, and there is no record on the muster-roll of their having been wounded at all. In other cases, men wounded and mustered out before the next muster-day did not appear on that roll as wounded or as having been wounded. In numerous instances men were reported on the muster-rolls, of June 30th, for instance, absent in hospital, wounded, without any statement as to when and where wounded. In others, men who were wounded were reported simply absent in hospital. Now all such cases as those mentioned were, necessarily, omitted from the list sent to General Badeau, and the number of wounded given by it falls much below the actual number. I learn that thousands of men have applied for pensions for wounds, respecting which no information is to be obtained from the regimental muster-rolls. The nominal lists of killed and wounded afford more reliable data than the muster-rolls. They are made out carefully as soon after the battle or action as possible, and contain every particular concerning each person killed and wounded, with a view to the interests of the Government and of the individual. But in the campaign of 1864 the marching and fighting were so continuous, and the losses in officers killed and wounded were so great, that the nominal lists are very incomplete.

The difference between the numbers which I have adopted and those given by General Badeau is 1,425 wounded. Badeau says, p. 132, Vol. II., "at least half of the wounded returned to the ranks without leaving the army."

Now, as already explained, such cases of wounded as those are not included in the numbers of the wounded given in Badeau's table, and if what he states were correct the number of wounded would be 17,570. But what he says is not correct.

On May 7th, Medical Director McParlin, in a communication to General Seth Williams, Adjutant-General, says: "Arrangements are made to send by railroad 7,000 wounded to Washington. Still more on hand, estimated apparently at 3,000." These 3,000 were also to go to Washington. A small number of the wounded, being very slightly hurt, did return to their regiments in a few days. But these men are not noted on the muster-rolls as wounded.

. In an account of the battle of the Wilderness by General C. M. Wilcox (commanding a division of Hill's corps), published in the Philadelphia *Weekly Times*, he states that by referring to the report of the Surgeon-General of the Army it will be seen that the losses of the Army of the Potomac " on the 5th and 6th of May, killed, wounded, and missirg, when added, amount to thirty-seven thousand seven hundred and thirty-seven ; and if to this prisoners be added, the entire loss to the Union side was over forty thousand."

In the Tabular Statement of the Surgeon-General referred to by General Wilcox, there are two alternative statements of losses, derived from different sources and placed one under the other, which have been added together by General Wilcox to obtain his total of thirty-seven thousand seven hundred and thirty-seven. Had he referred to the Appendix, Part I., which is pointed to for explanations in the column of the Table headed " Remarks and References," he would not have fallen into such an error. Further, prisoners are always included under the heading of "missing." The same statement as to the losses of the Army of the Potomac in the Wilderness is made by General Wilcox in the "Southern Historical Society Papers," August, 1878.

APPENDIX G.

HEADQUARTERS, ARMIES U. S.,
May 7, 1864, 6.30 A.M.

MAJOR-GENERAL MEADE, Commanding Army of the Potomac:

Make all preparations during the day for a night march to take position at Spottsylvan a Court House with one army corps, at Todd's tavern with one, and another near the intersection of Piney Branch and Spottsylvania road with the road from Alsop's to Old Court House. If this move is made the trains should be thrown forward early in the morning to the Ny River.

I think it would be advisable, in making the change, to leave Hancock where he is until Warren passes h m. He could then move and become the right of the new line. Burnside will move to Piney Branch Church. Sedgwick can move along the pike to Chancellorville, and on to his destination. Burnside will move on the plank-road to the intersection of it with the Orange and Fredericksburg plank-road, then follow Sedgwick to his place of destination. All vehicles should be got out of hearing of the enemy before the troops move, and then move off quietly.

It is more than probable that the enemy concentrate for a heavy attack on Hancock [1] this afternoon. In case they do we must be prepared to resist them, and follow up any success we may gain with our whole force. Such a result would necessarily modify these instructions.

All the hospitals should be moved to-day to Chancellorville.

Respectfully, etc.,

U. S. GRANT,
Lieut.-General.

[Copy to General Burnside.]

HEADQUARTERS ARMY OF THE POTOMAC,
May 7th, 3 P.M., 1864.

ORDERS.

The following movements are ordered for to-day and to-night :

1. The trains of the Sixth Corps authorized to accompany the troops will be moved at four o'clock P.M. to Chancellorville, and parked on the left of the road, and held ready to follow the Sixth Corps during the night march

2. The trains of the Fifth Corps authorized to accompany the troops will be moved at five o'clock P.M. to Chancellorville, following the trains of the Sixth Corps and parking with them, and held ready to follow those trains in the movement to-night.

3. The trains of the Second Corps authorized to accompany the troops will be moved at six o'clock P.M. to Chancellorville, and park on the right of the road,

---

[1] The words " on Hancock " not in copy furnished to General Burnside.

and held ready to move at same hour with the other trains by way of the Furnaces to Todd's tavern, keeping clear of the Brock road, which will be used by the troops.

4. Corps commanders will send escorts with these trains.

5. The Reserve Artillery will move at seven o'clock by way of Chancellorville, Aldrich, and Piney Branch Church to the intersection of the road from Piney Branch Church to Spottsylvania Court House, and the road from Alsop's to Block House, and park to the rear on the last named road, so as to give room for the Sixth Corps.

6. At half-past eight o'clock P.M. Major-General Warren, commanding the Fifth Corps, will move to Spottsylvania Court House by way of the Brock road and Todd's tavern.

7. At half-past eight o'clock P.M. Major-General Sedgwick, commanding the Sixth Corps, will move by the pike and plank roads to Chancellorville, where he will be joined by the authorized trains of his own corps and those of the Fifth Corps; thence by way of Aldrich's and Piney Branch Church to the intersection of the road from Piney Branch Church to Spottsylvania Court House and the road from Alsop's to Block house. The trains of the Fifth Corps will then join its corps at Spottsylvania Court House.

8. Major-General Hancock, commanding Second Corps, will move to Todd's tavern by the Brock road, following the Fifth Corps closely.

9. Headquarters during the movement will be along the route of the Fifth and Second Corps, and at the close of the movement near the Sixth Corps.

10. The pickets of the Fifth and Sixth Corps will be withdrawn at one o'clock A.M., and those of the Second Corps at two o'clock A.M., and will follow the routes of their respective corps.

11. The cavalry now under the command of Colonel Hammond will be left by General Sedgwick at the Old Wilderness tavern, and upon being informed by General Hancock of the withdrawal of his corps and pickets will follow that corps.

12. Corps commanders will see that the movements are made with punctuality and promptitude.

13. Major-General Sheridan, commanding Cavalry Corps, will have a sufficient force on the approaches from the right to keep the corps commanders advised in time of the approach of the enemy.

14. It is understood that General Burnside's command will follow the Sixth Corps.

By command of MAJOR-GENERAL MEADE.

S. WILLIAMS,
Asst. Adjutant-General.

APPENDIX H.

HEADQUARTERS, ARMY OF THE POTOMAC,
June 11, 1864.

ORDERS.

The following movements are ordered:

1. At dark on the evening of the 12th instant Brigadier-General Wilson will move the brigade of cavalry picketing the Chickahominy across the swamp at Long bridge or that vicinity, and out on the Long bridge road toward the crossing of White Oak Swamp, and toward the Charles City Central and New Market roads.

The brigade will move promptly and clear the road for the Fifth Corps.

The pickets at the crossings of the Chickahominy will remain until relieved by infantry pickets.

2. During Saturday, the 11th instant, Major-General Warren will move the two divisions of his corps now held in reserve to Moody's, by way of Parsley's mill and Prospect Church, etc., so as to avoid the observation of the enemy. At dark on the evening of the 12th instant he will move his whole corps to Long bridge, by the shortest route, across the Chickahominy, and move on the road to White Oak Swamp bridge (called Long bridge road) and hold that road, looking toward the crossing of White Oak Swamp and Charles City, Central, and New Market roads,

during the passage of the army toward James River. He will follow the Second Corps toward Charles City Court House.

General Warren will picket the crossings of the Chickahominy on his flank while moving to Long bridge, relieving the cavalry pickets.

3. Major-General W. F. Smith, Eighteenth Corps, will withdraw as soon after dark as practicable on the evening of the 12th instant, and move by way of Parsley's mill, Prospect Church, Hopeville Church, Tunstall's Station to White House, where he will embark and proceed to Bermuda Hundred. Upon reaching Tunstall's Station his artillery and trains will join the main trains of the army.

4. Major-General Burnside, Ninth Corps, will withdraw as soon after dark as practicable on the evening of the 12th instant, and move by way of Allen's mill (or by roads avoiding Smith's route), then north of the south fork of the Matadequin to Burtin's, thence past Hughes's, Watts's, Clapton's, Turner's store, etc , to Tunstall's Station, or by any adjoining route, avoiding Smith's, that may be found to Tunstall's Station.

At Tunstall's Station the corps of General Smith has precedence. When it has cleared the way, General Burnside will move to Jones's bridge, taking care not to interfere with routes of other corps, past Baltimore Cross Roads and Emman's Church.

Where the routes of the Sixth and Ninth Corps unite, about three miles from Jones' bridge, the corps that reaches the point first will have precedence.

After crossing at Jones' bridge, Major-General Burnside will take the route passing east of Charles City Court House, by Vandorn's, Clapton, and Tyler's mill.

5. Major-General Wright, Sixth Corps, will withdraw as soon after dark as practicable on the evening of the 12th instant to the intrenched line in his rear, from Allen's pond to Elder's swamp, and in conjunction with the Second Corps hold that line until the roads for the Second and Sixth Corps are well cleared by the Fifth Corps, when the two corps will withdraw.

General Wright will move by way of Cool Arbor, Taylor's, J. P. Parsley's, Widow Viss, Good's, and Hopkins' mill to Moody's, and thence by way of Emman's Church to Jones' bridge, preceding or following the Ninth Corps, as already indicated, when the routes unite.

After crossing the Chickahominy General Wright will take the route to Charles City Court House by Vandorn's.

6. Major-General Hancock, Second Corps, will withdraw as soon after dark as practicable on the evening of the 12th inst. to the entrenched line in his rear, from Allen's pond to Elder's swamp, and hold that line in conjunction with the Sixth Corps until the roads for the Second and Sixth Corps are well cleared, when he will move by routes in his rear to the Despatch Station road, avoiding the roads of the Sixth Corps, and by Despatch Station and the shortest route to Long bridge. He will look out for the crossings of the Chickahominy on his flanks while passing. After crossing the Chickahominy General Hancock will move toward Charles City Court House by way of St. Mary's Church, Walker's, etc.

7. Brigadier-General Ferrero will move his division at dark on the evening of the 12th inst., to the trains of the army near White House or Cumberland, and cover them during the movement.

8. The trains will move to the Window Shades and cross the Chickahominy in that vicinity.

They will take such routes as will not interfere with the movements of the troops.

9. The brigade of cavalry on the right will withdraw at the same time as the Sixth and Second Corps, and close in on the rear of the army and cover it and the trains during the movement.

10. Corps commanders will see that every precaution is taken to ensure the rapid execution of this movement, and that the troops move promptly and quickly on the march.

11. Headquarters during the movement will be at Pollard's or Cedar Grove, near Long bridge, and un il established there will be on the route of the Sixth Corps as far as Emman's Church.

12. Eight canvas and eight wooden pontons will accompany the Fifth Corps to Long bridge.

The engineers will establish bridges at Jones' bridge with the remaining eight canvas pontons and the wooden pontons of the Sixth Corps.

The wooden pontons of the Second Corps will accompany the main train of the army.

13. The pickets of the several corps will be withdrawn at the same hour from the line of intrenchments before daylight of the 13th inst., and will follow the routes of their respective corps.

14. The corps will take with them on the march merely those light headquarters wagons, ammunition wagons, ambulances, etc., specified for the march across the Rapidan. All others will be sent at once to the main trains of the army.

15. The dépôt at White House will be continued for the pre ent, with its permanent garrison, but all supplies, etc., for this army will be moved to the James River, leaving 50,000 rations subsistence and 30,000 rations of forage, in addition to supplies for the garrison. On the arrival of Major Generals Sheridan and Hunter the post at White House will be broken up and transferred to Yorktown, from which place the commanding officer will report his arrival to these headquarters.

By command of MAJOR-GENERAL MEADE.

S. WILLIAMS,
Asst. Adjutant-General.

APPENDIX I.

GENERAL HAMPTON says : " The recent publications of the enemy, together with some of their orders wh ch have been captured, show that Sheridan's object was to destroy Gordonsville and Charlottesville with the railroad near those places."

No order for the destruction of Gordonsville and Charlottesville, or any towns, was ever given by the Commander of the Army of the Potomac. Every care possible was taken by the Provost-Marshal-General of that army, under the orders of its Commander, to preserve private property from injury ; and what injury was done to it was done chiefly during night marches, and was the work of the cowardly skulks that infest, in some degree, all large armies.

The following is the copy of the order to General Sheridan :

HEADQUARTERS ARMY OF THE POTOMAC,
June 5, 1864, 3.30 P.M.

MAJOR-GENERAL SHERIDAN :

I am directed by the Major-General commanding to furnish the following instructions for your guidance in the ex cution of the duty referred to in the order for movements and changes of position to-night, a copy of which order accompanies this communication.

With two divisions of your corps you will move on the morning of the 7th inst. to Charlottesville, and destroy the railroad bridge over the Rivanna near that town. You will then thoroughly destroy the railroad from that point to Gordonsville, and from Gordonsville toward Hanover Junction, and to the latter point if practicable. The Chief Engineer, Major Duane, will furnish you a canvas ponton train of eight boats. The Chief Quartermaster will supply you with such tools, implements, and materials as you may require for the destruction of the road. Upon the completion of this duty you will rejoin this army.

A. A. HUMPHREYS,
Major-General and Chief of Staff.

APPENDIX J.

HEADQUARTERS ARMY OF THE POTOMAC,
June 21, 1864—9.20 A.M.

BRIGADIER-GENERAL WILSON, commanding Third Cavalry Division :

The Major-General commanding directs that you move your command at 2 A.M. to-morrow, the 22d instant, in execution of the duty assigned you of destroying certain railroads. Despatches received from the White House state that Hampton's cavalry was before that place yesterday evening, and that General Sheridan had also reached there. Hence it is desirable that you should march at the earliest moment. In passing Petersburg you will endeavor to avoid the observation of the enemy, and then move by the shortest routes to the intersection of the Petersburg and Lynchburg and the Richmond and Danville railroads, and destroy both those roads to the greatest extent possible, continuing their destruction until driven from it by such attack of the enemy as you can no longer resist. The destruction of those roads to such an extent that they cannot be used by the enemy in connection with Richmond during the remainder of the campaign is an important part of the plan of campaign The latest information from Major-General Hunter represents him to be a few miles west of Lynchburg. He may endeavor to form a junction with this army. You will communicate with him, if practicable, and have delivered to him, verbally, the contents of the accompanying copy of a communication from Lieutenant-General Grant to the Major-General commanding this army. Lieutenant Brooks, who will accompany your expedition part of the way, should be informed where General Hunter will probably be found. The success of your expedition will depend upon the secrecy with which it is commenced, and the celerity with which its movements are conducted.

Your command will therefore have with it the lightest supplies and smallest number of wheels consistent with the thorough execution of the duty, the supplies of the section of country you will operate in being taken into account.

Upon the completion of the work assigned you, you will rejoin this army.

The Chief Quartermaster was directed yesterday to supply you with the implements and material for the destruction of railroads obtained for General Sheridan.

A. A. HUMPHREYS,
Major-General and Chief of Staff.

Mr. SINAI CHURCH, June 21—6 P.M.

The instructions of the Major-General commanding of this date are received. I shall march in obedience thereto at 2 A.M. to-morrow.

Before starting, I would like to know if our infantry forces cross the Weldon Road.

I purpose striking the South Side Road first at Sutherland Station, or some point in that vicinity, tearing up the track sufficiently to delay railroad communication ten or twelve hours.

At this point I shall detach a force to strike the Richmond and Danville Road by a rapid march, at the nearest point, tearing up the track at every practicable point between there and Burkesville.

From Sutherland's I shall move the main body of my command by the Great Road, breaking the railroad at every convenient point, directly to Burkesville, which, if we succeed in capturing, will afford us the opportunity of prosecuting our work to great advantage. As soon as I have made dispositions for communicating with Hunter, and done all the damage possible to the road to Lynchburg, I shall move with all possible rapidity for Danville and Greenboro.

Circumstances must, however, in a great degree control our movements after leaving Burkesville. If Sheridan will look after Hampton, I apprehend no difficulty, and hope to be able to do the enemy great damage.

The ammunition issued to my command is very defective. The implements for destroying roads have not yet arrived, but I learn from General Ingalls that they will certainly be here to-morrow morning.

J. H. WILSON.

APPENDIX K.

HEADQUARTERS ARMY OF THE POTOMAC,
July 29, 1864.

ORDERS.

The following instructions are issued for the guidance of all concerned:

1. As soon as dark Major-General Burnside, commanding Ninth Corps, will withdraw his two brigades under General White, occupying the intrenchments between the plank and Norfolk roads, and bring them to his front. Care will be

taken not to interfere with the troops of the Eighteenth Corps moving into their position in rear of the Ninth Corps.

General Burnside will form his troops for assaulting the enemy's works at daylight of the 30th, prepare his parapets and abatis for the passage of the columns, and have the pioneers equipped for work in opening passages for artillery, destroying enemy's abatis, etc., and the intrenching tools distributed for effecting lodgment, etc.

2. Major-General Warren, commanding Fifth Corps, will reduce the number of his troops holding the intrenchments of his front to the minimum, and concentrate all his available force on his right, and hold them prepared to support the assault of Major-General Burnside. The preparations in respect to pioneers, intrenching tools, etc., enjoined upon the Ninth Corps will also be made by the Fifth Corps.

3. As soon as it is dark Major-General Ord, commanding Eighteenth Corps, will relieve his troops in the trenches by General Mott's division of the Second Corps, and form his corps in rear of the Ninth Corps, and be prepared to support the assault of Major-General Burnside.

4. Every preparation will be made for moving forward the field artillery of each corps.

5. At dark Major-General Hancock, commanding Second Corps, will move from Deep Bottom to the rear of the intrenchments now held by the Eighteenth Corps, resume the command of Mott's division, and be prepared at daylight to follow up the assaulting and supporting column, or for such other operations as may be found necessary.

6. Major-General Sheridan, commanding Cavalry Corps, will proceed at dark from the vicinity of Deep Bottom to Lee's mill, and at daylight will move with his whole corps, including Wilson's division, against the enemy's troops defending Petersburg on their right, by the roads leading from the southward and westward.

7. Major Duane, Acting Chief Engineer, will have the ponton trains parked at convenient points in the rear, prepared to move. He will see that supplies of sand-bags, gabions, fascines, etc., are in dépôt, near the lines, ready for use. He will detail engineer officers for each corps.

8. At half-past three in the morning of the 30th, Major-General Burnside will spring his mine, and his assaulting columns will immediately move rapidly upon the breach, seize the crest in the rear, and effect a lodgment there. He will be followed by Major-General Ord, who will support him on the right, directing his movement to the crest indicated, and by Major-General Warren, who will support him on the left. Upon the explosion of the mine the artillery of all kinds in battery will open upon those points of the enemy's works whose fire covers the ground over which our columns must move. care being taken to avoid impeding the progress of our troops. Special instructions respecting the direction of the fire will be issued through the Chief of Artillery.

9. Corps commanders will report to the Commanding General when their preparations are complete, and will advise him of every step in the progress of the operation and of everything important that occurs.

10 Promptitude, rapidity of execution, and cordial co-operation are essential to success, and the Commanding General is confident that this indication of his expectations will insure the hearty efforts of the commanders and troops.

11. Headquarters during the operation will be at the headquarters of the Ninth Corps.

By command of MAJOR-GENERAL MEADE.

S. WILLIAMS,
Assistant Adjutant-General.

***

OPINION.

The Court having given a brief narrative of the assault and "the facts and circumstances attending it," it remains to report that the following named officers engaged therein appear from the evidence to be "answerable for the want of success" which should have resulted.

I. Major-General *A. E. Burnside,* United States Volunteers, he having failed to obey the orders of the Commanding General :

1. In not giving such formation to his assaulting column as to insure a reasonable prospect of success.

2. In not preparing his parapets and abatis for the passage of the columns of assault.

3. In not employing engineer officers who reported to him to lead the assaulting columns with working parties, and not causing to be provided proper materials necessary for crowning the crest when the assaulting columns should arrive there.

4. In neglecting to execute Major-General Meade's orders respecting the prompt advance of General Ledlie's troops from the crater to the crest; or, in default of accomplishing that, not causing those troops to fall back and give place to other troops more willing and equal to the task, instead of delaying until the opportunity passed away, thus affording time for the enemy to recover from his surprise, concentrate his fire, and bring his troops to operate against the Union troops assembled uselessly in the crater.

Notwithstanding the failure to comply with orders, and to apply proper military principles, ascribed to General Burnside, the Court is satisfied he believed that the measures taken by him would insure success.

II. Brigadier-General *J. H. Ledlie*, United States Volunteers, he having failed to push forward his division promptly according to orders, and thereby blocking up the avenue which was designed for the passage of troops ordered to follow and support his in the assault. It is in evidence that no commander reported to General Burnside that his troops could not be got forward, which the Court regard as a neglect of duty on the part of General Ledlie, inasmuch as a timely report of the misbehavior migh have enabled General Burnside, commanding the assault, to have made other arrangements for prosecuting it before it became too late. Instead of being with his division during this difficulty in the crater, and by his personal efforts endeavoring to lead his troops forward, he was most of the time in a bomb-proof, ten rods in rear of the main line of the Ninth Corps works, where it was impossible for him to see anything of the movements of troops that were going on.

III. Brigadier-General *Edward Ferrero*, United States Volunteers:

1. For not having all his troops found ready for the attack at the prescribed time.

2. Not going forward with them to the attack.

3. Being in a bomb-proof habitually, where he could not see the operations of his troops, showing by his own order, issued while there, that he did not know the position of two brigades of his division, or whether they had taken Cemetery Hill or not.

IV. Colonel *Z. R. Bliss*, Seventh Rhode Island Volunteers, commanding First Brigade, Second Division, Ninth Corps:

In this, that he remained behind with the only regiment of his brigade which did not go forward according to the orders, and occupied a position where he could not properly command a brigade which formed a portion of an assaulting column, and where he could not see what was going on.

V. Brigadier-General *O. B. Willcox*, United States Volunteers:

The Court are not satisfied that General Willcox's division made efforts commensurate with the occasion to carry out General Burnside's order to advance to Cemetery Hill, and they think that more energy might have been exercised by Brigadier-General Willcox to cause his troops to go forward to that point.

Without intending to convey the impression that there was any disinclination on the part of the commanders of the supports to heartily co-operate in the attack on the 30th day of July, the Court express their opinion that explicit orders should have been given assigning one officer to the command of all the troops intended to engage in the assault when the Commanding General was not present in person to witness the operations.

WINFIELD S. HANCOCK,
Major-General U. S. Volunteers,
President of Court

EDWARD SCHRIVER,
Inspector-General U. S. A.,
Judge Advocate.

APPENDIX L.

The Morning Report of March 31, 1865, gives for the numbers of the Army of the Potomac 3,064 officers and 68,956 enlisted men of infantry, 147 officers and 5,715 enlisted men of artillery, with 243 guns, present for duty, equipped.

Morning Report, March 31, 1865, Army of the Potomac.

	Officers.	Enlisted men.	ARTILLERY.		
			Officers.	Enlisted men.	Guns.
Provost Guard...........	35	1,568			
Engineers	71	2,588			
Reserve Artillery	....	....	35	1,127	47 [1]
Post of City Point—Collis.	88	1,855			
Second Corps............	960	18,567	33	1,667	70 [2]
Fifth Corps..............	632	15,341	25	1,075	36
Sixth Corps..............	705	16,576	33	1,070	54
Ninth Corps.............	679	16,677	21	776	36
Total, exclusive of Provost Guard and Engineers...............	3,064	68,956	147	5,715	243

For the Army of the James, the Morning Report of the Twenty-fourth Corps of March 31st, Major-General Gibbon commanding, gives for its numbers 841 officers and 19,772 enlisted men of infantry ; 56 officers and 2,045 enlisted men of artillery, with 70 guns, present for duty, equipped.

The Morning Report of the Twenty-fifth Corps, of March 31st, does not comprise General William Birney's division. That of February 28th does, and gives for the numbers of the Corps 417 officers and 12,237 enlisted men of infantry, and 30 officers and 946 enlisted men of artillery, with 56 guns, present for duty, equipped.

---

[1] And some mortars.
[2] And four mortars.

Morning Report, March 31, 1865, *Twenty-fourth Corps*, GENERAL GIBBON *Commanding.*

	INFANTRY.		ARTILLERY.		
	Officers.	Enlisted men.	Officers.	Enlisted men.	Guns.
Foster's—First Division...	249	5,488			
Ames's -Second Division..	169	4,397			
Devens's—Third Division.	275	6,096			
Turner's Independent.....	148	3,791			
Total	841	19,772	56	2,045	70

Morning Report, February 28, 1865, *Twenty-fifth Corps*, GENERAL WEITZEL *Commanding.*

Twenty-fifth Corps	417	12,237	30	946	56

The cavalry of the Army of the James, General Mackenzie commanding, according to the Morning Report of March 31st, had 68 officers and 1,734 enlisted men present for duty.

The Army of the James, therefore, had present for duty 1,258 officers and 32,009 enlisted men of infantry, with 86 officers and 2,991 enlisted men of artillery, with 120 guns. Of this force General Ord took with him on the 27th of March 10,000 infantry of Gibbon's Corps, about 4,000 of Weitzel's, and all Mackenzie's cavalry, 1,700.

When General Sheridan united with the Armies of the Potomac and the James Gregg's cavalry division was assigned to him. The cavalry was an independent command, and consisted of Custer's and Thomas C. Devin's divisions, under the command of General Merritt, and General George Crook's division, formerly Gregg's.

The Morning Reports of March 31st give for the numbers of these divisions present for duty 611 officers and 13,209 enlisted men.

Morning Report, March 31, 1865, *Cavalry present for duty, not present for duty, equipped.*

	Officers.	Enlisted men.
Custer's—Third Division	209	4,355
Thomas C. Devin's—First Division..........	192	3,439
George Crook's—Second Division (Gregg's old division) ...	210	5,415
Total	611	13,209

The siege artillery is not included in the preceding.

The return of Lee's army of February 20, 1865, the last to be found among the Confederate archives in the War Department, gives the following for the number of officers and enlisted men present for duty :

Morning Report of February 20, 1865, Army of Northern Virginia.

	Officers.	Enlisted men.		Officers.	Enlisted men.
Longstreet's—First Corps	851	12,164	Pickett's Division .. Field's Division.... Kershaw's Division.	304 341 206	4,761 4,436 2,967
			Total...........	851	12,164

Gordon's — Second Corps	458	7,623	Evans's Division...
			   Terry's Brigade.
			   York's Brigade.
			   Evans's Brigade.
			 Grimes's Division..
			   Cox's Brigade.
			   Grimes's Brigade.
			   Doles's Brigade.
			   Battle's Brigade.
			 Walker's Division..
			   Toon's Brigade.
			   Lewis's Brigade.
			   Lilly's Brigade.
				....
				
				 ....
				
				 ....
					2,309
					
					 3,022
					
					 2,292

			Total........	458	7,623
Hill's—Third Corps..	865	13,567	Mahone's Division.. Heth's Division.... Wilcox's Division...	....	3,880 4,324 5,383
			Total...........	865	13,567
Anderson's Corps....	431	6,505	Johnson's Division...	431	6,505
	2,605	39,859			
Cavalry—W. H. F. Lee " Fitz Lee...	185 96	3,935 1,825			
	281	5,760			
Field Art.—Pendleton	244	5,155			

This evidently does not include Wise's brigade, which we know was present on the 29th of March, and was probably 2,000 strong.

Besides this force there was that of the Department of Richmond, commanded by General Ewell, consisting of General Custis Lee's command, whose effective force of infantry was 2,700, according to the return of March 20, 1865; Walker's brigade of Richmond and Danville Railroad defences, which on the return of February 20th is given at 1,414 enlisted men : the heavy artillery troops, the naval forces, and finally the local troops, which, although taking part in the defence of the intrenchments, would form no part of the army in the field.

Rosser's cavalry division took part in the defence of Petersburg, but does not appear to be included in the return of February 20th. Whether Gary's cavalry brigade, 1,100 strong, was included is not stated.

It appears, then, that on the 20th of February, and probably on the 25th of March, General Lee had an effective force of infantry of not less than 44,500, exclusive of Walker's brigade; of field artillery not less than 5,000, and of cavalry 6,000, a total of not less than 55,500. There were, besides, the heavy artillery, the local troops, and the naval forces.

COMMANDERS IN THE ARMY OF THE POTOMAC UNDER MAJOR-GENERAL GEORGE G. MEADE, ON MARCH 31, 1865.

GENERAL HEADQUARTERS AND UNATTACHED COMMANDS.

PROVOST GUARD.
COLONEL GEORGE N. MACY.

ENGINEER BRIGADE.
BRIGADIER-GENERAL HENRY W. BENHAM.

BATTALION U. S. ENGINEERS.
CAPTAIN FRANKLIN HARWOOD.

ARTILLERY.
BRIGADIER-GENERAL HENRY J. HUNT.

SIEGE TRAIN.
COLONEL HENRY L. ABBOT.

HEADQUARTERS GUARD.
CAPTAIN RICHARD G. LAY.

QUARTERMASTER'S GUARD.
COLONEL R. N. BATCHELDER.

SIGNAL CORPS.
CAPTAIN CHARLES L. DAVIS.

INDEPENDENT BRIGADE.
COLONEL CHARLES H. T. COLLIS.

SECOND ARMY CORPS.
MAJOR-GENERAL ANDREW A. HUMPHREYS.

FIRST DIVISION.
BRIGADIER-GENERAL NELSON A. MILES.

First Brigade.	*Second Brigade.*
Colonel GEORGE W. SCOTT.	Colonel ROBERT NUGENT.

Third Brigade.	*Fourth Brigade.*
Colonel HENRY J. MADILL.	Colonel JOHN RAMSEY.

SECOND DIVISION.
BRIGADIER-GENERAL WILLIAM HAYS.

First Brigade.	*Second Brigade.*	*Third Brigade.*
Col. WM. A. OLMSTEAD.	Col. JAMES P. MCIVOR.	Brig.-Gen. THOS. A. SMYTH

THIRD DIVISION.
BRIGADIER-GENERAL GERSHOM MOTT.

First Brigade.	*Second Brigade.*
Brig.-Gen. REGIS DE TROBRIAND.	Brig.-Gen. BYRON R. PIERCE.

Third Brigade.
Colonel Robert MCALLISTER.

ARTILLERY BRIGADE.
MAJOR JOHN G. HAZARD.

FIFTH ARMY CORPS.
Major-General GOUVERNEUR K. WARREN.

FIRST DIVISION.
Brigadier-General CHARLES GRIFFIN.

First Brigade.   *Second Brigade.*
Brig.-Gen. JOSHUA L. CHAMBERLAIN.   Colonel EDGAR M. GREGORY.

Third Brigade.
Brig.-Gen. JOSEPH J. BARTLETT.

SECOND DIVISION.
Brigadier-General ROMEYN B. AYRES.

First Brigade.   *Second Brigade.*   *Third Brigade.*
Col. FREDERICK WINTHROP.   Col. ANDREW W. DENISON.   Col. JAMES GWYN.

THIRD DIVISION.
Brigadier-General SAMUEL W. CRAWFORD.

First Brigade.   *Second Brigade.*   *Third Brigade.*
Col. JOHN A. KELLOGG.   Brig.-Gen. HENRY BAXTER.   Col. RICHARD COULTER.

ARTILLERY BRIGADE.
Colonel CHARLES S. WAINWRIGHT.

SIXTH ARMY CORPS.
Major-General HORATIO G. WRIGHT.

FIRST DIVISION.
Brigadier-General FRANK WHEATON.

First Brigade.   *Second Brigade.*   *Third Brigade.*
Col. WM. H. PENROSE.   Col. JOSEPH E. HAMBLIN.   Col. OLIVER EDWARDS.

SECOND DIVISION.
Brigadier-General GEORGE W. GETTY.

First Brigade.   *Second Brigade.*   *Third Brigade.*
Col. JAMES M. WARNER.   Brig.-Gen. LEWIS A. GRANT.   Col. THOMAS W. HYDE.

THIRD DIVISION.
Brigadier-General TRUMAN SEYMOUR.

First Brigade.   *Second Brigade.*
Colonel WM. S. TRUEX.   Colonel J. WARREN KEIFER.

ARTILLERY BRIGADE.
Captain ANDREW COWAN.

NINTH ARMY CORPS.
Major-General JOHN G. PARKE.

FIRST DIVISION.
Brigadier-General ORLANDO B. WILLCOX.

First Brigade.   *Second Brigade.*
Colonel SAMUEL HARRIMAN.   Lieut.-Colonel RALPH ELY.

Third Brigade.
Lieut.-Colonel GILBERT P. ROBINSON.

SECOND DIVISION.
BRIGADIER-GENERAL ROBERT B. POTTER.

First Brigade.
Colonel JOHN I. CURTIN.

Second Brigade.
Brig.-Gen. SIMON G. GRIFFIN.

THIRD DIVISION.
BRIGADIER-GENERAL JOHN F. HARTRANFT.

First Brigade.
Lieut.-Colonel WM. H. McCALL.

Second Brigade.
Colonel JOSEPH A. MATHEWS.

ARTILLERY BRIGADE.
COLONEL JOHN C. TIDBALL.

SHERIDAN'S CAVALRY.
MAJOR-GENERAL PHILIP H. SHERIDAN.

ARMY OF THE SHENANDOAH.
BRIGADIER-GENERAL WESLEY MERRITT.

FIRST DIVISION.
BRIGADIER-GENERAL THOMAS C. DEVIN.

First Brigade.
Colonel PETER STAGG.

Second Brigade.
Col. CHAS. L. FITZHUGH.

Third Brigade.
Brig.-Gen. ALFRED GIBBS.

THIRD DIVISION.
BRIGADIER-GENERAL GEORGE A. CUSTER.

First Brigade.
Col. ALEX. C. M. PENNINGTON.

Second Brigade.
Col. WM. WELLS.

Third Brigade.
Col. HENRY CAPEHART.

SECOND DIVISION (ARMY OF THE POTOMAC).
MAJOR-GENERAL GEORGE CROOK.

First Brigade.
B'g.-Gen. H. E. DAVIES.

Second Brigade.
Col. J. IRWIN GREGG.

Third Brigade.
Col. CHAS. H. SMITH.

ARMY OF THE JAMES.
MAJOR-GENERAL EDWARD O. C. ORD.

GENERAL HEADQUARTERS AND UNATTACHED COMMANDS.

SIGNAL CORPS.
CAPTAIN L. B. NORTON.

ENGINEERS
COLONEL JAMES F. HALL.

CAVALRY.
COLONEL FRANCIS WASHBURN.   COLONEL EDWIN V. SUMNER.
COLONEL CHARLES F. ADAMS, JR.

DEFENCES OF BERMUDA HUNDRED.
MAJOR-GENERAL GEORGE L. HARTSUFF.

PONTONIERS.
LIEUTENANT-COLONEL PETER S. MICHIE.

SEPARATE BRIGADE.
BRIGADIER-GENERAL JOSEPH B. CARR.

TWENTY-FOURTH ARMY CORPS.
MAJOR-GENERAL JOHN GIBBON.

FIRST DIVISION.
BRIGADIER-GENERAL ROBERT S. FOSTER.

First Brigade.	*Third Brigade.*	*Fourth Brigade.*
Col. THOS. O. OSBORN.	Col. GEO. B. DANDY.	Col. HARRISON S. FAIRCHILD.

THIRD DIVISION.
BRIGADIER-GENERAL CHARLES DEVENS.

First Brigade.	*Second Brigade.*	*Third Brigade.*
Col. EDWARD H. RIPLEY.	Col. MIC'L T. DONOHUE.	Col. SAMUEL H. ROBERTS.

INDEPENDENT DIVISION.
BRIGADIER-GENERAL JOHN W. TURNER.

First Brigade.	*Second Brigade.*	*Third Brigade.*
Lt.-Col. ANDREW POTTER.	Col. WILLIAM B. CURTIS.	Colonel THOS. M. HARRIS.

ARTILLERY.
CAPTAIN JAMES R. ANGEL.

TWENTY-FIFTH ARMY CORPS.
MAJOR-GENERAL GODFREY WEITZEL.

FIRST DIVISION.
BRIGADIER-GENERAL AUGUST V. KAUTZ.

First Brigade.	*Second Brigade.*	*Attached Brigade.*
Col. ALONZO G. DRAPER.	Bg.-Gen. EDW'D A. WILD.	Col. CHAS. S. RUSSELL.

SECOND DIVISION.
BRIGADIER-GENERAL WILLIAM BIRNEY.

First Brigade.	*Second Brigade.*	*Third Brigade.*
Col. JAMES SHAW, Jr.	Col. ULYSSES DOUBLEDAY.	Col. W. W. WOODWARD.

ARTILLERY BRIGADE.
CAPTAIN LOOMIS L. LANGDON.

CAVALRY DIVISION.
BRIGADIER-GENERAL RANALD S. MACKENZIE.

First Brigade.	*Second Brigade.*
Colonel ROBERT M. WEST.	Colonel SAMUEL P. SPEAR.

APPENDIX M.

No. 1.

April 7, 1865.

GENERAL--The result of the last week must convince you of the hopelessness of further resistance on the part of the Army of Northern Virginia in this struggle. I feel that it is so, and regard it as my duty to shift from myself the responsibility of any further effusion of blood, by asking of you the surrender of that portion of the Confederate States Army known as the Army of Northern Virginia.

U. S. GRANT,
Lieutenant-General.

GENERAL R. E. LEE.

No. 2.

April 7, 1865.

GENERAL—I have received your note of this date. Though not entertaining the opinion you express on the hopelessness of further resistance on the part of the Army of Northern Virginia, I reciprocate your desire to avoid useless effusion of blood, and therefore, before considering your proposition, ask the terms you will offer on condition of its surrender.

R. E. LEE,
General.

LIEUTENANT-GENERAL U. S. GRANT.

No. 3.

April 8, 1865.

GENERAL—Your note of last evening in reply to mine of same date, asking the condition on which I will accept the surrender of the Army of Northern Virginia is just received. In reply, I would say that peace being my great desire, there is but one condition I would insist upon, namely, that the men and officers surrendered shall be disqualified for taking up arms again against the Government of the United States until properly exchanged. I will meet you, or will designate officers to meet any officers you may name for the same purpose, at any point agreeable to you, for the purpose of arranging definitely the terms upon which the surrender of the Army of Northern Virginia will be received.

U. S. GRANT,
Lieutenant-General.

GENERAL R. E. LEE.

No. 4.

April 8, 1865.

GENERAL—I received at a late hour your note of to-day. In mine of yesterday I did not intend to propose the surrender of the Army of Northern Virginia, but to ask the terms of your propositi n. To be frank, I do not think the emergency has arisen to call for the surrender of this army, but as the restoration of peace should be the sole object of all, I desire to know whether your propos ls would lead to that end. I cannot, therefore, meet you with a view to surrender the Army of Northern Virginia, but as far as your proposal may affect the Confederate States forces under my command, and tend to the restoration of peace, I should be pleased to meet you at 10 A.M. to-morrow on the old stage road to Richmond, between the picket lines of the two armies.

R. E. LEE,
General.

LIEUTENANT-GENERAL U. S. GRANT.

No. 5.

April 9, 1865.

GENERAL—Your note of yesterday is received. I have no authority to treat on the subject of peace : the meeting proposed for 10 A.M. to-day could lead to no good. I will state however, General, that I am equally anxious for peace with yourself, and the whole North entertains the same feeling. The terms upon which peace can be had are well understood.

By the South laying down their arms they will hasten that most desirable event, save thousands of human lives, and hundreds of millions of property not yet destroyed.

Seriously hoping that all our difficulties may be settled without the loss of another life, I subscribe myself, etc.,

U. S. GRANT,
Lieutenant-General.

GENERAL R. E. LEE.

_____

No. 6.

April 9, 1865.

GENERAL—I received your note of this morning, on the picket line whither I had come to meet you, and ascertain definitely what terms were embraced in your proposal of yesterday, with reference to the surrender of this army. I now ask an interview in accordance with the offer contained in your letter of yesterday for that purpose.

R. E. LEE,
General.

LIEUTENANT-GENERAL U. S. GRANT.

_____

No. 7.

April 9, 1865.

GENERAL R. E. LEE, Commanding C.S.A. :

Your note of this date is but this moment, 11.50 A.M. received. In consequence of my having passed from the Richmond and Lynchburg road to the Farmville and Lynchburg road, I am, at this writing, about four miles west of Walker's Church, and will push forward to the front, for the purpose of meeting you.

Notice sent to me on this road where you wish the interview to take place will meet me.   Very respectfully, your obedient servant,

U. S. GRANT,
Lieutenant-General.

_____

No. 8.

APPOMATTOX COURT HOUSE, VA.,
April 9, 1865.

GENERAL—In accordance with the substance of my letter to you of the 8th instant, I propose to receive the surrender of the Army of Northern Virginia on the following terms, to wit : Rolls of all the officers and men to be made in duplicate, one copy to be given to an officer to be designated by me, the other to be retained by such officer or officers as you may designate. The officers to give their individual paroles not to take up arms against the Government of the United States until properly exchanged ; and each company or regimental commander sign a like parole for the men of their commands. The arms, artillery, and public property to be parked and stacked, and turned over to the officers appointed by me to receive them. This will not embrace the side-arms of the officers nor the private horses or baggage. This done, each officer and man will be allowed to return to his home, not to be disturbed by United States authority so long as they observe their paroles, and the laws in force where they may reside.

U. S. GRANT,
Lieutenant-General.

GENERAL R. E. LEE.

_____

No. 9.

HEADQUARTERS ARMY OF NORTHERN VIRGINIA,
April 9, 1865.

GENERAL—I received your letter of this date, containing the terms of the surrender of the Army of Northern Virginia as proposed by you. As they are substantially the same as those expressed in your letter of the 8th instant, they are accepted. I will proceed to designate the proper officers to carry the stipulation into effect.

R. E. LEE,
General.

LIEUTENANT-GENERAL U. S. GRANT.

INDEX.

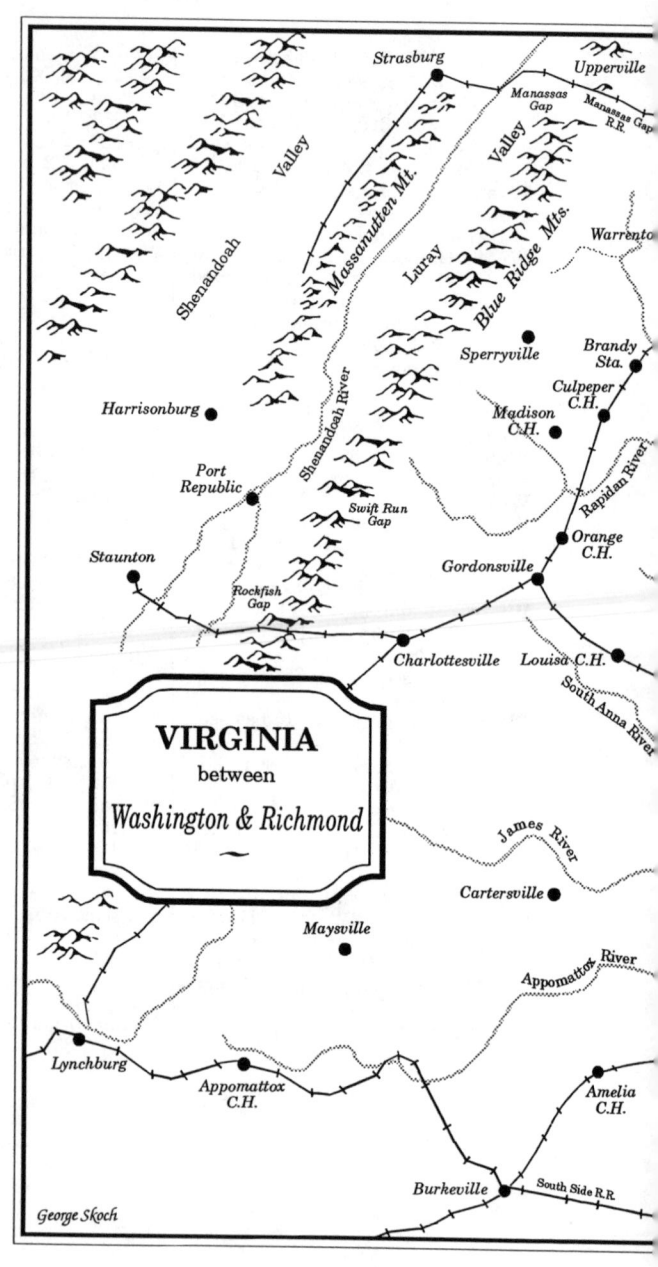

VIRGINIA
between
Washington & Richmond
—

George Skoch

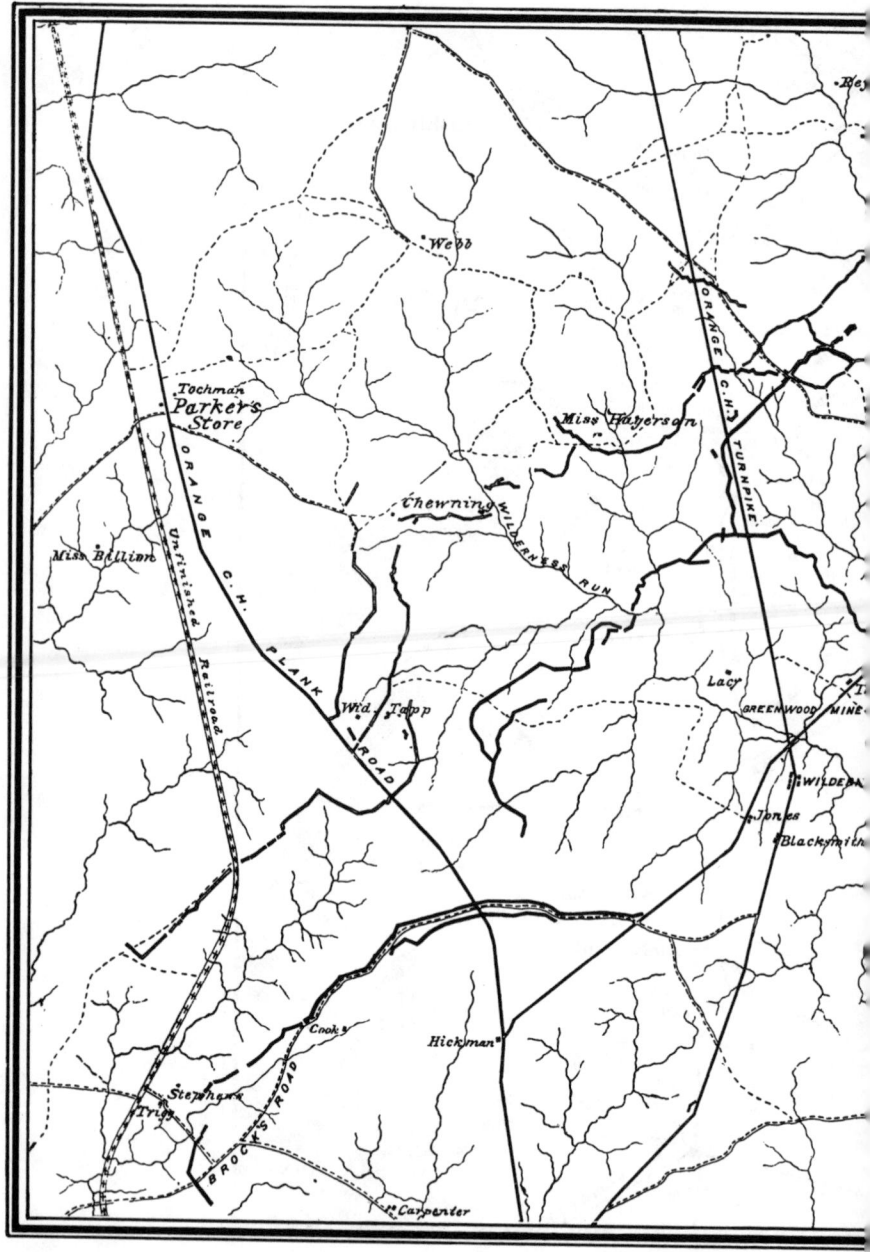

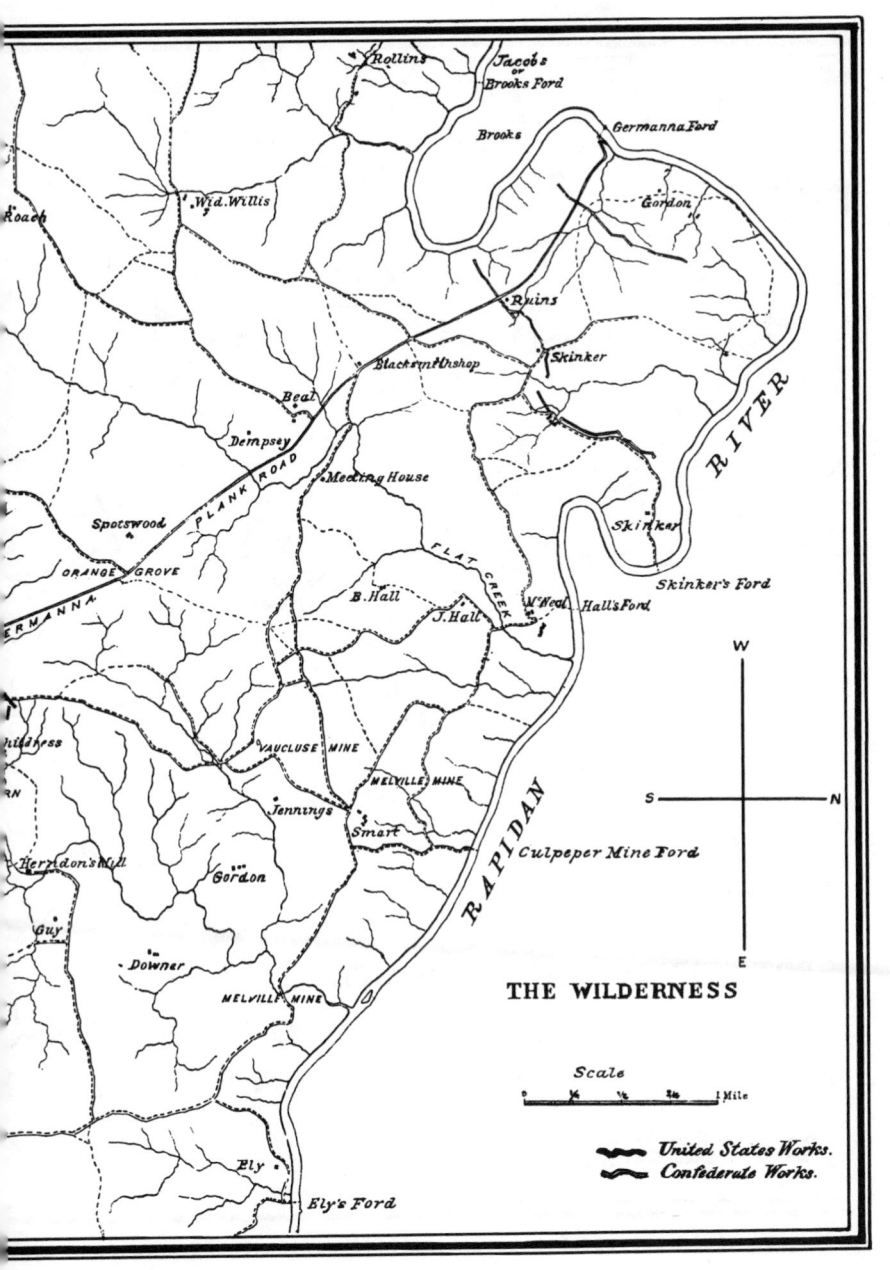

THE WILDERNESS

Scale

0   ¼   ½   ¾   1 Mile

〰 United States Works.
〰 Confederate Works.

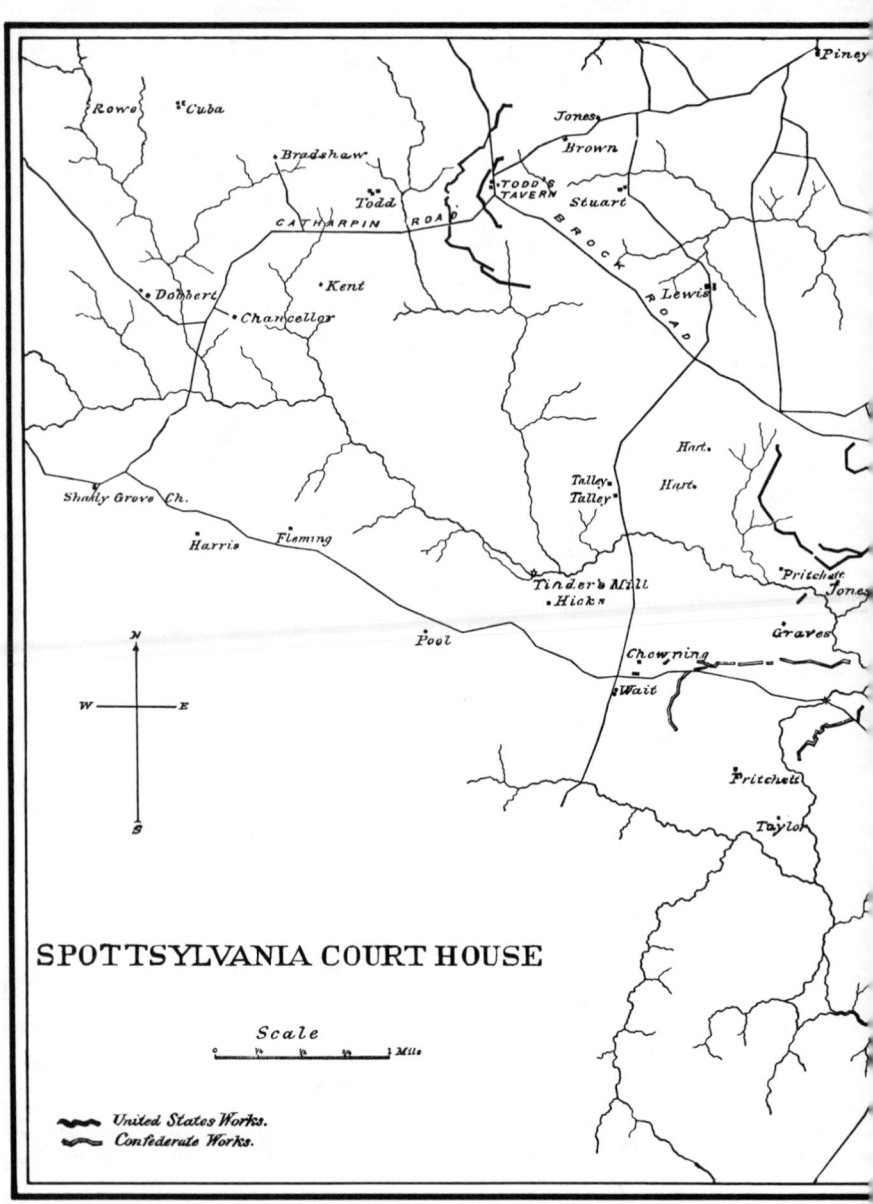

Piney

Rowe   "Cuba   Jones
                          Bradshaw   Brown
                                    Todd   TODD'S
                                             TAVERN   Stuart
                          CATHARPIN   ROAD
                                                        BROCK
    Dobbert   Kent   Lewis
        Chancellor   ROAD

                                                    Hart.

Shady Grove Ch.   Talley Hart.
                                             Talley
    Harris   Fleming
                                        Tinder's Mill   Pritchett
                                          Hicks   Jones

    N   Pool   Graves
                                              Chewning
W   E   Wait

                                                        Pritchett
    S   Taylor

SPOTTSYLVANIA COURT HOUSE

Scale
0   ¼   ½   ¾   1 Mile

〰 United States Works.
〰 Confederate Works.

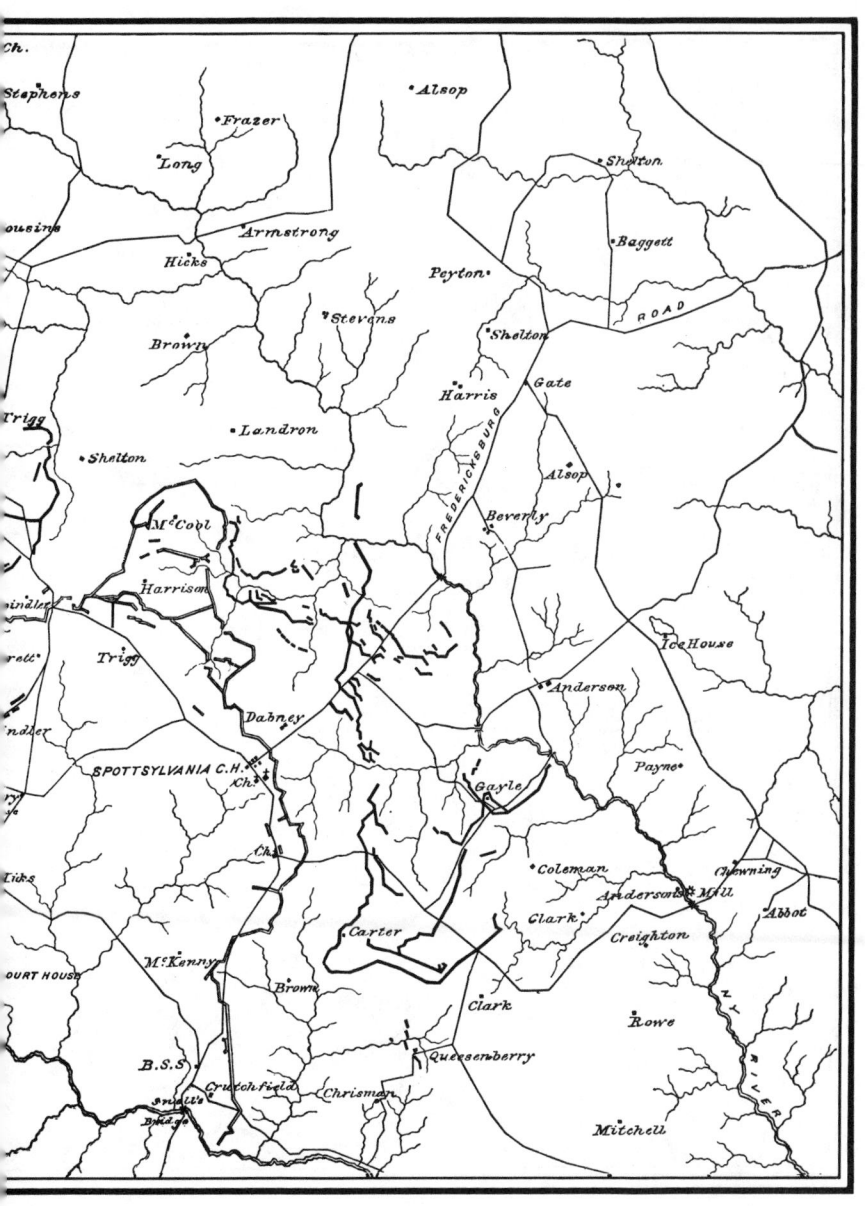

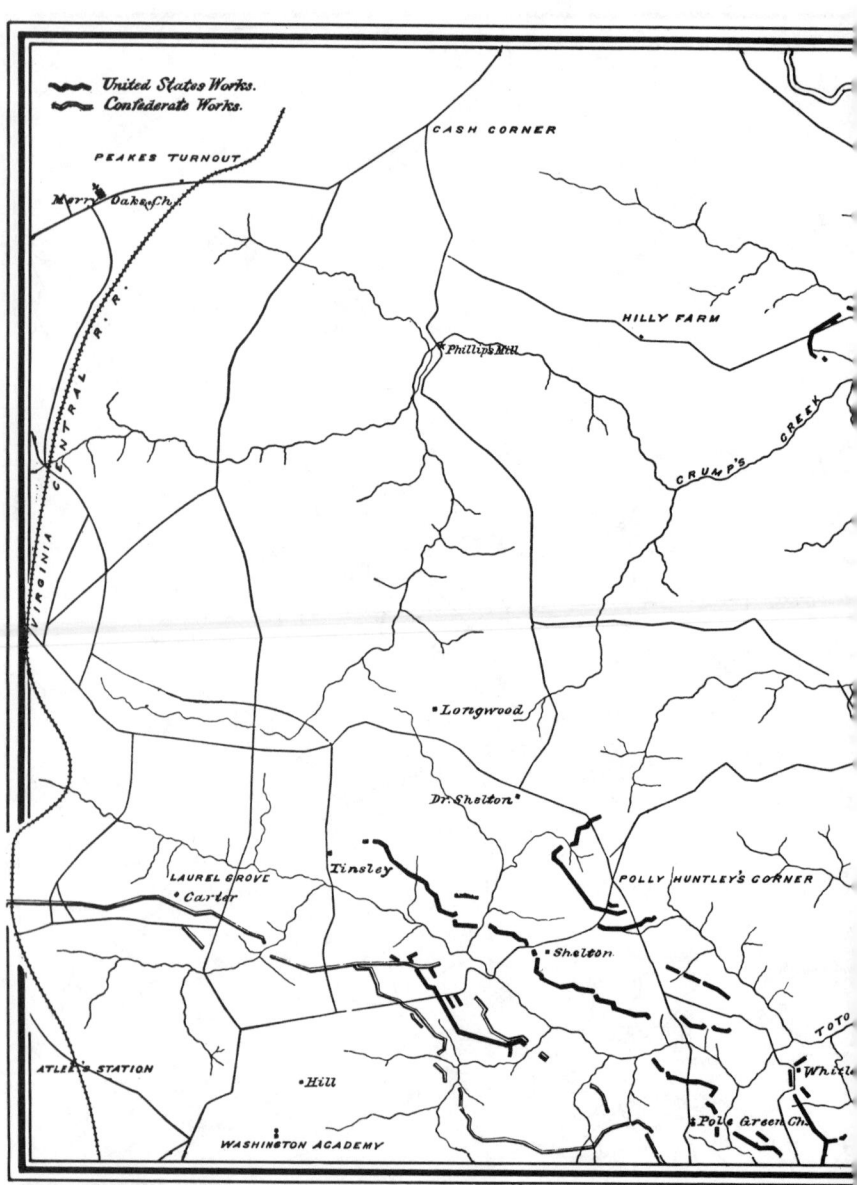

United States Works.
Confederate Works.

PEAKES TURNOUT

CASH CORNER

Merry Oaks Ch.

HILLY FARM

Phillips Mill

CRUMP'S CREEK

VIRGINIA CENTRAL R.R.

Longwood

Dr. Shelton

Tinsley

POLLY HUNTLEY'S CORNER

LAUREL GROVE
Carter

Shelton

TOTO

ATLEE'S STATION

Hill

Whit

Polla Green Ch.

WASHINGTON ACADEMY

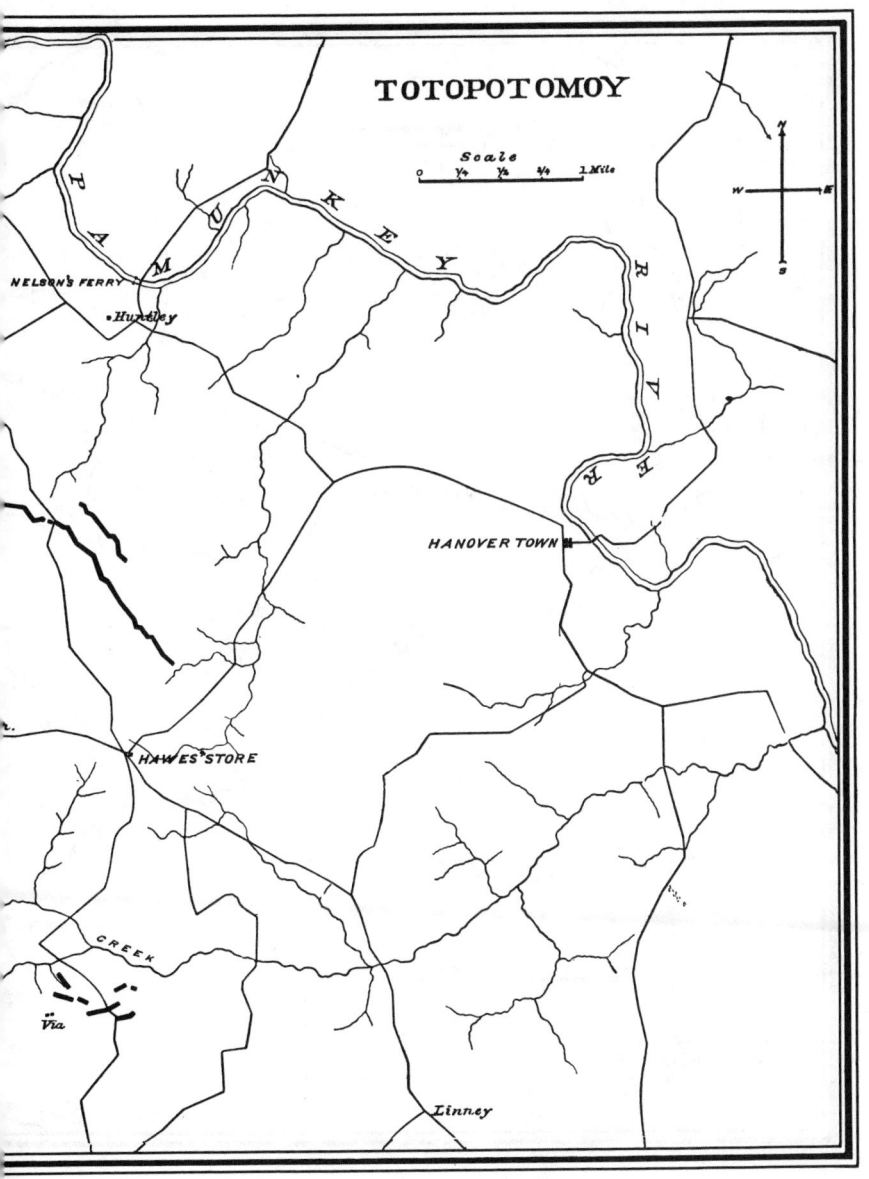

TOTOPOTOMOY

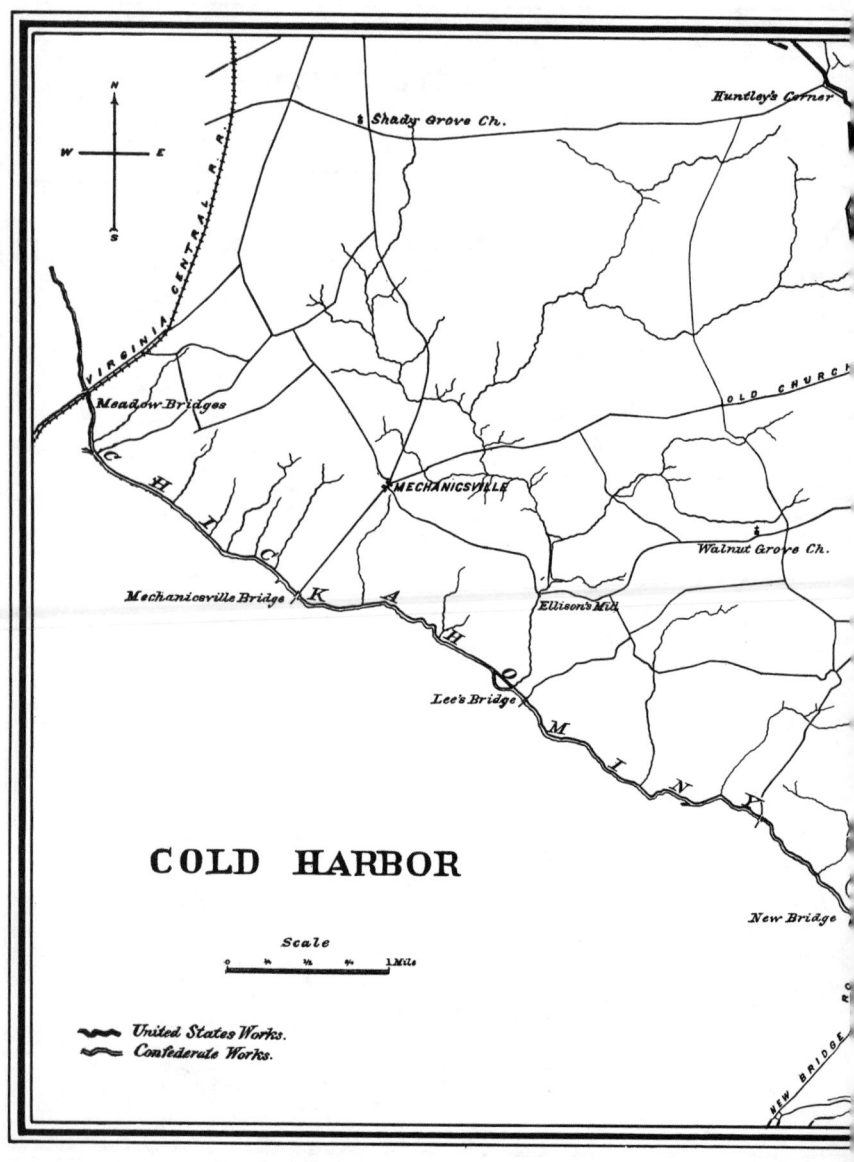

COLD HARBOR

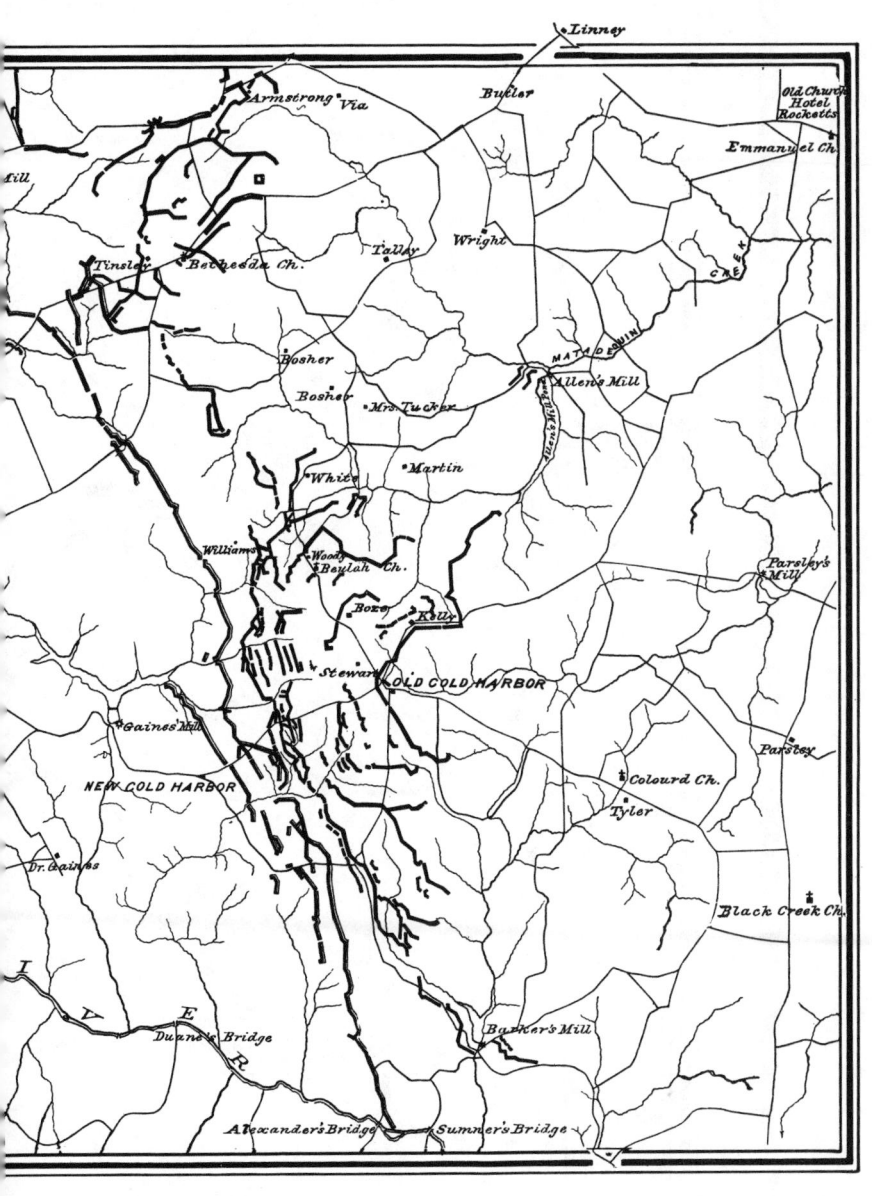

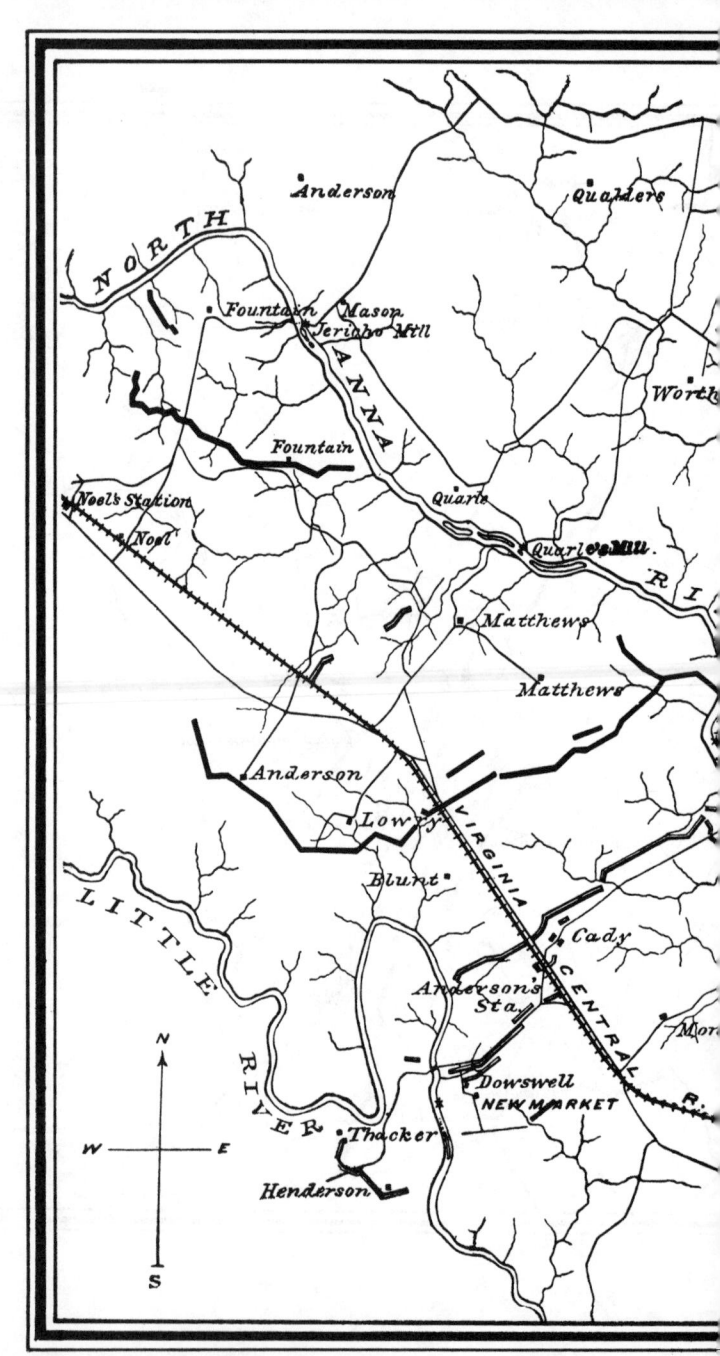

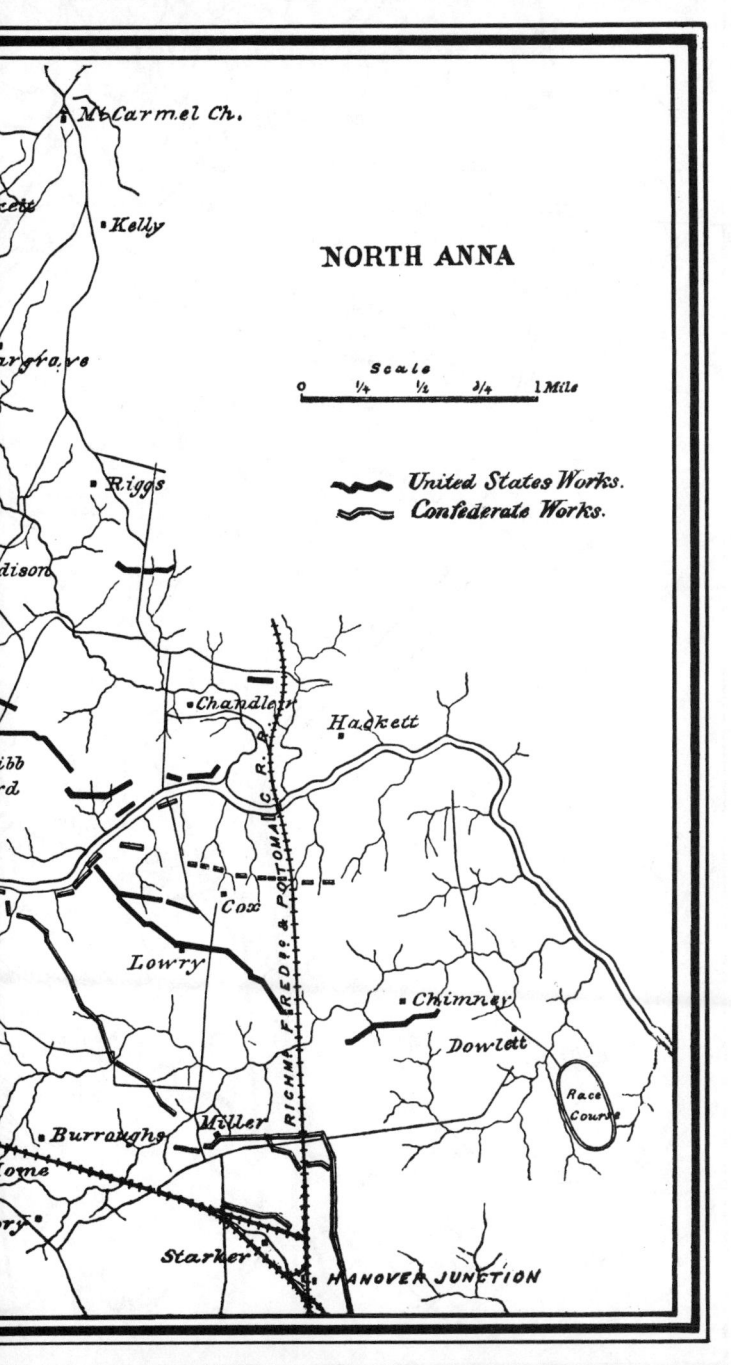

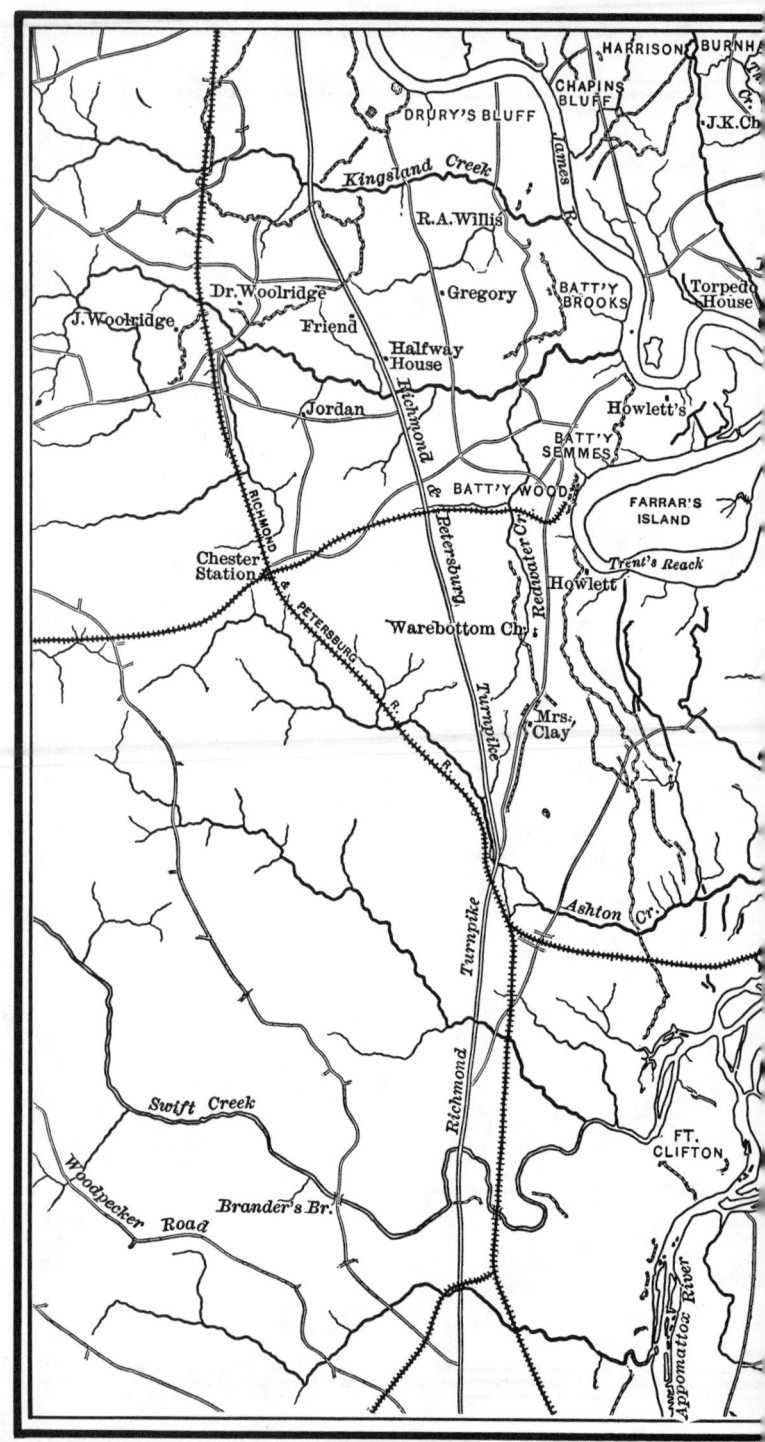

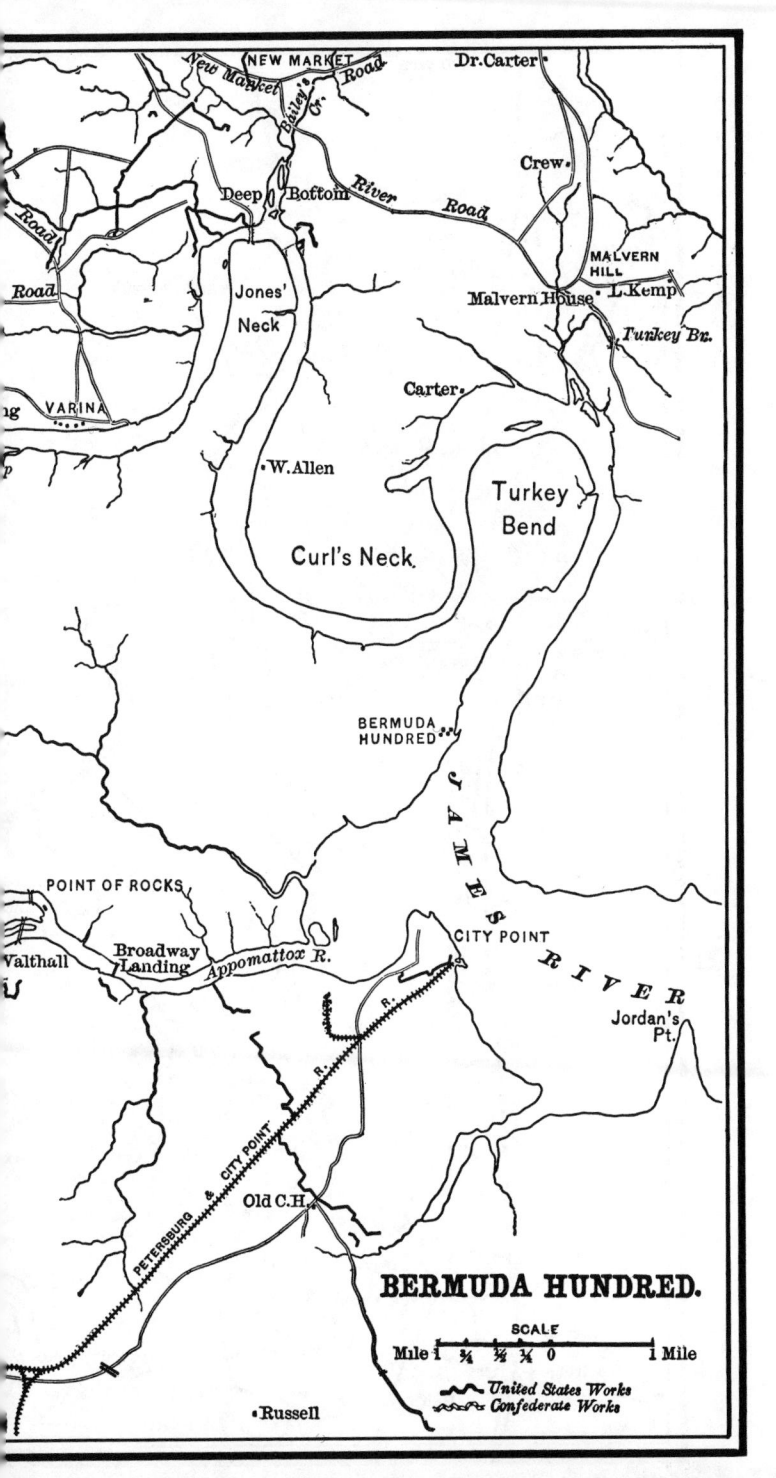

BERMUDA HUNDRED.

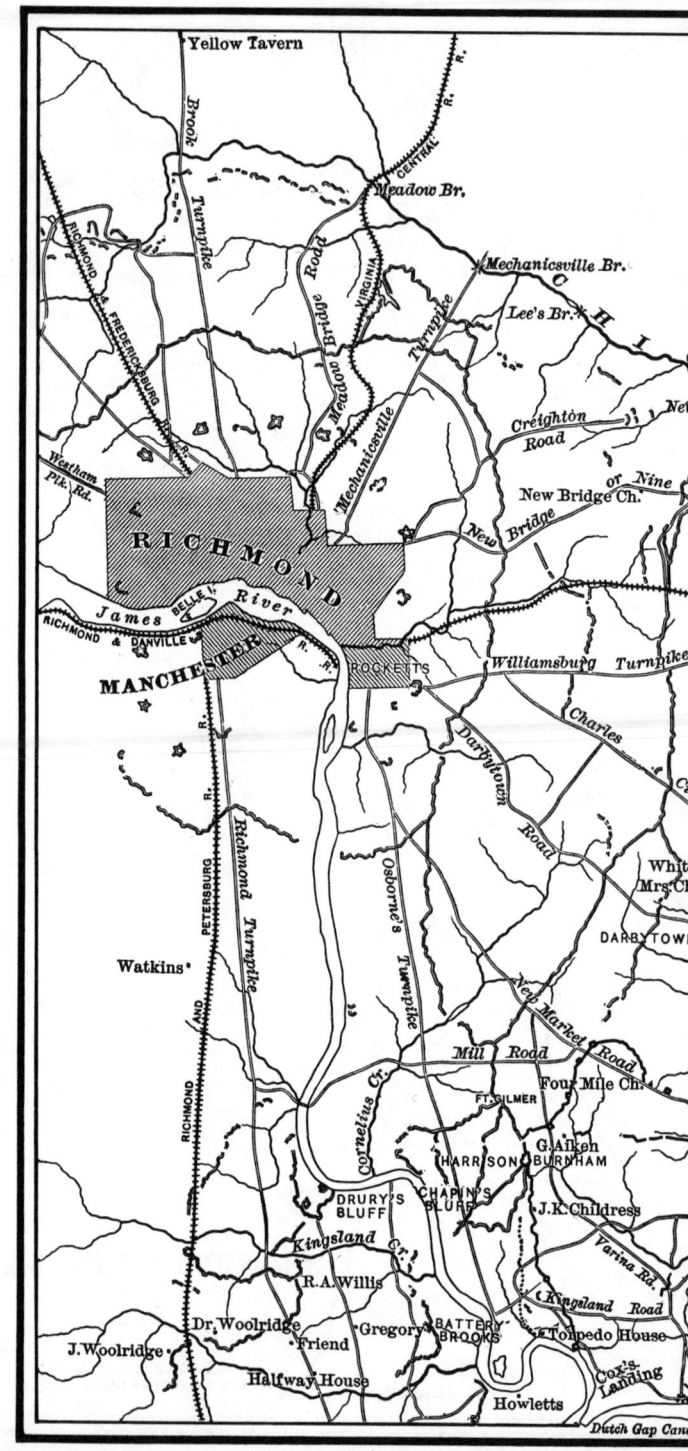

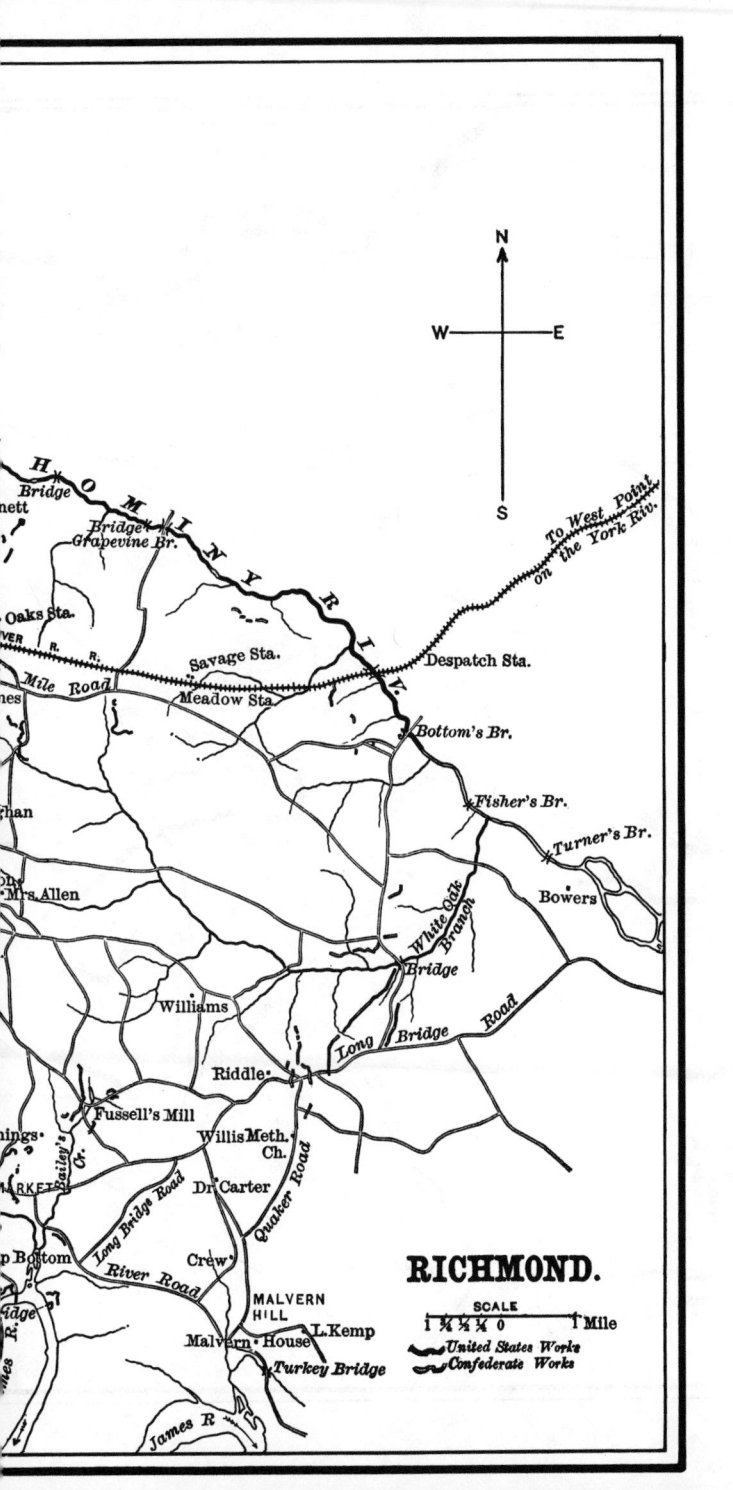

RICHMOND.

SCALE

1 ¾ ½ ¼ 0   1 Mile

~~~ *United States Works*
~~~ *Confederate Works*

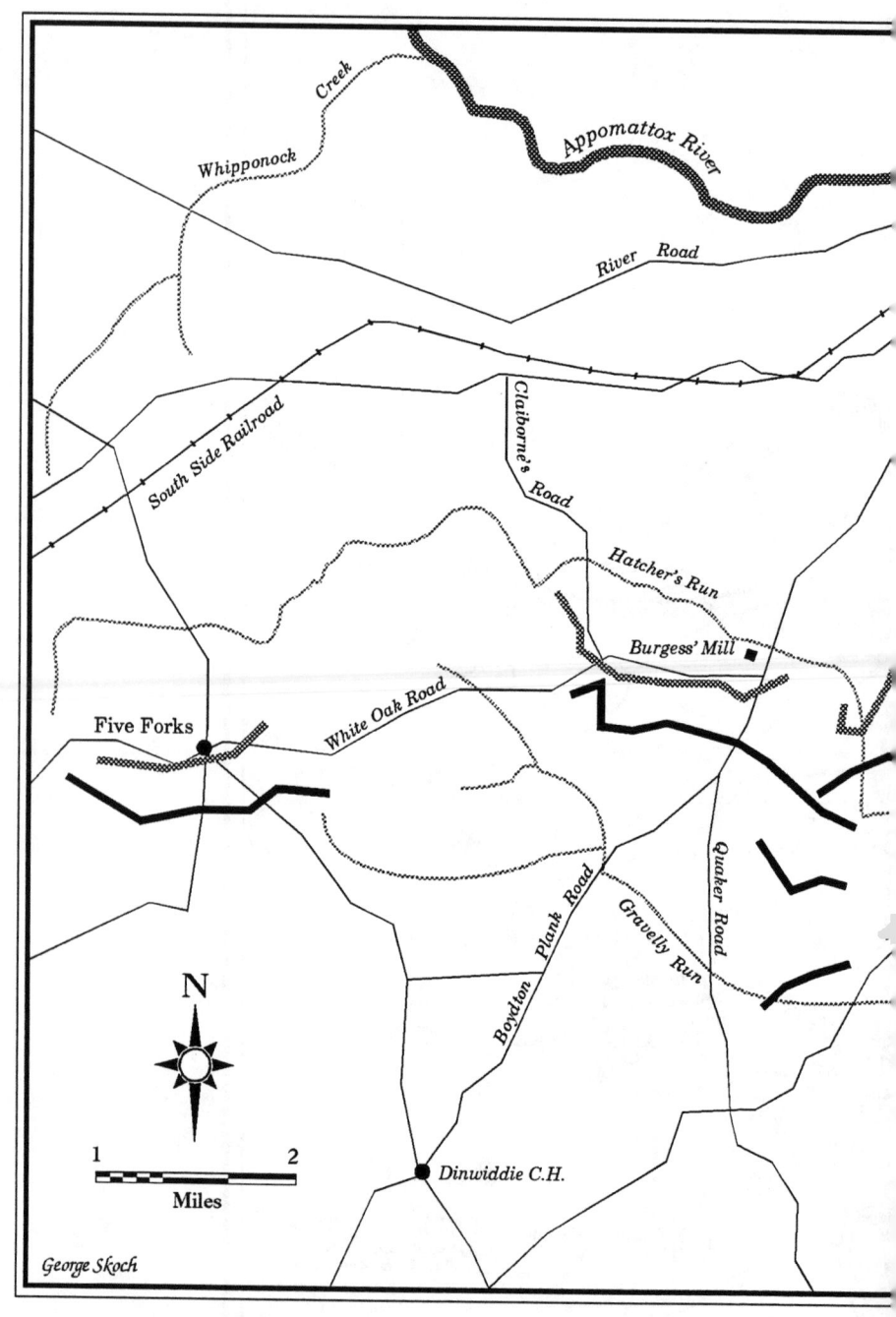

Whipponock Creek

Appomattox River

River Road

South Side Railroad

Claiborne's Road

Hatcher's Run

Burgess' Mill ■

White Oak Road

Five Forks

Boydton Plank Road

Gravelly Run

Quaker Road

N

1   2
Miles

Dinwiddie C.H.

George Skoch

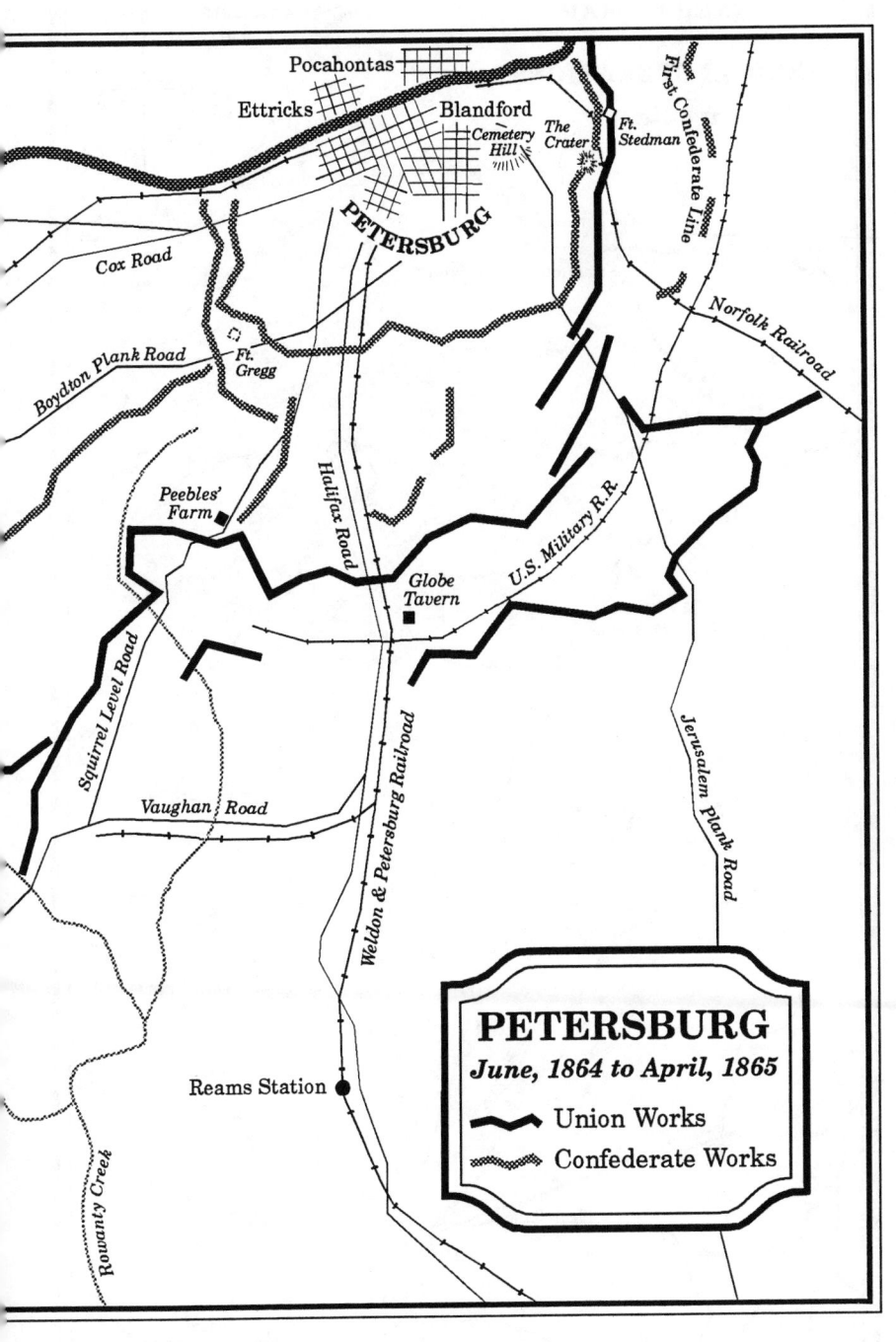

Pocahontas

Ettricks

Blandford

Cemetery Hill

The Crater

Ft. Stedman

First Confederate Line

PETERSBURG

Cox Road

Boydton Plank Road

Ft. Gregg

Norfolk Railroad

Halifax Road

Peebles' Farm

Globe Tavern

U.S. Military R.R.

Squirrel Level Road

Vaughan Road

Jerusalem Plank Road

Weldon & Petersburg Railroad

Reams Station

Rowanty Creek

PETERSBURG

June, 1864 to April, 1865

Union Works

Confederate Works

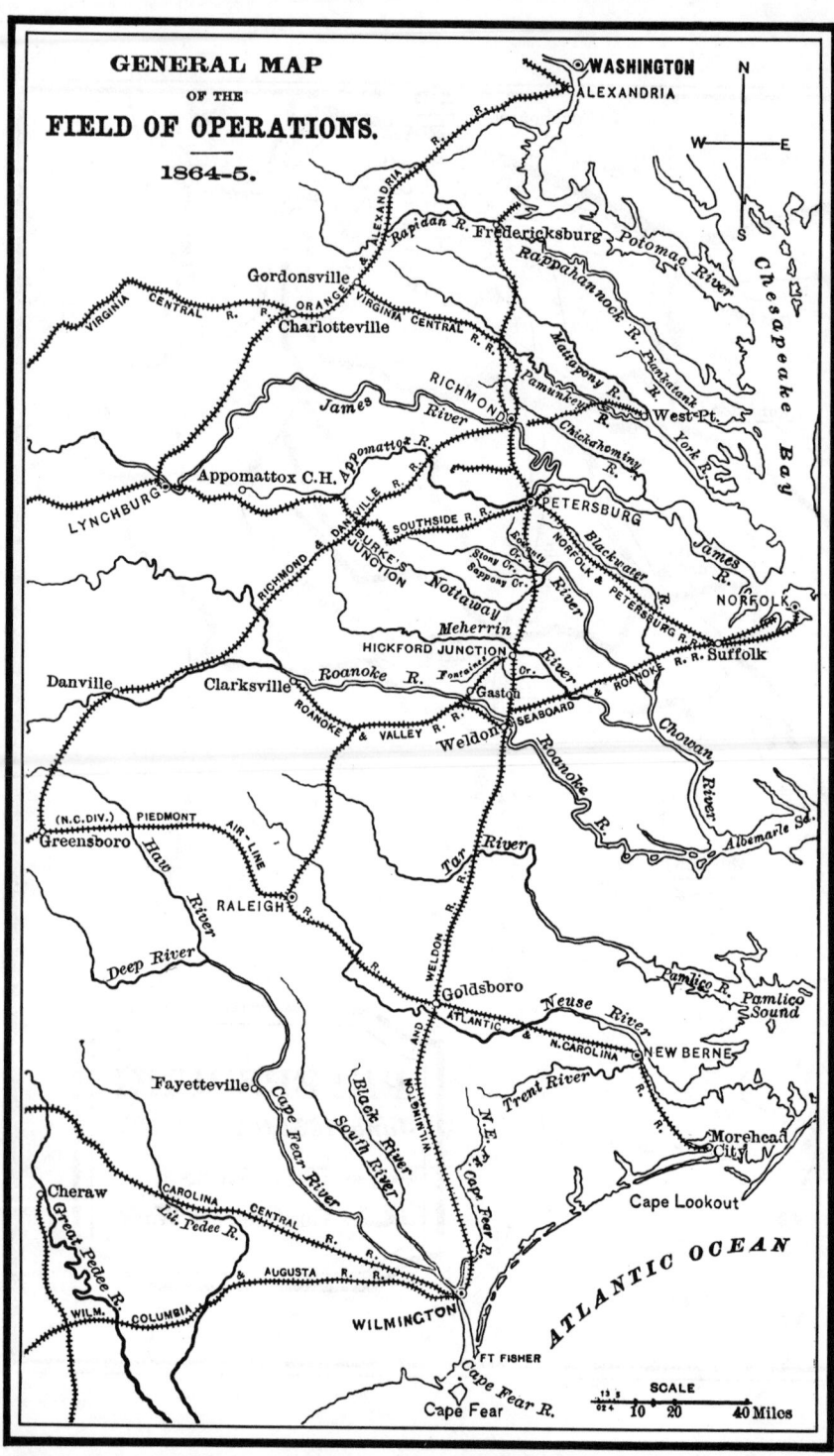

Other titles of interest

THE ANNALS OF THE
CIVIL WAR
Written by Leading Participants
North and South
New introd. Gary W. Gallagher
808 pp., 56 illus.
80606-1 $19.95

CHANCELLORSVILLE AND
GETTYSBURG
General Abner Doubleday
New introd. by Gary W. Gallagher
269 pp., 13 maps
80549-5 $12.95

FROM MANASSAS TO
APPOMATTOX
General James Longstreet
New introd. by Jeffry D. Wert
760 pp., 30 illus., 16 maps
80464-6 $17.95

GENERAL LEE
A Biography of Robert E. Lee
Fitzhugh Lee
Introd. by Gary W. Gallagher
478 pp., 2 illus., 3 maps
80589-8 $15.95

MEMOIRS OF GENERAL
WILLIAM T. SHERMAN
New introd. by William S. McFeely
820 pp. 80213-9 $17.95

PERSONAL MEMOIRS OF
U.S. GRANT
New introd. by William S. McFeely
Critical Notes by E. B. Long
xxxi + 608 pp.
80172-8 $15.95

SHERMAN'S BATTLE FOR
ATLANTA
General Jacob D. Cox
New introd. by Brooks D. Simpson
294 pp., 7 maps
80588-X $12.95

SHERMAN'S MARCH TO THE SEA,
Hood's Tennessee Campaign &
the Carolina Campaigns of 1865
General Jacob D. Cox
New introd. by Brooks D. Simpson
289 pp., 10 maps
80587-1 $12.95

STONEWALL JACKSON AND
THE AMERICAN CIVIL WAR
G.F.R. Henderson
New introduction by
Thomas L. Connelly
740 pp. 80318-6 $16.95

THE WARTIME PAPERS OF
ROBERT E. LEE
Edited by Clifford Dowdey and
Louis H. Manarin
1,012 pp. 80282-1 $19.95

BY SEA AND BY RIVER
A Naval History of the Civil War
Bern Anderson
344 pp., 20 illus.
80367-4 $13.95

THE GENERALSHIP OF
ULYSSES S. GRANT
J.F.C. Fuller
446 pp., 17 maps & plans
80450-6 $14.95

Available at your bookstore

OR ORDER DIRECTLY FROM

DA CAPO PRESS

1-800-321-0050